PATERNOSTER THEOLOGICAL MONOGRAPHS

Mission and the Coming of God

Eschatology, the Trinity and Mission in the Theology of Jürgen Moltmann and Contemporary Evangelicalism

PATERNOSTER THEOLOGICAL MONOGRAPHS

A full listing of titles in this series and
Paternoster Biblical Monographs will
be found at the close of this book.

PATERNOSTER THEOLOGICAL MONOGRAPHS

Mission and the Coming of God

Eschatology, the Trinity and Mission in the Theology of Jürgen Moltmann and Contemporary Evangelicalism

Tim Chester

Paternoster:
thinking faith

First published 2006 by Paternoster
Paternoster is an imprint of Authentic Media
9 Holdom Avenue, Bletchley, Milton Keynes, MK1 1QR, UK
and
PO Box 1047, Waynesboro, GA 30830-2047, USA

09 08 07 06 12 11 10   7 6 5 4 3 2 1

British Library Cataloguing in Publication Data
A catalogue record for this book is available from the British Library.

ISBN 1-84227-320-5

Typeset by D.J. Potter
Published by Paternoster
Printed and bound in Great Britain
by Nottingham Alphagraphics.

PATERNOSTER THEOLOGICAL MONOGRAPHS

Series Preface

In the West the churches may be declining, but theology—serious, academic (mostly doctoral level) and mainstream orthodox in evaluative commitment—shows no sign of withering on the vine. This series of *Paternoster Theological Monographs* extends the expertise of the Press especially to first-time authors whose work stands broadly within the parameters created by fidelity to Scripture and has satisfied the critical scrutiny of respected assessors in the academy. Such theology may come in several distinct intellectual disciplines—historical, dogmatic, pastoral, apologetic, missional, aesthetic and no doubt others also. The series will be particularly hospitable to promising constructive theology within an evangelical frame, for it is of this that the church's need seems to be greatest. Quality writing will be published across the confessions—Anabaptist, Episcopalian, Reformed, Arminian and Orthodox—across the ages—patristic, medieval, reformation, modern and counter-modern—and across the continents. The aim of the series is theology written in the twofold conviction that the church needs theology and theology needs the church—which in reality means theology done for the glory of God.

Series Editors

Contents

PREFACE

Since the publication of *Theology of Hope* in 1964 (first published in English in 1967), Jürgen Moltmann has been one of the most influential Protestant theologians of his generation. Despite a number of new directions, his theology has remained consistently focused around his commitment to the centrality of eschatology in Christian theology and to the transforming nature it imparts to the mission of the church.

The relationship between eschatology and mission has also been a central concern in evangelical missiology over the last forty years, especially as evangelicals have re-emphasised social involvement. The nature and significance of continuity between historical activity and the new creation, and the nature and significance of the presence of the kingdom in history continue to be recurring issues.

This study explores these themes, pointing to the strengths in the approaches taken by Moltmann and within evangelicalism. It also highlights the limits and ambiguities of hope as an incentive for socio-political transformation. It indicates the all too common confusion caused when proximate hopes for social change and the eschatological hope of a new creation are not clearly distinguished.

The main organising principle for the material on Moltmann is thematic, all the time exploring (as the chapter titles indicate) the relationship of the different themes to Moltmann's central interest in eschatology and mission. There is, however, some progression in the chapters and this is best viewed as a movement out from the centre of Moltmann's theology. Presentation and criticism (both my own and that of others) is mingled throughout the chapters on Moltmann. Occasionally I have 'digressed' to present a constructive, alternative proposal, usually building on Moltmann, but making modifications in the light of the critique.

The material on evangelicalism also works out from a central point. That centre is evangelical interaction with Moltmann. Two figures favourably disposed towards Moltmann are considered first: Richard Bauckham, an expositor and apologist for Moltmann, and Miroslav Volf who takes Moltmann's theology in new directions. This is followed by a more critical evangelical: Stephen Williams. Williams' criticisms, and especially his interaction with Volf, bring us naturally to more exclusively evangelical debates over the relationship between mission and eschatology. First, we consider 'the future of the present' with a discussion of the nature of continuity between pre- and post-eschaton existence as well as the relevance of that continuity for social and cultural engagement. Second, we consider 'the presence of the future,' that is, the nature and extent of the kingdom of God in history prior to the new creation. Three alternative evangelical proposals are then considered: those of Stephen Mott, Richard Mouw and Oliver O'Donovan. These proposals highlight the need not to isolate the theme of eschatology, but to locate it within the biblical drama as a whole.

Taking Calvin's understanding of the union of the believer with the crucified and risen Christ as a starting point, the concluding chapters highlight a missing element in the discussions: that of *patience*, a common New Testament correlate of hope. We propose that an emphasis upon future blessing need not function as 'opium for the people', but can, if such action is established on other grounds, sustain one's commitment to social involvement. This leads to the development of an eschatology of the cross – an extension of Luther's *theologia crucis*. We suggest that there is in history and in Christian discipleship a pattern of suffering followed by glory which corresponds to the pattern of cross and resurrection. The sacrificial love of the cross is the mark of Christian discipleship in history. We experience resurrection life in the present through the eschatological Spirit, but it is a hidden reality prior to the 'apocalypse' or unveiling at the parousia. Prior to that unveiling, our resurrection life is revealed in a contrary manner through our conformity to the cross.

All theological reflection, of necessity, reflects certain assumptions. As an evangelical I assume the normative role of Scripture in theology and my interaction with evangelical thought reflects this shared presupposition. In discussing the thought of Moltmann, however, I have sought primarily to examine it in Moltmann's own terms, only discussing biblical exegesis where he does. The definition of 'evangelical' is becoming increasingly difficult, not to say controversial. It is the not the purpose of this book to explore these debates. Instead we have followed the simple rubric of including as evangelicals those who readily fit the definition outlined by the historian, David Bebbington. Bebbington says: 'These are the four qualities that have been the special marks of evangelical religion: *conversionism*, the belief that lives need to be changed; *activism*, the expression of the gospel in effort; *biblicism*, a particular regard for the Bible; and what may be called *crucicentrism*, a stress on the sacrifice of Christ on the cross. Together they form a quadrilateral of priorities that is the basis of evangelicalism.' (1989:3)

I am profoundly grateful to Prof. Stephen Williams who supervised the PhD upon which this work is based. He not only guided me through the academic process, but has repeatedly inspired me both to love my theology and live my theology. Thanks, too, belong to Dr Dewi Hughes of Tearfund from whose input I have often benefited and Jeremy Mudditt of Paternoster Press for his patience through the publication process.

With the exception of my first book, it has always been my practice to use annotations only for citations. I prefer to decide whether material should be included or omitted rather than avoiding the decision through the use of a footnote. Since in the current work the citations are made in the text with reference to the bibliography, there are no footnotes.

Abbreviations

The following abbreviations are used for the major works of Jürgen Moltmann throughout this book.

TH   *Theology of Hope: On the Ground and the Implication of a Christian Eschatology* (London: SCM, 1965, ET 1967)

CG   *The Crucified God: The Cross of Christ as the Foundation and Criticism of Christian Theology* (London: SCM, 1973, ET 1974)

CPS   *The Church in the Power of the Spirit: A Contribution to Messianic Ecclesiology* (London: SCM, 1975, ET 1977)

TKG   *The Trinity and the Kingdom of God: The Doctrine of God* (London: SCM, 1980, ET 1981)

GC   *God in Creation: An Ecological Doctrine of Creation*, The Gifford Lectures 1984-1985 (London: SCM, 1985, ET 1985)

WJC   *The Way of Jesus Christ: Christology in Messianic Dimensions* (London: SCM, 1989, ET 1990)

SL   *The Spirit of Life: A Universal Affirmation* (London: SCM, 1991, ET 1992)

CoG   *The Coming of God: Christian Eschatology* (London: SCM, 1995, ET 1996)

ET   *Experiences in Theology: Ways and Forms of Christian Theology* (Minneapolis, MN.: Fortress Press, 2000, ET 2000)

PART ONE

Jürgen Moltmann

CHAPTER 1

Eschatology and the Coming of God

The Centrality of Eschatology

Traditionally eschatology has been thought of as the doctrine of the last things; the events surrounding and following the end of time. According to Jürgen Moltmann, however, 'the relegating of these events to the "last day" robbed them of their directive, uplifting and critical significance for all the days which are spent here, this side of the end, in history' (*TH*, 16). In other words, eschatology has been divorced of any relationship to history and to mission. In dogmatics eschatology became an irrelevant appendix at the end, bearing no relation to the central themes. It is Moltmann's contention that a theology of hope is the central task for theology today. 'A theology of love was developed in the Middle Ages and a theology of faith at the time of the Reformation; now it is important to develop a universal theology of hope which directs the church and humanity, humanity and nature, towards the kingdom of God and prepares them for it' (1983:272; see also *CG*, xii; 1975:186-189; 1991:169; *ET*, 52).

Historically, argues Moltmann, as Christianity became intertwined with the state, so it replaced its orientation to the future with a support of the status quo, relegating the future to a vague beyond; to the eternal. Messianic hope 'emigrated as it were from the church and turned in one distorted form or another against the church' (1983:272; see also *CG*, xii; 1975:186-189; 1991:169; *ET*, 52). In contrast to this, Moltmann asserts that eschatology, the doctrine of Christian hope, is not an appendage to dogmatics, but the framework or starting point, for dogmatics; and not only dogmatics, but Christian life and mission as well. Furthermore, that which has been seen as making Christianity incredible in the modern age, namely a future eschatology, is seen by Moltmann as precisely the way to make it credible and relevant to the modern world (see Bauckham, 1989i:200-1).

> From first to last, and not merely in the epilogue, Christianity is eschatology, is hope, forward looking and forward moving, and therefore also revolutionising and transforming the present. The eschatological is not one element *of* Christianity, but it is the medium of Christian faith as such, the key in which everything in it is set, the glow that suffuses everything here in the dawn of an expected new day. For Christian faith lives from the raising of the crucified Christ, and strains after

the promises of the universal future of Christ. Eschatology is the passionate longing kindled by the Messiah. Hence eschatology cannot really be only a part of Christian doctrine. Rather, the eschatological outlook is the characteristic of all Christian proclamation, of every Christian existence and of the whole church. (*TH*, 16; see also 1980:11-12)

So Christianity *is* hope. The basis of this hope is the raising of the crucified Christ. This is the promise which gives birth to the hope in the universal future of Christ. And this hope is not a sterile, impotent hope for a future beyond, but a hope which is 'revolutionising and transforming the present'. Moltmann resolutely rejects any eschatology in which the individual's future beyond history has replaced a true eschatological hope for history and the world (*ET*, 53). Such a theology, claims Moltmann, is escapism rather than eschatology and is closely associated with the individualism which Moltmann identifies as pervasive in our society. 'This theology threatens to become a religious ideology of romanticist subjectivity, a religion within the sphere of the individuality that has been relieved of all social obligations' (*TH*, 316).

Eschatology and Transformation

Traditionally the role of philosophy had been seen as describing and understanding the world. The philosopher is an objective observer of the world. But Karl Marx famously said: 'The philosophers have only interpreted the world in various ways; the point, however, is to change it' (*Theses on Feuerbach*, 1845). It is not good enough to be an observer. One must be a participant. One must be involved in changing the world. Moltmann says: 'The theologian is not concerned merely to supply a different *interpretation* of the world, of history and of human nature, but to *transform* them in expectation of a divine transformation.' (*TH*, 84; see also *ET*, 124) The echo of Marx is clear and Moltmann has been influenced by his dialogue with Marxists and the Marxist philosopher Ernst Bloch in particular. Marx argued that the role of philosophy was not to interpret the world, but to change it. For Moltmann theology takes the place of philosophy, but the principle is the same. According to Moltmann, the task of theology is to serve processes of transformation. To complete the picture: since for Moltmann 'Christianity is eschatology', to say that theology promotes transformation is to say that eschatology promotes transformation. And indeed Moltmann's theology can be seen as the exposition of how eschatology serves the task of transformation. '"The theology of hope" ... does not merely want to interpret the world differently. It wants to change it.' (*SL*, 110) Richard Bauckham comments: 'If the purpose of Bloch's philosophy of hope is to promote Marxist revolutionary praxis, the purpose of Moltmann's theology of hope is to promote the revolutionary praxis of the Christian mission.' (1987:14)

The task of theology, then, is to demonstrate the relevance of this hope to the transformation of the present: 'The coming lordship of the risen Christ cannot be merely hoped for and awaited. This hope and expectation also sets its stamp on life, action and suffering in the history of society. Hence mission means not merely the propagation of faith and hope, but also historic transformation of life.' (*TH*, 330) Born in 1926 into a secular German family, Moltmann became a Christian while a prisoner of war in Britain. After serving for a five years as a pastor, he entered the academic world, most notably as Professor of Systematic Theology at Tübingen from 1967 to 1994. Throughout his theological career, Moltmann has consistently engaged with historical events and social movements: the Jewish holocaust, the nuclear threat, liberation theology, the civil rights movement, feminism and ecological threat.

Because the Lord of the kingdom is the one who raised Christ from the dead, we know him as *creator ex nihilo*. This means the kingdom does not come in history or as a result of human effort – it is a *nova creatio*. Nevertheless, 'the coming lordship of God takes shape in the suffering of the Christians, who because of their hope cannot be conformed to the world, but are drawn by the mission and love of Christ into discipleship and conformity to his sufferings' (*TH*, 222). Just as the kingdom is inclusive, so too is its love, which, as such, seeks to embrace everything in hope. 'Love is the praxis of God's coming kingdom and his righteousness and justice in this world.' (*ET*, 58) Moltmann concludes, 'The *pro-missio* of the kingdom is the ground of the *missio* of love to the world' (*TH*, 224).

Recovering the Relevance of Eschatology

The rediscovery of the central role of eschatology in the ministry of Jesus at the end of the nineteenth century by Johannes Weiss and Albert Schweitzer had a shattering effect on nineteenth century liberal theology. 'The recognition of the eschatological character of early Christianity made it clear that the automatically accepted idea of a harmonious synthesis between Christianity and culture was a lie' (*TH*, 37). To Liberal theology the historical Jesus and his message were foreign. Yet, because Weiss and Schweitzer, according to Moltmann, failed to relate biblical eschatology to contemporary history, Jesus remained an alien figure (*CoG*, 7-10).

This challenge, of relating biblical eschatology to the modern world, was taken up by the dialectical theologians. They sought to do this by transforming the eschaton into a transcendental eternity. Thus Barth speaks of eternity as 'un-historical' and 'supra-historical'. In his commentary on *The Epistle to the Romans,* Barth regards the eschaton as the transcendental boundary between time and eternity and, as such, ever present; it is at hand in every age. Revelation takes the form of divine encounter, an encounter between time and eternity. According to Moltmann, however, this means Easter is already an eschatological fulfilment and, as such, robs revelation of its true content, namely the promise which creates hope and opens up the future. This transcendental eschatology, as Moltmann calls it, obscures the future orientation of Christian faith. 'Christian revelation does not introduce something ... which was always beginning or is eternal. Rather it makes present that which does not yet exist.' (1971:15) The revelation of Jesus is not a revelation of eternity, but of the future.

Whereas Barth bases revelation on the subjectivity of God, Bultmann bases it on the subjectivity of humanity. He interprets knowledge of God existentially by equating it with knowledge of self. As such, he offers 'no proof of the existence of God, but a proof of God through existing authentically' (*TH*, 61). The eschatological statements of scripture are an objectification of existential experience and so, in order to be interpreted for modern people, they must be demythologised. For Bultmann eschatology is not the goal of history, but the individual's goal of self-fulfilment. Thus Bultmann speaks of the 'eschatological moment'. In the eschatological moment the word is proclaimed and faith responds. This is the content of revelation and its goal is self-understanding or self-authenticity. This, Moltmann believes, makes faith its own goal: it is the climax, the eschaton, of revelation. In reality, argues Moltmann, faith is directed to promise (Hebrews 11:1) and has a goal beyond itself (1 Peter 1:9). Furthermore, 'man's self-understanding is socially, materially and historically mediated' (*TH*, 67). True selfhood is not achieved apart from the resurrection of the body; neither is it achieved apart from the redemption of history and the world. In this respect, we are one with the cosmos which likewise 'waits in eager expectation' (Romans 8:18-25). Moltmann concludes that the eschatological cosmology of Romans 8 cannot be reconciled with the Kantian cosmology and transcendental eschatology of Barth and Bultmann.

That Moltmann traces the origins of the transcendental eschatology of Dialectical Theology back to the influence of Kant (*TH*, 46-51) is significant because it allows him to introduce Hegel's critique of Kant, a critique which Hegel developed further in opposition to Romanticism. Hegel's concern in both cases is with the dualism in which they result: the split of a person into believing person and knowing person; the split between the private, subjective, religious world of faith and the public, objective, political, scientific world. Fiorenza claims that Moltmann's critique of Bultmann, and of Dialectical Theology as a whole, has a 'formal similarity' to Hegel's critique (1968:144).

In contrast to nineteenth century Liberalism, Dialectical Theology stressed the absolute transcendence of God over against humanity. By stressing the centrality of eschatology (as they interpreted it), they condemned the immanent, this-worldly eschatology of Liberalism which associated the eschaton, the kingdom of God, with human achievement in history. Hence Bultmann says, 'the object of theology is God, and the objection to liberal theology is, that it treated not of God but of man. God means the radical negation and cancellation of man.' (cited, *TH*, 59) Yet it is precisely this for which Moltmann criticises Bultmann; for locating the knowledge of God in the subjectivity of humanity by equating knowledge of God with knowledge of oneself. In doing so, God's relationship to the world and to history is undermined. That it is with reference to Hegel – who 'knew so much about human things, but nothing of God' – that Moltmann makes this critique, Fiorenza claims 'is surprising above all' (1968:9, 152).

Kant sought to overcome rationalism by limiting human knowledge to knowledge of experienced objects. Knowledge of the infinite is beyond the scope of reason and belongs to practical faith. Hegel claims that in doing this Kant fails to achieve his objective of establishing knowledge of humanity's limitation and finiteness. Instead this limited knowledge, based on a marriage of rationalism and empiricism, becomes an absolute by which everything else is measured. Hegel believes humanity only comes to knowledge of its limitations as it comes to knowledge of the true absoluteness of the infinite. The Romanticism of, for example, Schleiermacher arose as a way around what amounts to a denial by Kant of the possibility of rational, objective knowledge of God. Romanticism responds by basing knowledge of God, not on objective reasoning, but on religious experience; upon human subjectivity. Hence the result of both Kant's transcendental philosophy and Romanticism was a dualism between objectivity and subjectivity; between science and faith; between citizen of the state and private individual; and the form which, because of his missiological concerns, Moltmann is ultimately concerned to overcome, between the world and God. Moltmann's critique of both Barth and Bultmann is that in their different ways they perpetuate this dualism. Barth bases knowledge of God on the subjectivity of God, while Bultmann bases it on the subjectivity of man. In doing so neither of them overcome the problem of dualism identified by Hegel. Indeed for Dialectical Theology this dualism, between 'a theoretic atheism and a believing heart' (Kierkegaard; see *TH*, 64), is the mark of authentic faith.

The Death of God and the Resurrection of Jesus

Fiorenza claims that Dialectical Theology understood Hegel's assertion 'God is dead' via Nietzsche and, as such, saw it as representing a theoretic atheism which had emerged in the Enlightenment and as the antithesis of private faith. In fact, for Hegel 'God is dead' had a double function. First, it was a polemical statement used against the dualism of the transcendental philosophy of his day. Primarily, however, it was an expression of the dialectic of reality. Moltmann contrasts Nietzsche's assertion that 'God is dead! God stays dead! And it is we who have killed him!' with Hegel's belief that the death of God represents 'God's expending of himself' (*TH*, 170). The experience of godforsakenness and the absence of God in the practical atheism of post-Enlightenment society is paralleled by the experience of Good Friday. Hence God himself identifies with his own negation. In this way the two sides of the dualism can be reconciled and overcome in the hope of resurrection.

If this very atheism – as it has been most profoundly understood by Hegel and Nietzsche – derives from the nihilistic discovery on the 'speculative Good Friday', that 'God is dead', then the only real way of vindicating theology in face of this reality, in face of this reason, and in face of a society thus constituted, will be in terms of a theology of the resurrection – in fact, in terms of an eschatology of the resurrection in the sense of the future of the crucified Lord. (*TH* , 84)

Christian faith in God is not a naïve basic trust. It is unfaith that has overcome: 'Lord, I believe, help thou my unbelief.' In the fellowship of the assailed and crucified Christ faith grows up in the pains of one's own suffering and the doubts of one's own heart. Here the contradictions and rebellions do not have to be suppressed. They can be admitted. Those who recognise God's presence in the face of the God-forsaken Christ have protest atheism within themselves – but as something they have overcome. (*ET*, 17)

Moltmann follows Ernst Bloch's criticism of Hegel's 'closed system', but he does so in his own explicitly Christian way: 'The god-forsakenness of the cross cannot, as in Hegel, be made into an element belonging to the divine process and thus immanent in God' (*TH*, 171). Moltmann agrees with Hegel that on the cross God himself identifies with the experience of godforsakenness and, as such, with contemporary practical atheism. What Moltmann cannot accept is the abstraction of this into a process within the absolute Spirit. Hegel is in danger of making the cross and resurrection a temporal picture for something which is essentially eternal. Moltmann cites Hegel – 'concept cancels time' (*TH*, 172). The effect of this is to make the cross and resurrection essentially a-historical. 'Hegel attempted to reconcile faith and knowledge – but at the price of doing away with the historicity of the event of revelation and understanding it as an eternal event' (*TH*, 172). While for Hegel the cross-resurrection symbolises the dialectical process that takes place as the self-movement of absolute Geist, for Moltmann the cross-resurrection is an historic event which took place at a specific time. As such, it is not an eternal event within a divine process, but the event which set the dialectical process in motion. It is neither a symbol of the eternal, nor an eternal event in itself, but the historic revelation of promise and the historic event which forms the basis of the eschatological *novum*. For Hegel the negation of God paralleled by the cross is itself negated by the resurrection; this is the dialectic of absolute Spirit in the world – a process complete within itself. In contrast for Moltmann, 'the cross is the mark of an eschatological openness which is not yet closed by the resurrection of Christ and the spirit of the Church, but remains open beyond both of these until the future of God and the annihilation of death' (*TH*, 172). As Moltmann sees it, Hegel describes a process which is resolved in the eternal consciousness of absolute Spirit and as such is closed to the future. Moltmann's understanding is of a process still outstanding which will only be resolved by the eschaton and the kingdom of God.

Moltmann himself believes that the statement 'God is dead' 'is not merely a statement of philosophical metaphysics or of theology, but is one which also seems to lie at the foundations of modern experience of self and the world and to provide the ground for the atheism that characterises the methods of science' (*TH*, 167). It is against this background that the missionary proclamation that Christ is risen has real content and meaning for contemporary society. If present reality makes God questionable (the position of protest atheism), then, conversely, God, in raising the crucified One from the dead, makes present reality questionable (see Bauckham, 1989i:206).

> Only when, along with the knowledge of the resurrection of Jesus, the 'God of the resurrection' can be shown to be 'God' in terms of the 'death of God' that has become familiar to us from history, from the world and from our own existence – only then is the proclamation of the resurrection, and only then is faith and hope in the God of promise, something that is necessary, that is new, that is possible in an objectively real sense. (*TH*, 168)

Moltmann takes this further by linking it to Bonhoeffer's thought in *Letters and Papers from Prison*. He quotes Bonhoeffer:

> And we cannot be honest unless we recognise that we have to live in the world *etsi deus non daretur*. And this is just what we do recognise – before God!... God would have us know that we must live as men who manage our lives without him. The God who is with us is the God who forsakes us... Before God and with God we live without God. God lets himself be pushed out of the world on to the cross. He is weak and powerless in the world, and that is precisely the way, the only way, in which he is with us and helps us. (1971:360; cited *TH*, 171)

Not until we recognise the reality of godforsakenness and godlessness in the world will we see that our hope lies in the weakness of the cross and the hiddenness of God, and so move beyond the cross to the power and hope of the resurrection.

It is by means of an eschatological understanding of the resurrection as the contradiction of the godforsakenness of the cross that Moltmann wants to break the impasse into which, as he sees it, theology has fallen. Theology remains caught between objectivity and subjectivity; swinging between the poles of the total affirmation of eternity and the transcendence of God on the one hand, and the affirmation of history and involvement in the world on the other. This is a form of what Moltmann calls Christianity's 'identity-involvement dilemma' (*CG*, 7). On the one hand the cosmology of natural science obscures reality as history, while on the other hand subjective transcendentalism only finds meaning in the supra-historical. By restoring a sense of history as the interval between promise (the resurrection) and fulfilment (the new creation) Moltmann wants to break the impasse and make the antithesis 'fluid once more' (*TH*, 50). He wants to assert that Christian theology is 'public theology' (*ET*, 65; 1999ii).

The contradiction between cross and resurrection, between reality and promise, means that the question of revelation is a question of hope. Revelation is ultimately validated in the new creation (see 1971:16).

The identity of the risen Lord with the crucified One is of central importance to Moltmann. It is not the resurrection *per se* that brings hope to the world, but the resurrection of the One who was crucified, and more than that, the One who was crucified as a blasphemer, as a political rebel, and forsaken by God. 'The new and scandalous element in the Christian message of Easter was not that some man or other was raised before anyone else, but that the one who was raised was this condemned, executed and forsaken man' (*CG*, 175). As a blasphemer, Jesus placed himself above the law and, instead of proclaiming judgment on sinners, he accepted them and claimed to forgive their sins. As one crucified by the Romans, Jesus was crucified as a political rebel; as one who had caused political unrest. Although he had similarities to the Zealots, he denied the right to vengeance (whether by the Romans or the Zealots) and proclaimed love for enemies and acceptance of sinners and traitors. The kingdom he proclaimed was not the kingdom of judgment for which the Zealots looked, but a kingdom of grace. Finally, although Jesus had proclaimed God as 'Abba', he dies abandoned by God and as such identifies with every experience of godforsakenness (*CG*, 126-153).

Against this background the resurrection is the vindication of the Jesus who was crucified. It is as if his historical trial was eschatologically re-opened and the verdict reversed by God himself. Jesus' message concerning the kingdom and the fatherhood of God is so identified with his person that it appears to die with him (*CG*, 117-125), but with his resurrection it is endorsed by God himself.

> If God raised this dishonoured man in his coming righteousness, it follows that in this crucified figure he manifests his true righteousness, the right of the unconditional grace which makes righteous the unrighteous and those without rights ... It shows the cross of Christ as the unique and once-for-all anticipation of the great world judgment in the favour of those who otherwise could not survive at it. (*CG*, 176)

'Are You the One Who is to Come?'

Both the early church and modern Protestant theology start christology from a universal question. For the early church it was the question of the eternal, immutable God and hence they asked, 'Is Jesus true God?' For modern Protestantism the question is the existential problem of humanity's existence and hence they ask, 'Is Jesus true man?' These approaches reveal something of Jesus, but, argues Moltmann, they both have problems when faced with his individuality and his abandonment by God on the cross. The former resorts to 'a mild docetism' (*CG*, 89). The latter compromises Christianity's absolute claim by making Christ simply a moral archetype for true humanity before God.

We come closer to discerning who Jesus was when we set him against his Jewish background and ask the eschatological question, 'Are you the One who is to come?' 'There is no such thing as a christology without presuppositions; and its historical presupposition is the messianic promise of the Old Testament ... What does christology mean except messianology.' (*WJC*, 1)

Taking up recent study in Old Testament theology and using the tools of comparative religion, Moltmann identifies the distinctive feature of Israelite thought as the concept of *promise*. The revelation of God in the Old Testament is not a revelation of the present, but of promise; and knowledge of God is knowledge of his faithfulness to that promise (*TH*, Pt. II; *ET*, 54-55). By announcing a coming reality that does not yet exist, the promise orients people to the future and causes them to experience reality as history. As Israel's history progresses the promises are not 'liquidated' in history either by fulfilment or disappointment, but are constantly renewed and widened by each partial fulfilment. Moltmann comments: 'The reason for the overplus of promise and the fact that it constantly overspills history lies in the inexhaustibility of the God of promise, who never exhausts himself in any historic reality but comes "to rest" only in a reality that wholly corresponds to him' (*TH*, 106; see also 1975:49-50). It is not only the Old Testament concept of promise in general which shapes eschatological christology, but also its specific expectation of the Messiah (*WJC*, 5-27).

Coming to christology from this background, Moltmann stresses that the God who raises Christ from the dead is Yahweh, the Old Testament God of exodus and of promise. The basis of the promise is the power of God 'who gives life to the dead and calls things that are not as though they were' (Romans 4:17) and of this we can be certain because God has raised Christ from the dead (Romans 4:24).

> The gospel has its inabrogable presupposition in the Old Testament history of promise. In the gospel the Old Testament history of promise finds more than a fulfilment which does away with it; it finds a future. 'All the promises of God in him are yea, and in him Amen' (2 Corinthians 1:20). They have become an eschatological certainty in Christ, by being liberated and validated, made unconditional and universal. (*TH*, 147)

> Because [Paul's] gospel proclaims the promise as validated in the event of Christ, it starts the traditional promise to Abraham off on a new history. (*TH*, 152)

The Future of Christ

Christian eschatology, however, is not the same as Old Testament faith, nor is it merely an examination of general possibilities in history. Rather it speaks of the future of Christ. Hence true Christian eschatology is in fact christology from an eschatological and messianic perspective. 'There can be no christology without eschatology and no eschatology without christology' (1991:95). When we ask what is the content of Moltmann's eschatology, the answer is, in essence, the future of Christ. It is to the future of Christ that the promise is given and all our hopes are directed. We do not simply look to the past of Christ (his resurrection) and so hope for a repetition of it for ourselves (resurrection of the dead). Rather we see in Christ's resurrection the promise that he has a future which is cosmological in scope (and therefore one which includes the resurrection of the dead).

In *Theology of Hope* Moltmann acknowledges that what he calls the future of Christ 'is described elsewhere as the "parousia of Christ" or the "return of Christ"' (227). As such, he speaks of the parousia as 'first and foremost the completion of the way of Jesus: "the Christ on the way" arrives at his goal. His saving work is completed. In his eschatological person he is perfected and is universally manifested in the glory of God.' (*WJC*, 314) The 'process', in which the promise of the resurrection finds fulfilment in the glory of Christ and the new creation, is an historical process – it is not supra-historical. 'It works upon the present by awaking hopes and establishing resistance' (*TH*, 227) and it culminates in the consummation of history. As such the parousia cannot be called 'return' or 'second coming' for this presupposes an absence of Christ from history (*CPS*, 130; 1980:33-4). On the other hand, this 'process' cannot, and must not, be reduced to the historical. It will not 'emerge out of the forces and trends of growth and decay' (*CPS*, 130). The parousia will not develop out of the present (*GC*, 133), instead it is a coming presence. 'As compared with what can now be experienced, [the parousia of Christ] brings something new' (*TH*, 227).

This is the reason, according to Moltmann, why the Latin word used for parousia is *adventus* (coming), and not *futurum* which has the sense of that which develops out of the present (*CPS*, 130; *GC*, 132-135; *WJC*, 206; *CoG*, 25; 1970:11-16; 1975:52; 1979i:29-31,55; 1991:95; *CoG*, 22-29). Likewise, Luther translates parousia with the German word *Zukunft* which means future rather than return, but future in the sense of something coming towards the present rather than something developing (becoming) out of the present. The parousia comes as something new, not as the culmination of an historical process. As such, it does not come in history. but represents the end, the fulfilment, of history (*CPS*, 131; *WJC*, 327-328). In *The Coming of God* Moltmann critiques the modern understanding of time with its emphasis on linear development (see also *ET*, 31-33). At issue is not whether time is linear, but the extent to which the linear predominates the way modern people think about time. Moltmann critiques this because it makes the future appear to be a development of present trends while the present is viewed simply as a transition from the past to the future. As a result, the unexpected possibilities contained within the present are ignored and an uninterrupted progress into the future is assumed. It assumes an homogeneity between past, present and future with only quantitative differences between them (see also Bauckham, 1999:155-226). This view of time serves to obscure the parousia as something qualitatively new. The parousia is reduced to a further development within time.

Moltmann's use of the term 'future of Christ' instead of parousia in *Theology of Hope* may have arisen out of a fear of being labelled a literalist. Yet in *The Church in the Power of the Spirit*, after having made the distinctions described above, he goes further: 'The character of promise in the history of Jesus, the eschatological character of his cross and resurrection from the dead, the hopeful character of faith and the unique nature of the experiences of the Spirit, which point beyond themselves, would be incomprehensible without this future orientation towards Christ's parousia and would hence ultimately themselves be null and void.' (*CPS*, 131) Finally, in *The Way of Jesus Christ*, in a section entitled 'A Little Apologia for the Expectation of the Parousia' (*WJC*, 313-321), Moltmann confronts the 'embarrassment' engendered by the parousia. 'For modern theology the early Christian expectation of the parousia is an embarrassment which it thinks it can get rid of with the help of demythologisation' (*WJC*, 313). In reality, loss of the parousia is a sign of Christianity becoming a civil religion aligned with the status quo; it is a sign that it has lost its revolutionary edge (see also 1980:33).

What the future of Christ will mean is illumined by the more specific dimensions of the promise. In *Theology of Hope*, Moltmann identifies these as:
1. the promise of the righteousness of God
2. the promise of life as a result of resurrection from the dead; and
3. the promise of the kingdom of God in a new totality of being.

1. The Future of Righteousness

Righteousness means standing in a right relationship both to God and to others. It also involves, according to Moltmann, being able to stand, having subsistence, and, as such, God's righteousness is that by which everything is held together. Its future will involve 'a new ground of existence and a new right to life ... a new creation' (*TH*, 204). Or again, 'Out of this new creation will arise a new being that will put an end to the ambivalence of all created beings between being and non-being.' (1969:36) Thus, the ontological ambivalence determined through *creatio ex nihilo* is overcome in the *participatio in Deo* (1969:106). Therefore Christ's 'act of righteousness' (Romans 5:18) is 'for those who, both in a juridical and in an ontological sense, cannot stand before the wrath of God' (*TH*, 205). It embraces *remissio peccatorum*, reconciliation and the gift of life. Nevertheless, despite present assurance, it remains something hoped for (Galatians 5:5). It is present now as promise, as 'a gift that is pledged' (*TH*, 206), but ultimately it is eschatological.

2. *The Future of Life*

In Israelite religion resurrection arises not in an anthropological context (the continuation of the individual), but in a theological context, on the basis of the power of the God of promise. Death was seen not just as the individual's loss of life, but also of his loss of God and of the divine promise. Against this background, the death of Christ is to be seen not just as the end of his life, but as the end of hope and the death of God in his Messiah; it represents the supreme expression of godforsakenness. But this means the resurrection is the conquest of death in all its godlessness, the conquest of godforsakenness, the 'negation of the negation of God'. Of this future resurrection life, the life-giving Spirit is an earnest and pledge who enables us to participate in the present sufferings, the fellowship of Christ's death, which lead on to glory (2 Corinthians 13:4).

Here, and elsewhere, Moltmann seems to be employing a form of the *via negativa*; what Moltmann calls 'the dialectical principle of knowledge'. If theology is not to be ghettoised, revelation must be expressed in relation to present experience and reality. This is the justification for views of revelation that centre on existence, whether God's, humanity's or the existence of reality and history as whole. But, as we have seen, Moltmann has been deeply critical of these. His alternative is based on the fact that the promise is directed to something new, that the future of Christ will be discontinuous with the present and hence eschatology is defined in terms of what it is not. Hope, then, places us in contradiction to present reality and, as such, we see the nature of the future in its contrary, as the opposite of the present experiences of suffering and godforsakenness. As Moltmann reminds us, the Reformers spoke of the kingdom of God as *tectum sub cruce et sub contrario*, dwelling in suffering and what is contrary (*TH*, 223). Moltmann himself says, 'the positive content of the ideas is all supplied by negation of the negative' (*TH*, 131; see also 1991:78). This is how the Old Testament understanding of promise developed and this is how God has revealed the eschatological future in the death and resurrection of Christ.

3. *The Future of the Kingdom of God and of the Freedom of Man*

Moltmann calls the kingdom of God and the lordship of God 'the real heart of eschatology' (*TH*, 216). The idea of the lordship of Yahweh is central in the Old Testament and the resurrection universalizes this. This means eschatology should not be confined to the lordship of God in a subjective sense, but should speak of the expectation that the whole cosmos will be brought to salvation, peace and life in the kingdom of God.

The kingdom of God in the New Testament can refer 'both the actual rule of God in the world, and the universal goal of that divine rule' (*CPS*, 190). Moltmann believes that both of these aspects must held in tension. He affirms that both rule and kingdom (the realm over which rule is exercised) must be maintained: rule expresses the present reality; kingdom the future order. This double definition prevents the relegation of the kingdom to the future and its reduction to the present. Recent Protestant theology has restricted it to rule, making it moralistic and neglecting the new creation. In doing so, they have failed to do justice to the kingdom of God as good news to the poor to whom it brings hope and dignity through incorporation into the people of God (see *WJC*, 97-102).

In his kingdom, God's rule is undisputed. In history, however, 'God rules through the word of promise and the Spirit of freedom ... God rules in a disputed and hidden way' (*CPS*, 190). His rule may thus be assailed, resisted and contradicted. Nevertheless, the present rule of God points forward to the universal rule of God. 'If we view history, with its conditions and potentialities, as an open system, we are bound to understand the kingdom of God in the liberating rule of God as a transforming power immanent in that system, and the rule of God in the kingdom of God as a future transcending the system' (*CPS*, 190). The kingdom is, then, both the transforming power which is able to realise the possibilities opened up by the promise and it is the fulfilment of these in the coming new creation of righteousness. When potentialities are seized this is not a matter of eschatological indifference, they are 'part of the history of the new creation' (*CPS*, 191).

So then, 'the coming kingdom is present in history as "liberating rule"' (*CPS*, 191). This takes place through (i) the word of promise calling and liberating people, and (ii) the Spirit of freedom, who as its earnest is the beginning of the new creation. The kingdom, the new order begun in the midst of the old, is given 'the mediating name of *messianic*' (*CPS*, 192). The messianic is the mediation between history and the kingdom. This is how Moltmann defines the word which he gives to his whole theological project (*GC*, xv).

In *The Trinity and the Kingdom of God* Moltmann outlines what he calls a *trinitarian doctrine of the kingdom*. Following Joachim of Fiore, the medieval mystic, Moltmann speaks of the kingdom of the Father, the kingdom of the Son and the kingdom of the Spirit (*TKG*, 202-220; 1991:91-109; *SL*, 295-98). The kingdom of the Father consists of creation, its preservation and its openness to the future of the kingdom of glory. Creation is only the beginning of God's creative activity; it unfolds in *creatio continua* and is fulfilled in *creatio nova*. The kingdom of the Son consists in the liberating lordship of the crucified one. It is the liberty of God's children gained through the servitude of the Son. It, too, is open for the kingdom of glory. The kingdom of the Spirit is experienced in the gift conferred on the people liberated by the Son – the gift of the Holy Spirit's energies. Through this gift the new creation is already experienced (as anticipation and pledge) and the new community is formed. Although in this way it is open to it, it is not the kingdom of glory; it is historical.

This has parallels with traditional Protestant theology which speaks of three kingdoms: the *regnum naturæ*, the *regnum gratiæ*, and the *regnum gloriæ*. In fact, however, Joachim of Fiore's schema has four kingdoms because the kingdoms of the Father, Son and Spirit are fulfilled in the kingdom of glory. In Protestant theology the Spirit anticipates the kingdom of glory, but is not said to have a kingdom apart from the Father and Son. Moltmann rejects Joachim's dispensationalism. The kingdoms of the Father, Son and Spirit are not three successive eras. Instead Moltmann speaks of 'continually present strata and transitions in the kingdom's history' (*TKG*, 209). 'These transitions are present in every experience of freedom' (*TKG*, 221). There is a 'trend' (from servants to children to friends), but this should not be thought of in terms of strictly successive events, but as overlapping stages in 'the process of maturing through experiences that are continually new' (*TKG*, 222).

Out of this, Moltmann believes, comes a true doctrine freedom. The fear of God becomes the trust of children and then, through rebirth, God rules directly through his indwelling Spirit. In the kingdom of the Father the relationship is one of dependence; freedom is found in serving God. In the kingdom of the Son there is a new relationship: the servants have become children. In the kingdom of the Spirit, the relationship becomes the reciprocal relationship of friends. In the kingdom of glory 'freedom means the unhindered participation in the eternal life of the triune God himself' (*TKG*, 222).

The Future of the Natural World

The universal and cosmic scope of the kingdom leads in Moltmann's thought to an affirmation of the body and of this world. In *God in Creation* Moltmann cites Friedrich Oetinger, 'Embodiment is the end of all God's works' (244; see also *SL*, 93). This is in contrast to those who have maintained the primacy of the soul over the body. Moltmann believes we should look to a perichoretic pattern (analogous to the trinitarian life) as a preferable model for the relationship between body and soul. Moltmann speaks of the human *Gestalt*; 'the configuration or total pattern of the lived life' (*GC*, 259). Not that the body is everything. Moltmann believes that we must take a broader view of health than is currently held, one which includes a total wholeness of being so that one can speak of health even in sickness (*GC*, 270-275). 'The ethos of the *struggle for existence* must be turned into the ethos of *peace in existence*' (1973ii:98; see also 1975:158-171; 1979i:131-148).

In a similar way, Moltmann looks at the natural world in the light of the cross and resurrection. '[Christ] did not merely die the violent death which belongs to human history. He also died the tragic "death of nature"' (*WJC*, 253). As such his resurrection is the hope of a new creation in which there will be an end to death and decay (see *CoG*, Part IV). This is the basis for the cosmic christology of, for example, Colossians 1. All things are reconciled in Christ; 'mutual destruction is replaced by a community of peace' (*WJC*, 255). Thus, just as the dignity of people derives from the fact that Christ died for them, so, too, does the dignity of all life. 'The special thing about Christian eschatology is its surmounting of the enmity between soul and body, spirit and matter, and its full affirmation of the body and the matter of which earthly things are composed' (*WJC*, 259). The resurrection of the body is the basis for what Bonhoeffer called 'Christianity's profound this-worldliness'. Hope for the redemption of the world leads to the affirmation of the natural world now. Community with nature, rather than its exploitation, is to be our aim (*CoG*, 279).

Moltmann speaks of Christ's death as being in solidarity not only with all human beings, but also in solidarity with all living things. 'Does death really have the same significance for every kind of creature?' asks Bauckham (1991:529). Is the annual cycle of death and new life of a marigold of the same order of tragedy? According to Bauckham's reading of Moltmann, the implication is, that every living creature that ever died – 'every marigold, every termite, every smallpox virus' – will be resurrected in the new creation – a concept that Bauckham acknowledges to be 'bizarre' (1995:210). (Arguably Bauckham's explanation that for Moltmann in eternity 'all the times [of redeemed history] will be simultaneous' so that 'all creatures as they are diachronically in the process of their history ... will be resurrected and transfigured in eternity' is just as bizarre!)

In *God in Creation* Moltmann expands upon this cosmological dimension. The crown of creation, he argues, it not humanity, but the blessing and the rest of the Sabbath (276-96; see also *SL*, 96-7). As such, the Sabbath points forward to the eschatological blessing and rest of creation in the fulfilment of God's purposes for creation. 'The Son of Man did not become man simply because of the sin of men and women, but rather for the sake of perfecting creation' (*TKG*, 116). Christian eschatology is not an 'apocalyptic final solution'. 'In the end is the beginning,' Moltmann has become fond of saying (*CoG*, xi; 2004i): 'In God's creative future, the end will become the beginning, and the true creation is still to come and is ahead of us.' (*CoG*, xi) In *The Spirit of Life* Moltmann adds a pneumatological dimension: 'Through the fellowship of the Spirit, the experience of God will reach beyond experience of the self and the experience of sociality, and become experience of nature too; for the Spirit is the Creator, and the new Creator, of all things.' (*SL*, 221)

The Coming of God

Moltmann says, 'the crucified Christ does not disappear when fulfilment comes, but rather becomes the ground for redeemed existence in God and the indwelling of God in all' (*CG*, 266). The work of Christ does not simply cancel out the effects of sin; there is a 'surplus of Christ's resurrection over his death'

(*WJC*, 186) which leads to a 'surplus of grace' (*CPS*, 31; *TKG*, 116; *WJC*, 186; 1969:21,23; 1979i:168-170). This is the only way the resurrection can qualify as a redemptive event in and of itself (*CPS*, 1). The history of Christ 'is not totally absorbed by the forgiveness of sins but, through the operation of forgiveness, leads to new life and the new creation' (*CPS*, 31; *CoG*, 264, 272). The 'extra' of the new creation over the first creation is the presence of God's Shekinah in space and time, anticipated in the space of the temple and the time of the Sabbath (*CoG*, 265-267, 294). Drawing on Eastern Orthodoxy, Moltmann calls this the 'deification of the world' (CoG, 272-274). This does not mean that we become gods, but that we participate in divine nature and immortality through our union with Christ – and along with us 'nature' as a whole. And so by the time we reach *The Coming of God*, Moltmann concludes: 'the different horizons of eternal life, the eternal kingdom and the eternal creation draw together to a single focus: *the cosmic Shekinah of God.*' (*CoG*, xiii; see also *ET*, 310, 313-320)

CHAPTER 2

Eschatology and Proclamation

An Apologetic for the Resurrection

Moltmann wants to extend the idea of mission beyond simple proclamation. Nevertheless, the proclamation of hope has a place in his missiological agenda. Besides which, given its centrality in his thought, he is concerned to show that the resurrection is credible in the modern world. To these ends he engages in an apologetic of the resurrection.

Since Descartes, the traditions which provided continuity with the past have been increasingly undermined by the method of doubt. Indeed, now they are frequently thought of as representing inherited prejudice. Underlying this is the 'eschatological, messianic passion of the "'modern age"' (*TH*, 294) where the 'old' is left behind in favour of the 'new'. In reaction, Romanticism wants to reverse this and return to the pure origin. It views history as a falling away from the holiness of the beginning. Are these the only options for the church in the modern age? Moltmann thinks not.

The content of Israel's traditions were Yahweh's promise and faithfulness, and so their traditions were oriented to the future. In the same way, argues Moltmann, Christian tradition is not the recounting of doctrinal statements or rules of living, but the proclamation of the eschatological event of the raising of the crucified one. So Christian tradition is proclamation; the proclamation of the presence of Christ and of his future. In order, however, for it not to degenerate into a myth about a heavenly being, the gospel requires a continuity with the earthly Jesus. 'Historical knowledge of Jesus must therefore be constitutive of the faith which awaits the presence and future of God in the name of Jesus' (*TH*, 300). This continuity is provided by the identity of the risen one with the crucified one in the Easter appearances. Nevertheless, the very nature of those appearances orients the tradition to the future.

Because Christian tradition takes the form of proclamation, it is universal. That is to say, it does not pass along the generations, parent to child, but moves outwards in the process of mission. 'It is not through birth, but through rebirth, that faith is propagated' (*TH*, 301; on this basis Moltmann argues against infant baptism, *CPS*, 226-242). 'Christian tradition is then not to be understood as a handing on of something that has to be preserved, but as an event which summons the dead and the godless to life' (*TH*, 302). It is through this proclamation that the godless are justified and, as such, proclamation points to the *nova creatio ex nihilo*. Its basis is the resurrection which makes proclamation both possible and necessary. Christian tradition 'is thus identical with eschatological mission' (*TH*, 302).

Having established a view of tradition that has resurrection at its heart and so is oriented, not to the past, but to the future, how is the concept of resurrection to be proclaimed in a post-Enlightenment, scientific age? The rise of the historico-critical approach to the Bible and Christian tradition has led to a questioning of the historicity of the resurrection. This is legitimate, says Moltmann, to the extent that the Easter records present the resurrection, not as an experience of faith, but as an historical event. What is questionable, however, is the anterior understanding of history behind this historical criticism. History is assumed to have an anthropocentric character, that is to say, its subject is assumed to be humanity. Furthermore, it presupposes there is a common core of similarity throughout history. The result is that it is supposed that history must be judged in relation to present human experience. As a result, by modern standards, resurrection is impossible. Moving from the universal – 'I don't believe in resurrection' – modernity comes to the particular – 'I don't believe in the resurrection of Christ'.

Moltmann, however, asserts that the question of the resurrection recoils on the questioner, questioning his or her view of history. 'It becomes quite a different matter if we stop looking at Christ's resurrection in the perspective of history and look at history in the perspective of the resurrection' (1980:29). If God created *ex nihilo* then the resurrection can be understood as *nova creatio*. There is, then, no analogy with the resurrection short of the new creation. This leads to a view of history at the heart of which is the resurrection. 'The resurrection of Christ is without parallel in history known to us. But it can for that very reason be regarded as a "history-making event" in the light of which all other history is illuminated, called in question and transformed.' (*TH*, 180)

If history is eschatological in this way then a view of history which automatically precludes the resurrection itself becomes questionable. In the worldview of the modern age the resurrection is historically impossible; for the Christian the resurrection defines history. The mistake in apologetics is, for strategic reasons, to concede the modern worldview and so end up arguing the impossible. The shape of Moltmann's argument corresponds closely to Karl Barth's condemnation of those apologists who, for strategic reasons, start with the possibility of knowledge of God rather than starting with the reality of revelation. In the same way, Moltmann works from the reality of the resurrection to a view of history which includes the possibility of resurrection. Both work from reality to possibility rather than from possibility to reality.

In *The Way of Jesus Christ* Moltmann outlines this apologetic in opposition to the historiographical axioms of Troeltsch (1898) which Moltmann believes have 'enjoyed authoritative status for the theology of the resurrection' (*WJC*,

228). These are: (i) historical research can never arrive at absolute knowledge only probable knowledge; (ii) all the phenomena of historical life mutually interpret one another – this provides their ontological foundation; (iii) thus all historical events must have an underlying identity of kind – hence the category of analogy for historical knowledge is based on the homogeneity of all historical events. Moltmann shows how, for example, Barth (with his 'category of divine history') and Bultmann (with his 'category of existential history') shaped their theology of the resurrection in the light of Troeltsch's axioms. Both, he believes, involve a reductionist approach.

Moltmann emphasises the resurrection as an event without analogy; it is qualitatively new and thus a history-making and history-determining event. 'To talk about Christ's resurrection is meaningful only in the framework of the history which the resurrection itself opens up ... In the framework of a history determined in any other way it has no meaning.' (*WJC*, 237) Without belief in the resurrection, there can be no belief in the redemption of the world, and, conversely, without a view of history shaped by the belief in *nova creatio*, there can be no meaning to the resurrection. 'The Christian resurrection faith is thus historically unverifiable ... it is subject to eschatological verification' (1969:51). Thus, the question of what we can know is related to the question of what we hope for and what we must do. 'The resurrection of Christ is *historically* understood in the full sense only in the unity of knowing, hoping and doing' (*WJC*, 237). Or again: 'seeing history in the perspective of resurrection means participating through the Spirit in *the process of resurrection*' (*WJC*, 240).

In discussing the form-critical approach to the question of the resurrection, Moltmann takes this further. The form-critics locate the event of resurrection in the missionary faith of the early church. Thus, the Easter texts are not accounts of events as they happened in history, but are expressions of the church's faith. 'The place of the substantio-metaphysically conceived common core of similarity in all events, which makes analogical understanding possible, is taken by a similarity in the historic character of human existence, which is conceived in terms of fundamental ontology and makes understanding possible between one existence and another in encounter' (*TH*, 185). The problem with this, according to Moltmann, is that it makes anthropology constant and christology variable. In fact, the Easter accounts speak not of human experience, but first and foremost of the actions of God. The narratives themselves present the events of Easter not only as experiences of faith but as narrative, that is as history; as something that took place at a given time. The modern distinction between historical realities and existential calls for decision is alien to the texts.

But what then are we to make of the form-critics' insight that it was the missionary, and not the archivist, who shaped the Easter tradition? Moltmann replies: 'If the reality of the resurrection of Jesus is transmitted and mediated to us only in the form of missionary proclamation, and this form of transmission and mediation manifestly belongs to the reality of the resurrection itself, then it must be asked whether the inner compulsion to this kind of statement and communication is not grounded in the peculiarity of the event itself.' (*TH*, 188; see also 1970i:34-40) It is Moltmann's contention that the very nature of the resurrection, that is its orientation to the future, means of necessity that it is transmitted in the form of proclamation. The commission and basis of the mission of the church, which lies in the resurrection, becomes itself part of the proclamation of that mission. If the event of resurrection points to and strains after the future, then it cannot be reported as an event complete in itself, but instead it must be proclaimed along with its future, that is the future of the one who was raised. In other words, to speak of the resurrection is of necessity to be engaged in missionary proclamation. 'Only missionary proclamation does justice to the historical and eschatological character of this event' (*TH*, 189). And only a missionary and liberating hermeneutic will do justice to the Bible (1975:6-8). This approach to the truth of the resurrection defines a role for theology in the mission of the church. 'As the church is engaged with its surrounding society in the struggle for the truth, so theology has a part in the mission of the church. It must engage with the views of history and historical world-views in a struggle for the future of the truth and therefore also in a battle for the reality of the resurrection of Jesus.' (*TH*, 182)

Proclaiming the Resurrection in the Modern World

Moltmann, as we have seen, refuses to speak of the resurrection as historical in the same way as we can speak of the cross as historical (see, for example, *WJC*, 214; *CoG*, 69). He insists that we must call it eschatological – as opposed to historical – since it is the first act of new creation; the initiation of the eschatological age. The resurrection does not speak the 'language of facts' but the 'language of promise' (see *CG*, 172-173). Has Moltmann solved the historicity problem or merely side-stepped it? The problem is confused by the fact that Moltmann goes beyond simply saying that the resurrection, as an eschatological event, is not historically verifiable, to say that it is not an historical event. It is 'not a historical revelation of God *in* history; on the contrary, the eschatological revelation of God is "the end of history"' (*CG*, 136). This, however, is not necessarily to say that it is unhistorical (that it did not take place), but rather that it is eschatological. The contrast is not between historical and unhistorical but between historical and eschatological. The result is a situation in which Moltmann does not say the resurrection is historical, but neither does he say it is unhistorical. He can talk about it as if it happened, but because he fails to define the ontological status of his language or use of biblical imagery, we cannot be certain of – how shall we put it? – its factuality. On the one hand, the importance which it plays in his thought suggests he believes in a factual resurrection; on the other hand, his use of Blochian language suggests a more symbolic interpretation (the power of the future etc.) may lie behind his usage. Macquarrie believes Moltmann fails to give 'any clear meaning to "resurrection"' (1978:102). Thus, while Bauckham can claim, 'Moltmann is quite clear that the resurrection of Jesus was a real event in space and time' (1989i:210), Grace Jantzen, for one, suspects the resurrection in Moltmann's thought is 'merely a term used as a symbol of hope' (1982:5).

Does this matter? Jantzen thinks so. She believes that if Jesus is not literally raised from the dead then this 'symbol of hope' is 'a grotesquely misguided symbol' (1982:5). For if Jesus is not raised then his cry of godforsakenness must be the last word. Certainly the *word* of resurrection can hardly have the same status as promise as the *fact* of resurrection. And, if the *word* of resurrection is that God will create a new future for us, it is hard to see what this amounts to if he has not done this for his Son, the crucified one, or for that matter, how Christ's resurrection can be called a *firstfruit* of what is to come.

Nevertheless, as an apologetic for the resurrection, Moltmann's exposition has much to commend it. His belief in the questionableness of the preconceptions of modern historiography when used on the resurrection is welcome. He is surely right to say that the resurrection creates its own perspective on history, the perspective of the God who creates *ex nihilo* and who raises from the dead, and that it is not verified in historical terms, but in eschatological terms. The problem is that this creates a closed circle of faith in which the Easter accounts are only understandable from the perspective of resurrection faith and hope. The problem is further compounded by Moltmann's assertion that the resurrection has no analogy in history. It is questionable what basis hope can have if it has no relation to present experience (see Gilkey, 1970:88; Harvey, 1970:129; Hodgson, 1971:240; Macquarrie, 1990:322-323). As Macquarrie says, 'Past and future cannot be used to verify each other without reference to the present' (1970:122).

Langdon Gilkey believes the missing element in Moltmann's approach is the *sensus divinum*, as Calvin puts it, mediated by the Holy Spirit. Gilkey writes:

> Perhaps the authority of *das Wort* in the German theological tradition is sufficient to explain psychologically the authority, for theologians, of [the Easter] reports, but, as the authority of the church was not sufficient for Calvin, such traditional authority, even in such an impressive theological tradition, is not sufficient when one is asking *theological* questions. Only the immediate presence of the Holy Spirit, said Calvin, can be a basis for faith in these words – and that is an immediacy of the divine which witnesses in our hearts to the truth of the apostolic witness. (1970:88)

Putting it in Moltmann's terms: while the resurrection has no historical analogies, it does have eschatological analogies. That is to say, if the resurrection is an eschatological event which takes place in history then we should look for analogies to the resurrection in other eschatological events which take place in history. Moltmann's theology is capable of providing these. He talks, for example, about the experience of new birth as an anticipation of the new creation (*CPS*, 279; 1988:86). In more general terms, if 'eschatology is the work of the Spirit', if the Spirit is the 'advance payment' (*CPS*, 34) of the future, then we should expect analogies of the resurrection in the work of the Spirit. This brings us back to Gilkey and Calvin. And indeed in responding to Gilkey, Moltmann says: 'If in the history of death there are no analogies of Jesus' resurrection, there are at least analogies in the category of the Spirit and his effects. For us today, the experienceable form of the resurrection is the "the Spirit of the resurrection" or "the power of the resurrection".' (1970i:163)

While Moltmann continues to speak of the resurrection as an event without analogy in his later theology (*WJC*, 229), in *The Spirit of Life*, Moltmann places significant emphasis upon our experience of God. Indeed, the book is called *The Spirit of Life* because Moltmann wants 'to bring out the unity between the experience of God and the experience of life' (x). To experience the spirit of life is to experience God's Holy Spirit. Although Moltmann does not comment upon it, this emphasis upon what is known and experienced in the present stands in contrast to the emphasis in his early theology upon the God who is known through promise. Throughout *The Spirit of Life* the emphasis is upon the experience of the Spirit in the experiences of life, whereas in *Theology of Hope* the emphasis was upon the contradiction with the present into which the promise brings us. (See Bauckham, 1995:213-47.) Not that the eschatological dimension is lost. 'The more deeply the presence of the Spirit is experienced in the heart and in fellowship with one another, the more certain and assured the hope for the Spirit's universal coming will be' (74; see also 151-2). Neither is the notion of contradiction lost, for, as Moltmann puts it, '*when freedom is close, the chains begin to hurt*' (75). We experience what is positive in 'the determined negation of what has been experienced as negative' (75). Nevertheless, while in *Theology of Hope* Christian experience is only known in the contradiction between reality and the promise, in *The Spirit of Life* it seems almost any experience counts as Christian experience. 'Every experience that happens to us or that we have, can possess a transcendent, inward side ... It is therefore possible to experience God in, with and beneath each everyday experience of the world' (34; see also 18, 35, 39). This experience of God in all things allows Moltmann to relate pneumatology to his ecological concerns (10, 36). The Spirit is not simply the Spirit of redemption but also the Spirit of nature and the body (8).

The Spirit of Life involves a deliberate determination 'to start ... with the personal and shared experience of the Spirit, instead of with the objective word of proclamation' (17). The result is not simply the correction called for above by Gilkey, namely an emphasis upon the subjectivity of revelation in the anticipatory work of the Spirit, but an activity of the Spirit in the experiences of life which is complementary to revelation in the Word. According to Moltmann: 'The Holy Spirit is not simply the subjective side of God's revelation of himself' (7). Moltmann here displays the influence of ecumenical theology (in which he has been an enthusiastic participant), with its emphasis upon understanding the signs of God's activity in the world – in both secular and religious movements – and making these normative for determining the shape of mission (see Chester, 1993:62). The theology of revelation, Moltmann claims, is 'church theology, a theology for pastors and priests'; whereas the theology of experience is 'pre-eminently lay theology' (*SL*, 17). The implication – albeit not one spelt out by Moltmann – is that revelation is the property of the clergy and used by them to control the laity; whereas experience is a liberating and democratic force.

In *The Way of Jesus Christ*, Moltmann says, 'All knowledge of God begins with the terrible perception of the Wholly Other' (*WJC*, 245). Such a statement would have been impossible in 1968 when Moltmann said (at the same consultation at which Gilkey's comments, cited above, were made): 'God is not "beyond us" or "in us", but ahead of us in the horizons of the future opened to us in his promises' (1970i:10). Gilkey's question is, If God is future then how can we experience the presence of God through the Holy Spirit, the experience which gives rise to faith? Moltmann's answer appears in the long run to be a modification – albeit unacknowledged – in his theology. In *The Spirit of Life* Moltmann says, 'experiences of the Holy Spirit ... are of unfathomable depth, because in them God himself is present *in us*, so that in the immanence of our hearts we discover *a transcendent depth*' (*SL*, 155; emphasis added) – a long way from 'God is not "beyond us" or "in us"'.

This shift affects his critique of Dialectical Theology. In his early theology, as we have seen, Moltmann claimed that dialectical theologians had made revelation a timeless, transcendent event instead of an eschatological promise. In so doing, claimed Moltmann, they perpetuate the dualism between fact and faith, public and private, the world and God. In *The Spirit of Life* Moltmann claims the dialectical theologians held a false distinction between the emphasis of the Romantics upon human experience – which they rejected – and the emphasis upon the Word from God – which they advocated. 'Anyone who stylises revelation and experience into alternatives, ends up with revelations that cannot be experienced, and experiences without revelation' (*SL*, 7).

In the same way, Moltmann's response to Troeltsch's historiographical principle of analogy also appears to change. In *Theology of Hope* the response centred on the *resurrection* – the resurrection is an eschatological event with no analogies (*TH*, 172-182). In *The Way of Jesus Christ*, however, it is the underlying principle – that like is known by like – which is questionable (*WJC*, 244-245). Although not explicitly identified, it is clear that behind this stands Moltmann's understanding of the dialectical principle of knowledge which has its roots in the *cross* (see *CG*, 25-28,212-213; 1979i:77-79; and also Bauckham, 1977:301-311; 1987i:67-72).

Moltmann's Theological Method and Style

The ambiguous way in which Moltmann treats the 'factuality' of the resurrection is typical of his theological method as a whole. Richard Bauckham, perhaps Moltmann's strongest advocate and expositor in the evangelical world, points to a lack of concreteness in much of Moltmann's thought, especially in his early theology (1987i:41; 1995:99-100,104-5,115-6). Even Moltmann's later work, says Bauckham, can be 'disappointingly, sometimes frustratingly, lacking in concreteness' (1995:184). There is a lack of analytical rigour. Moltmann himself says: 'For me, theology was, and still is, as adventure of ideas. It is an open, inviting path ... I was not concerned to collect up correct theological notions, because I was much too preoccupied with the perception of new perspectives and unfamiliar aspects.' (*ET*, xv; see also *CoG*, xiv) The result, according to Bauckham, is a tendency to uncritically favour revolutionary change since this more fittingly corresponds to the radicalness of the future (1989ii:308-9).

Bauckham's criticisms of Moltmann's theological method have been stated even more strongly by others. Henri Blocher says, 'Moltmann is *first of all* an orator' (1985:119). Carl Braaten decries his tendency towards overstatement (1976:120; see also Brown, 1985:307-308 and McGrath, 1986:193). Webster contrasts Moltmann to other writers on the Trinity who are characterised by their careful analytical style (Webster, 1985:4). Stephen Williams notes 'Moltmann's habit of apparently denying in one place what he apparently partially allows elsewhere (the word 'not' slides uneasily into 'not only' occasionally in his literature)' (1989:13). Thus, for example, in *The Crucified God* Moltmann says we must 'abandon the traditional theories of salvation' (*CG*, 33), while later speaking of the need to 'go beyond' them (*CG*, 184) and the importance of 'the representative saving significance of [Christ's] death on the cross' (*CG*, 185-6). More provocatively than most, Don Cupitt writes: 'Moltmann is desperately ambiguous ... Is it all safe, pious talk, and action guiding rhetoric? I do not know, for I do not understand how an academic can be content to be so deeply ambiguous and evasive as this.' (1980:216)

Moltmann fails to define the ontological status of his language – even though such a process would seem apposite when discussing eschatology. This is evident from the radically varying understandings of Moltmann's thought. Some claim Moltmann demythologizes the eschaton (Gilkey, 1976:229; Hoekema, 1978:316; Blocher, 1990:19-20), while others accuse him of taking it too literally (O'Collins, 1968:49; Hick, 1976:214; Macquarrie, 1980:5). Is Moltmann engaged in *de*-mythologization or, as Macquarrie puts it, *re*-mythologization? Nobody seems to know. When you read Moltmann you are left asking, 'What exactly does he mean by this?' This is not because his thought is excessively complex, but because one is never certain how he is using language. Moltmann's use of Blochian terminology does not help. A phrase such as 'the moving horizon of the future' is a case in point. What Wayne Hudson said of Bloch could well be said of Moltmann. His work is '...enchanted language, full of foreboding and ontological significance, which finally remains cipher talk, metaphorical drama which cannot be precisely glossed ... unnecessarily mystifying ... including the tendency to an excessive categorical innovation which proclaims the discovery of a new category too often to be convincing.' (1982:157-158)

Bauckham also identifies a tendency towards 'undisciplined speculation' (1989ii:308-9; 1995:167), citing as examples Moltmann's contribution to the *Filioque* debate, his discussion of feminine images of God and his use of Joachim of Fiore's three kingdoms typology (1995:167-70, 181). To this list we might add the concept of *zimsum*, the idea that the incarnation was necessary apart from humanity's sin, the idea that God's Shekinah presence becomes alienated from God in the alienation of individuals and Moltmann's panentheism – none of which find clear, concrete support in the Scriptures (Braaten, 1976:118; Mackey, 1983:205; D. Brown, 1985:307; Walsh:1987:73). One is left asking from where Moltmann gets his special knowledge of the trinitarian life! Describing *God in Creation*, Bauckham says, 'at its worst this is a book whose argument takes flight into a kind of pure speculation in which Moltmann in his more recent work seems to have developed a tendency to indulge' (1995:184). Bauckham begins to sound like a frustrated, yet committed, fan whose team is playing badly! Carl Braaten speaks of Moltmann 'flying on his own' (1976:118) and Paul Wells complains of a 'lack of theological humility' (1990:66-7; see also Berkouwer, 1977:255 and Dumas, 1978:104). Speculation must be accompanied by a delineation of the limits of our knowledge, a recognition of the unknowability of God, otherwise it slips uneasily into dogmatic statements. Furthermore, the limited usefulness of speculation for practical theology and missiology must be recognised. Such criticisms are all the more striking in the light of Moltmann's own eschatological re-formation of Luther's understanding of the hiddenness of God (God is hidden because full revelation is future). It would seem that Moltmann goes beyond his own limits!

This indulgence in speculation is coupled with a tendency 'to ignore historical-critical interpretation' (Bauckham, 1989ii:309; 1995:167; *ET*, xxi). The result, says Bauckham, is that Moltmann leaves 'his hermeneutical principles dangerously unclear' (1989ii:309; see also 1995:191). Moltmann himself concedes: 'sometime in the 1970s, the exegetical discussion became hazy and confused for me, and the hermeneutic discussion even more. I found it more of a hindrance in listening to the biblical texts ... Finding myself as a loss, I then doubtless developed my own post-critical and "naïve" relationship to the biblical writings.' (*ET*, xxi) Bauckham believes that Moltmann's drift towards speculation and away from firm hermeneutics are linked. 'Unable to find a real basis in the biblical history for the kind of speculation in which he engages, Moltmann freely employs inferences from biblical phrases and metaphors which, he sometimes admits (e.g. *GC* 218), cannot be warranted by historical-critical exegesis' (1995:167). Looking back on his theological journey, Moltmann himself says, 'in my dealings with what the biblical writings say I have also noticed how critical and free I have become towards them ... I take scripture as a stimulus to my own theological thinking, not as an authoritative blueprint and confining boundary.' (*ET*, xxi-xxii) In developing a doctrine of scripture Moltmann makes the text of scripture subservient to 'the matter of scripture' (*ET*, 134-139). As a result, 'if we look at scriptural texts from the angle of "the matter of scripture", then the canon remains open: we can, for objective reasons, judge the Epistle of James to be "an epistle of straw", as Luther did, and might prefer to exclude the book of Revelation; but we can also preach from non-biblical texts if they accord with "the matter of scripture".' (*ET*, 138) Bauckham accuses Moltmann of 'mere citation of texts in a pre-critical manner' and 'hermeneutical irresponsibility in the service of speculation' (1995:167-168). It is ironic that an evangelical should level such criticisms against such a prominent non-evangelical theologian given that an uncritical or pre-critical approach to scripture is a frequent accusation made against evangelicals.

'God is dead' … And on the Third Day He Rose Again

Despite these concerns, there is in Moltmann apologia for the resurrection something which is suggestive. I want to suggest how it is possible to build on Moltmann through a dialogue with Nietzsche and Bonhoeffer.

Friedrich Nietzsche (1844-1900) was perhaps the apotheosis of the modern rejection of God. He was radically anti-Christian. The whole notion that human beings needed God and needed redemption was obnoxious to Nietzsche. He believed that Christianity undervalues bodily life, deprecates all that is aesthetic and restrains human freedom. Nietzsche says: 'I call Christianity the *one* great curse, the *one* great intrinsic depravity, the *one* great instinct for revenge for which no expedient is sufficiently poisonous, secret, subterranean, *petty.*' (*Antichrist*, 62) What really annoyed Nietzsche was the call to self-denial. Nietzsche said that people should assert a will to power. He talked about a new *Übermensch* ('superman'). Nietzsche valued every expression of human self-will. When it comes to God, it is Nietzsche who first said that 'God is dead'. And what is more, it is we who have killed him. For Nietzsche this is the triumph of human freedom. We no longer need God to make our way in the world. We can live without him. Nietzsche's presence is everywhere in Western thought. His shadow pervades the twentieth century. We see it existentialism, radical secularism, materialism and even consumerism. The twenty-first century society exists as if God is dead and often seems to rejoice in its deicide.

Dietrich Bonhoeffer also recognised that God was absent from modern society. Bonhoeffer argued that we must live today as if God did not exist, that we must develop 'religionless Christianity'. These suggestive motifs were taken up by the death-of-God theologians and the Christian secularists such as Harvey Cox. What is more suggestive, however, is Bonhoeffer's focus on the powerlessness of God. Here we approach Bonhoeffer's solution to the problem rather than his analysis of it which is what Cox *et al* have focused on.

And we cannot be honest unless we recognise that we have to live in the world *etsi deus non daretur* ('as if God did not exist'). And this is just what we do recognise – before God! God himself compels us to recognise it. So our coming of age leads us to a recognition of our situation before God. God would have us know that we must live as men who manage our lives without him. The God who is with us is the God who forsakes us (Mark 15:34). The God who lets us live in the world without the working hypothesis of God is the God before whom we stand continually. Before God and with God we live without God. God lets himself be pushed out of the world on to the cross. He is weak and powerless in the world, and that is precisely the way, the only way, in which he is with us and helps us. Matt 8:17 makes it clear that Christ helps us, not by virtue of his omnipotence, but by virtue of his weakness and suffering.

Here is the decisive difference between Christianity and all religions. Man's religiosity makes him look in his distress to the power of God in the world: God is the *deus ex machina*. The Bible directs man to God's powerlessness and suffering; only the suffering God can help. To that extent we may say that the development towards the world's coming of age outlined above, which has done away with a false conception of God, opens up a way of seeing the God of the Bible, who wins power and space in the world by his weakness, This will probably be the starting - point for our 'secular interpretation'. (Bonhoeffer, 1971:360-361)

The problem with so many modern readings of Bonhoeffer is that they stop at the end of the first paragraph and in doing so miss the point. The second paragraph quoted is so thoroughly Lutheran (and Bonhoeffer was steeped in Luther). It is simply a restatement and re-application of Luther's *theologia crucis*. The point is not that God is powerless or absent from the world, but rather that he is powerful through the weakness of the cross, present through the godforsakenness of the cross.

What do we say in a world in which God is dead? We certainly do not try to pretend that it is otherwise. Nor can we retreat into our subculture, our private world of faith – that is to abandon the world. Nietzsche cries: '"Whither is God?" he cried; "I will tell you. *We have killed him* – you and I. All of us are his murderers ... God is dead ... And we have killed him." (*The Gay Science*, III.125) After this the madman comes and says: '"I have come too early," he said then: "my time is not yet. This tremendous event is still on its way, still wandering; it has not yet reached the ears of men ... and yet they have done it themselves." (*The Gay Science*, III.125.) Williams comments: 'Fresh from the biblical narrative, one can find fault with only one sentiment, but an important one. Far from the fact that the madman has come early and the deed is on its way, the story has come late and the deed is long since accomplished.' (Williams, 1995:106)

We respond to a world that cries 'God is dead' by acknowledging that God is dead, but proclaim that on the third day he rose again. This is not to attach some symbolic sense to Calvary (as Hegel did). Humanity rebelled against God, choosing to live without God: as such the world is quite literally god-less.

In response, God cursed the world; he forsook it. God's punishment against humanity's sin is the withdrawal of his presence, of his love, of relationship. On the cross Christ takes upon himself the effects of humanity's rebellion; both the godlessness and godforsakenness of the world. But he does so in order to redeem the world, to restore a relationship with God and to claim all of life afresh as Lord.

The resurrection is promise, not fulfilment. After all, the cross and resurrection precede the advent of modernity. It is no good simply saying God died and then rose again if the world continues to feel god-less and indeed feels it more than ever. In that case the world would make the resurrection questionable – as indeed it does. Instead, in reality, it is the resurrection that makes the world questionable, in other words, provisional. In the light of the world we see around us – godless and godforsaken – the concept of God becomes questionable. But in the light of God in Christ the world – godless and godforsaken – becomes questionable. The world judges God and declares him absent. But in Christ God judges the world and claims it as his own.

The resurrection is not the fulfilment, but the promise because salvation is eschatological. The gospel is promise (it is this that provides the continuity between the Old and New Testaments). It is received in hope. The world is still godless and godforsaken, but already God is present with his people, he speaks through his word and through his Spirit, and he lays claim to the whole cosmos through the risen Christ. Ultimately he will redeem and recreate the world. Ultimately a world without God and forsaken by God will be filled with the glory of God as the waters cover the sea. And so the message we proclaim to a secular, post-modern society is the same as ever: Christ has died, Christ has risen, Christ will come again.

Until the time when Christ comes again there is a very real sense in which we cannot say that God is present in the world, nor can we say that he is absent. Rather we can say with the Reformers that he is hidden; or rather, he is hidden in what is opposite. His glory, power and wisdom are seen in the shame, weakness and foolishness of the cross. And they are seen in the cross-centred lives of those who follow Christ. Our life, that is our conformity to Christ's resurrection, is hidden in our conformity to Christ in his death (2 Corinthians 4:10-12; Colossians 3:3). How will we make God known to a post-Christian world? By revealing him in cross-centred discipleship.

Has God died? Has God forsaken the world? Must we live in a world without God? The answer to all these questions must be Yes. But Christ has risen, he has redeemed the world from God's curse and now as Lord he claims all of life. The startling thing is this: the message of secularism and the message of the cross is the same: the world has been forsaken by God, he is dead, we must live in the world without him. The difference is that this is where the message of secularism ends, but it is where the message of the cross begins. The Reformation, the scientific revolution, the Enlightenment, modernity: all lead to this terrible conclusion: God is dead and we live in the world without him. All that can follow is the non-truth or relativism of postmodernity. This is as true for many Christians as it is for non-Christians. God is present in our private faith sub-culture, but as we live in the world, we do so without God. He does not impinge upon our public relationships, our social attitudes or our actions.

But if this is where the message of secularism ends, it is where the message of the cross begins. God has died, the world is forsaken by God, it is without God. But 'on the third day he rose again'. Christ has died, but now he has risen. He took upon himself the curse of humanity – to be forsaken by God (Mark 15:57) – in order to redeem the world. Raised as Lord he lays claim to all of life. The reason we are sent out in mission is that all authority has been given to the Son: the world was without God, but now in Christ the whole world is claimed in his name.

CHAPTER 3

Eschatology and the Trinity

The Trinitarian History of God

The fundamental premise of Moltmann's missiology and ecclesiology is that
the church participates in the mission of God to the world. The mission of the
church must be placed within the context of what Moltmann calls *the
trinitarian history of God.*

> In the movements of the trinitarian history of God's dealings with the world the
> church finds and discovers itself ... It is not the church that has a mission of
> salvation to fulfil to the world; it is the mission of the Son and the Spirit through
> the Father that includes the church, creating a church as it goes on its way ... The
> church participates in Christ's messianic mission and in the creative mission of
> the Spirit. We cannot therefore say *what* the church is in all circumstances and
> what it comprises in itself. But we can tell *where* the church happens ... Thus the
> whole being of the church is marked by participation in the history of God's
> dealing with the world. (*CPS*, 64-65; see also *ET*, 310-312)

Although the trinitarian history of God is most systematically elaborated in
The Trinity and the Kingdom of God, it arises first in *The Crucified God*. This is
significant for, according to Moltmann, an understanding of the trinitarian
history of God begins with the cross. The cross 'divides God from God to the
utmost degree of enmity and distinction'. There is between the Father and the
Son a separation 'which takes place within God himself; it is *stasis* within God
– "God against God"' (*CG*, 152). The Son suffers abandonment by the Father,
but the Father himself suffers, though in a different way – he suffers the loss of
his Son. Moltmann speaks of a 'death *in* God' (*CG*, 207). Yet in this absolute
and terrible separation of Father and Son there is, through the Spirit (see, for
example, *SL*, 63-4), a volitional unity; a unity of purpose. In taking upon
himself the godforsakenness of the world, its suffering and its death, the Son
takes up the world and unites it to God. Christ's death is a death 'for us'. The
resurrection prefigures the eschatological unity of God in glory. 'The
resurrection of the Son abandoned by the Father unites God with God in the
most intimate fellowship' (*CG*, 152).

Through the event of the cross and resurrection, however, the unity of God is now open to humanity and to the world. In *The Coming of God* Moltmann says that the process of God's glorification must be understood 'not exclusively but inclusively': 'the fellowship between Christ and God in the process of mutual glorification is so wide open that the community of Christ's people can find a place in it' (*CG*, 335). Through Christ, God takes up the world and makes in part of himself, not just that which is good but also the suffering of the world, so that the world might participate in the divine unity and glory. Indeed the very protest of theodicy, heard on the lips of the Son of God (Mark 15:34), now exists in God.

This schema has a number of important theological consequences. Moltmann is quite clear that it requires what he calls a 'revolution in the concept of God' (*CG*, 335; see also 1979i:93). It is this revolution which lies behind Moltmann's response to 'protest atheism' (see, for example, Bauckham, 1987:ii). In the light of the cross, theology either becomes impossible or distinctly Christian (*CG*, 153).

The Passibility of God

Following Bonhoeffer (1971:360-361), Moltmann argues strongly for the passibility of God (*CG*, 126-127). He rejects the classical idea of *apatheia* as a metaphysical axiom and ethical ideal, and instead, drawing on Jewish theology, he outlines an understanding of the *pathos* of God. God's *Shekinah* implies his passionate involvement and co-suffering with his people (*CG*, 267-278; *TKG*, 21-30; *SL*, 47-51,62; 1979i:69-71; 1991:23-4). Moltmann criticises the classic argument for the impassibility of God because it fails to recognise the alternative to impassibility on the one hand, and unwilling suffering and change on the other; namely willing suffering, the suffering of love (*CG*, 229-231). We cannot talk about the immutability, the impassibility and the invulnerability of God if these mean that 'in the freedom of his love' God could not choose to change, to suffer and to be vulnerable on the cross (*CPS*, 62; see also 1979i:92-93). Indeed, Moltmann even says, 'God is *not perfect* if this means that he did not in the craving of his love want his creation to be necessary to his perfection' (*CPS*, 62). The cross involves 'a new experience for God' (*CPS*, 62). If God is love then we cannot talk about his freedom not to love even if this love is suffering love. 'In God *necessity* and *freedom* coincide' (*TKG*, 107). The highest form of freedom is not the power of choice (that leads to the language of domination), but the unreserved determination to, and realisation of, good. '[God's] freedom therefore lies in the *friendship* he offers to men and women, and through which he makes them his friends' (*TKG*, 56).

God's Openness to the World

This conception of God's freedom lies behind Moltmann's understanding of

God's openness to the world. The central thesis of Moltmann's theology could well be summarised as, 'For eschatological faith, the trinitarian God-event on the cross becomes the history of God which is open to the future and which opens up the future' (*CG*, 255). The Trinity is not a closed circle, but 'eschatologically open history ... If Christian belief thinks in trinitarian terms, it says that forsaken men are already taken up by Christ's forsakenness into the divine history and that we "live in God", because we participate in the eschatological life of God by virtue of the death of Christ.' (*CG*, 255)

Moltmann maintains that 'the *missio ad extra* reveals the *missio ad intra*' (*CPS*, 54). That is to say, 'the Trinity in the sending reveals the Trinity in the origin as being from eternity an open Trinity ... It is open for men and for all creation' (*CPS*, 55; 1979i:85). This understanding of the Trinity as open to humanity in *sending* which culminates in the cross and resurrection must be balanced by an understanding of the Trinity as open in the corresponding event of the Trinity after the cross and resurrection, namely glorification. The goal of God's history is his glorification and 'the trinitarian history of glorification leads to the eschatological unity of God' (1979i:91). The trinitarian history of God is a movement from unity to unity, but, with the cross at its centre, it becomes 'soteriologically imbued' (1979i:92) because through the cross and resurrection Christ unites men and women with God. 'In this union God is glorified through men and in it they partake of the glory of God himself' (*CPS*, 59). 'The Trinity in the glorification is open for the gathering and uniting of men and creation in God' (1979i:91; see also *ET*, 322-323). It is the Spirit who creates this unity with God in Christ and he does so even now, making the coming glory efficacious in present life. 'Wherever on the way to this goal the gospel is preached to the poor, sins are forgiven, the sick are healed, the oppressed are freed and outcasts are accepted, God is glorified and creation is in part perfected' (*CPS*, 60).

Panentheism

God's openness to the world from creation and the eschatological unity of creation *in* God leads Moltmann to develop a doctrine of panentheism as an expression of the dialectic of God's relationship to the world; the dialectic of transcendence (monotheism) and immanence (pantheism). 'The "history of God", whose nucleus is the event of the cross, cannot be thought of as history in the world, but on the contrary makes it necessary to understand the world in this history ... the world is a possibility and a reality in this history ... The history of God is ... the horizon of the world.' (*CG*, 218-219) Theism, by stressing God's differentiation from the world, has allowed humanity (as God's image) to likewise differentiate itself from the world and so justified the domination and exploitation of the earth where there should have been participation and community with creation. That is why Moltmann entitles his 'ecological doctrine of creation', *God in Creation* (1985).

In working out a doctrine of creation in panentheistic terms, Moltmann draws upon the Jewish mystical idea of *zimsum* (*TKG*, 109-111; *GC*, 86-93; *WJC*, 328-330). Traditional Christian theology has considered creation an act of God outwards. But can an omnipresent God have an 'outward' aspect? Moltmann believes that in creation God withdrew from himself to leave a realm 'outside' God; a realm of 'nothingness' out of which, or in which, God creates the world. Thus, creation presupposes God's self-limitation. 'It is only God's withdrawal into himself which gives that *nihil* the space in which God then becomes creatively active' (*TKG*, 109). This *nihil* is godforsakenness, hell, absolute death. *Creatio ex nihilo* points forward to the redeeming *annihilatio nihili*. The resurrection, the firstfruits of the new creation, is an act of life out of *nihil* and, as such, it corresponds to *creatio ex nihilo*. Much the same idea applies to time. Time is only ever created time and it, too, presupposes a self-limitation of God in that he creates time within his eternity.

Moltmann stresses the involvement of all the members of the Trinity in creation concluding that 'creation can only be conceived of in trinitarian terms' (*TKG*, 105). Or again: 'In the panentheistic view, God, having created the world, also dwells in it, and conversely the world which he has created exists in him. This is a concept which can only be thought and described in trinitarian terms.' (*GC*, 98; see pp.9-13, 94-98). Furthermore, in Moltmann's panentheism, through the cross, even the godforsakenness of life exists in God (*CG*, 277; *SL*, 211-3). God's self-limitation in creation corresponds to his self-humiliation on the cross – they presuppose each other. God's freedom in both cases is defended by Moltmann in the same way: on the basis of the necessity of his love.

The Cross and the Trinity

The cross and the Trinity, perhaps the two most distinctive features of Christianity, are integrally connected in Moltmann's thought. Moltmann believes that the cross can only be truly understood as the death of God if one thinks in trinitarian terms and speaks of a death *in* God (*CG*, 200-207). Thus, the cross and the Trinity mutually interpret one another: the cross is the starting point for understanding the Trinity; the Trinity is necessary for an understanding of the cross (1979i:74,91; 1980:16; *ET*, 305). Where experience (Schleiermacher) or practice (Kant), rather than the scandal of the cross, are made the starting point for theology, the Trinity has been undermined (*TKG*, 2-9). Moltmann, in contrast, looks at the history of Jesus from a trinitarian perspective, examining the involvement of each of the persons of the Trinity at the different stages in that history. He notes, furthermore, that the Trinity does not always function according to the same pattern (traditionally understood to be Father-Son-Spirit).

Behind the failure of modern theology to articulate an understanding of the Trinity, argues Moltmann, is the understanding of God either as Supreme

Substance, based upon the cosmological proof of God's existence, or Absolute Subject, based upon the existentialist proof of God's existence (*TKG*, 10-16). Starting with the question of God in this way meant the Trinity was always examined within the context of the unity of God. Ever since Aquinas broke the pattern of Peter Lombard's *Sentences*, *De Deo uno* has preceded *De Deo trino* (*CG*, 239; *CPS*, 370, fn.107; *TKG*, 17; 1979i:91). This has led in turn to the three-ness of the Trinity being reduced to 'modes of being' in order to preserve the unity of God (*TKG*, 18). (Barth and Rahner are guilty of this, according to Moltmann, even though formally they return to Lombard's pattern, *TKG*, 139-148; *SL*, 290.)

Starting from the history of Jesus and from the cross, Moltmann has no hesitation in speaking of three persons – this is after all, he notes, the way the Bible encourages us to speak. For Moltmann three-ness is a presupposition for an examination of God's unity (and not vice versa). Given this, we must 'dispense' with one substance and identical subject, and speak of God's 'unitedness' (*TKG*, 150). The unity of the Trinity, says Moltmann, is volitional rather than ontological. It is expressed as community rather than *una natura* (*CG*, 243-244; *CPS*, 62; *TKG*, 95-96, 150; 1979i:92). Following John of Damascus, Moltmann describes the Trinity in terms of *perichoresis*: the persons of the Trinity are alive in one another and through one another to such an extent that they are one. Through this, the persons of the Trinity mutually reveal one another's glory (*TKG*, 174-176; 1991:xv-xvi,86,131-2).

A Social Trinity

This understanding of the Trinity has social consequences, according to Moltmann. The perichoretic fellowship of the Trinity provides a pattern for human association. The social Trinity is a model for human society. We are both to participate in, and reflect, this trinitarian model. And, therefore, a feature of mission is a concern for perichoretic fellowship in human relationships. This social model is itself rooted in the trinitarian history of God. From the terrible separation of Father and Son on the cross, the trinitarian history of God, now open to the world, moves through the unifying love of the Spirit towards eschatological unification and glorification, towards an eschatological perichoretic fellowship which includes the world.

The doctrine of the Trinity, far from upholding monarchy and patriarchy, actually undermines them. 'The inner fellowship of the Father, the Son and the Holy Spirit is represented in the fundamental human communities, and is manifested in them through creation and redemption' (*GC*, 241; see also *TKG*, 191-222; *CoG*, 183; 1981i:53; 1984ii:91-104; 1991:xi-xvi,1-25; *ET*, 303-304,332-333). It also has ecological consequences for Moltmann speaks of 'a perichoretic doctrine of creation'. 'What is normative for all relations in creation is not the structure of command and obedience within the Trinity, but the eternal perichoresis of the triunity' (1991:127; see also *GC*, 16-17).

Moltmann, then, sees in the social doctrine of the Trinity a model for all human relationships. 'The triune God is community ... and makes himself the model for a just and liveable community in the world of nature and human beings' (1991:xii-xiii).

Moltmann's use of the Trinity as a model of social interactions, however, has been criticised. David Brown questions whether such a social Trinity in fact achieves what Moltmann intends it to. He points out that three-person juntas are as equally capable of domination as a one person dictatorship (1985:308). Moltmann, however, does not stress plurality *per se*, but rather the mutuality of the plurality as a model for social organisation. Bauckham's comment that Moltmann confuses authority with domination is perhaps more pertinent (1987i:135). This confusion between authority and domination means ultimately that Moltmann is wary of any form of hierarchy – ultimately even between God and humanity (*TKG*, 219-22).

To say that we are to participate in the trinitarian fellowship and that we are to reflect the trinitarian fellowship is to say two distinct things, argues Bauckham (1995:177). While the former, that we participate in the trinitarian life, is true; the latter Bauckham finds to be somewhat questionable, despite being a feature of the work of other contemporary theologians. 'To stand outside this participation in the Trinity and our specific relationship to the three Persons and to view the Trinity as an external model which human relationships should reflect ... has no biblical basis' (1995:177). We are asked to see the Spirit as one of the divine community whose fellowship we are to reflect. Yet, while the terms Father and Son refer to mutual relationships, the Spirit as a subject in relation to the Father and the Son can only be conceived as 'a bare colourless subject' (1995:1963). Bauckham's point is not to deny the personhood of the Spirit. Instead, his argument is twofold. First, all the biblical images of the Spirit characterise his relationship to us, not to the Father and the Son. We cannot know the nature of the Spirit's relationship to the Father and Son, not even in the analogical way that scripture allows us to describe the relationship of the first and second Persons as the relationship of a Father and Son. To think of the Spirit as feminine, as Moltmann encourages us to do, does not help. Moltmann himself does not suggest the feminine image of the Spirit refers to a motherly relationship within the Trinity, but to his motherly relationship to us. And second, those biblical images that speak of the Spirit in relation to us – power, water, breath, fire – are impersonal. While the Spirit is a Person in relation to the Father and Son, albeit in a way which we cannot know, he does not relate to us in the same way, for we do not have a relationship with the Spirit, but, through the Spirit, with the Father and Son.

These two arguments are related. If we relate to the divine Persons in a differentiated way, then this reflects the differentiated character of the relationships of the trinitarian Persons to one another (which, in some way, which we cannot know, is the basis for their differentiated relationship with us). Just as the Son is God's ability to be incarnate, so the Spirit is God's ability to indwell us (1995:164). 'The point of Christian talk of the Trinity is to ground precisely this highly differentiated threefold relationship, in which Christians come to know God and to participate in the divine life' (1995:178). This differentiated relationship means we cannot think of the Trinity simply as a group of friends, who include us in their circle of friendship as yet further friends. If we could, then it might be natural for those who are so included to share a similar pattern of friendship among themselves. But instead, 'we enjoy a highly differentiated relationship to the three divine persons.' (1995:177) Criticising Moltmann's proposal that we think of the Spirit as Mother, Bauckham says: 'The argument overlooks the peculiar character of the Spirit as known to us in the trinitarian history: that the Spirit is a Person in relation to the Father and the Son, but not in relation to us (since we experience the Spirit not in a person-to-person relationship but as our own relationship to the Father and the Son).' (1995:169).

In fact, Scripture encourages us at least to think of the Spirit as a Person in relation to us to the extent that he is a Person whom we can grieve (Ephesians 4:30). Bauckham's point, however, remains for we cannot conclude from this anything of the inter-trinitarian relationships.

> The only way in which, from the resources of Scripture and tradition, we can conceive the Spirit's personal relation to the Father and the Son is by bringing ourselves into the picture: the Spirit inspires our relationship to the Father and the Son. We cannot stand outside the trinitarian fellowship and see it as a model for our own relationships. We can only enter it and experience the Spirit's relationship to the Father and the Son as our relationship to the Father and the Son. (1995:163)

Moltmann's mistake, argues Bauckham, is to abstract the Trinity in itself from God's trinitarian history with the world (1995:163). Bauckham does not say so, but in effect, he is arguing that Moltmann has abstracted the immanent Trinity from the economic Trinity. If Moltmann's identification of the immanent Trinity with the economic Trinity allows him to speak of the inner trinitarian life, he cannot then divorce this from the economic Trinity. The identification of economic and immanent Trinity may open up the possibility of talking about the immanent Trinity, but at the same time, it imposes tight limits on such talk. (For Bauckham's comments on Moltmann's identification of the immanent and economic Trinity see 1995:156-7.)

Bauckham believes that Moltmann's intention to ground our social relationships in the Trinity can be maintained, but only by reference to the Trinity's relationships to the world. The perichoretic unity of the Trinity is open to our participation because one person of the Trinity, the Spirit, is the means by which God relates to us. In other words, human fellowship cannot be an image of the Trinity as it is in itself, but it can be a participation in the Trinity's history with us. 'It means human community comes about, not as an image of

the trinitarian fellowship, but as the Spirit makes us like Jesus in his community
with the Father and with others' (1995:178).

Mission and the Trinitarian History of God

It is of central importance in Moltmann's missiology that the mission of the
church be seen in the light of the trinitarian history of God as a participation in
the mission of God. 'A theology of liberation sees all individual sufferings and
failures in the world against the background of God's patient suffering. It
therefore sees all partial movements towards liberation against the horizon of
God's own perfect and final history of liberation.' (1979:99) Thus, 'it is not the
church that has a mission of salvation to fulfil to the world; it is the mission of
the Son and the Spirit through the Father that includes the church, creating a
church as it goes on its way' (*CPS*, 64; see *CPS*, 64-65). Richard Bauckham
comments:

> The church is understood as a *movement* within the living, moving relationships
> of the trinitarian history of God with the world, created by the missions of the Son
> and the Spirit ... *The Church in the Power of the Spirit* attempts to work out this
> principle consistently by understanding every aspect of the church's life and
> activity as a function of the mission of Christ and the Spirit, a participation in
> God's trinitarian history with the world'. (1987i:120,121)

That which mediates between the trinitarian history of God and the mission
of the church is the Holy Spirit. Through the Holy Spirit, 'the church is the
concrete form in which men experience the history of Christ ... It lives in the
experience and practice of the Spirit from the eschatological anticipation of the
kingdom.' (*CPS*, 35; see also 1978i:18-19) The Spirit is the earnest and
foretaste of the new creation. Thus, 'eschatology is the work of the Spirit. For
through the Spirit the believer is determined by the divine future.' (*CPS*, 34) It
is the Spirit who effects the eschatological unity of God and, as such, the
Spirit's work now is an anticipation of that glory. This is why Moltmann's
book of 'messianic ecclesiology' is entitled *The Church in the Power of the
Spirit* (1975).

Drawing some conclusions from his assertion that the mission of the church
is a participation in the trinitarian history of God, Moltmann gives the
missiological formula, *ubi Christus, ibi ecclesia* – 'where Christ is, there the
church is' (*CPS*, 121-132; 1975: 116). And Christ is where he has promised to
be: in the apostolate ('Christ is present in the apostolate, in the sacraments, and
in the fellowship of the brethren', *CPS*, 123); in the poor (Matthew 25:31-46);
and in the parousia (Christ's presence is a coming reality).

Mission in an eschatological perspective has a number of consequences.
Israel must be recognised as still having a special relationship with God. Israel
reminds the church that redemption is not yet complete and the church exists to

make Israel jealous that she too might yet be redeemed (*CG*, 134-135; *CPS*, 136-150; *WJC*, 28-37; 1975: 60-68; 1984i:189-217; 1991:107-8,121).

Although Moltmann says he has 'no intention of disputing ... or belittling' the traditional view that mission should be concerned 'to awaken faith, to baptise, to found churches and to form a new life under the lordship of Christ' (*CPS*, 152), he does want to include along with this 'quantitative approach' to mission a 'qualitative approach'. 'Mission has another goal as well. It lies in the *qualitative* alteration of life's atmosphere' (*CPS*, 152). In relation to other religions 'qualitative mission takes place in dialogue'; it is 'vulnerable in openness' (*CPS*, 152). In this it shows God's openness, vulnerability and power in helplessness (*CPS*, 161). In relation to the processes of the world's life, Christianity must encourage a 'passion for living' (*CPS*, 167) and the 'kindling of live hopes' (*TH*, 328). In economic life this will mean challenging the concept of progress with the concept of community or symbiosis. In political life it means challenging the monopolisation of power and encouraging democracy. And in cultural life it means encouraging an open identity which replaces the self-justification that creates the 'culture-conflicts' of racism, sexism and prejudice. This is the agenda Moltmann sets out in *The Church in the Power of the Spirit* (163-189). Although not contradicting his basic principles, he sets out slightly different agendas elsewhere (see *CG*, 329-335; *WJC*, 64-69; 263-273; 1969:38-41; 75:180-184; *Future*, 1979:109-114; 1989:8-15). Furthermore, throughout his writings, Moltmann has shown himself to be passionately concerned with the issues that face the church and the world today on a practical level (1991:166-8).

Finally, in the light of the passion and pathos of the trinitarian God, a person becomes *homo sympathetikos* rather than *homo apathetikos* (*CG*, 270-274; 1975:69-84). 'The divine pathos finds its resonance in the sympathy of man, in his openness and sensitivity to the divine, the human, and the natural ... He is angry with God's wrath. He loves with God's love. He suffers with God's suffering. He hopes with God's hope.' (1975:76) The *homo sympathetikos* is open to others, is concerned for them, and does not measure everything in terms of 'the idols of action and success' (1975:83).

The Future God

Given that God is a community of persons, Moltmann believes we must speak of 'God' as an event (*CG*, 247). This is not to say that God is not personal; in fact he is three persons! Prayer, for example, is addressed to the *persons* of the Trinity 'but *in* this event' (*CG*, 247). In other words, 'God' consists of the unity of the three persons of the Trinity, but this unity has a history – the history of sending, cross, resurrection and glorification. This is why Moltmann prefers to speak of 'the trinitarian history of God' rather than the Trinity as such (1979i:82).

In his early work Moltmann spoke of 'God with "future as his essential nature"' (*TH*, 16) and the future as the 'mode of God's being' (1970i:10; see also *CoG*, 24). This was Moltmann's response to 'death of God' theology. God is not dead, but ahead of us in the future (though present now through his promises). He is not 'not'. Instead he is 'not yet'. This idea of God as future, however, received a great deal of criticism (see, for example, Gilkey, 1970:96; Hodgson, 1971:15-17; Hunsinger, 1973:278-279). In particular some felt that Moltmann had simply shifted Barth's vertical transcendence ninety degrees to form a new horizontal transcendence (Alves, 1969:61; Gilkey, 1976:234; Olson, 1983:218). Between *Theology of Hope* and *The Crucified God*, Moltmann drops the idea of God as exclusively future (see O'Donnell, 1982:163 and Bauckham, 1987i:94). Instead, the Trinity comes to the fore (the doctrine of the Trinity was largely absent in *Theology of Hope*). Yet the eschatological perspective is maintained with Moltmann preferring to speak of 'the trinitarian history of God' (1979i:82; Bauckham, 1980:129). At first Moltmann said 'in the Christ event God *becomes* the Trinity' (1970i:27; see also *CG*, 247), but again at times he seems to draw back from this ontological sense (Bauckham, 1980:121). He speaks instead in noetic terms of the cross 'revealing' God as Trinity (*CPS*, 96) and allows a more prominent role for the immanent Trinity, although always in close relation to the economic Trinity (*TKG*, 152; Blocher, 1990:19).

Traditionally a distinction has been made between the immanent and the economic Trinity in order to preserve the freedom of God. The immanent Trinity is the Trinity which, as it were, could have been free not to create the world. Yet, as we have seen, Moltmann believes that God's freedom does not consist in his freedom not to create the world, but is expressed in the determination of his self-communicating love which cannot be restricted and which derives from his essential nature. Moltmann, therefore, concludes that the immanent and economic Trinity 'form a continuity and merge into one another' (*TKG*, 152).

In fact, Moltmann speaks of the immanent Trinity as the goal of the trinitarian history of God; in this sense that it is the perfecting of the economic Trinity in the eschatological unity and glory of God. 'The economic Trinity completes and perfects itself to immanent Trinity when the history and experience of salvation are completed and perfected. When everything is "in God" and "God is all in all", then the economic Trinity is raised into and transcended in the immanent Trinity. (*TKG*, 162) It is in this sense that Moltmann speaks of 'the future as the mode of God's being' (1975: 41). The immanent Trinity has a place now in the worship of the church as the church prefigures the eschatological glory of God. Thus 'the "economic Trinity" is the object of kerygmatic and practical theology; the "immanent Trinity" the content of doxological theology' (*TKG*, 152).

Moltmann speaks of the economic Trinity having a 'retroactive' effect on the immanent Trinity (*TKG*, 160) and of the economic Trinity being completed and perfected in the immanent Trinity (*TKG*, 161). 'God's future is not that he will be as he was and is, but that he is on the move and coming towards the world. God's Being is in his coming, not in his becoming.' (*CoG*, 23) This would suggest the immanent Trinity should be conceived of as the eschatological goal of the trinitarian history of God and yet Moltmann also says 'the divine relationship to the world is primarily determined by that inner relationship' (*CoG*, 23). Does the economic Trinity determine the immanent Trinity or does the immanent Trinity determine the economic Trinity? Moltmann appears to want to have it both ways. And if the immanent Trinity is eschatological how does it relate to the protological Trinity? Olson comments: 'If the immanent Trinity is conceived as future, and thus not a completed reality at any point in the historical process of the divine life (how could it be if it is really "affected" by the events in the history of this life?), how does it "primarily determine" that process and life? Moltmann fails to explain.' (1983:221)

It would appear that Moltmann speaks of the immanent Trinity in two senses: protologically and eschatologically. The trinitarian history of God moves from unity to unity with the cross in between. That is to say, it begins with the unity of the protological immanent Trinity which in turn determines the relationship of the economic Trinity to the world which itself determines the open unity of the eschatological immanent Trinity. Yet this leaves the question, What of the immanent Trinity now? In Moltmann it seems the immanent and economic Trinity are not concurrent ways of looking at God, but consecutive stages in the history of God. It appears doubtful whether economic and immanent are appropriate terms for describing that which Moltmann seeks to describe.

Olson believes that Moltmann's description of the Father as 'the fount of all divinity' requires him to make what Olson describes as a 'dubious distinction' between 'the inner life' and 'the constitution' of the Trinity (1983:220). In other words, Moltmann seems to talk about two levels of the divine life: on the level of substance, the Father is the source of all (*TKG*, 165-6); on the level of particular existence, the persons of the Trinity are mutually interdependent. Thus, for example, the Spirit receives his divine being from the Father alone, but his particular relational form from the Father and the Son. *Filioque* can be affirmed on the latter level, but not on the former (*TKG*, 178-87; see also *SL*, 8,71-2,306-9; 1991:58-9,88; *ET*, 307). This, argues Olson, threatens to reintroduce that which Moltmann has so firmly sought to reject: a God who is above the events of salvation history. Thus Olson believes 'he seems to affirm an ontological monarchism himself' (1983:226). Extending Olson's thought we might ask whether Moltmann, having redefined the distinction between immanent and economic in terms of eschatology and history, then goes on the replace the original distinction with a distinction between the trinitarian constitution and inner life; between the ontological Trinity and functional Trinity.

Creation, Fall and the (Be)Coming of God

John Milbank believes what he calls 'the "strong" Protestant version of Rahner's axiom which declares the identity of the economic with the immanent Trinity' creates 'the tendency of these theologians to do without a doctrine of the fall, or to elide fall with creation' (1986:224). Milbank believes argues that the distinction between the immanent and economic Trinity corresponds to the distinction between the world as God intended it to be and the world as it is affected by the fall. This brings us to the question of the fall and of sin in Moltmann's theology. As we shall see, Moltmann does not to see death as a consequence of sin; instead creation is oppressed by Nothingness with sin as one consequence. Moltmann says:

> When we talk about the history of the Spirit ... we mean the dialectical process of interactions which is opened up and urged on by the future of the thing that is entirely new. The history of the creative Spirit embraces human history and natural history, and to that extent is to be understood in dialectical-materialist terms as 'the movement', 'the urge', 'the spirit of life', 'the tension' and 'the torment' which – as Marx said with Jacob Böhme – is matter's pre-eminent characteristic. (*CPS*, 34)

The significant thing is that for Moltmann the power of death and the *nihil* experienced in the cross are contradicted by the resurrection and resolved in the history, the dialectical-process, the movement of the Spirit. It would be hard to avoid the strong Hegelian overtones here and also in Moltmann's description of the cross as an event within the life of the Trinity. Moltmann calls Hegel 'the philosopher of the Trinity' (1979i:82) This conjures up ideas of history as a process of self-realisation for God. World events are seen as events of the inner life of the Trinity. Not only does God change, but all change exists in God (Wells, 1990:64,67). Particularly significant is a section in *The Crucified God* (*CG*, 253-256) in which Moltmann discusses and cites Hegel at length to support his argument that the doctrine of the Trinity makes it possible to understand the cross in terms of the history of God. Bauckham, for example, believes an Hegelian reading of *The Crucified God* is the most obvious (1987i:107; see also Walsh, 1986:59; Williams, 1989:11 fn. 29). Thus Milbank says, 'the Trinity itself is seen in terms of God's involvement in historical becoming, and the Spirit as God's eschatological arrival in the kingdom or *as* the kingdom, already anticipated in the church' (1986:222). Likewise Gilkey believes that in Moltmann's thought there is an identity between God's being and the eschatological future of the world' (1976:232; see also O'Donnell, 1983:147-149).

Hill believes that in Moltmann's early theology the Spirit was not a person, but 'the Christian symbol for the Father's sacrifice of his Son as that goes out to humanity and becomes a formative influence in history ... the power of futurity insofar as that is a mode of God's own being' (1982:174). Moltmann qualifies this, however, as Hill goes on to acknowledge, in *The Trinity and the Kingdom of God* where the Spirit is specifically identified as a person (*TKG*, 125-126). This can be done because the Spirit does not just act as the Spirit of God or the Spirit of Christ (in which case the Spirit could be seen as the energy of God), but also as a separate subject. The Spirit is a separate subject through whose activity the Father and the Son are glorified and receive their unity. Indeed in *The Spirit of Life* Moltmann criticises traditional Protestant soteriology with its emphasis upon the objective work of Christ appropriated by the subjective work of the Spirit, arguing that there is a 'reciprocal relationship' between Son and Spirit (81-2).

Thus, whatever Moltmann's Hegelian influences, and Moltmann never repudiates Hegel's philosophical trinitarianism, in his affirmation of the persons of the Trinity, Moltmann clearly parts company with Hegel. This is even more striking because Moltmann does so in deliberate contrast to any form of modalism and any theology of absolute subject. Indeed Moltmann's emphasis on three persons has been such that he has been accused of tritheism. It remains open to question whether Moltmann's volitional, as opposed to ontological, unity of a community of persons is adequate to overcome this criticism. It may well be that Moltmann wants to affirm the unity of the Trinity, but has problems doing so because of his stress on the three persons of the Trinity. On the other hand, of course, it is Moltmann's contention that the Western tradition has often so stressed the unity of God that it has not given an adequate account of the three-ness of the Trinity.

A key question raised by Moltmann's Hegelianism is whether, as John Milbank believes, Moltmann embraces 'a Hegelian theodicy in which necessary estrangement is justified by the final outcome' (1986:224; see also Blocher, 1985:121). If the problem of death does not arise from sin, but is in some way inherent in a creation *ex nihilo*, does this imply that this negative element is in some way necessary? Is the cross itself necessary to the Trinity in its becoming? Walter Kasper believes that the understanding that God needs history in order to come to himself is unavoidable in Moltmann. The concern here is that if the cross is in any way necessary to God, the grace of God is undermined. 'Is there not the danger here, that the miracle of the love of God, the cross, is dissolved in a dialectic, which changes into identity?' (Walter Kasper, cited and translated by O'Donnell, 1982:164).

In response, Moltmann does not so much affirm the freedom of God's love in the cross as deny the relevance of a freedom-necessity polarity when speaking of God. If God *is* love we cannot talk of him acting in any way except according to that love (*TKG*, 52-56; 1979i:76-77). Yet despite this, the problem remains: if the immanent Trinity is in any way dependent upon the economic Trinity or the two are identical then the cross is determinative for God's being and 'godlessness, godforsakenness and death are necessary to the dialectic which constitutes God's trinitarian being, so that either evil is necessary or God's trinitarian being is contingent on unnecessary evil' (Bauckham,

1987i:107-108).

It is hardly enough to say, as Bauckham does, that Moltmann 'avoids this dilemma only by retreating from the position if he ever really intended it, that God is Trinity only through the cross' (1987i:108). Instead, argues Bauckham, Moltmann sees the grounds for the cross in the eternal love and openness of the Trinity. Yet such a move allows Moltmann to say, 'The pain of the cross determines the inner life of the triune God from eternity to eternity' (*TKG*, 161). If the economic Trinity previously determined the eschatological immanent Trinity then now it also retroactively determines the immanent Trinity from eternity. The problem perhaps lies in the strength of the word 'determine'. If Moltmann had said 'reveals the inner life ...' then we could concur that God's love is from eternity open to the possibility of an event such as the cross should such an event prove necessary (necessary, that is, for humanity's salvation, not God's being). This would be true whether or not the fall of humanity (and hence the cross) had taken place although, arguably, it is only *revealed* to be true to humanity because of the cross. In other words, the cross, in a way no other event could, *reveals* the extent of God's love and openness. Because God is from eternity self-communicating love and because 'creation is part of the eternal love affair between the Father and the Son' (*TKG*, 59), Moltmann himself refuses to speak of a God without the world, of a God who could have chosen not to create; and indeed such speculation may not always be helpful.

The root of the problem, however, lies, not so much in Moltmann's exaggerated use of language when speaking of the trinitarian history of God, but in his understanding of the fall. Paul Wells says Moltmann 'links suffering to ontological finitude as a pre-condition for the opening of creation to the future of God ... However, if this sort of reciprocity between immanence and transcendence is established with regard to suffering, how can it be avoided for sin and evil?' (1990:64) Certainly Moltmann explicitly rejects the idea that evil is in some way necessary. Sin cannot be given any positive quality and evil cannot be excused or declared necessary for the sake of good (1979i:77). It is doubtful, however, whether Moltmann can sustain this given his view of the fall. If the sin of humanity in the fall is not seen as the reason for the presence of death in creation, but instead, sin is seen as a consequence of a creation created *ex nihilo* and so threatened by the *nihil*, then is hard to see how death can be seen as anything but an inherent part of creation as created by God. The problem is, that, because Moltmann cannot conceive of creation apart from the threat of *nihil* and because he sees the suffering of death as inherent to creation, he cannot envisage God apart from that suffering and death. Indeed, ultimately the logic of Moltmann's theodicy requires him to abandon the omnipotence of God, or at least to reinterpret it as 'the all-endurance of divine love' (1988i:77).

The significance of these problems with Moltmann's understanding of the trinitarian history of God for his view of mission should not be underestimated. If there are problems with his trinitarianism then there are problems with his missiology because, for Moltmann, the mission of the church *is* its participation in the trinitarian history of God. As we have seen, the relationship between the economic and immanent Trinity is far from clear in Moltmann's work. The result of this is to jeopardise the sovereignty of God and, as a result, the grace of God. Moltmann is certainly right to point out that the freedom of God does not consist in his ability to act contrary to his nature. We might call this the *inner compulsion* of divine love or divine grace. God is free in his love because that love is free in the sense of being unreserved, liberal and unbounded. God's freedom, however, does not consist simply in this (as Moltmann seems to imply, *TKG*, 52-56). It also consists in the fact that God is not under any *external compulsion*. Only then is God's inner compulsion to love truly free and unbounding. Certainly it may well be inappropriate to argue that the freedom of God implies he could have acted differently towards the world. A God who is love must act in love. Yet Moltmann goes beyond this when he says, for example, that the economic Trinity is determinative for the immanent Trinity. To argue that creation and cross are necessary for God's self-becoming is clearly to impose an external necessity upon God. The immanent Trinity becomes the economic Trinity because of God's inner compulsion to love – herein lies the grace of God. To say, in contrast, as Moltmann does, that the economic Trinity determines the immanent Trinity (whether eschatologically or retroactively) is to make God's relationship with the world determinative for God himself. And that is to place God under external compulsion and so undermine his sovereignty and grace.

Even Bauckham, one of Moltmann's most faithful advocates, recognises the problems posed by Moltmann's Hegelian tendencies. By identifying the economic and immanent Trinities, Moltmann leaves little room for God's independence from the world. History, including the history of suffering, and supremely the cross, becomes a vehicle for the resolution of God's identity; a necessary part of his becoming. Bauckham identifies two dangers with this. The first is that it compromises the freedom of God in relation to the world. The world becomes necessary to God for his self-becoming. The second danger is that evil is justified as part of the process of God's becoming. If world history is necessary for God's identity then so is the evil it contains (see Bauckham, 1987i:106-7).

With the first of these dangers Bauckham characteristically defends Moltmann by a careful exposition of his views. It is not Moltmann's intention to dissolve God into history, but to see history as a reciprocal relationship between God and the world. God is genuinely affected by this relationship, but only because of his voluntary openness and love. This, suggests Bauckham, would have been enough to protect divine freedom. Moltmann, however, goes further. To argue that God is affected by the world, through his voluntary openness, suggests that in his freedom he could have chosen not to do so. This is to introduce the sort of distinction between the immanent and economic Trinity which Moltmann is so determined to avoid. Moltmann instead denies that freedom and necessity is real in God. According to Bauckham, 'God's freedom is not arbitrary choice but the inner necessity of his being, i.e. the God who is love cannot chose not to love' (1987i:109).

As for the second danger, that Moltmann makes history, and therefore evil, necessary to God's self-becoming, Bauckham believes that Moltmann 'attempted to resolve [such problems] both by clarification and by further developments of his thoughts' (1987i:107). However, Bauckham clearly doubts whether this has been entirely successful. In *The Crucified God*, Moltmann suggests that in the event of the cross God becomes the Trinity, and, as such, that the cross is the self-constitution of the Trinity. The implication is that godlessness and godforsakenness are necessary for God's becoming, making evil necessary for the sake of good. Yet it is essential to Moltmann's theodicy that evil is not explained nor justified (Bauckham, 1987i:84).

Moltmann avoids this problem, argues Bauckham, by retreating from the position that God is Trinity only through the cross. Typically, Bauckham adds 'if he ever really intended it', although he himself acknowledges that an Hegelian reading of *The Crucified God* is 'the most obvious' one (1987i:108, 107). Bauckham acknowledges Moltmann's debt to Hegel (1987i:107; see also pp. 6,56-7), but also argues that while Moltmann's trinitarian dialectic is Hegelian in structure, it is not necessarily Hegelian in content. After *The Crucified God*, argues Bauckham, Moltmann sees the cross as having a central, but not unique, determinative place in the history of God. Moltmann speaks of God as Trinity prior to the cross; indeed, this trinitarian structure is a condition for Jesus' cry of dereliction. God's trinitarian being has been open from eternity to human history. There is mutual involvement between God and the world. 'The cross (and, by extension, the rest of God's history with the world) is *internal* to the divine trinitarian experience' (see Bauckham, 1989ii:304; see also Bauckham, 1995:16).

But while Bauckham defends Moltmann from the charge of Hegelianism by – typically – clarifying his thought and tracing its development, he nevertheless remains critical. Moltmann not only wants to speak of the cross revealing God's eternal open love, but still as a constitutive event for the trinitarian relationships, even retroactively in God's eternity. It is one thing to say, argues Bauckham, as Moltmann does, that 'God's essence is from eternity a love which is *capable* of suffering, ready to sacrifice and to give itself up' (1981ii:54; cited by Bauckham, 1987i:108; emphasis added). It is another thing to say 'the pain of the cross *determines* the inner life of the triune God from eternity to eternity'; or again, that 'the Son's sacrifice of boundless love on Golgotha is from eternity *already included* in the exchange of the essential, the consubstantial love which constitutes the divine life of the Trinity' (*TKG*, 161,167; cited Bauckham, 1987i:109; emphasis added). The first means God's nature is from eternity such that it is ready to suffer when his love is contradicted. With the second, believes Bauckham, evil determines the inner life of God from eternity: 'we seem to be back with the original problem'.

If this does not makes evil necessary, then contingent evil not only affects God in the course of his trinitarian history, but essentially determines his inner life from eternity. This conclusion results from the temptation, which Moltmann from *The Crucified God* onwards seems unable to resist, to see the cross as the key to the doctrine of God, not only in the sense that it reveals God as the kind of love which is willing to suffer, but in the sense that the actual sufferings of the cross are essential to who God is. (1987i:109)

The result, according to Bauckham, is that 'this attempt to take God's temporal experience as seriously as possible oddly ends by eternalising it.' (1987i:109)

If an Hegelian reading of, for example, *The Crucified God* is the correct one, then for Moltmann the trinitarian history of God consists of the negation (on the cross) of the negative (the inherent oppression of the *nihil* in creation as created by God) and the resolution of this dialectic in the movement of the Spirit. It is the story of God's self-becoming of which creation and cross are necessary parts. It is doubtful, however, whether talk of God's self-becoming makes any sense once Moltmann has allowed for (as he does in *TKG*) a protological immanent Trinity, unless that protological Trinity is in some way deficient. Moltmann reads salvation history in this way because he reads it without the fall. The immanent Trinity becomes the economic Trinity (without ceasing to be the immanent Trinity) not to realise itself, but in response to the fall of humanity, a response engendered by the inner compulsion of divine love rather than a need for self-realisation. In its mission the church seeks to participate in the history of the Spirit who is the 'advance payment', anticipating the resolution of all things in the new creation. As such, it proclaims and affirms life. For Moltmann, however, this is not so much life in contrast to the spiritual death brought about by sin, but life in contrast to the oppression of the *nihil*. The result is that Moltmann no longer sees faith as trust in a being (for God is becoming), but as identification with God through suffering (see Eckardt, 1985:23) and that the church proclaims its participation in the self-becoming of God rather than its experience of the grace of God.

CHAPTER 4

Eschatology and History

Eschatology is always thought to deal with the end, the last day, the last word, the last act: God has the last word. But if eschatology were that and only that, it would be better to turn one's back on it altogether; for 'the last things' spoil one's taste for the penultimate ones, and the dreamed of, or hoped for, end of history robs us of our freedom among history's many possibilities, and our tolerance for all the things in history that are unfinished and provisional. We can no longer put up with the earthly, limited and vulnerable life, and in eschatological finality we destroy life's fragile beauty. The person who presses forward to the end of life misses life itself. (*CoG*, x-xi)

So says Moltmann in the preface to *The Coming of God*. Eschatology may be central to Moltmann's theology, but it must always be an eschatology that impinges on history. History cannot be left behind, untouched. Eschatology must lead to an engagement in history.

Promise and Possibilities

The form that future hope has in the present is *promise*. 'The future of the risen Lord is accordingly here present in promise' (*TH*, 87). 'The promised future is already present in the promise itself; and mobilizes people concerned through the hope it awakens.' (2004i, 3) Promise is something received, a present reality; nevertheless it is a present reality which always points to the future. 'Hope's statements of promise anticipate the future. In the promise, the hidden future already announces itself and exerts its influence on the present.' (*TH*, 17)

It is not so much that the promise *discloses* history as that it *opens up* history to a new reality (see 1971:18; *ET*, 54,93-95,98,102). This is because the revelation of promise is at the same time a call and commission. Moltmann asserts, 'The *pro-missio* of the universal future leads of necessity to the universal *missio* of the church to the nations' (*TH*, 225). This it does by announcing the future which in turn leads to those receiving the promise seeking to anticipate that future in the present. Such anticipations are partial fulfilments of the promise, but at the same time they are pointers to the wider future of the promise (1979i:46).

The eschatological future illumined by the promise makes it impossible for the church to resign itself to the world. Instead the church will seek to guide all things in the direction that the promise points. For example, 'the promise of divine righteousness in the event of the justification of the godless *leads immediately* to the hunger for divine right in the godless world, and thus to the struggle for public, bodily obedience' (*TH*, 225, emphasis added). The revelation of the future in the form of promise leads the Christian to seek and search for that future and to anticipate it in the here and now. The promise directs present action through the development of 'the social imagination to conceive the desirable future of a habitable earth' (1979i:56).

In its missionary enterprise the church gives an answer for its hope (1 Peter 3:15) and so involves the world in 'the exodus from the present of a self-contained existence into the promised future' (*TH*, 89). The history of this process is the history which corresponds to the promise – the interval between promise and fulfilment. Thus defined, 'awareness of history is awareness of mission' (*TH*, 89; see also 1971:165). The Christian understands history to the extent that he understands, and is involved in, mission because it is in mission that the promise becomes historical.

From the Marxist philosopher Ernst Bloch, Moltmann inherited a kind of eschatological metaphysics; Bloch's not-yet ontology. This centres on the concept of 'possibilities' or 'potentialities'. Reality is full of possibilities; that is to say it is not a closed system of laws, but always open to change. For Moltmann, however, these do not arise, as for Bloch, from the dynamic nature of matter in its becoming, but from the promise and the resurrection. '[Christian eschatology] sets out from a definite reality in history and announces the future of that reality, its future possibilities and its power over the future. Christian eschatology speaks of Christ and *his* future.' (*TH*, 17) Christian eschatology is not concerned with the possibilities in history in a general sense, but with the possibilities opened up by the resurrection of Christ (*TH*, 192) – and, in Moltmann's later work, from the operation of the Holy Spirit (*SL*, 103).

The difference between Bloch and Moltmann over the ultimate cause of the openness of reality towards the future (eschatological metaphysics and promise respectively) leads in turn to two further differences between them. First, there is no guarantee in Bloch's system that the result of the dialectical process will be concrete utopia. It might alternatively be destruction. Block labels this uncertain element 'hazard' and it forms the basis of his call to action. For Moltmann, in contrast, the faithfulness of the God of promise is the basis for confident hope that eschatological righteousness will be the outcome of history (*TH*, 145). Second, for Moltmann, Christian eschatology starts with 'the deadliness of death' (1975:37) and proclaims the hope of resurrection. In contrast, death remains for Bloch 'the strongest non-utopia' (1986:1103). Bloch can only speak of a 'solidarity' of existence, a collective consciousness, which is not destroyed by death. Even then, whereas Moltmann begins with the hopelessness of the weak and suffering, Bloch speaks only in relation to 'red heroes' whom he describes as 'revolutionary materialists ... the most powerful idealists ... enlightened seafarers ... steadfast individuals' (1985:1172). Moltmann believes that Bloch's view, like belief in the immortality of the soul, extracts from reality one element which is accorded immortality while the major part of reality is afforded no hope at all.

According to Moltmann, the possibilities created by the resurrection of Christ are not necessarily possible in a realistic sense, but only from the perspective of the God who creates *ex nihilo* and raises from the dead. Only in this context 'can hope become effective in love' (*TH*, 92). The word of promise, the gospel, not only proclaims freedom but 'makes it possible and empowers it'. 'The call to freedom is founded on, and made possible by, the approaching rule of God, already present in gospel. In the proximity of the rule of God, what was till then impossible becomes possible.' (*CPS*, 78) In this way 'hope becomes realistic because reality is full of every potentiality' (*CPS*, 78). In other words, the liberating power of God's rule comes so near in the promise and resurrection that its effects can be experienced in history. The coming kingdom is present in the liberating rule of Christ and, as such, hope, inspired the word of promise, is able to realise itself in anticipation through the power of that rule.

The openness to the future engendered by the promise has, then, both a subjective side and an objective side. Subjectively it creates in people hope for the future, passionate expectation, and places them in contradiction with the present. Objectively it represents the transforming and liberating power of God's rule, which Moltmann speaks of in Blochian terms as the possibilities and potentialities of the resurrection. 'Without real chances, the hope of man is meaningless' (1975:25).

Since history is fundamentally open to the future, the present is full of possibilities. And since this is the case, we have every reason to expect change and no reason to accept any status quo short of the kingdom of God. 'Revelation, recognised as promise and embraced in hope, thus sets an open stage for history, and fills it with missionary enterprise and the responsible exercise of hope, accepting the suffering that is involved in the contradiction of reality, and setting out towards the promised future.' (*TH*, 86; see also *ET*, 100-101) Thus the Christian is not to be concerned with the maintenance of the status quo, but with discovering possibilities for change which correspond to the promise.

Moltmann believes it is important to retain an understanding of heaven, the invisible aspect of creation (*GC*, 158-184; *WJC*, 331-333). The reality of heaven means that the earth can never be a unity in and of itself and, as such, heaven represents earth's openness. Moltmann defines heaven in the following way. 'For the earth, "the heavens" mean the kingdom of God's creative potentialities ... Heaven is, as it were, the preparing and making available of the potentialities and potencies of the world's creation, redemption and glorification.' (*GC*, 163, 166) Since the fall, judgment has been perceived in terms of a 'closed heaven'. In Christ 'the *coelum gratiæ* opens and is perceived

in the movement of God towards the liberation and redemption of the world'
(*GC*, 170). Heaven 'opening' represents the appearance of God's energies,
potentialities and potencies; that is to say, the transforming power of his
liberating rule, and this justifies attempts to anticipate the *coelum gloriæ*, the
coming glory of God, here on earth.

Promise and Process

What is the relationship between anticipations and the future? On the one hand,
we could say that the kingdom emerges from its anticipations; on the other
hand, we could say that there is no relationship between the kingdom and its
anticipations. Richard Bauckham argues that such a polarity represents an
incorrect way of looking at the issue: 'The causal connection is the reverse: the
eschatological kingdom by arousing hope and obedience produces anticipations
of itself in history' (1987i:45). In other words, it is not that the kingdom
emerges from its anticipations, but that those anticipations arise from the
coming kingdom which, furthermore, is genuinely present in its anticipations. If
Bauckham were right in his interpretation of Moltmann there would be no
problem. Moltmann, however, frequently hints at a greater connection,
although again he is characteristically ambiguous.

In particular, Moltmann's talk of a 'process' created by the promise or of the
universal mission of the church as a process is potentially problematic. The
term 'process' implies an idea of progress or development in history.
Berkouwer for one believes that the theology of hope 'focused so concretely on
the *process* of history' that 'it was eschatological without being futuristic'
(1977:200). Yet Moltmann also asserts that the kingdom comes about through a
decisive act of God in which history is brought to a close rather than that it
grows in history until it climaxes in the eschaton. What is to come, says
Moltmann, 'does not emerge out of the forces and trends of growth and decay'
(*CPS*, 130; see also *CPS*, 72). He clearly does not want to be regarded as going
back to nineteenth century Liberalism in which the kingdom was associated
with the progress of human culture and society. But if the term 'process' does
not refer to movement or progress in history, in what sense is Moltmann using
it?

One solution is to see it in the context of the language that Moltmann
inherits from Hegel and Bloch. In Hegel's thought the term refers to the
dialectical process of absolute spirit. And it is possible to see the term 'process'
in this way in Moltmann's thought. Generally Moltmann only uses the term in
the context of the dialectic. As such it could be said that 'process' is a technical
term in relation to the dialectic. This 'dialectic' consists, in Moltmann's
thought, of the contradiction of the cross by the resurrection and the eventual
resolution of these antitheses in the eschaton. As such, it does not refer to
something which progresses in history. Yet we have to be careful here because
Moltmann maintains that the dialectical process is historical, even though it

cannot be reduced to history, for it exerts a transforming influence on history.

This immanence and transcendence in history corresponds to the present and future of the kingdom: 'If we view history, with its conditions and potentialities, as an open system, we are bound to understand the kingdom of God in the liberating rule of God as a transforming power immanent in that system, and the rule of God in the kingdom of God as a future transcending the system.' (*CPS*, 190) The 'process' is present in history in the form of promise and the liberating rule of Christ. Moltmann calls history 'the reality instituted by promise' (*TH*, 224); that is to say history is defined as the interval between promise and fulfilment. As such the 'process' refers to the events which frame it: the event of promise (cross-resurrection) and the event of fulfilment (the eschaton). Thus, when Moltmann speaks of 'the process of the resurrection' (*WJC*, 240-242), he does so in order to indicate that the resurrection is neither a completed past event – it has a future – nor simply future fulfilment – it affects history in the present.

Thus, the term 'process' is used by Moltmann to signify the history of Christ. Moltmann says of Paul that 'he talks about an End-time process, which the resurrection of the crucified One has irrevocably set going ... The history of Christ manifests the *trend* which points to his future' (*WJC*, 319, 320). The context of these statements is the necessity of affirming Christ's future in the light of the fact that his history points beyond itself. As such, 'trend' here does not refer to growth or culminative development, but to the fact that the events of Christ's history, and the effect that it causes in human history through his liberating rule, point forward to his future. They indicate and reveal a reality beyond themselves. The process itself transcends this historical trend. 'With God's raising of the Christ murdered on the cross, a universal theodicy *trial* begins which can only be completed eschatologically with the resurrection of all the dead and the annihilation of death's power – which is to say through the new creation of all things.' (*WJC*, 183) The resurrection reopens the trial of Jesus and it will remain unresolved until Christ is fully vindicated and glorified through the new creation. Significantly the word translated here as *trial* is the German word *Prozeß* which can mean both trial (in a legal sense) and process (see *WJC*, 183 fn.). Thus, the process is called *The Way of Jesus Christ*. This title was chosen by Moltmann in part because 'the symbol of the way embodies the aspect of process, and brings out christology's alignment towards its goal' (*WJC*, xiv). This transcendent process is historically mediated by the Holy Spirit (*WJC*, 240-241). Thus, when we speak of the history of the Spirit 'we mean the dialectical process of interactions which is opened up and urged on by the future of the thing that is entirely new' (*CPS*, 34).

The process creates potentialities in the world which can be realised in immanent futures that anticipate and are fulfilled in the resolution of the process (the new creation). Thus, Moltmann distinguishes between 'the quality of the created potentialities of God towards the world, and the quality of the world's own potentialities' which are 'made possible by the divine ones'. This corresponds to the distinction 'between the world's historical future and its eschatological future' (*GC*, 182). In other words, although the term process does not refer to the development of history, the dialectical process does involve a radical openness of history to the future (and as such to change) and the presence in history of God's liberating rule. Nevertheless, all such fulfilments of this openness and these possibilities fall short of the full content of the promise. The process 'will be completed only at the parousia of Christ' (*TH*, 206). As such, these fulfilments do not belong directly to the dialectical process (although caused by it) but instead they *anticipate* it; they 'give a foretaste of the promised future' (*TH*, 108).

The problem is that we are forced to make sense of Moltmann by making him use words in an abnormal sense; that is to say, when he uses 'process' he does not mean process as such but dialectic. Furthermore, we are still left asking, What do 'setting out towards the promised future' or 'the exodus ... into the promised future' (*TH*, 86, 89) involve if that future comes upon us *ex nihilo* and is discontinuous with the present? Although we should not talk of an historical process, the way seems left open for a process *in* history, albeit one which contradicts reality (see *TH*, 86). Bauckham says the dualism in Moltmann's thought between godforsaken reality and the kingdom of God 'functions in *Theology of Hope* to exclude the possibility of a process towards the kingdom arising immanently out of present reality, but not to exclude a process created by the promise. On the contrary, Moltmann is maintaining precisely that the promise discloses for the world a wide open horizon of new possibility and sets in motion already a dialectical process of negating the present in order to create the future.' (1987i:40) Quite what 'a dialectical process of negating the present' amounts to is unclear. That a principle (such as the cross-resurrection) should negate the present is understandable, but how this can have a process is less obvious. Does the resurrection increasingly negate reality? Would that imply history was getting progressively worse? How can, as a result of the promise, reality be 'full of every potentiality' (*CPS*, 78) and yet at the same time be negated by that promise?

One might say that the promise negates reality in order to make it open to possibility. That is to say, a person is placed in contradiction as a result of the promise and as such looks for possibilities for change and seeks to realise them in history. The problem is that in Moltmann's thought the relationship between immanent possibilities and the ultimate future is unclear. Thus, for example, he can say, 'In the light of this hope [of resurrection], freedom is the creative passion for the possible' (*SL*, 119). If immanent possibilities were only realised in anticipations of the future there would be no problem – although process would hardly be the most appropriate word to describe this. For Moltmann, however, the creation of potentialities and possibilities by the promise frequently appears to be a condition for the new creation. Thus Walsh asks: 'Is the "new" which eschatological language anticipates a totally new future or a realisation of the possibilities of the past and present? Moltmann's answer has not been clear.' (1987:56) Likewise, Bauckham says, 'in *Theology of Hope* the relation between immanent and transcendent possibilities, between the future that is not yet and the future that is created out of nothing, is not properly established' (1987i:22).

Ultimate Hope and Penultimate Possibilities

Moltmann needs to distinguish between hope created by possibilities and hope created by promise. The former is open to disappointment since possibilities are not necessarily realised in history. The latter is a certain hope based on the faithfulness of the One who promises. If such a distinction is not made then false hope may well be given to those who suffer or are oppressed (1989ii:7). Bauckham warns of the danger of creating 'unrealistic expectations of revolutionary change' (1987i:43) and Preston says Moltmann is in danger of presenting 'impossibilities as possibilities' (1975:161). Moltmann's fear of giving eschatological opium to the people appears at times to get the better of him. In the New Testament patience and long-suffering are more frequently seen as eschatological virtues than revolutionary fervour.

One reason why immanent possibilities are ambiguously related to ultimate hope is found in Moltmann's inheritance from Ernst Bloch. For Bloch the *novum* is the culmination of the dialectical process through the realisations of the potentialities inherent in the open system of reality. Although the process will have an end, its outcome is not certain. There is *hazard* in the process. The process could end in *Alles*, but it could also end in *Nichts*. Bloch says, 'Since it is still an undecided process ... its outflow can just as easily be Nothing as All, just as easily total In-Vain as total success' (1986:193). For Bloch reality is genuinely open, does not have a pre-ordained end and as such the *novum* cannot be guaranteed.

For Moltmann, in contrast, the outcome of history is assured even in the midst of death (see in particular 'Hope and Confidence: A Conversation with Ernst Bloch', in 1969:148-176; especially 171-176). The process is not dependent on the struggles of humanity or the dynamic nature of matter, but upon the God who promises – the God who raises the dead. As such, Moltmann introduces transcendence over the process and thus he is able to speak of its outcome as assured. Speaking of Paul's argument in Romans 4, Moltmann says: 'As in Judaism, so also he, too, is certain that God keeps his promises. Yet the ground of this assurance is new: because God has the power to quicken the dead and call into being things that are not, therefore the fulfilment of his promise is possible, and because he has raised Christ from the dead, therefore the fulfilment of his promise is certain ... Unbelief does not let God be God, for it doubts the dependability of God which guarantees his promises.' (*TH*, 145)

In this way Moltmann removes the problem of *hazard* in Bloch's system. As Bauckham points out, and as we have seen, however, 'the introduction of transcendence creates a problem which Bloch did not have to face: how do the new possibilities which God creates relate to the immanent possibilities of the world?' (1987i:21-22). Furthermore, Bloch's call to revolutionary action follows naturally from his concept of *hazard*. If the outcome of history is not certain then clearly human involvement is going to be needed in order to ensure that *Alles* is the outcome. For Moltmann, however, the outcome rests upon the faithfulness of the One who promises; upon that which transcends the process. This means he must relate the human activity of realising immanent possibilities to the eschaton on a different basis. Yet his dependence on Bloch ultimately appears to obscure such a clear delineation. Indeed, particularly in his earlier work, he spoke in terms of *risk* and of 'hope as an experiment' (1975:186-190). In a sense, Moltmann wants it both ways. On the one hand, following Bloch, he wants an element of risk, of uncertainty, which leads naturally to a resolute call to involvement. On the other hand, he wants to say that hope arises from the promise and rests secure on the faithfulness of the One who promises, the God who raises from the dead. The former reflects the influence of esoteric Marxism on his thought; the latter the influence of biblical theology. The only way, however, that Moltmann can get away with this is to blur the distinctions between ultimate hope and penultimate possibilities.

The Millennial Reign of Christ

The millennial reign of Christ, having not featured strongly in Moltmann's theology, suddenly appears as a key theme in *The Coming of God*. And with this appearance comes the claim that 'Christian eschatology – eschatology, that is, which is messianic, healing and saving – is millenarian eschatology.' (CoG, 202) As Richard Bauckham notes, 'Moltmann's extensive discussion of millenarianism … is notable for the seriousness (rare in a contemporary theologian) with which he treats the Christian millenarian tradition.' (1997:264)

   Moltmann makes a distinction between 'eschatological millenarianism' and 'historical millenarianism' (*CoG*, 146, 192).

1. Eschatological Millenarianism

'Eschatological millenarianism' is the expectation that Christ will reign on the earth in the future with the saints. 'Eschatological millenarianism hopes from the kingdom of Christ as the future which will be an alternative to the present, and links this future with the end of "this world" and the new creation of all things.' (*CoG*, 146) This future reign will act as a transition to the new creation. It promises a qualitative better future in contrast to the sufferings and injustices of the present. Moltmann charts the way this approach flourished in the patristic period, waned under the influence of Augustine, re-emerged in the theology of Joachim of Fiore and various forms of Protestantism. This is the millennial hope that Moltmann wants to espouse. It remains, however, unclear what shape he thinks it will take in history (Bauckham, 1999:22).

2. Historical Millenarianism

Moltmann uses the term 'historical millenarianism' (or 'presentative millenarianism', *CoG*, 154) to refer to those who see the millennial reign of Christ as already present in history: 'historical millenarianism interprets the present as Christ's Thousand Years' empire and the last age of humanity' (*CoG*, 146). The present age is therefore also the last age. This is akin to 'amillennialism'. The view is a-millennial if the millennium is defined as a *future* reign on earth, but in fact amillennialism has tended to be defined as the belief that the millennial reign is already taking place. Moltmann calls this a kind of realized millenarianism. The hope of a millennial reign is already being realized within history so that the millennium does not belong exclusively to the future. Moltmann identifies three forms that historical millenarianism has taken over the centuries:

1. POLITICAL MILLENARIANISM. Moltmann highlights two forms of political (historical) millenarianism. The first is the 'holy empire' of Christendom that began with the adoption of Christianity by Constantine as the official religion of the Roman Empire (CoG, 159-168). Eusebius of Caesarea portrayed the resulting 'Christian' empire as the realisation of Christ's kingdom on earth. This continued in the east in the Byzantium Empire and in the West in the Holy Roman Empire. This political millenarianism leads to a 'mission of violence' in which Christ's reign is extended through political power; first in Europe and then throughout the world through Europe's imperial expansion from the seventeenth century onwards.

But its legacy continues in a second form of political millenarianism, that of the 'Redeemer Nation' (*CoG*, 168-178). From the Pilgrim Fathers down to the present day, Moltmann provides ample evidence of the notion of 'chosen people' and 'manifest destiny' in the self-identity of the United States. Deep in American culture is the belief that the United States possesses a God-given universal mission to spread democracy and freedom throughout the world; a notion that justifies its own 'mission of violence'. It manifests itself both in political rhetoric and popular culture as, for example, westerns and science-fiction films portray good overcoming evil through force. Moltmann also highlights the flipside of the American dream: the American nightmare. In particular he argues that 'the American experiment' cannot in fact be universalized. 'Politically, humanity cannot afford more than "one America", and the same can be said ecologically of the earth. If the whole world were "America", the whole world would already have been destroyed.' (*CoG*, 177).

2. ECCLESIASTICAL MILLENARIANISM (COG, 178-184). This Moltmann sees embodied in the medieval and Roman Catholic church. The church 'ceases to see itself as the struggling, resisting and suffering church; it is now the church victorious and dominant. It no longer participates in the struggle and sufferings of Christ, but already judges and reigns with him in his kingdom.' (CoG, 179). This lead to a hierarchical understanding of church polity as the church's self-identity is

understood in terms of rule and power. 'The hierarchical concept of the church is a [historical] millenarian concept of the church ... What counts as the church is now the hierarchy, no longer the gathered congregation.' (*CoG*, 179, 182)

3. EPOCHAL MILLENARIANISM (CoG, 184-192). This is Moltmann's term for the secularised millenarianism of modernity (*CoG*, 135). He claims that the Enlightenment Project of human progress is a humanist version of a millennial reign. In modernity the divine plan of salvation was seen as being replaced by education. Technology was overcoming nature. Human reason and scientific knowledge were creating an era of enlightenment and freedom. Moltmann argues that this hope was shaped by messianic motifs. In particular, Joachim of Fiore's prediction of 'the third age to the Spirit' was seen as being realized in the Enlightenment.

The problem with all these versions of historical millenarianism is not only that they claim too much, but that they justify too much. In the light of the millennium or its progress, imperialism and the subjugation of nature come to be seen as legitimate means. The millennial reign justifies the destructive exercise of power.

Eschatological millenarianism, in contrast, is a form of resistance to the powers of this world for it relativises the present by pointing to a better future. Moltmann sees eschatological and historical millenarianism as existing in conflict. Historical millenarianism idealises the present while eschatological millenarianism calls this idealization into question. Historical millenarianism legitimises the power of the powerful. Eschatological millenarianism sustains resistance to the status quo (although, as Moltmann acknowledges, in the case of American dispensationalism it can also take the form of spiritual escapism). As a result, historical millenarianism has often sought to suppress eschatological millenarianism. 'The churches of the Christian imperium condemned the hope for a coming kingdom of Christ because they thought that they themselves were already that kingdom; so the hope that the kingdom was still to come, and would replace them, had to be viewed as subversive criticism of their own authority.' (*CoG*, 147; see also *CoG*, 135, 154)

Richard Bauckham has engaged with Moltmann's millenarianism in an essay entitled 'Must Christian Eschatology Be Millenarian? (1997). Bauckham questions some of the emphases of Moltmann's account of the historical developments of millennial views. The pre-Contantinian church was not universally millenarian, nor were those who rejected millenarian views always triumphalistic about the church or state. He also suggests that the influence of Platonism was as significant a factor, if not more significant, in the demise of millenarian views. The move to historical millenarianism was not so much an attempt to legitimise the status quo as a result of unease at an 'unspiritual' millennial, earthly reign (1997:268-269).

But the thrust of Bauckham's criticism is that the millennial reign is unnecessary to secure what Moltmann wants it to secure. Moltmann has consistently insisted that Christian hope is hope for *this* world rather than an escapist hope for another, 'spiritual' world. In *The Coming of God* he employs millenarianism to safeguard this. Millennial hope directs our attention to an earthly reign. It is by definition this-worldly hope. Where churches have excluded millennial hope 'all that was left to them was hope for souls in the heaven of a world beyond this one' (CoG, 147). Bauckham comments:

> Why should the exclusion of hope for a future millennium not leave us with hope for the new creation as Moltmann envisages it – not a purely spiritual other world, but precisely this world renewed and transfigured in all its material as well as spiritual reality? In most of Moltmann's earlier theology, the millennium goes unmentioned, but the eschatological motivation and direction of Christian praxis in the present appears to be supplied by the hope of the eschatological new creation of all things. It seems that Moltmann now thinks the millennium alone, as a this-worldly future prior to the new creation, can supply such motivation and direction: 'Without millenarian hope, the Christian ethic of resistance and consistent discipleship lose their most powerful motivation' (CoG, 201). The question we must ask is: what theological function does the millennium fulfil which the new creation cannot? (1997:272; see also Volf, 1999:243-245)

In other words, Moltmann has consistently emphasised that the new creation is a renewal of this world rather than its replacement by another, 'spiritual' world. And he has done so precisely to safeguard the kind of concerns that he now claims can only be safeguarded through eschatological millenarianism. Bauckham, as it were, remains convinced by Moltmann's earlier arguments and so is unconvinced by Moltmann's new claim that eschatological millenarianism is necessary.

Moltmann does says that 'the millenarian expectation mediates between world history here, and the end of the world and the new world there. It makes the end as transition imaginable ... The transition will be brought about through a series of events and the succession of various different phases.' (*CoG*, 201). So perhaps the issue is that Moltmann cannot imagine an apocalyptic 'apocalypse' (unveiling) of Christ's glory. He can only conceive of a process – 'a series of events'. The problem is that Moltmann leaves the nature of Christ's future millennial reign undefined and unexplored with the result that it is no less imaginable. How will we know when the 'series of events' and 'various different phases' have begun? How can we avoid repeating the mistake of historical millenarian? Might we find ourselves falsely interpreting 'events' as the millennial reign when we should be relativising them by pointing to a future, eschatological millennium? Or might we find ourselves rejecting the millennial reign in the name of a future eschatological millennium?

Bauckham also points to Moltmann's failure to distinguish adequately between pre- and post-millenarianism (not withstanding Moltmann's comments in *CoG*, 147). Both are forms of eschatological millenarianism in that both look to a future millennial reign. But, whereas premillenarianism tends to the see the millennial reign as something for which believers can only wait and pray, postmillenarianism sees it coming about through the Holy Spirit prospering the mission of the church. It was this form of millenarianism that drove the rise of the Western missionary movement in the seventeenth and eighteenth centuries (see Edwards, 1774; Murray, 1971). Bauckham comments that this postmillenarianism is closer than premillenarianism to the secularised millenarianism of modernity. We might go further and say that it is the (eschatological) millenarianism of postmillenarianism that mutated into the secularised millenarianisms of both the Enlightenment project and the American millenarianism of 'manifest destiny'. In other words, these may not be forms of historical millenarianism as Moltmann claims, but forms of eschatological millenarianism. They push forward to as yet unattained futures, justifying the use of power over nature and other nations en route.

This brings us to a more significant response to Moltmann's millenarianism, one to which Bauckham points. Bauckham says: ' The issue of when Christ's earthly rule with his saints occurs – now or in the future millennium – needs supplementing with a discussion of the nature of that rule. otherwise Moltmann's argument is in danger of suggesting that while it is premature for Christians to attempt to exercise absolutist and violent domination over the world now, they will exercise such domination in the coming millennium.' (1997:274) Moltmann sets up false alternatives. We just choose between an oppressive historical millenarianism and a resisting eschatological millenarianism. I want to argue for a 'cruciform millenarianism' (an argument that anticipates the eschatology of the cross proposed in the conclusion).

The millennium is the form Christ's reign takes in history. It is the reminder that the kingdom is not wholly future. The kingdom is present in history, but it is not yet present in power and glory. The Jews expected that God's kingdom would come in glory and power leading to the complete victory of God and the defeat of his enemies. Jesus claims that the kingdom has come, but he himself is resisted and opposed. How can this be the promised coming of God's kingdom. The parables of the kingdom in Matthew 13 and Mark 4 are the response of Jesus to this question. They suggest that the kingdom has come, but in a secret, gracious manner. It comes now through the word of God as that word is 'sown'. And the kingdom grows in a secret, unseen way. The promised judgment falls, but it falls on the king at the cross. The fact that the Messiah is opposed does not mean the kingdom has not come. The kingdom has truly come, but in a secret way. But the fact that the kingdom has come in a secret way does not mean it will not also come in glory in the future. The proverbially small seed will one day encompass the whole earth. God will be victorious and his enemies will be judged. The Crucified and Risen Christ is given all authority. He sends his followers out in that authority to claim the all nations in his name.

Throughout the biblical narrative God reigns through his word just as he creates through his word. And God reigns today through the proclamation of his word in the mission of the church. This is the sense in which the saints share in the reign of Christ (Revelation 2:26-27). It is because the Risen Christ has been given all authority that he sends out his disciples to claim the nations by calling on them to obey all his teaching (Matthew 28:18-20). But when the reign of God is uncoupled from the word of God then people begin to interpret that reign in terms of earthly government – either in the present rule of Christendom or a nation's manifest destiny (Moltmann's historical millenarianism) or in a future earthly government (Moltmann's eschatological millenarianism).

The millennium is the reminder that the kingdom of Christ is present in history. But the kingdom has not yet come in resurrection glory. It is present in history under the sign of the cross. Christ will one day return to defeat his enemies and renew creation. In the meantime he reigns through the message of the cross – through his self-sacrificial love. The One on the throne of heaven is the Lamb who was slain. The millennial reign is given to the martyrs (Revelation 20:4). This is a cruciform reign. It is the present reign of an historical millenarianism, but it is not an absolutist or oppressive reign. It is a reign given to those who overcome by the blood of the Lamb and the word of their testimony, who do not love their lives so much as to shrink form death, who do not worship the beast, who patiently endure (Revelation 12:11; 13:8, 10; 14:10).

The millennial reign is the present reign of Christ over his people through his word. But this reign is a hidden reign – hidden under what is contrary (glory in shame, power in weakness, victory through death). It is thus a shaped by the cross. It is expressed not in the domination of others, but in the mission to the nations and the suffering of Christ's people. 'They overcame him by the blood of the Lamb and by the word of their testimony; they did not love their lives so much as to shrink from death' (Revelation 12:11).

CHAPTER 5

Eschatology and Soteriology

The Absence of Soteriology

Moltmann is susceptible to the criticism that he has failed to work out an adequate soteriology. Carl Braaten points out that in The Crucified God Moltmann never even uses the word 'atonement' (1976:114). He believes this fact arises from Moltmann's failure to engage with the history of tradition. Missing, believes Braaten, is any dialogue with Irenaeus, Origen, Athanasius, Augustine, Anselm, Abelard and others on the doctrine of atonement (1976:114; see also Williams, 1989:13). The traditional treatments of atonement get at best only fragmentary references (see, for example, CG, 183; see also 1991:52). In The Spirit of Life Moltmann rather dismissively says, 'Modern insights into the dignity and personhood of human beings make the old notions about propitiation and satisfaction, expiatory offerings and ransom obsolete' (134-5). They are 'inadequate images' (136). Elsewhere the idea of expiation is dealt with in a rather ambiguous way. One moment we are told it is very difficult to harmonise the idea of expiation with the resurrection, then we find that expiation is partially allowed. Braaten himself concludes, 'A fundamental treatment of the concept of substitution would seem to be absolutely essential if the Father's participation in the suffering and death of the Son would carry ultimate salvific meaning for those who suffer alone and die forgotten deaths today' (1976:115). That God suffers with us may be a comfort in our suffering, but it does not in and of itself redeem us from our suffering. Nor does it get to the heart of the reason for the cross – the atonement and defeat of sin (see Cook, 1990:88-9). Bauckham defends Moltmann by saying: 'God's suffering is with those who suffer for the sake of their redemption from suffering' (1990:99). This, however, begs the question: How?

It is perhaps ironic that, while Moltmann fails to give any sustained treatment of the atonement, and of substitution and vicarious suffering in particular, that element of the atonement which has often been considered the most problematic is an integral part of his understanding of the cross. The doctrine of atonement can be expounded in such a way as to apparently set God against God, the Father against the Son. Yet it is the idea of a *stasis* in God which is the starting point of Moltmann's understanding of the cross: 'God overcomes himself, God passes judgment on himself, God takes the judgment on the sin of man upon himself. He assigns to himself the fate that men should by rights endure. The cross of Jesus, understood as the cross of the Son of God, therefore reveals a change in God, a *stasis* within the Godhead.' (*CG*, 193) In *Theology of Hope* Moltmann speaks of 'the overcoming of God by God – of the judging, annihilating God by the saving, life-giving God, of the wrath of God by his goodness' (131). Bauckham comments: 'It is ... a serious weakness of Moltmann's theology that he is only able to speak of the judgment of God in these near-Marcionite terms ... For Moltmann the God who condemns the sinner and the 'human God' who justifies the sinner are so far opposed as to be either two Gods or to represent such a transformation of God as amounts to much the same thing.' (1977:309-310; see also Hill, 1982:169)

John Macquarrie, while welcoming *The Crucified God*, finds in it one major flaw namely the fact that Moltmann continues to speak of Christ as forsaken by God. 'The ghost of God the executioner is still lurking on the fringes' (1980:6). What Macquarrie seems to have failed to realise is the central place that Christ's experience of godforsakenness plays in Moltmann's thought. Indeed, as John Stott recognises, by the cross Moltmann 'means more than anything else the cry of dereliction' (1986ii:216). Moltmann's christology, trinitarianism, theodicy and political theology (including all that Macquarrie welcomes) all hinge of the fact that Christ experiences in a very real sense godforsakenness. In responding to similar criticisms from Dorothy Sölle (see also O'Donnell, 1983:153-156), Moltmann emphasises the fundamental underlying community of will between the Father and the Son (*WJC*, 175-177). Those who regard the God who 'surrenders' Jesus to the cross as a 'brutal' or 'sadistic' God fail to recognise that Jesus is not the passive subject in this process and they fail to recognise the suffering the Father undergoes in surrendering his dearly beloved Son.

What is remarkable is that in this context Moltmann criticises the idea of expiatory sacrifice because 'then the Father and the Son are not one. They are divided ... They are opposed to one another' (*WJC*, 176). This from the man who can say, 'The cross of the Son divides God from God to the utmost degree of enmity and distinction' (*CG*, 152)! In other words, Moltmann's own response to Sölle's (and Macquarrie's) criticisms can be used against his criticism of expiation. Once again one feels the want of any full discussion of the atonement. On the one hand, Moltmann is forced into using the language for which Bauckham criticises him. On the other hand, he criticises others for using not dissimilar language.

Underlying the absence of atonement is the fact that in Moltmann's theology, and in *The Crucified God* in particular, it is the question of theodicy which predominates over soteriology (1991:xvii, 172). Thus, for example, one of Moltmann's most explicit substitutionary phrase – '[God] assigns to himself the fate that men should by rights endure' (*CG*, 193) – comes in the context of a discussion, not of the significance of the cross to humanity, but of its significance to God himself. In *The Crucified God* Moltmann says that the cross 'embraces both the question of human guilt and man's liberation from it, and also the question of human suffering and man's redemption from it' (*CG*, 134). Yet it is arguable that Moltmann goes beyond this in that, while it is true that the question of human suffering predominates, he deals with this more in terms of the justification of God in the light of suffering than man's redemption from it. Thus, in general, (i) the question of the justification of God predominates over the question of the justification of humanity (see *ET*, 304); and (ii) the solidarity of Christ's sufferings with those of humanity is emphasised to the exclusion of the redemptive uniqueness of Christ's suffering. It is possible that Moltmann has sacrificed atonement – the justification of humanity – for the sake of theodicy – the justification of God.

The Relationship Between Sin and Death

But we must go further and ask, within the context of Moltmann's wider theology, whether the world is godless because of the sin and rebellion of humanity or because of God's self-limitation at creation. Throughout *The Crucified God*, Moltmann uses the expression 'godlessness and godforsakenness' to describe the human situation (Bauckham, 1987i:60-61). Moltmann's understanding of this divine absence is crucial for it impinges more than once on Moltmann's conception of mission and eschatology. Moltmann says:

> Sin cannot be merely understood in anthropological terms as transgression of the law, guilt, and distress of conscience on man's part. Law and conscience reveal the oppression of 'the power of sin', which is at once godlessness and godforsakenness. That is why behind sin is death – absolute death and the total end. Sin is not merely the anthropological problem of man's self-division and self-alienation, nor is it merely the theological problem of remoteness from God. It is an apocalyptic pressure of affliction for everything that wants to live and has to die. (1979i:164)

What is striking here is that death does not enter creation as a result of sin; quite the opposite: 'behind sin is death'. Moltmann has reversed the biblical order. For Moltmann death precedes sin rather than sin preceding death. He even speaks of an 'imperfect creation' (*CoG*, 91). In *The Coming of God* Moltmann rejects the view that 'death is the result of original sin', replacing it with the assertion that death is 'a characteristic of frail, temporal creation which will be overcome through the new creation of things for eternal life' (*CoG*, 78). In a self-conscious reversal of the biblical order, Moltmann describes sin as 'the wages of death' (*CoG*, 94). 'Death is only the consequence of sin,' says Moltmann, 'inasmuch as sin exists because of death: we cannot endure morality, and by killing we can make other people die' (*CoG*, 91).

Moltmann acknowledges that what he sometimes calls the Augustinian position that human death is the consequence of human sin was the dominant view of the Church until nineteenth century Liberal Protestantism (*CoG*, 85-90). But he rejects this view. 'If death is the consequence of human sin,' says Moltmann, 'then when Adam and Eve were in the Garden of Eden they must have been immortal. That, however, makes their sexual reproduction impossible.' Quite why it might make sexual reproduction impossible he does not explain. He points out that non-human living things are subject to death – in their case there is death without sin (*CoG*, 90). He cites Romans 8:20: 'For the creation was subjected to frustration, not by its own choice, but by the will of the one who subjected it, in hope.' But creation become subject to frustration as a result of humanity's failed stewardship. Instead of caring for creation under God's rule, we rejected that rule. We rule creation not in the image of God's good, liberating and life-giving rule, but in the image of Satan's lie – his portrayal of God's rule as harsh and tyrannical. Moltmann dismisses human culpability in the frustration of non-human creation as 'hubris' (*CoG*, 90). But, in the Romans 8 passage cited by Moltmann, Paul links creation's liberation with the 'the glorious freedom of the children of God'. Humanity's slavery to sin brings frustration to non-human creation. Humanity's redemption will bring liberation to non-human creation.

Moltmann does not view sin in objective terms, but in subjective terms as 'distress of conscience' or 'self-alienation'. And this is the reason why Moltmann is so ambiguous on atonement. For him sin is a symptom, but not the root problem. Because it is not the root problem, Moltmann denies that the solution consists in the expiation of sin. Because it is a symptom, Moltmann allows the forgiveness of sin as one consequence of the cross.

The underlying problem is 'the intruding Nothingness' (1979i:163; *SL*, 213), the 'apocalyptic pressure of affliction of everything that wants to live and has to die' (1979i:164; see also *CPS*, 34). 'Everything which exists is *burdened with transitoriness*, but burdened in hope because it wants to be free' (1969:217; see also p. 36). This affects Moltmann conception of salvation. He says, 'Creation, new creation and resurrection are external works of God against chaos, nothingness and death' (*CG*, 192-193). Quite apart from the questionableness of the belief that creation was a salvific work against chaos (see Walsh, 1987:64-67), this conception puts the emphasis of salvation upon ontological transitoriness and not upon the problem of sin and judgment (in *Theology of Hope* Moltmann saw divine righteousness '*both* in a juridical *and* in an ontological sense', 205, my emphasis). This is why the resurrection and the new creation are *ex nihilo*; because they are set against the fundamental tendency of reality towards nothingness. The problems of sin, alienation and guilt are an expression of this underlying ontological instability. To support his view Moltmann refers to Romans 8 and the 'frustration' and 'bondage to decay' of creation. As Walsh points out, however, 'Romans 8:19f portrays the groaning of creation in terms of Adam's sin, not the inherent structure of creatureliness' (1987:64).

In Moltmann there is little place for *re*-generation, *re*-newal, *re*-creation, *re*-mission and so on (see, for example, *SL*, 145). For Moltmann, creation has always been oppressed by the *nihil*, so there is no place in his conception of salvation for restoration; no significance for the prefix re- in soteriology (Walsh, 1987:61; Wells, 1990:65). Moltmann, unnecessarily, wants to force us to choose between restoration and fulfilment. Indeed, Douglas Schuurman believes that, because Moltmann, without the sharp distinction made in Genesis 3, collapses sin and creation into each other, 'he views salvation as redemption not only from sin but also from creation' (1987:65).

Against this background, Moltmann sees sin in terms of 'closedness' to the future and, specifically, to the future opened up by the word of promise (see *TH*, 22-24; *GC*, 69; 1979i:122-123). As Langdon Gilkey notes, however, the future can be a menace as well an opportunity (1976:258). Brian Walsh comments, 'The future is thus ambiguous ... openness to the future *per se* is no guarantee of redemption because it is precisely this openness which affords us the freedom which has the potential to sin' (1987:63). Rubem Alves puts it somewhat differently. He says: 'History is not open. The problem of future and hope in history is not related primarily to decay and death but to the powers that keep history captive. The cross does not stand for dying, but for killing, for the powers that destroy men. History is thus not closed by organic realities but by active powers of political nature.' (1969:64)

Walsh seeks to clarify the issue by distinguishing between the ontological *structure* of reality and the historical, existential *direction* that creation has taken' (1987:63). While Moltmann's analysis of the freedom and openness of the structure of reality is convincing to Walsh, he believes 'it becomes confused with the directional question of sin or obedience when [Moltmann] speaks of things like suffering being ontologically constitutive of matter' (1987:64). In contrast, Walsh wants to retain the openness of the structure of reality, but to maintain the distinction between structure and direction by saying that reality is open to two directions, namely obedience and disobedience. It is not the ontological structure of reality which is judged by God, but its direction in response to God.

Absent, then, from Moltmann's thought is an adequate understanding of the fall. In Moltmann the fall is subsumed into creation itself; it is an expression of the threat of Nothingness in a world created *ex nihilo*. This idea is found in embryonic form in Kierkegaard who sees the fall arising from anxiety, anxiety which in turn arises from the freedom of humanity, a freedom which is 'infinite and arises out of nothing' (cited by Blocher, 1984:138). Yet such an understanding stands in contrast to the biblical account of the fall. However one views the historicity of the Genesis account, it is clear that its intention is to describe an origin for evil apart from creation. Creation, as originally created, is characterised as entirely good and not as oppressed by the *nihil* from which it was created. Blocher (who believes that in Genesis 3 we have the account of an historical fall, albeit a highly pictorial account) cites Ricoeur (who in contrast believes that Genesis 3 is mythic): 'The etiological myth of Adam is the most extreme attempt to separate the origin of evil from the origin of the good; its intention is to set up a *radical* origin of evil distinct from the more *primordial* origin of the goodness of things.' (Blocher, 1984:160; see also Schuurman, 1987:65-6)

Not only in Genesis 3, but throughout the Scriptures, the presence of evil is regarded not as that which arises from the inherent structure of creation, but as a terrible and disastrous intrusion into creation. Indeed, as we saw when we considered Moltmann's understanding the trinitarian history of God, unless evil is seen in this latter sense then it is impossible to separate evil from God himself. If there is no disjunction between creation and sin, a disjunction expressed in terms of the fall, then some form of duality of good and evil is required either within God or between God and non-contingent Evil. And so we find ourselves returning not to the Judæo-Christian account of creation, but to the Babylonian creation myths.

In *The Spirit of Life* Moltmann goes further, criticising the Reformation doctrine of justification, which he acknowledges to be based on Paul's teaching. This doctrine, says Moltmann, has the universality of sin – the doctrine of original sin – as its premise and a christological foundation which sees Christ's death and resurrection as vicarious. 'The weakness about the universal concept of sin underlying the Pauline and Protestant doctrine of justification is that collective guilt of this kind makes people blind to specific, practical guilt' (*SL*, 126). The generality of the traditional view of sin, Moltmann argues, allows people to hide their individual guilt for specific sins. Moltmann detects an alternative view in the Synoptic Gospels where 'sinners' are those on one side of the social conflicts that characterise history. With this alternative reading of sin comes an alternative reading of the fall: 'The real history of human sin begins with Cain's fratricide (Gen. 4) and with the spread of wickedness on earth through "violence" (Gen. 6). The eating of the forbidden fruit in the Garden of Eden (Gen. 3) belongs to the world of myth, which offers a metaphysical interpretation of the physical history of the world.' (*SL*, 125-6)

Once again Moltmann's habit of sliding between 'not' and 'not only' is evident. He says the doctrine of original sin makes the Protestant doctrine of justification unconvincing to 'many people', but does not specify whether this includes himself. He appears to deny the traditional Protestant view of the fall, original sin and justification. But then he adds statements like, 'it is important for Christian *not merely* to look at the mythical story' of the fall (*SL*, 126; emphasis added); or that the Protestant doctrine of justification and liberation theology 'can correct and enrich one another mutually' (*SL*, 128). Nevertheless, he himself offers no understanding of the significance of the 'mythical story' of the fall; nor an understanding of the universality of sin and the universal need for justification. The nearest he gets is arguing that in situations of injustice, the perpetrators too need liberation – liberation from their guilt through the justifying righteousness of God (*SL*, 133).

Against the background of his view of reality (as 'oppressed by Nothingness', 1979i:171), the human condition (godlessness and godforsakenness), and sin (a subjective experience of guilt and distress of conscious), Moltmann views salvation first and foremost on a social and cosmic level. The problem is that Moltmann is unable to give a satisfactory account of individual salvation. It is seen simply in relation to cosmic salvation, as an anticipation of the future. In practice it is little more than 'psychological liberation' (chapter 7 of *CG*) or freedom from anxiety (1980:48-50). Furthermore, it is striking how little is the attention Moltmann gives to individual life after death. In a sense he finds himself in a cleft stick. He wants to affirm the resurrection of the body and life after death, particularly in his discussion of death in relation to Bloch (1975:36-39). Yet he does not make too much of it because he wants to stress the importance of the body now and of action now. When in *The Coming of God* he does address issues of personal eschatology, he portrays death not as judgment or separation, but as a positive experience which 'de-restricts' people:

> Through death the human person is transformed from restricted life to immortal life, and from restricted existence to non-restricted existence. Death de-restricts the human being's spirit in both time and space. The dead are no longer there as temporally limited and spatially restricted "contract person', but we sense their presence whenever we become aware that we are living "before God"; and wherever we sense their presence, we feel the divine "wide space" which binds us together. (*CoG*, 76-77)

It is difficult to see how this view of death as that which removes the restrictions of finitude squares the biblical portrayal of death as 'the last enemy'.

The result of Moltmann's view of sin and death is that he sees personal salvation as a noetic experience rather than an ontological or juridical reality. The cross and resurrection communicate to us the fact that God is the God who justifies the godless. In *The Coming of God* he asks: 'Is sin the cause of physical death, or dies it simply turn physical death into a mental and spiritual torment?' (*CoG*, 83). Moltmann's clearly believes it is the latter and salvation is not atonement from sin, but release from the unnecessary mental torment of death. So, in his discussion of the atonement in his most recent works, Moltmann appears to see the soteriological significance of the cross in noetic rather than ontological terms. 'It is God himself', he says, 'who atones for the sins of his people ... Atonement .. is realised by God, who transforms human guilt into divine suffering by "bearing" human sins' (1991:50). God in himself atones for sin as he bears and suffers the injury to his love (*SL*, 134). The cross, then, 'can only be understood as atonement for the sins of the world if in Christ we see God' (*SL*, 135; 1991:52). As such, the cross does not so much *effect* atonement as *reveal* atonement through 'the pain of God'. 'The Christ who atones is *the revelation* of the God who has mercy'. Or again: 'God's representative action is *manifest* in the representative action of Christ. In Christ's suffering and death for us it becomes certain that "God is for us"' (1991:51-52, emphasis added; see also *SL*, 136).

Judgment and Universalism

Battista Mondin bemoans the fact that there is in Moltmann no concept of judgment, no 'eschatology of fear and perdition' (1972:62; see also Page, 1984:98). This, however, is not strictly true. Moltmann is dismissive of 'a more modern evangelical idea about *conditional immortality*' because it means people 'would not have to answer before God's judgment' and because annihilation is incompatible with God's 'faithfulness to what he has created' (*CoG*, 109). In *The Crucified God* Moltmann says, 'God passes judgment on himself, God takes the judgment on the sin of man upon himself' (*CG*, 193). This allows him to go on to argue that the cross does not allow the distinction between Christian and non-Christian to be maintained. 'The theology of the cross is the true Christian universalism. There is no distinction here, and there cannot be any more distinctions. All are sinners without distinction, and all will be made righteous without any merit on their part by his grace which has come to pass in Jesus Christ.' (*CG*, 194-195; *CoG*, 251) Moltmann makes this claim with reference to Romans 3:22b-24. In particular he makes much of the phrase 'there is no distinction' in verse 22b (RSV). Yet he fails to refer to verse 22a: 'This righteousness from God comes through faith in Jesus Christ *to all who believe*'. The 'no distinction' is among those who believe and must surely, given the context in the epistle to the Romans, refer to the distinction between Jews and Gentiles.

Turning to the idea of the last judgment or the day of judgment, Moltmann views it in the context of the unqualified grace of the God who justifies the godless. The Last Judgment 'is solely the victory of the divine righteousness that is to become the foundation of the new creation of all things' (*WJC*, 315). Thus Moltmann can say: 'He will not judge in order to punish the wicked and reward the good, but so as to make the saving righteousness of God prevail among them all. He will "judge" in order to raise up and to put things right.' (*WJC*, 315) The images of terror and perdition associated with the last judgment arose, according to Moltmann, because it was not viewed in the context of the joyous expectation of Christ, of the glorious future of God and his righteousness. The judgment, then, is to be seen, believes Moltmann, as the establishment of God's justice which is the essential precondition for the universal reign of peace.

Does then the final judgment lead to damnation for any? This is 'the Christian dilemma' (*WJC*, 336-338) and in his early theology Moltmann refused to answer it dogmatically. Yet it becomes clear which side of the dilemma he favours. He reminds us that God's love is unconditional and that its most perfect form is love for one's enemies. At the heart of the gospel is the reconciliation of all things through the cross. 'Is is conceivable', he asks, 'that in the final judgment the coming Christ will act in contradiction to Jesus and his gospel, and will judge according to the penal law of retaliation?' (*WJC*, 337). He concludes:

> [The final judgment] is not an end but a beginning. If it is seen like this, then it of course raises the question about universal reconciliation and the redemption of the devil. But this does not have to be affirmed in order to spread confidence about the judgment, any more than a double outcome of the judgment for believers and the godless has to be affirmed in order to emphasise the seriousness of the human situation. Whatever the outcome of Christ's judgment of the living and the dead – whether all will be saved or only a few – this is *Jesus'* judgment, and Christians can wait for it only in the light of the gospel of Jesus Christ which they know and believe. But this Jesus does not come to judge. He comes to raise up. That is the messianic interpretation of the expectation of Christ's judgment. (*WJC*, 338; see also 1980:34-5)

In *The Coming of God* Moltmann's universalism becomes even more explicit. 'The hope of Christians is not exclusive, and not particularist either. It is an inclusive and universal hope for the life which overcomes death. It is true not only for Christians but for everything living that wants to live and has to die.' (*CoG*, 110) 'The judgment that consists of the consequences of evil action does not take place. Anyone who teaches "the principle of grace" cannot at the same time teach "the Last Judgment" as apocalyptic karmic law.' (*CoG*, 115) He cites Johann Christoph Blumhardt saying 'Good Friday proclaims a general pardon to the whole world' (*CoG*, 254). Indeed for Moltmann this general pardon extents to the Devil: 'In this divine Judgment all sinners, the wicked and the violent, the murderers and the children of Satan, the Devil and the fallen angels will be liberated and saved from their deadly perdition through the transformation into their true, created being, because God remains true to himself, and does not give up what he has once created and affirmed, or allow it to be lost.' (*CoG*, 255)

Moltmann claims the belief in divine judgment was originally the hope of the victims of oppression that God's justice would prevail over their persecutors. Only with the advent of Christendom did this morph into a prototype of imperial judicial power in which evil-doers are tried (*CoG*, 235, 250). It is, however, to reconcile this assertion with the opening chapters of Romans where Paul's argument is precisely that all humanity is under God's wrath. On 'the day of God's wrath, when his righteous judgment will be revealed,' says Paul citing Psalm 62:12 and Proverbs 24:12, 'God "will give to each person according to what he has done".' (Romans 2:5-6) Moltmann asserts that 'universal salvation and a double outcome of judgment are therefore both well attested biblically. So the decision for the one or the other cannot be made on the ground of "scripture"'. (*CoG*, 241) But the review of scripture that precedes this conclusion (and it is not clear why he places the words 'scripture' in inverted commas) is unconvincingly for Moltmann takes statements of the universal scope of salvation (encompassing all people especially including Jews and Gentiles) for statements of universal salvation. He ignores the fact that such statements implicitly or explicitly assume faith as the condition of salvation. It is all who have faith in Jesus Christ who will be saved.

Moltmann quotes the evangelical Lausanne Covenant: 'Those who reject Christ repudiate the joy of salvation and condemn themselves to eternal separation from God.' He comments: 'Is this theologically conceivable? Can some people *damn themselves*, and others redeem themselves by accepting Christ? If this were so, God's decisions would be dependent on the will of human beings. God would become the auxiliary who executes the wishes of people who decide their fate for themselves. If I can damn myself, I am my own God and judge. Take to a logical conclusion this is atheistic.' (*CoG*, 109). But this is to twist the meaning of the Lausanne Covenant. The Covenant is not saying people are their own judges. It is saying that they make decisions that lead to their righteous condemnation by the divine Judge. The divine Judge does not make arbitrary judgments. He judges people on the basis of their decisions and actions. Moltmann can only deny this by advocating a kind of hyper-Calvinism in which human choices have no meaning. Reformed evangelicals certainly would affirm God's sovereignty over human decisions, but this does not mean human choices are illusory. If the only means of salvation – Jesus Christ – is rejected then there can be no salvation.

But Moltmann wants to deny a link between actions and judgment. 'If at "the Last Judgment" we were to be judged only according to what we have done, then the outcomes of the proceedings would be in our own hands ... We ... should need no God for it. We should only have to know the law, in order to will, or not to will, the consequences of what we do. A God who bound to his law, and who can do more than implement it, is neither free nor godlike.' (*CoG*, 115; see also *CoG*, 245) Two points need to be made. First, God is not bound by some universal law of justice that stands over God himself. He is bound by his own righteous character and his own words of warning. He is the holy God before whom sin and sinners cannot stand. Far from being ungodlike, judgment on the basis of human actions is a consequence of the holiness and righteousness of God. Second, Moltmann is right to assert God is not bound to judge us on the basis of our actions. This is the message of justification through the atoning death of Christ. On the cross God reconciled his justice and his mercy; his holiness and his love. He upheld his judgment while justifying sinners through the propitiatory death of Christ (Romans 3:25-26). Salvation from judgment comes through faith in the saving work of Christ as Paul repeatedly affirms his epistle to the Romans. This faith is itself a gift from God through the regenerating work of the Spirit so that God's gracious freedom is maintained in salvation. Nevertheless, contrary to Moltmann's claims, without faith in Christ there is no salvation from judgment. Those who do put their faith in Christ will be judged according to their actions. Ultimately in Moltmann's theology justification is a universal act of God cut loose from the cross and independent of faith. The cross does not achieve justification, it merely reveals it. And therefore faith in cross of Christ is not necessary for justification, it is necessary only for comfort in the face of death and judgment. Christ becomes, in Moltmann's theology, the revealer of salvation rather than the means of salvation. It is ultimately an un-christological soteriology.

Soteriology and the Church

Does Moltmann's view of judgment affect his view of the church and its mission? The answer must clearly be, 'Yes'. Andrew Kirk believes 'Moltmann does not distinguish too clearly between the special community of the redeemed, who experience at first-hand Christ's power to produce a new kind of existence, and the rest of humanity who may expect some kind of benefit from Christ's eschatological victory over the idolatries of power, race and economic privilege' (1980:66).

Moltmann's refusal to allow a distinction along the lines of Christian and non-Christian creates difficulties for him in defining the church in relation to the world – a definition at the heart of any missiology. Thus, Moltmann says the church 'is not "the not-world"' (*CPS*, 83). Instead the church must be seen as the eschatological vanguard of the new humanity under the reign of God. The church is 'the beginning of the liberation of man and creation ... the present form of messianic liberation' (*CPS*, 84). The distinction between the church and the world is, for Moltmann, temporal (and indeed temporary) rather than eschatological.

This, however, ignores the biblical images of the church as Christ's bride which suggests that the church is an eschatological reality as well as an historical one. We might speak of the church as the eschatological vanguard in the sense that its present experience of salvation anticipates that of the whole cosmos (Romans 8:20-21; James 1:18). Moltmann, however, cannot retain a distinction between the church and the world after eschatological judgment because of his universalism.

The result is a merging of the church with the mission of the church so that ecclesiology equals missiology. The church, says Moltmann, 'exists as a factor of present liberation' (*CPS*, 75). The church is defined not by what it is but by what it does, specifically in terms of its participation in the trinitarian history of God. As such, 'we cannot therefore say *what* the church is in all circumstances and what it comprises in itself. But we can tell *where* the church happens.' (*CPS*, 65) The church, then, exists to the extent that it 'participates in the glorifying of God in creation's liberation... in the uniting of men with one another, in the uniting of society with nature and in the uniting of creation with God... in the history of God's suffering... in the history of the divine joy' (*CPS*,

65).

Although Moltmann acknowledges that 'it is one goal of mission to awaken faith, to baptise, to found churches and to form a new life under the lordship of Christ' (*CPS*, 152), he wants to emphasise a qualitative view of mission alongside, what he calls, this quantitative view. Yet in practice the qualitative view predominates in his thought to the exclusion of the quantitative view. Thus, for example, dialogue predominates to the exclusion of evangelism.

An inadequate soteriology leads to an inadequate ecclesiology. If we can hope for the salvation of all people then the distinction between the church and the world can at best be a temporary or provisional one. The church is then inevitably defined in terms of activity. It is no longer defined by its experience of God's grace but by what it does, that is to say, where it shares in the anticipation of the coming kingdom. And so an inadequate ecclesiology leads in turn to an inadequate missiology. Because Moltmann sees salvation almost exclusively in cosmic and social terms so he sees mission almost exclusively in these terms as well. To the extent that personal salvation is largely noetic and psychological, mission on a personal level is more pastoral than evangelistic.

CHAPTER 6

Eschatology and the Church

The Exodus Church

The last chapter of *Theology of Hope* is entitled 'Exodus Church' by which
Moltmann means the eschatological character of the church as a pilgrim people.
Those who accept the scandal of the cross are not integrated into society, but
are made 'homeless' in this world (*CG*, 39). Although it serves the world and
identifies itself with the world, the exodus church is not subject to the pressures
society places upon it, but is subject instead to the lordship of Christ (*CPS*, 4-7;
1975:58-59).

Moltmann outlines how modern society has rejected its traditional religious
orientation. From being central to society and to its aims, religion has become a
private affair, a matter of individual choice in a society operating along purely
functional lines. Although scientific 'facts' are regarded as absolutes, value
judgments have become subjective and relative. Such a society exerts pressure
on the church to fulfil certain roles which it, society, accords to the church (see
TH, 304-324; 1969:110-117; 1971:130-140). If the church is to be true to its
eschatological calling then, Moltmann believes, these pressures must be
resisted.

The first pressure is to provide a transcendental context for the new cult of
subjectivity. If value judgments are individual then the church is called upon to
provide a framework in which individuals can make their personal choices. The
problem with this is that it operates within the dichotomy of the private,
subjective world and the public world in which there remains a cosmological-
metaphysical atheism. 'God' belongs only to the existential subjective plane.
The church no longer has any relation to the socio-political order. Justice and
political righteousness are, as it were, off limits. The object of Christian love,
our neighbour, is reduced to someone we personally encounter, divorced of
their social and economic context. The result threatens to become 'a religious
ideology of romanticist subjectivity that has been relieved of all social
obligations' (*TH*, 316)

A second pressure upon the church is for it to fill the gap created by the
radical individuality of modern society, indeed the radical loneliness. The
pressure is for the Christian community to 'offer human warmth and nearness,

neighbourliness and homeliness' (*TH*, 320). Certainly the church is a new community in contrast to the loneliness common in the world. Its function, however, cannot be reduced to this. It is more than just a 'club'. It is the eschatological community under the cross, straining after the promise of the new creation. This pressure denies the church its critical role in society. Society becomes increasingly dehumanised and the church becomes increasingly ghettoised.

A third pressure upon the church is institutionalism. In the contemporary world, argues Moltmann, ideologies are being replaced by institutions as that which provides a framework for existence. They relieve people of the pressure of making critical decisions for themselves. In this context, the pressure is for the church to become that institution which makes a person's theological decisions for him or her. The effect of this is 'the religious attitude of an institutionalised non-committal outlook' (*TH*, 323). In other words, when an individual's decisions are made for him or her they carry little personal conviction and become effectively meaningless and irrelevant.

The exodus church must resist these pressures in favour of the will of its Lord. If the church, 'according to the will of him in whom it believes and in whom it hopes, is to be different and to serve a different purpose, then it must address itself to no less a task than that of breaking out of these its socially fixed roles' (*TH*, 324). In contrast to what society would have it be, the church is 'the community of eschatological salvation' (*TH*, 325). This means that an eschatological orientation pervades its whole life. As a people who are not of this age, but of the age to come, under the eschatological lordship of Christ, the church's existence is geared to the mission of Christ and following Christ's pattern of service to the world. This mission is conducted, not in accordance with the expectations of society, but in accordance with the eschatological expectation of the kingdom of God and, as such, the church 'lays claim to the whole of humanity in mission' (*TH*, 327). The church's service to the world is not geared to the preservation of society, but to its transformation as it seeks to anticipate eschatological shalom and reconciliation. 'In the light of the eschatological person of Christ, the church does not live from the past; it exists as a factor of present liberation, between the remembrance of his history and hope of his kingdom' (*CPS*, 75). The church is to be an agent of eschatological unrest. For this reason Moltmann prefers to speak, not of 'the church for the world' which is a 'very vague' term, but of 'the church for the kingdom of God' (*TH*, 327-328).

Furthermore, the church must not conform to the ethics of society, but, as the messianic community, it is to exhibit a messianic lifestyle. Its ethical basis is not natural theology, but christology. In response to those who argue that ethics is impossible on the basis of christology, Moltmann believes that what is at stake in Jesus' call to messianic lifestyle is nothing less than his messiahship (*WJC*, 116-119). The messianic community is to practise 'the new corporate justice of God's messianic people' (the justice of Jubilee), and as such to be 'the great alternative to the world's present system' (*WJC*, 122). This it does as it follows 'the messianic Torah': the gospel is a fulfilment rather than antithesis of the law (*WJC*, 122-127). This means, for example, that we are to break the vicious circle of (retaliatory) violence, exercise creative love for our enemies and seek to fulfil, as the early church saw itself doing, the messianic promises of peace in Isaiah 2 and Micah 4 (*WJC*, 127-136).

Moltmann takes up the Reformers' understanding of the universal priesthood of all believers and the vocation that all believers are given in the world. 'Callings' in the sense of specific roles given to specific believers in a given historic situation are controlled and function only in relationship to the irrevocable and immutable 'call' given universally to all. This call is 'the call to join in working for the kingdom of God that is to come' (*TH*, 333). All callings are to serve that end and are therefore pursued not for self-fulfilment, but for the incarnation of faith, concretion of hope and for their correspondence to the future kingdom (*TH*, 334). Similarly, the messianic community, 'the fellowship of friends' (*CPS*, 316), cannot be hierarchically structured. 'Assignments' – Moltmann prefers this to the term 'ministries' because of the exclusive overtones the latter has come to have – are given to all through the Spirit for the good of all. There are no 'higher' offices. Moltmann uses 'callings' in *Theology of Hope* to refer to roles in society (329-338) and 'assignments' in *The Church in the Power of the Spirit* to refer to roles within the church (300-314). Moltmann wants to recover the sense of the church as a voluntary association (1979iii:37-42), a church *of* the people rather than a church *for* the people. Moltmann says, 'My thesis is a simple one: the local congregation is the future of the church' (1979ii:21).

In the light of its character as the Exodus church, Moltmann interprets the traditional elements in a doctrine of the church from an eschatological perspective. The proclamation of the word is a proclamation of the future in the form of promise. 'In the gospel and in the evangelisation of the world this future becomes present in the Word' (*CPS*, 219). Or again: '[The church's] word of gospel is the anticipation of the eschatological manifestation of God in all areas of the world. It thus bears in itself the character of promise. It is, in a hidden way, the anticipatory epiphany of God in the world.' (1969:215) Baptism demonstrates 'the dawn of the rule of God in personal life and the common conversion to the future of that rule' (*CPS*, 226; see also 1979iii:46-51). The Lord's Supper is an inclusive 'sign of hope' (*CPS*, 243); it is celebrated in Christ's Easter presence through the hope-awakening remembrance of his passion (see also *WJC*, 204-211; 1979iii:52-56). Worship is the anticipation of the eschatological glory of God and of the feast and rest of creation. (It is these elements of joy and doxology which prevent praxis becoming simply activism, see 1973; 1991:179; Bauckham, 1989ii:296-297). In the experience of faith, the rebirth of all creation is already experienced in an individual's life as he or she is born again into living hope.

Promise and Contradiction

As the church of the crucified one and the church in the power of the Spirit, the church in the world experiences an 'unrest' which is 'implicit to itself' (*CPS*, 3). This unrest is created by the promise. Augustine said, 'My heart is restless until it finds its rest in you'. Moltmann claims the source of Augustine's *cor inquietum* is the *promissio inquietum* (*TH*, 88) and as such it 'is not a universal human presupposition for the Christian understanding of God, but is a mark of the pilgrim people of God and a goal of the Christian mission to all men' (*TH*, 276; see also 1980:12).

The truth of most statements is judged by the extent to which they conform to existing reality. Moltmann maintains, however, that this is not the case with statements of Christian hope; hope contradicts reality and present experience. It speaks not of present existence, but of new possibilities of existence, of the new creation. The promise of Christian hope is for a new and better future; in other words, a future unlike the present. 'Hope's statements of promise ... must stand in contradiction to the reality which can at the present be experienced' (*TH*, 18).

'Present and future, experience and hope, stand in contradiction to each other in Christian eschatology, with the result that man is not brought into harmony and agreement with the given situation, but drawn into the conflict between hope and experience' (*TH*, 18; 1979i:104; *CoG*, 139; *ET*, 100-101). This eschatological *contradiction* allows no harmony with the present, instead it brings us into conflict with it. 'If there were no God, then perhaps one could accept violence and injustice, because that was the way things were. But if there is a God and this God is just, then one can no longer accept them.' (1989:7) The Christian is no longer content with the status quo, but only with change that corresponds to hope. In this way, argues Moltmann, eschatology provides a powerful dynamic for change and mission. 'It is in this contradiction that hope must prove its power' (*TH*, 19). And it is for this reason that eschatology is frequently expressed in negative terms because 'eschatology ... must formulate its statements of hope in contradiction to our present experience of suffering, evil and death' (*TH*, 19). This, too, is how eschatology will speak with relevance to contemporary society. 'Atheists and Christians find themselves in solidarity in the contradiction that is disclosed. For unbelief, this contradiction becomes the occasion to put God in the wrong. For faith, it becomes the occasion to put reality, as it presents itself, in the wrong.' (1971:16)

As a person receives revelation in the form of promise, they are identified as what they are (in the sense that they are part of the godforsaken world seen in the cross) and differentiated as what they will be. As they believe, so they stake their future on the risen Christ; as they hope, so they find themselves in contradiction with what they will be. So revelation does not leap over the present to what is not yet nor does it ignore the present. Instead it creates a painful contradiction which the believer embraces. 'He gains himself by abandoning himself. He finds life by taking death upon him. He attains to freedom by accepting the form of a servant. That is how the truth that points forward to the resurrection of the dead comes to him.' (*TH*, 92)

The reality that the contradiction of present experience takes in the world is the kingdom of God. It is in this way that the kingdom becomes this-worldly; as it 'becomes the antithesis and contradiction of a godless and god-forsaken world' (*TH*, 222). The kingdom, then, is present as promise and hope. And the form the kingdom takes in the world is the suffering experienced by believers as its contradiction is imposed upon them. 'The coming lordship of God takes shape here in the suffering of the Christians, who because of their hope cannot be conformed to the world, but are drawn by the mission and love of Christ into the discipleship and conformity to his sufferings' (*TH*, 222).

If the contradiction of hope is the incentive for mission, the possibilities opened up by the resurrection make it possible to bring about change and the promise gives direction to that change. 'If the promise of the kingdom of God shows us a universal eschatological future horizon spanning all things – "that God may be all in all" – then it is impossible for the man of hope to adopt an attitude of religious and cultic resignation from the world. On the contrary, he is compelled to accept the world in all meekness, subject as it is to death and the powers of annihilation, and guide all things towards their new being. (*TH*, 224)

The source of the contradiction which arises from hope is the contradiction of the cross and resurrection. The sin, death, suffering, and hatred of the cross are contradicted by the righteousness, life, glory and peace of the resurrection. In the same way, the promise of Christian eschatology is that sinners are justified, the dead live and so on. 'The contradiction to the existing reality of himself and his world in which man is placed by hope is the very contradiction out of which this hope itself is born – it is the contradiction between the resurrection and the cross' (*TH*, 18). As such, the resurrection is more than merely consolation in suffering. Its contradiction of the cross is no accident. It is 'the protest of the divine promise *against* suffering' (*TH*, 21). In this way, the contradictory aspects of our existence are transformed into the not-yet of Christian hope. That the resurrection is the contradiction of the cross is confirmed by the identity of the crucified one with the risen one. This claims Moltmann is the main thrust of the Easter appearances, that the one who appears as risen is the same one as the one who was crucified. This 'identity in infinite contradiction' (*TH*, 85) is to be understood as an act of God's faithfulness. In this way the resurrection functions as promise: the contradiction of the godlessness of the cross by the resurrection points to a time when all godlessness will be contradicted by an analogous act of new creation. We can only hold on to this truth as we hold on to the *contradiction* of the cross-resurrection *and* the *continuity* of the cross-resurrection in the identity of the crucified one with the risen one. This leads to what Moltmann calls 'an open dialectic' (*TH*, 201); a dialectic which will find its resolution only in the eschaton.

The influence of Hellenistic epiphany religions, and of the Judaizers with whom Paul struggled and who regarded the Christ event as fulfilled already in a renewed covenant and people, led to a danger of an over-realised eschatology in the early church. The Christ event, instead of being seen as promise, is regarded as a redemptive act fulfilled in itself and repeated in the cultus. The sacraments come to represent the mystical union of the believer with Christ. Instead of being regarded as hidden in the present, Christ is regarded as already exalted and fully glorified. No longer is the cross 'the abiding key-signature of his lordship in the world' (*TH*, 158) prior to the eschaton. Now it is merely a transitional stage, the climax of the incarnation, before his heavenly lordship which is already established. Instead of citizens of the coming kingdom, we have people who at death share in the eternal bliss of heaven. The eschaton involves nothing more than a revelation of what is already the case. Moltmann sums up this view by calling it an *eschatologia gloriæ.*

He has in mind here Luther's phrase *theologia gloriæ.* By this Luther meant those who look for revelation and knowledge of God in acts of power. In contrast, Luther proposed a *theologia crucis* in which God is revealed in the cross; as such he is revealed in his contrary. That is his power is revealed in weakness, his wisdom in folly, his glory in suffering, and so on. Likewise, Moltmann proposes an *eschatologia crucis* in contrast to the *eschatologia gloriæ.* Those who hold to the latter emphasise what is fulfilled, that is they emphasise the power, victory and glory of the resurrection. Moltmann, however, maintains that these correctly belong to that to which the resurrection points – the new creation. The effect of an *eschatologia gloriæ* is to pass over the cross to the resurrection and, in so doing, to abandon the earth on which the cross stands in all its godlessness. Moltmann is sensitive to the Jewish inability to accept Jesus as the Messiah on the basis of the fundamentally unredeemed character of history. True Christianity, Moltmann maintains, unlike an *eschatologia gloriæ*, acknowledges that redemption is future (*CG*, 100-102; *WJC*, 28-37; 1975: 60-68; *SL*, 209-10).

So, in contrast to an *eschatologia gloriæ*, true eschatology leads to an *eschatologia crucis.* The believer, inspired by promise and hope, enters into the reality of the world in its godlessness and in doing so takes up his cross and experiences the fellowship of Christ's sufferings. The Reformers talked of the kingdom of God as *tectum sub cruce et sub contrario,* dwelling in suffering and what is contrary. Moltmann says: 'The cross of Christ is the presently given form of the kingdom of God on earth' (1975:57). The believer who embraces the *eschatologia crucis* is led into the discipleship of the cross and participation in the sufferings of the world. 'By accepting the cross, the suffering and the death of Christ, by taking upon it the trials and struggles of obedience in the body and surrendering itself to the pain of love, it proclaims in the everyday the future of the resurrection, of life and the righteousness of God. The future of the resurrection comes to it as it takes upon itself the cross.' (*TH*, 163; see also 1979i:52-54) True apostolic mission is, then, not only active, but also 'leads inescapably into *tribulation, contradiction and suffering*' (*CPS*, 361). The joy in the resurrection 'turns dumb suffering into articulate pain' (*CPS*, 112). In other words, the eschatological promise, while it brings hope, also, through the experience of that hope, causes a person to experience the suffering of present reality all the more acutely.

Political Theology

Moltmann's so called 'political theology' (see, for example, 1974ii; 1975:101-118; *ET*, 114-117) arises from his understanding of the church as the exodus church. Its guiding principle is that the resurrection of the crucified one is the critique of human ideas about power. This critique is exercised by the exodus church as it accepts the scandal of the resurrection of the crucified one and lives in its light.

Political theology, which is particularly associated with Moltmann and Johannes-Baptist Metz, arose first in the 'sixties as a response to Auschwitz and, in particular, the silence of German Christians. 'The incomprehensible thing about "Auschwitz" for us was not the executioners ... [nor] the hiddenness of God. For us it was the silence of people who watched or looked away or closed their eyes in order to deliver the victims alone and forsaken to mass murder.' (1989:25) The reason for this, according to Moltmann, was not lack of courage, but the privatisation of faith, and the separation of religion and politics. Since that time, political theology has been extended by its contact with the various theologies of liberation and the peace movement (for an account of this in Moltmann's own theological development see *ET*, Pt. III). 'Since the middle of the 1970's, the political theology which we began in the 1960's in the awareness of the Jewish holocaust in Auschwitz has increasingly become a theology of peace in the face of the nuclear holocaust which threatens all mankind' (1989:29).

As we have noted, Moltmann describes what he calls the 'identity-involvement dilemma' of the church (*CG*, 7; see also 1975:1-4; 1979i:59). In the search for relevance, the church seeks involvement in the world, but in so doing is left wondering how it is distinctly Christian. In the search for identity, it can find itself becoming dogmatic or ghettoised and so irrelevant. Although identity and involvement will always have to be held in tension, *The Crucified God* is an attempt to outline a way of involvement on the basis of the cross which will thereby also preserve identity.

Jesus was crucified by the Romans as a political rebel; 'crucifixion at that time was a political punishment for rebellion against the social and political order of the *Imperium Romanum*' (*CG*, 136; see also *WJC*, 160-164). Jesus was not just concerned with inner dispositions, but also for social relationships. Yet, unlike the Zealots, he denied the right to vengeance, proclaiming instead reconciliation between enemies and the acceptance of traitors. He proclaimed a kingdom, not of judgment, but of grace. This political stance appears to end in failure and despair, but it is vindicated through the raising of the crucified one.

The risen Christ's identity as the crucified one is significant in this respect. Moltmann claims that in the confession 'Jesus is Lord' the emphasis should not be on 'Lord', but on 'Jesus'. In other words, the one who is the Lord is Jesus. We must not in this phrase attach to Jesus the usual ideas about what lordship means, but see it as it truly is – a revolutionary new understanding of lordship. It represents a lordship exercised through service, in the love and the acceptance of all, which leads to freedom. This is the antithesis of human lordship which is exercised through power and domination. Furthermore, the gods of the world, of civil religions, which sustain and justify dominating power, stand in radical contrast to the God of the cross. Thus Moltmann turns round Bloch's phrase, 'Only an atheist can be a good Christian', and says, 'Only a Christian can be a good atheist' (*CG*, 195). In other words, the resurrection of the crucified one is a radical critique of the gods and ideologies which sustain the powers of this world. 'The equation of *Pax Christi* with *Pax Romana* could never really succeed because of the infinite quality of Christian hope' (1975:108). In other words, the quality and universal scope of Christian hope means it can never be fulfilled in an earthly kingdom.

Moltmann sees this as an extension of Luther's *theologia crucis* and, in fact, criticises Luther for not having worked out the *theologia crucis* as social criticism (*CG*, 72-73). Indeed, since Constantine, the church has itself all too frequently taken the role of the civil religion rather than exercising a critique of earthly power on the basis of the cross (*CG*, 321-329):

> The consequence for Christian theology is that it must adopt a critical attitude towards political religions in society and in the churches. The political theology of the cross must liberate the state from the political service of idols and must liberate men from political alienation and loss of rights. It must demythologise state and society. It must prepare for the revolution of all values which is involved in the exaltation of the crucified Christ, in the demolition of relationships of political domination. (*CG*, 327)

Furthermore, traditional Christian theism has led, Moltmann believes, to what he calls political and clerical monotheism; that is, to hierarchical structures of authority. In the fact that it is more monotheistic than trinitarian, Christian theology has, according to Moltmann, been shaped by the concept of monarchy (one-rule) and this has led in turn to a justification of political authoritarianism (*TKG*, 129-132, 191-202). Trinitarian theology reveals the God who rules as the Father of the crucified one, as the one who raised him from the dead and so vindicated him. The Trinity itself is a social community and its perichoretic form is a model for human social organisation. 'An absolute sovereign in heaven does not inspire liberty on earth. Only the passionate God, the God who suffers by virtue of his passion for people, calls the freedom of men and women to life.' (*TKG*, 218)

Political theology for Moltmann is not an attempt to replace the spiritual with the political (*CPS*, 15; 1989:7,27). Rather it is the critique of the political by the spiritual; that is, in the name of the coming rule of the crucified one who was vindicated by the resurrection.

An Evaluation of Moltmann's 'Exodus Church'

While Moltmann has wanted to associate himself with liberation theology (see *ET*, Pt. III) – believing there to be a continuity between the theology of hope and liberation theology – liberation theologians have sometimes distanced themselves from Moltmann. Central to the criticisms of the liberation theologians has been the contention that Moltmann is simply not practical enough for the contexts in which they work. Although Moltmann calls for 'concrete realisations', James Cone says 'the future about which [Moltmann] speaks is too abstract and too unrelated to the history and culture of black people' (cited by Chapman, 1979:199; see also Alves, 1969:55-68; Gutierrez, 1974:217). José Miguez Bonino cites Moltmann's failure to engage in any sociological analysis as the root of the problem (1975:147). The problem, however, lies at a more fundamental level. Despite his stated intentions and despite the rhetoric of his theology, Moltmann has arguably failed to satisfactorily relate eschatology and mission.

Problematic is Moltmann's insistence upon the future as entirely new and, correspondingly, upon the absolute contradiction of present existence by the promise of God (see especially Schuurman, 1987). Only the acts of resurrection and of new creation, acts *ex nihilo*, can truly correspond to the promise. Yet any transformation in history is clearly not the new creation and so, by Moltmann's own criteria, is judged to be contradicted by the promise. In other words, no transformation in history can be positively affirmed if the present itself cannot be positively affirmed – hardly a sound basis for a transforming involvement in history! Thus Langdon Gilkey, for example, argues that Moltmann's position on the utterly new of the future, works against his own political and revolutionary interests: 'In any political understanding of history and even more in an effective revolutionary one, the relevant idea for the future cannot be understood as *utterly* new, as a *creatio ex nihilo* out of the future, as totally unrelated to the latent forces or conditions of the past and present.' (1976:235; see also Preston, 1975:156)

In fact, Moltmann seems to argue that the radical contradiction of the present by the promise implies that change must itself be radical and revolutionary. Yet, quite apart from the questionableness of the advocacy of revolution in the light of the lessons of history, even radical change cannot be affirmed if the promise totally contradicts the present. 'Since all possible consequences of Christian striving for justice will be annihilated as a prelude to another *creatio ex nihilo*, it is impossible to affirm the significance of such striving for the eschaton' (Schuurman, 1987:57). Furthermore, we must ask what sense can be made of possibilities and potentialities in the present if that present is contradicted by the promise? How can the promise create possibilities and potentialities while at the same time contradicting them? And what relationship can these possibilities and potentialities have to a future that is utterly new and *ex nihilo*?

Rubem Alves doubts Moltmann's contention that only the promise places humanity in contradiction to the present (see, for example, *TH*, 224); in reality humanity is all too painfully aware of the contradiction and negative of the present (1969:59; see also Gutierrez, 1974:217). Alves believes Moltmann has created a 'gap' between the cross and resurrection which can only be traversed by an act of *creatio ex nihilo*. Yet, because such an act never becomes history but is only made present as promise, Alves believes that Moltmann is unhistorical, that he has abandoned history in favour of the future.

Now this is clearly not Moltmann's intention. In response to criticism on this issue, Moltmann expresses surprise. He maintains that he only intended to criticise 'the negative and dangerous aspects of the modern world, that is, the repressive structures of society and the increasing crisis aspect of modern civilisation' (1970ii:156). He did not intend, he adds, to imply the negation of all relationships. Yet in his discussion of the contradiction of reality by the promise, his statements express the unqualified totality of the contradiction: 'Hope's statements of promise ... must stand in contradiction to the reality which can at present be experienced'. Or again: 'Present and future, experience and hope, stand in contradiction to each other in Christian theology'. He speaks of 'the conflict between hope and experience' (*TH*, 18). Walsh doubts whether Moltmann can affirm the present at all despite his attempts to: the theology of hope is 'ultimately devoid of any meaningful affirmation of the present' (1987:59). And Schuurman points out that, while Moltmann may claim that the negative which is negated is sin, without an adequate understanding of the fall, Moltmann does not carefully separate creation and sin. Moltmann himself says that the new in the new creation is 'not only new as compared with sin, but also as compared with creation' (1970i:29).

Richard Bauckham, however, believes that Moltmann retains some measure of continuity between this world and that new creatio, even while speaking of a new creation *ex nihilo*. He maintains that the continuity between creation and new creation arises, for Moltmann, from the identity of Jesus in the contradiction of cross and resurrection (1989ii:299). He argues that the new creation in Moltmann's thought 'is not, strictly speaking, creation *ex nihilo*, but creation from no-longer-being' (1987i:152, fn. 17). Again we must remember that for Moltmann creation is constantly threatened by the *nihil* out of which it was made. Creation was not only made *from* the *nihil*, but the *nihil* continues as an ever present threat. The new creation is, then, an act in which this threat is removed. It takes away the presence of the *nihil* and in this sense can be called *ex nihilo*. In other words, the resurrection and the new creation are *ex nihilo* because they are set against the fundamental tendency of reality towards nothingness. Bauckham believes it is important to Moltmann to affirm the continuity between this world and the new creation as a motive for action in the light of hope (1987i:38; 1989i:207; see also O'Donnell, 1983:152-153).

Yet even if Bauckham is right, this only explains one feature of Moltmann's language (the new creation as *ex nihilo*). Are we to believe that all Moltmann's talk of 'the utterly new' is simply rhetoric? Surely his distinction between *adventus* and *futurum* is employed precisely in order to stress the contradiction between present and future. And if this is rhetoric, what in fact is meant by it? That the new creation is 'mostly' new? Once again Moltmann's position is ambiguous. Indeed Schuurman believes that Moltmann's statements in this regard are 'contradictory' and 'irreconcilable' (1987:47,50). In other words, Moltmann seems to want to have it both ways: the future is utterly new and it is continuous with the present. In *God in Creation* Moltmann argues that only hope in a God who creates *ex nihilo* can give us hope in an age which faces the possibility of man-made annihilation (*GC*, 93). It would seem that Moltmann can envisage the new creation at the very least as a creation from annihilation, *ex annihilo* (or should that be *post annihilinem*?). Clearly, then, the future life is not necessarily life in *this* body and in *this* world. In other words, for Moltmann hope is 'this-worldly' in its effect, rather than its content. Yet, as we have said, Moltmann is characteristically ambiguous at this point.

Mediating Categories

The heart of the problem is the need for *mediating categories* between the future and the present, between the eschatological new creation and history, between hope and mission. If the future is utterly new, then without some form of mediation it is irrelevant. If the promise contradicts reality, then it must also contradict actions in that reality. If history is in no way continuous with eschatology, then neither is action in history. If the present has the potential to be annihilated, then so have actions in that present. Some form of mediating categories are needed to bridge the gulf between the present and the future if hope is going to be related to mission.

Moltmann identifies his position as being in contrast to those who advocate 'orders of creation' (see Gustafson, 1974:192), since the creation order has always been threatened by *nihil*. The continuity of history is provided instead by its orientation to the future. Yet how can a future which is discontinuous with history (the significance of Moltmann's *adventus-futurum* distinction) provide the continuity of history necessary for historical analogy and hence historical ethics? And how is this future to be made concrete? James Gustafson believes 'Moltmann's answer to these questions is more psychological than ethical or theological' (1974:186). Although Moltmann says the people of God are to act as a source of eschatological unrest and are to provide a directive for society, Gustafson believes that 'there is an appalling paucity of content to that directive' (1974:187). His conclusion is that the eschatological proviso is the sum total of Moltmann's ethics. Likewise Chapman believes that the price Moltmann pays for the relativization of everything by the *novum* is 'a certain nagging abstractness that pervades [his] ethics, ironically in the face of [his] very insistence in concretion' (1983:459). The failure is not so much a failure of application (Moltmann cannot be expected to speak on every issue or in every situation), but rather a failure to outline principles of eschatological application, mediating principles between the future and the present.

Hunsinger believes: 'Words such as 'desacralisation', 'democratisation' and 'humanisation' may suggest a certain direction, but they remain vague and empty without more details and historical examples' (1973:393). Chapman and Bonino, however, go further. Bonino criticises Moltmann for finding refuge in a 'critical function' – a supposedly ideologically neutral position from which theology can criticise all socio-political positions. Bonino says that Moltmann, along with other European theologians, needs to 'recognise the human, ideological content that it carries' (1975:149). In an similar way, Chapman believes that Moltmann's 'eschatological resistance toward conceptualisation' creates a 'vacuum' which 'is inexorably filled'. Thus, for example, in the case of anthropology '"the negation of the negative" rejects positive declarations and instead relies on *a priori* recognition of what (of course!) is "de-humanising".' In fact, the pre-conceptual norm resembles that of the Enlightenment which 'arouses doubt as to whether Moltmann has sufficiently rethought the substance of the conventional Western ideals about man' (1974:328). Likewise, Bonino believes that 'what emerges is one form of the liberal social-democratic project which progressive European theologians seem to cherish particularly' (1975:149). And Schuurman believes that 'Moltmann's creation-annihilating conception of the eschaton leads to a world-denying ethic', that is to say 'a negative form of social responsibility' in which Christian moral action is primarily to critic existing social institutions. As such, Schuurman believes, the positive guidance which Moltmann gives 'is not connected to or based upon his eschatology' (1987:50-51,56-57).

In the light of such criticisms a more complete discussion of the presence of the kingdom might have seemed apposite. The presence of the future kingdom could well be the mediating category which Moltmann lacks. Moltmann himself can say, 'the coming kingdom is present in history as liberating rule' (*CPS*, 191). In history God rules through his word and his Spirit, although in a hidden and resisted way. These ideas, however, receive no sustained treatment and figure little in his understanding of mission (see *CPS*, 190-192; *WJC*, 97-99). Or again, if Moltmann had expressed the absolute contradiction between the present and the future in terms of the contradiction between the old age and the new age then, by affirming the presence of the new age in history ahead of the eschaton, he could have maintained the contradiction while at the same time having a more positive attitude to the present.

Instead Moltmann, in his later work, has increasingly stressed the importance of 'anticipations' as a mediating category. Thus, he concludes *The Way of Jesus Christ* with a call for '*life in anticipation* of the Coming One' (*WJC*, 340; see, for example, *CPS*, 193-195; 1979i:45-48). And with anticipation goes *resistance* against the forces which oppose life (*CPS*, 194). Alternatively, Moltmann sometimes expresses the same idea in terms of 'correspondence': those who hope seek to live, and seek the renewal of life, in correspondence to their hope (see, for example, 1969:218). Moltmann claims that, since the World Council of Churches assembly in Uppsala in 1968, anticipation along with promise, hope and mission have become key expressions in ecumenical thought (*CPS*, 13; *WJC*, 341; 1989:7-8). The future, although not in its fulness, is present now when it is anticipated. In this sense anticipation is the form in which the possibilities created by the promise and resurrection are realised in history. Anticipations, though of the future, take place in the present and represent a form of realised eschatology. In particular, the church is the anticipation of the kingdom of God in history. In this sense the church is, albeit in a fragmentary way, the representation in history of the whole that is to come for the sake of that whole (see *CPS*, 193-196).

> Human beings do not live by traditions but also in anticipations. In fear and in hope we anticipate the future and commit ourselves to it in the present. Those who despair today and say 'No future' anticipate their end and destroy the life of others. But Christians anticipate the future of the new creation, the kingdom of justice and freedom, not because they are optimists but because they trust in the faithfulness of God. Certainly we shall not realise the kingdom of righteousness in the world. But we cannot dispense ourselves from this task for God's sake. An anticipation is a foretaste, a sign of hope and a beginning of new life. (1989:8)

The eschatological orientation of New Testament paranesis has a twofold effect. Where it is strongly apocalyptic it stresses the need to endure. Where it is characterised by hope for the parousia, however, 'it calls men and women to reshape their lives in the community of Christ' (*WJC*, 339). Hope leads people to 'reshape' their lives and the world around them in the light of their expectation of the coming kingdom. Christian life becomes more than simply holding fast to the faith: 'It goes far beyond that, reaching out to the active shaping of life. It is *life in anticipation* of the coming One, life in "expectant creativity".' (*WJC*, 340). In this way the messianic kingdom takes shape in history in and through the messianic community and the future kingdom is experienced now through the Holy Spirit.

Anticipation is 'a defence against fervent enthusiasm – "the kingdom of God is already present and we are already risen" – and tragic resignation – "the world is unredeemed and everything is still ambivalent"' (*CPS*, 194). This is because anticipation is not the eschaton as such, but nor is it some other, unrelated reality. The pursuit of anticipations creates personal and social openness to the future and so to change, and this in turn leads to resistance and suffering. Anticipations point not to themselves, but beyond themselves to the future which they represent and of which they are part. 'Future as *adventus Dei*, however, cannot be extrapolated from history (as future as *futurum* is), but is historically *anticipated*, insofar as it announces itself' (1970i:14). Anticipations, then, stand in contrast to the extrapolation of the present into the future (as *futurum*). Nevertheless, hope which looks to the *adventus* of God is able to give *direction* to planning which looks to the *futurum*. 'The people of God who travel in hope ... provide a *directive* for ... society.' (1971:124) In this sense, hope has a creative role to play: the hope of faith must become a source of creative and inventive imagination in the service of love' (1969:121).

'Christian hope,' claims Moltmann, 'is a creative and militant hope in history. The horizon of eschatological expectation produces here a horizon of ethical intentions which, in turn, gives meaning to the concrete historical initiatives.' (1969:217-218) In other words, eschatological hope provides a set of values and sets an agenda which has a directive role to play in history. Thus, 'only when sociological extrapolations and socio-ethical anticipations are combined, when knowledge is joined with wisdom and planning with hope, social politics can result' (1970i:14, fn. 20). Yet once again we must ask, Without an adequate emphasis on the presence of the future kingdom, how can hope play a directive role if it is hope for the utterly new? What kind of practical agenda can hope set if it stands in utter contradiction to the present? In the context of such ambivalence what is to prevent other values coming uncritically to the fore in the way Chapman and Bonino fear?

PART TWO

Evangelical Trajectories

CHAPTER 7

Evangelical Interactions with Moltmann: Richard Bauckham

In 1966, two years after the publication of Moltmann's *Theology of Hope*, more than a thousand evangelicals from over 100 countries gathered in Berlin (Padilla, 1985i:27-8). Developments in ecumenical theology, of which evangelicals were highly critical, created an impetus towards an 'evangelical ecumene' (Bosch, 1980:181). Evangelicals saw themselves as taking up the task of world evangelisation which, as they saw it, had been discarded by the ecumenical movement. But at Berlin there were, too, signs of a renewed emphasis on social involvement. The following years have seen a remarkable change in evangelical attitudes towards social concern with a rediscovery of the social involvement that characterised evangelicalism prior to the twentieth century. With this has developed an 'integrated' or 'transformational' understanding of mission.

It was the follow-up conference to Berlin, the Lausanne Congress in 1974, that truly established social involvement as a dimension of the evangelical understanding of mission (Padilla, 1985i:29; Chester, 1993:69-78). In the opening plenary session, John Stott argued that mission should not simply be equated with evangelism. Instead, we should speak of the total mission the church, including both evangelism and social concern (Stott, 1986i:15-34; especially p. 24). This, Stott acknowledged, was a change from the view he expressed at Berlin in 1966 (1986i:22-23; see also Chester, 1993:72-73,210 fns. 13 and 14). But it was the new generation of Third World evangelicals that really set the conference alight, particularly the contributions of the Latin Americans, Samuel Escobar (1975) and René Padilla (1975). At the heart of their concerns was the fear that the Congress would endorse a strategy that, for the sake of numerical results, would compromise the claims of discipleship, particularly as these affected social issues. The resulting Covenant, drafted by a committee of John Stott (chair), Samuel Escobar and Hudson Armerding, said 'we affirm that both evangelism and socio-political involvement are both part of our Christian duty' (Paragraph 5, 'Christian Social Responsibility').

The Congress and Covenant have been the most significant events in what has proved to be the re-emphasis upon social concern among evangelicals. René Padilla says of Lausanne, 'social involvement had finally been granted full citizenship in evangelical missiology' (1985i:29). That such a representative gathering should endorse social involvement gave legitimacy and confidence to those evangelicals whose social commitments had been viewed with suspicion by their fellow evangelicals (see the comments of Michael Cassidy and Chris Sugden, cited Chester, 1993:77, 212 fn. 39). The Congress also led to the Lausanne movement, with the formation of the Lausanne Committee for World Evangelisation. The place of social action in the activities of the Committee has been much disputed (see Chester, 1993:85-87,101,116-8,122-4,163-6), but it has sponsored, and co-sponsored with the World Evangelical Fellowship, influential conferences on culture (in 1978; see Chester, 1993:92-3), lifestyle (in 1980; see Padilla, 1985i:29-30) and, perhaps, the most significant, the 'Consultation on the Relationship between Evangelism and Social Responsibility' (Grand Rapids, 1982; see Padilla, 1985i:30-1). The Theological Commission of the World Evangelical Fellowship was also part of this process. In 1980 it sponsored an international conference on development (in 1980; see Chester, 1993:93-94). This conference, in turn, initiated a period of study culminating in a major conference in Wheaton in 1983 which placed 'transformation' at the heart of an integrated view of mission (see Padilla, 1985i:30-1).

These conferences have not only been significant in shaping evangelical thought, but provide a gauge of the development of evangelical thought. For the most part, the conferences did not create a renewed emphasis in evangelicalism on social concern, rather they provided a clear picture of changing evangelical attitudes. A number of factors contributed to this shift of thinking.

The 1960s saw growing confidence within evangelicalism (Chester, 1993:17-26). Because liberalism had taken over mainstream denominations in the first half of the century, evangelicalism became defensive and inward-looking, concerned with the maintenance of truth. But as their numbers increased and as evangelical academics began to provide a credible defence of evangelical orthodoxy, so evangelical confidence grew and with it a growing concern to be outward-looking, applying their understanding of the faith to all areas of life.

At the same time, the radical movements of the sixties forced many within evangelicalism to look afresh at the Bible for teaching on social issues (Chester, 1993:47-59). Christians, particularly in the Third World, needed a response to the Marxist critique of Christianity, and in so doing discovered a critique of pietistic evangelical attitudes. A key factor in the rediscovery of evangelical social concern has been the coming of age of Third World evangelicalism, and the opportunities to contribute to mainstream evangelical debates afforded to them by the new international gatherings (Chester, 1993:34-5,73-6,111-20). The thinking of Third World evangelicals has inevitably been shaped by the day to day reality of poverty which they faced. At the same time, the growth of television ownership brought the reality of that poverty, in some measure, into the living rooms of Western evangelicals (Chester, 1993:43-6).

The latter third of the twentieth century, then, witnessed a remarkable change in evangelical attitudes towards social involvement. In a period which saw evangelicals become a major force in many parts of the church, they re-emphasised the place of social action in the life of the church and its mission. From this has grown the now widespread commitment to 'holistic mission' or 'integrated mission'; a view of mission in which evangelism and social action are seen as inseparable and interrelated components. According to Vinay Samuel and Albrecht Hauser, 'Within the evangelical tradition groups of people in a variety of contexts have developed an understanding of mission and evangelism which integrates proclaiming the gospel and inviting people to respond to Christ as Saviour and Lord with involvement in action for justice, bringing social transformation to structures and communities.' (Samuel and Hauser, 1989:10)

Evangelical Social Involvement and Eschatology

After Lausanne, as evangelicals sought to place social involvement in the broader context of evangelical theology, eschatology has played a key role. Much of the theological debate has revolved around the question of the relationship between eschatology and mission. David Bosch said in 1983, 'The main area of difference among evangelicals about the relation of evangelism and social responsibility lies in the area of eschatology' (1987:182). Commenting on the movement for integrated mission, Samuel and Hauser say, 'The theological themes that emerged were the themes of the kingdom of God, the lordship of Christ, his lordship over history today, the role of human action in history, and the place of that in God's plan of salvation. The dominant theological theme was essentially salvation in relation to history.' (1989:13)

Thus, while Moltmann was bringing eschatology to the theological forefront with his theology of hope, evangelicals were rediscovering a transformational view of mission which includes both evangelism and social action; and the relationship between mission and eschatology was a central theological concern of this movement, perhaps *the* central concern. It is, therefore, not surprising that calls should come for a dialogue between evangelicals and Moltmann. Stephen Travis, the British evangelical theologian, has called for 'a synthesis between these "worldly hopes" [of the theology of hope, political theology and liberation theology] and a theology of immortality in fellowship with God' (1980:138). At the Consultation on the Relationship between Evangelism and Social Responsibility (Grand Rapids 1982), Peter Kuzmic called for a dialogue between the theologies of hope and evangelical thought: 'evangelical theology can be corrected and fruitfully enriched by openly and humbly, even though critically, entering into dialogue with contemporary theologians like Pannenberg, Moltmann, and many others, with their stimulating attempts to relate theology to ethics.' (1985:155)

Even more so than Moltmann, the concerns of the evangelical debate on social concern have been missiological rather than dogmatic; practical rather than academic. Indeed, much of the debate, at conference level at least, has been conducted by missiologists, missionaries and social practitioners rather than by academic theologians. Indeed, the *activity* of evangelicals is one reason why their theology is worthy of attention. Nevertheless, more theologically substantial figures have interacted with Moltmann from an evangelical perspective. First, we shall look at Richard Bauckham, who has been perhaps Moltmann's more prominent expositor and defender in the Anglo-Saxon world. Second, we shall turn to Miroslav Volf, who studied under Moltmann and has sought to use his eschatological understanding as a basis for a theology of work. And third, we shall examine the criticisms of Moltmann offered by Stephen Williams.

The latter two figures, Volf and Williams, form a bridge to evangelical debates on the place of eschatology in mission in general and social involvement in particular. Two issues have predominated.

1. The Future of the Present

The first issue we might call 'the future of the present' or 'the present in the future'. It has to do with the nature and significance of the continuity between pre- and post-eschaton existence; an issue which has already been raised in our discussion of Moltmann. Volf and Williams have entered into dialogue on this issue and their dialogue will form the focus for our discussion. It should, however, be noted that consideration of this theme is wider than the social involvement debate within evangelicalism with the Dutch Reformed tradition, in particular, making a significant contribution to the issue (see Schuurman, 1991:157, fn. 12 and Schuurman himself, 1991).

2. The Presence of the Future

The second issue we might call 'the presence of the future' or 'the future in the present'. This has to do with the nature and extent of the kingdom in history. Specifically, it considers the questions of whether the kingdom of God is present in history outside the conscious confession of Christ and whether the coming of social justice within history should be regarded as an act of divine salvation, as a coming of the kingdom. This debate closely parallels another, namely the question of whether social involvement should be shaped primarily by our understanding of creation (creation ethics) or by our understanding of the kingdom of God (kingdom ethics).

Finally in our discussion of eschatology and mission within evangelicalism we will consider three alternative proposals: those of Stephen Mott, Richard Mouw and Oliver O'Donovan. What they have in common in their different ways is a focus not on one theological theme (such as creation, kingdom or the new creation), but on the biblical drama as a whole.

Evangelical Interactions with Moltmann – Richard Bauckham

Any assessment of Moltmann's thought will inevitably draw upon the work of Richard Bauckham and this has been true of the previous chapters. There reference was made to Bauckham in order to illumine and critique the thought of Jürgen Moltmann. Here the focus will be on the more complex task of assessing Bauckham's approach Moltmann as an example of evangelical interaction with Moltmann. Moltmann himself describes Bauckham's books *Messianic Theology in the Making* and *The Theology of Jürgen Moltmann* as 'far and away the best accounts of my theology.' He adds 'he knows my theology, with its strengths and weaknesses, better than I do myself ... He knows not only my conscious intentions but my unconscious preferences and suppressions. So from his accounts of my theological progress I can learn more than I would if I were to look back on it myself.' (1999i:35)

In the preface to his study of Moltmann's theology, *Messianic Theology in the Making*, Bauckham describes how he first read Moltmann, one cold, wet week in Suffolk in 1973. 'I remember that first reading as one of the most exciting theological experiences of my life ... I owe Jürgen Moltmann himself a very considerable debt of gratitude' (1987i:vi). It is no surprise, then, to find that Bauckham has become one of Moltmann's staunchest apologists in the English-speaking world. He acknowledges that 'my overall evaluation of Moltmann's massive contribution to contemporary theology is strongly positive,' and he speaks of 'my considerable sympathy for the nature and directions of Moltmann's theological enterprise.' (1995:x). His first main work on Moltmann is subtitled 'an appreciation' and Moltmann himself writes the foreword (1987i). His second work on Moltmann is dedicated 'to Jürgen Moltmann from whose work I have learned rather less than I think and a lot more than I realise' (1995:v; see also Bauckham and Hart, 1999, xiii-xiv). Bauckham is, however, critical of certain significant aspects of Moltmann thought. Bauckham acknowledges that 'I find some developments in his theology problematic and some arguments open to serious criticism' (1995:x). Yet even his criticisms, Bauckham argues, are consistent with Moltmann's aim of writing theology which is open to dialogue. Moltmann sees his theology as an unfinished project and expects readers to interact creatively with it. We have noted some of Bauckham's criticisms at various points in our assessment of Moltmann. The focus here will be on Bauckham's evangelical reading of Moltmann and on some of the problems evangelicals face appropriating Moltmann's theology.

At times, Bauckham's own perspective appears to colour his exposition of Moltmann. Often Bauckham's exposition is clearer and more attractive than Moltmann's own – and sometimes, one suspects, more than Moltmann's warrants. Thus, for example, on one page in *Moltmann: Messianic Theology in the Making*, Bauckham twice says 'it seems to me': 'Although Moltmann does not make any of this very clear, it seems to me the only way to understand his argument consistently ... It seems to me that Moltmann thinks ...' (1987i:88) This sort of approach, in which Bauckham clarifies Moltmann's thought, is utilised by Bauckham to defend Moltmann from his critiques. Typical is: 'It could be said ... Moltmann is ... What Moltmann is really doing, however ...' (1995:141 fn 20). Or again: 'At this point Moltmann tends to give a misleading impression ... Moltmann's point is rather that ...' (1990:101-2). A simple example is found in Bauckham's essay 'Moltmann's Eschatology of the Cross' (1977:304-6). Bauckham describes Moltmann's 'dialectical principle of knowledge' in which truth is known in its opposite. God's love is revealed in hatred. Anticipating the charge that revelation in the opposite makes it hard to understand how any revelation can take place, Bauckham argues that what is really meant is that God's love is revealed in the *context* of hatred; in other words, the extent of God's love is revealed in contrast to its opposite.

Bauckham, then, often indicates an area of criticism and then defends Moltmann by clarifying Moltmann's thought. Sometimes, however, one suspects the clarification is determined by an attempt to absolve Moltmann. Indeed, sometimes the clarification has the feel of being what Bauckham thinks Moltmann ought to mean. Bauckham in effect ties up Moltmann's loose ends or, to change the metaphor, irons out some of the difficulties in his thought.

If Bauckham does not suggest Moltmann can be defended by clarification, then often he will suggest that Moltmann's own thought provides a ready solution. Bauckham regularly indicates the criticisms of others, or raises questions himself, and then answers them on Moltmann's behalf. Typical is a statement like, 'The remedy is simple and at hand in Moltmann's own work' (1995:164). In his essay 'In Defence of *The Crucified God*' (1990), Bauckham sets out to defend Moltmann from his critics by carefully expounding his thought 'since the best defence of a theologian is often a careful and sympathetic account of his views' (1990:93). Such an approach only makes sense if Bauckham anticipates that his exposition of Moltmann will be more careful and less problematic than Moltmann's own. The evidence of the essay bears this out: 'Although Moltmann does not perhaps make this point as clear as he might ... The inattentive reader may succumb to ... His general discussion of ... could mislead ... could seriously mislead ...' (1990:102,105,112-3) In the essay, Bauckham goes on to outline 'a line of argument, different from, but complementary to Moltmann's, which will in general support his view of divine passibility, but with some qualification' (1990:93). This argument is careful and qualified – typically Anglo-Saxon, lacking the rhetorical flourish or dialectical form of Moltmann's approach.

Bauckham is good at tracing the development of Moltmann's thought. He describes, for example, how Moltmann is able to re-appropriate concepts of which he has previously been critical and transform them into his own thought. Bauckham's essay 'Mysticism' provides a good example of how Moltmann does this with the idea of the epiphany of the eternal present (1995:213-47). Nevertheless, Bauckham usually defends Moltmann's consistency. Moltmann's developing thought can throw up 'superficial inconsistencies' (1995:221), but Bauckham is quick to identify their superficial nature by constantly relating the development of Moltmann's thought back to his early theology.

The result of these clarifications, explanations and answers is that, as we shall see, in many ways Bauckham presents us with *an evangelical reading of Moltmann*: he makes Moltmann's thought not only accessible to evangelicals, but also palatable to them. Bauckham's presentation, for example, lacks the strong Hegelianism which he concedes is present in Moltmann's thought.

The Dialectic of Cross and Resurrection

Bauckham's exposition of Moltmann is thorough and careful. Nevertheless, when one asks what is characteristic of his exposition of Moltmann, there are perhaps two themes which emerge: first, the grounding of eschatology in the dialectic and cross and resurrection; and second, the emphasis upon solidarity and its missiological consequences.

Eschatology is famously central to Moltmann's theology, but it is an eschatology grounded in the dialectic of cross and resurrection. Central for Bauckham is the correspondence between the cross and resurrection, on the one hand, and present godforsaken and godless reality, and the promise of the new creation, on the other. This promise has substance because of the identity of Jesus in the radical contradiction of cross and resurrection (see, for example, 1989i:299). This is the starting point of Bauckham's exposition, and he regularly relates aspects of Moltmann's thought back to it.

Two fundamental concepts combine to constitute the core of the meaning of the resurrection in *Theology of Hope*. The first is the *identity* of Jesus in the total contradiction of cross and resurrection ... The second fundamental concept is that this divine act of raising the crucified, dead and buried Jesus to new life is an event – the definitive event – of eschatological promise ... By bringing these two fundamental interpretative concepts together we can see the resurrection of Jesus as an event of *dialectical* eschatological promise ... [Jesus] resurrection is God's promise of new creation for the whole of the godforsaken reality which the crucified Jesus represents. (1989i:202-4; 1999:5)

While there is little doubt that this is a correct reading of Moltmann, this dialectical eschatology predominates in Bauckham's interpretation, not only of Moltmann's early theology, but also his later theology. Despite all the new points of departure taken by Moltmann, Bauckham argues that 'the essential dialectical character of his early eschatology survives' (1991:525). As such, this basic exposition of Moltmann's thought recurs in a number of Bauckham's essays on Moltmann as the framework in which Bauckham looks at different aspects of Moltmann's thought (see, for example, 1977:302-3,8; 1989i:202-4; 1989ii:295-6,9; 1995:82-4, 100-2;). At the same time, Bauckham understands all of Moltmann's theology in the light of this dialectic, and often defends

Moltmann from his critics by identifying how his ideas are rooted in this dialectical understanding of the cross (1995:166). Bauckham says, 'The most important controlling theological idea in Moltmann's early work is his dialectical interpretation of the cross and the resurrection of Jesus, which is then subsumed into the particular form of trinitarianism which becomes the over-arching principle of his later work' (1995:4). To the extent that this trinitarianism arises from the dialectic interpretation of the cross, Bauckham welcomes it. But when Moltmann's understanding of the Trinity diverges from its roots in the cross into speculation, Bauckham becomes uncomfortable.

It is no surprise to find Bauckham acknowledging a preference for Moltmann's early work. Bauckham describes *Theology of Hope* as 'arguably one of the truly great theological works of the last few decades and indisputably one of the most influential.' Although Moltmann's theology has developed over the years, '*Theology of Hope,*' says Bauckham, 'remains one of his greatest achievements, rivalled only by his second major work, *The Crucified God.*' 'These two books, which constitute the core of Moltmann's early theology, have, it seems to me, a concentrated power of argument, focus on their central integrating ideas, which is lacking in the more diffuse structure and argument of the later works ... Personally, I still prefer the intensity of theological vision in Moltmann's early work to the greater breadth of view in the later writings.' (1989i:199)

Solidarity

Arising from the dialectical interpretation of the cross is the second aspect of Moltmann's thought which features strongly in Bauckham's exposition, and one which gives missiological expression to the dialectic, namely that of solidarity (see especially 1995:108-113). The dialectic is given substance through the identification of Jesus on the cross with the godlessness and godforsakenness of the world. Through his solidarity with suffering humanity, 'God does not merely enter by empathy in the suffering of all who suffer, but by an act of solidarity makes their suffering his own' (1990:105; see also 115).

This solidarity features heavily in Bauckham's understanding of Moltmann's political theology and soteriology. God's solidarity with humanity on the cross leads to 'a praxis of loving identification or solidarity with the world' (1995:109). In particular, Christian mission will be shaped by our solidarity with the victims of injustice, with the poor and with the marginalised. This, claims Bauckham, helps to root Moltmann's vague and somewhat romantic commitment to revolutionary change in *Theology of Hope*. Revolution may be appropriate, but it must result from real solidarity with the victims of injustice and serve their interests.

Second, solidarity features strongly as Bauckham defends Moltmann's doctrine of the atonement. God suffers to overcome suffering (1990:99). God suffers *with* his people and *because* of his people (as they reject him). Together these constitute his redemptive suffering *for* his people. (1990:115). It is through his solidarity with people that Christ's sufferings become redemptive (1984:12). One might almost suggest that solidarity plays the same role in Moltmann's theology as substitution does in evangelical theology. And Bauckham seems caught in the middle, pushing Moltmann towards an evangelical understanding of atonement, but at the same time, happy to speak of this in terms of solidarity, and reluctant to challenge Moltmann's rejection of substitution. The problem is, that unless solidarity is seen in substitutionary terms, the talk of solidarity still leaves unanswered the question as to how Christ's sufferings are redemptive. But both Moltmann and Bauckham seem reluctant to go this far.

Furthermore, as Bauckham is quick to point out, godforsakenness as well as godlessness is key in Moltmann. 'Moltmann understands the soteriological significance of the cross more broadly than it has usually been understood ... including both "the question of human guilt and man's liberation from it. and also the question of human suffering and man's redemption from it"' (1990:98; citing *CG,* 134). What Bauckham does not explore, however, is why, in Moltmann's thought, the world is godforsaken. For Moltmann the answer lies in creation. For evangelicals the answer lies in the fall. For Moltmann we experience godforsakenness in the world because it is a world created with the ever-present threat of the *nihil.* For evangelicals, God's judgment, and hence the experience of godforsakenness, arises in response to human sinfulness.

Bauckham cannot go as far as Moltmann when Moltmann speaks of Christ's death as being in solidarity not only with all human beings, but also in solidarity with all living things. 'Does death really have the same significance for every kind of creature?' asks Bauckham (1991:529). Is the annual cycle of death and new life of a marigold of the same order of tragedy? According to Bauckham's reading of Moltmann, the implication is, that every living creature that ever died – 'every marigold, every termite, every smallpox virus' – will be resurrected in the new creation – a concept that Bauckham acknowledges to be 'bizarre' (1995:210). Arguably Bauckham's explanation that for Moltmann in eternity 'all the times [of redeemed history] will be simultaneous' so that 'all creatures as they are diachronically in the process of their history ... will be resurrected and transfigured in eternity' is just as bizarre.

Kingdom and Church in Eschatological Perspective

Moltmann sees the church as a provisional reality which will be superseded by the kingdom. As such, it exists in mission, and the purpose of this mission is the fostering of every anticipation of the kingdom – whether inside the church or not. The aim of mission is not the extension of the church *per se,* in other words, it is not evangelism. The purpose of mission 'is not to spread the church but to spread the kingdom' (*CPS,* 11).

Bauckham attempts to retain an evangelical commitment to evangelism as a component of mission by arguing that Moltmann's belief in the church as the missionary anticipation of the kingdom does not necessitate the distinction Moltmann makes between spreading the church (which Moltmann rejects) and spreading the kingdom (see *CPS*, 11,69,84; cited by Bauckham, 1987i:136-137). Bauckham argues that if the church is the anticipation of the coming kingdom, then it would seem natural that the church should serve this kingdom by calling upon people to be part of that kingdom's anticipation in the church. This would not make the church self-serving, for it would do this for the sake of those outside the church. Although Moltmann does not deny the importance of preaching the gospel, for him it is preached, not that the people might become part of the messianic fellowship of the church, but instead that the liberation of the kingdom might be furthered – the crucial point being that the liberation of the kingdom does not take place exclusively within the church. There are movements towards the kingdom outside the church, and the church mediates the kingdom in ways other than making disciples. Bauckham, however, comments, 'this need not invalidate the Christian desire that all should join the messianic fellowship as Christian disciples: such a goal could remain desirable in addition to the church's liberating activity of other kinds' (1987i:138; see also 1995:148).

Moltmann believes, that while the church is part of the mission of the Son and Spirit towards the kingdom, this mission is not confined to the church. The liberating activity of the Spirit extends beyond the church. While Moltmann rejects Rahner's notion of anonymous Christianity, he does believe there are 'saving efficacies outside the church' which are related to the saving work of Christ (1995:149; citing *CPS*, 64-5). Again, however, Bauckham asks why the church should not seek to include these elements in its mission. 'Why should it not be desirable that this anonymous work of the Spirit comes to explicit confession of Jesus Christ?' (1995:149)

Finally Moltmann erects what Bauckham calls 'the uncrossable barrier' (although Bauckham attempts to cross it; 1995:149), namely the church's 'partners in history' – Israel, the world religions and secular movements. The church will never supplant Israel, and the other religions and secular movements cannot be ecclesiasticized nor Christianized. The presence of these partners safeguards the church from triumphalism. The church, then, must be open to the eschatological potentialities of each partner (1995:14). Again, Bauckham asks whether this necessitates a limit on the explicit response to the gospel through confession of Christ? The church, for example, according to Moltmann, is not to suppress the potentialities in other religions, but to give them 'messianic direction'. Bauckham asks, 'In gaining this messianic direction, why should they not also, without forfeiting their distinctive potentialities for the kingdom, come to believe in Jesus as the Messiah of the kingdom?' (1995:150).

Step by step, Bauckham argues that Moltmann's theology need not negate the place of proclamation and evangelism. In arguing that this can be reconciled to Moltmann's ecclesiology, however, Bauckham appears, from an evangelical perspective at least, to achieve too little and concede too much. He argues that calling people to faith in Christ is admissible in the light of the coming kingdom, but in the process loses the gospel imperative to go to all nations, making disciples. The result is, that the proclamation of the gospel appears a rather secondary activity. Making disciples is almost seen as a concession rather than as the core of mission. This may not be Bauckham's own position, but it is the best he can do given the constraints of Moltmann's ecclesiology which Bauckham seems reluctant to challenge. Ultimately Bauckham believes: 'It may well be that Moltmann's ecclesiological concerns can be maintained without setting any limits on the church's mission to call people to faith in Jesus Christ' (1987i:139). What is less certain, however, is whether Moltmann's soteriological commitments can provide an adequate basis for such missiological concerns.

Despite these criticisms, Bauckham offers a weak critique of Moltmann from an evangelical perspective. He does not address one of the most fundamental criticisms of Moltmann advanced by evangelicals, namely, that Moltmann merges creation and fall with all the consequences this has for soteriology, eschatology and missiology (see the above chapters on 'Eschatology and the Trinitarian History of God' and 'Eschatology and Soteriology'; and Schuurman, 1987 and Walsh, 1987). Bauckham fails to relate the theme of solidarity in Moltmann to substitution in evangelical soteriology. His plea for the inclusion of evangelism in Moltmann's mission only highlights the weakness of his critique. Given Bebbington's assertion that two of the defining features of evangelicalism are 'crucicentrism, a stress on the sacrifice of Christ on the cross' and 'conversionism' (1989:2-10,14-17), Bauckham's critique of Moltmann leaves a lot to be desired from an evangelical perspective.

Bauckham reveals some of the difficulties involved for evangelicals in the appropriation of Moltmann's theology. Bauckham's evangelical reading of Moltmann certainly has its attractions. In the process, however, Bauckham concedes too much, or at least, lets too much go unchallenged. At best it remains an evangelical reading of Moltmann, one step removed from the real thing. And even at one step removed it retains problematic features.

CHAPTER 8

Evangelical Interactions with Moltmann:
Miroslav Volf

Miroslav Volf, a native of Croatia and now Henry B. Wright Professor if Systematic Theology at Yale Divinity School, undertook his doctoral research on Karl Marx's understanding of work under the supervision of Moltmann in Tübingen. Volf is relevant to our subject for two reasons. First, he is an evangelical who has interacted with Moltmann. His theology of work is a conscious attempt to build upon the eschatological thought of Moltmann. As a young man, Moltmann wondered whether theology was possible after Barth. Volf asks whether eschatology is possible after Moltmann, concluding: 'eschatology needs to be "after Moltmann" by continuing to press further in the same direction as he was moving.' (1999:235) Volf has done this by extending Moltmann's dialogue between Christian eschatology and modernity into a dialogue with postmodernity (see Volf, 1999 and Volf and Katerberg, 2004). Below, however, we will focus on Volf's application of eschatology to the theme of *work*.

Second, although the word 'mission' is not to the fore in Volf's theology of work, underlying it all is a commitment to a transformational view of mission. Volf explicitly states that his discussion of work is not simply an attempt to understand the nature of work, but an attempt to contribute to its transformation. He wants to contribute to the church's theology of mission because he wants to contribute to the church's mission, particularly as that relates to social involvement in the field of work. Throughout his work, Volf assumes an integrated or transformational view of mission. Indeed, Volf tends to use the term 'transformation' synonymously with 'mission' throughout his work. Volf's theology of work is not simply a static description. His intention throughout is to facilitate and direct change. A foundational presupposition is that mission includes working for social change. Indeed, eschatology is central to Volf's understanding of work precisely because he believes it orients mission, and social involvement in particular, towards change.

Volf has also been a participant in evangelical debates. After the Consultation on the Relationship between Evangelism and Social Responsibility (Grand Rapids, 1982), Volf contributed, as we shall explore, to the continuity-discontinuity debate through a dialogue with Stephen Williams (see Volf, 1990i and Williams, 1990i). And Volf has contributed East European perspectives on politics and democracy to evangelical debates through his contributions to *Transformation*, a journal established after Wheaton 1983 to provide 'an international dialogue on evangelical social ethics'. Volf also played a key role in the first two Oxford Conferences on Faith and Economics (in 1987 and 1990; see Volf, 1991:xi, 6, 155-6). This process of evangelical reflection on economics was initiated in 1985 by the International Fellowship of Evangelical Mission Theologians (INFEMIT) as part of the developments coming out of Lausanne 1974. The third Oxford conference was held in Agra, India, in 1995, reflecting upon the impact of the market economy upon the poor. The second Oxford conference involved a broad spectrum of evangelical economists, theologians, ethicists and development practitioners, after criticism that the first conference was too biased towards 'the left'. This broad spectrum makes the resultant *Oxford Declaration on Christian Faith and Economics*, a highly acclaimed comprehensive statement on economics from a Christian perspective, all the more remarkable. Volf, who was a drafter of the Oxford Declaration, 'incorporated ... some key formulations' of the manuscript of *Work in the Spirit* in the Declaration (1991:xi), and a good number of these, he claims, survived the conference process. He was, he says, 'especially pleased to see the "Oxford Declaration" follow me in basing its theological reflection on work on the concept of *charisma,* rather than vocation' (1991:xi).

Work, Eschatology and Transformation

In *Work in the Spirit*, Volf sets out to develop a theology of work. In doing so, he is concerned to do more than simply provide ethical reflection on work (71-74) and to provide more than an inductive synthesis of biblical texts (76-9; see Moltmann, 1984i:43). Instead, he argues that a right understanding of work must be set in a broad theological framework. And the framework with which Volf chooses to work is that provided by Moltmann, particularly in *Theology of Hope*. In an essay entitled 'The Right to Meaningful Work', Moltmann elaborates a critique of vocation, viewing work instead as co-operation with God in the renewal of creation – key themes taken up by Volf (1984i:37-58). Nor is the interaction one-way for in *The Spirit of Life* Moltmann acknowledges the comments of Volf and develops the idea of *charisms*, a central theme in Volf's approach to work. (SL, xiii, 180-4)

Volf wants to approach the question of human work from the perspective of the new creation.

> The broad theological framework within which I propose to develop a theology of work is the concept of the *new creation* ... I am following the basic insight of Moltmann's *Theology of Hope* that at its core, Christian faith is eschatological. Christian life is life in the Spirit of the new creation or it is not Christian life at all. And the Spirit of God should determine the whole life, spiritual as well as secular,

of a Christian. Christian work must, therefore, be done under the inspiration of the
Spirit and in the light of the coming new creation. (79)

Thus, although Volf provides no sustained treatment of Moltmann's thought,
Moltmann's theology of hope is central to Volf's undertaking. Indeed, this
eschatological framework is treated as a given, with no attempt to justify it
other than pointing to Moltmann's *Theology of Hope* (79). If eschatology is
central to Christian theology, then it will be central to a Christian theology of
work. A Christian theology of work will be developed 'on the basis of a
specifically Christian soteriology and eschatology, *essential to which* is the
anticipatory experience of God's new creation and a hope of its future
consummation' (79, emphasis added). If Volf does not stop to justify the
eschatological as the framework for a theology of work, it is because 'the
reasons for opting for an "eschatological" and pneumatological theology of
work are best given in the process of its development' (79). The proof of the
pudding, we might say, is in the eating. Even before beginning 'the process of
its development', Volf outlines two advantages of an eschatological approach
to work.

First, citing Moltmann, he says the task of a theology of work 'is not merely
to interpret the world of work in a particular way, but to lead the present world
of work "towards the promised and the hoped-for transformation" in the new
creation' (83; see also 1983). In common with Moltmann, the new creation is
important for Volf because he believes it orients mission towards change. 'A
theological interpretation of work is valid only if it facilitates transformation of
work towards ever-greater correspondence with the coming new creation' (83).
As such, Volf believes a theology of work must reflect, not only upon the
biblical revelation, but also upon the contemporary situation of work, for its
task is to facilitate the transformation of that contemporary situation in the light
of biblical revelation. Identifying key contemporary factors which must shape a
transforming theology work, Volf points first to the great change in the nature
of work with technological developments, increased automation and a
frequently mobile workforce. Second, he identifies a number of areas in which
there is a crisis with work, specifically child labour, unemployment,
discrimination, dehumanisation, exploitation and ecological crisis (35-42).

So, in developing his understanding of work, Volf is taking two key features
of Moltmann's theology, namely, that mission is an all-embracing commitment
to transformation, and the centrality of eschatology as the framework for
theology, and making them concrete in the area of work. It is an attempt by an
evangelical to build on the work of Moltmann, and apply it to mission,
understood as including social transformation.

The second advantage of an eschatological approach to work is that a
theology of work based on the new creation will be comprehensive since 'the
new creation is a universal reality' (84 and 1987:61). As such, an
eschatological theology of work will address the relationship of work to God,

other human beings and the non-human environment since human work 'is related to the goal of all history, which will bring God, human beings, and the non-human creation into "shalomic" harmony' (84). Since an eschatological theology of work is comprehensive, Volf believes it provides a normative understanding of work, reflecting not only what he or a particular subculture desires work to be, but 'what human beings *should* desire their work to be' (81).

The comprehensive nature of an eschatological framework is more appropriate than an anthropological framework, according to Volf, since it allows for the inclusion of the non-human environment. It is not clear, however, why the anthropological should be viewed as the only alternative. The theme of creation, and with it themes such as stewardship and Sabbath, might also be chosen and would arguably be as comprehensive, if not more so, than the eschatological motif. It could, for example, be argued that while not all will share in the new creation, all are part of creation and, as such, creational principles are more comprehensive.

Volf seems, at times, a little over-enthusiastic about possibilities of using the new creation as 'the main ethical norm'. He believes economic systems should be judged by three principles: freedom of individuals, satisfaction of the basic needs of all people, and the protection of nature from irreparable damage. All three, he believes, 'can be derived from the notion of "new Creation"' (1987:61 and 1991:15). New creation, says Volf, implies the dignity of individuals, who should therefore be treated as a free and responsible agents. This is because 'each person is created in the image of God and is called to a personal relation with Christ as his brother or sister' (1991:15). Yet this could conceivably be the case even if there were no new creation. New creation may well add something to the notions of human beings as God's image and called to a relationship with Christ, but Volf does not elaborate what this might be. Likewise, we are told that new creation means 'practising solidarity', a phrase redolent of Moltmann, and therefore meeting everyone's basic needs. This is because 'every person is called to be an heir with Christ in the community of God's people' (1987:61 and 1991:16). Again, to be called into the community of God's people is not a specifically eschatological notion. And since not all respond to this call this seems a somewhat tenuous basis for universal solidarity.

Work, Eschatology and the Spirit

There are, broadly speaking, two dimensions to Volf's eschatological theology of work. First, Volf outlines the implications of his conviction that there is a degree of continuity between history and the new creation (1990i and 1991:88-102). The issue of eschatological continuity has played a central role in broader evangelical debates concerning social action and we will return to it in the next chapter.

Second, he examines how the eschatological new creation impinges on work and mission in the present through the Holy Spirit (1991:102-122). Since we have no present experience of the new creation, except through the Holy Spirit – described by Volf as 'the power of eschatological salvation' (153) – work viewed from an eschatological perspective must, argues Volf, be set in a pneumatological framework. In Paul, the Spirit is seen as the 'firstfruits' and 'down payment' of the new creation (Romans 8:23; 2 Corinthians 1:22). And in the gospels it is through the Spirit that the future kingdom is anticipated.

The Spirit is the reason that we can have hope for change in the present. 'The presence of the Spirit of the resurrected Christ in the whole of creation, and in particular in those who acknowledge Christ's lordship, gives hope that work *can* also be transformed in ever greater correspondence to this ideal' (168). Volf speaks of the opportunity we have 'to anticipate' the new creation and – without further elaboration – of the possibility 'to image' the new creation. 'Human beings should strive to image the new creation in the present world as the good God ultimately desires for them ...' (173; see also 1990ii:13). In response to an article by Richard John Neuhaus entitled 'Democracy – A Christian Imperative' (1990), Volf suggests that the vision of the new creation allows us to go beyond the way of justice as a social goal to the way of love (1990ii:13; see also 1991:82-3). In response Neuhaus is less sanguine: 'Short of the End Time (i.e. the genuinely "new politics" of the kingdom of God) the business of politics is justice. Justice is the form that love assumes in the public arena' (1990:19). Reflecting on the experience of the church under communism, Volf describes the prevailing 'theology of martyrdom': 'the imperative for uncompromising Christian living in the face of what seemed an all-out attack on the churches' (1990ii:15). While acknowledging the validity of this approach, Volf also finds it lacking. 'There is no hope that the kingdoms of this world would even in a small way be willing to image the justice and peace of the kingdom of God (1990ii:15).

According to Volf, then, the presence of the Spirit means that anticipating the new creation now is a genuine possibility. The Spirit mediates the life of the eschatological future in the present. As such, any eschatological theology of work will be pneumatological. 'Without the Spirit there is no experience of the new creation! A theology of work that seeks to understand work as active anticipation of the *transformatio mundi* must, therefore, be a *pneumatological theology of work.*' (1991:102)

Protestant theology, however, has not traditionally given the Spirit a significant role in relation to human work. The Spirit has been thought to have little to do with work because, argues Volf, the activity of the Spirit has been restricted to the sphere of salvation, and the locus of that salvation has been restricted to the human spirit, to Luther's 'inner man' (102-3). In contrast, Volf believes we need look no further than the gospels to see that the exclusion of materiality from salvation is unfounded. The gospels portray Jesus' healing miracles as the in-breaking of God's kingdom. Through the power of the Spirit, they not only point to the future rule of God, but are 'realisations' of its presence in history. God's salvific purposes extend to the whole of creation, including its materiality. 'Because the whole creation is the Spirit's sphere of operation, the Spirit is not only the Spirit of religious experience, but also the Spirit of worldly engagement' (104).

From Vocation to *Charisms*

Central to Volf's pneumatological approach to work is the idea that a Christian approach to work should be governed by *charisms*. 'The Spirit of God calls and gifts people to work in active anticipation of the eschatological transformation of the world'. Volf closely relates his view of work shaped by *charisms* to his general eschatological approach:

> Since human beings were created to live on earth as God's co-workers in anticipation of the new creation, the Spirit imparted to them various gifts to accomplish that task. These gifts form part of their personality that they are responsible to respect and to develop, both because of the intrinsic value of their personalities as integral part of the new creation, and because the more they are developed, the better they can anticipate the new creation through their work. (173)

Volf presents *charisms* as an alternative to the traditional understanding of vocation as the key motif in the Protestant understanding of human work. Luther, for example, held that all Christians (and not just monks!) have a vocation from God, and that every type of work, or station in life, can be viewed as a divinely ordained vocation. Although Volf accepts the value that this understanding gave to all human work, he remains critical of it. Luther's understanding of work as vocation, Volf argues, is indifferent towards alienating work. 'It seems that virtually *every* type of work can be a vocation, no matter how dehumanising it might be' (107). In fact, Luther's advocacy of vocation was qualified: the calling applies 'insofar as this can be done without sin'. In practice, however, this was often overlooked (see Moltmann, 1984i:47). Vocation can give value and consolation to those whose work is 'sordid and base', but 'at the expense of the transforming potential for overcoming alienation in situations when transformation is both necessary and possible' (1991:107). In other words, the notion of vocation cannot satisfy Volf's missiological concern to develop a transforming view of work. Indeed, vocation can be ideologically misused to ennoble dehumanising work rather than changing it.

But vocation is also inadequate in an increasingly mobile society. In modern industrial and information economies a person rarely remains within one job for a lifetime – what Volf calls 'diachronic plurality'. The pace of technological change means that a person's skills can soon become redundant, forcing a change of career. Not only so, but it is increasingly common for a person to take on more than one job at the same time – what Volf calls 'synchronic plurality'. In such a context, argues Volf, vocation is too static. For Luther the external calling corresponds to the single, permanent, spiritual calling. Luther expects a person to remain within their vocation throughout their life, charging them to 'remain' and 'be satisfied' within their calling.

Volf rejects any attempt to reform the understanding of vocation. He argues that Luther misunderstood his main proof text, 1 Corinthians 7:20. The 'calling' in this verse is not the situation to which a person was called, but the call to become a Christian. Paul is arguing that those called to be Christians should not infer from their new liberty the right to, or necessity of, changing their circumstances, unless the opportunity should present itself (1 Corinthians 7:21). Instead, they are called to conduct consistent with their faith, in whatever situation they find themselves. In essence, Volf argues, that 'calling' in the New Testament refers always to the calling to become a Christian and to live a consistent Christian life rather than to a particular job or life situation. Vocation, then, is 'both inapplicable to modern societies and theologically inadequate' (vii).

The alternative which Volf advances is that of *charisma*. Volf argues that *charisma* should not be defined too widely as encompassing the whole sphere of Christian activity. Paul distinguishes between the fruit and gifts of the Spirit: 'The gifts of the Spirit are related to the specific tasks or functions to which God calls and fits each Christian' (111). But neither should *charisma* be defined too narrowly as only ecclesiastical activities. 'The place of operation does not define *charisms*, but the manifestation of the Spirit for the divinely ordained purpose' (112). *Charisms* belong neither to an elite group within the church, nor are they confined to the 'extraordinary'. The calling to enter the kingdom and live accordingly, becomes, for the believer, a call to bear the fruit of the Spirit and, 'as they are placed in various situations, the calling to live in accordance with the kingdom, branches out in multiple gifts of the Spirit to each individuals' (113).

By approaching human work from the perspectives of *charisma*, Volf claims to avoid the ideological misuse to which vocation is open when one's station in life is seen as divinely appointed and therefore immutable. Individual giftings are given by God, through the Holy Spirit, but these 'remain different from their mediations and should not be reduced to, or confused with, them' (115). Indeed, the divine gifting of a person implies the need to take their gifts seriously. 'The point is ... to transform work into a charismatic co-operation with God on the "project" of the new creation' (116). Not only does Volf's understanding of *charisma* not restrict his missiological concerns, but it actively encourages the transformation of work, so that gifts are used to the full, and people participate in God's eschatological purposes.

But such a pneumatological view of work also overcomes the problems of the diachronic plurality and synchronic plurality of work. In different and changing circumstances the expression of a person's gifting may change accordingly. Indeed, while a person cannot pick and choose their *charisms,* since they are sovereignly dispensed by the Holy Spirit, this does not preclude a person 'earnestly desiring' certain spiritual gifts (1 Corinthians 12:31; 14:1,12). Furthermore, Volf argues that since a person may possess more than one gift, or may express their gift in more than one context, his view of *charisma* does not find having more than one employment problematic in the way that he argues vocation does. This is because Volf has broken the link between the one, immutable spiritual calling and an external vocation, which is, by implication, also one and immutable. 'The pneumatological understanding of work is free from the portentous ambiguity in Luther's concept of vocation, which consists in the undefined relation between spiritual calling through the gospel and external calling through one's station' (115). The call to service, and to the faithful use of one's gifts, remains the same even as the expression of this gifting changes. Occupational decisions need not be irrevocable, but instead will be determined and changed by a person's talents, preferences and the prevailing job opportunities. Indeed, whereas vocation tended to reduce work to employment, a person can express their *charisms* in a meaningful way even in the absence of paid employment. 'Since an unemployed person has not been deprived of all *charisms,* in a pneumatological understanding of work he is not left without a divinely appointed, significant activity' (156).

Furthermore, by placing work in a pneumatological and eschatological context, Volf claims that work is no longer 'first and foremost' the result of divine command, but rather is the result of divine empowering and gifting. It arises not from duty, but from the inspiration and enabling of the Spirit. 'The appropriate response to an experience of grace is not so much naked (though thankful!) obedience, as it is joyful willingness to employ the capabilities conferred in the entrusted "project"' – the project being for Volf co-operation with God in the eschatological transformation of the earth (125).

Charisms in the Church and in the World

Despite the advantages of Volf's pneumatological approach, and the refreshing seriousness with which he grapples with the modern working environment, it is susceptible to a number of theological questions relating to the applicability of *charisma* to human work as a whole.

In the New Testament *charisms* are given in the context of church life. They are given specifically for the edification of the body of believers. Indeed, there are some gifts described in the New Testament – such as tongues and prophecy – which appear to have no relation to the world of work. Volf is not unaware of this problem. He argues that *charisms* should not be defined so narrowly as to include only ecclesiastical activities. He points to the gift of an evangelist (cited in Ephesians 4:11) as one which must relate to activity towards *non*-Christians (111). Yet, this is to confuse activities which build up the church and its ministry, with activities within the church. While evangelism takes place outside the ecclesiastical sphere, it clearly contributes to the building up of the church. This could be said even of giving to the needy (another gift outside the ecclesiastical sphere cited by Volf; Romans 12:8) when this is done as a ministry of the church and as a demonstration of God's love. Volf himself says, 'As the firstfruits of salvation, the Spirit of Christ is not only active in the Christian fellowship, but also desires to make an impact *on the world through the fellowship*' (111). While this is true, it is nevertheless 'through the fellowship'. Again, Volf goes on: 'All functions *of the fellowship* – whether directed inward to the Christian community or outward to the world – are the result of the operation of the Spirit of God and are thus charismatic' (111, emphasis added).

This highlights a confusion which pervades the book. It is not always clear whether Volf is talking to Christians alone or presenting an understanding of work applicable to all people in society. He can say, citing 1 Corinthians 14:12-26, that the purpose of *charisms* is 'the *oikodome* of the community'. '*Charisms* link a person to a larger community, a whole in which the *charisms* of each are a contribution to the good of all' (190). The passages which Volf cites – 1 Corinthians 12; 14 and 1 Peter 4 – are all addressed to the Christian community, but, by speaking in terms of 'a larger community' and 'the good of all', Volf allows an ambiguity to remain.

Problems lie not just with the purpose for which charisms are given, but also to whom they are given. If the charisms are given for the edification of the church, then in the same way they are given to Christians. How can the work of non-Christians be understood in the terms of the gifts of the Spirit? And how, for that matter, can their work be understood in relation to the new creation?

Again Volf is not unaware of these problems. Volf believes 'the work of non-Christians has in principle the same ultimate significance as the work of Christians: insofar as the results of non-Christians' work pass through the purifying judgment of God, they, too, will contribute to the future new creation' (118). And Volf believes, too, that we can understand the work of non-Christians pneumatologically. If Christ is Lord of all humanity, and rules through his Spirit, then, argues Volf, we must assume that the Spirit is active 'in some way' in all people, even those who do not consciously acknowledge that activity. While the Spirit is present in the church, redeeming and sanctifying the people of God, the Spirit is also active in the world of culture, sustaining and developing humanity. The difference in these activities of the Spirit is, argues Volf, not so much their different purpose, but 'the nature of the receptivity of human beings' (119). Finally Volf says, citing Moltmann, 'the goal of the Holy Spirit in the church and in the world is the same: the Spirit strives to lead both the realm of nature (*regnum naturæ*) and the realm of grace (*regnum gratiæ*) toward their final glorification in the new creation (*regnum gloriæ*)' (119.). Volf argues that since the Spirit is active in the *regnum gratiæ* as the firstfruits of the *regnum gloriæ* and the *regnum gloriæ* is also the goal of the *regnum naturæ*, we can think of the Spirit's activity in the *regnum naturæ* as analogous to his activity in the *regnum gratiæ*. As such, 'what can be said of the work of Christians on the basis of the biblical understanding of *charisms* can also be said by analogy of the work of non-Christians' (119). The work of non-Christians, to the extent that they are open to the Spirit, is a co-operation with God in anticipation of the new creation, 'even though they may not be aware of it' (119).

Whatever the validity of these arguments, and we will examine the broad issues involved in the next chapter, it remains questionable whether they adequately defend a general theology of work based on the concept of *charisms*. At one point, Volf cites examples from the Old Testament of the anointing of individuals by the Spirit, enabling them to complete particular tasks. His point is the wide range of tasks for which people were so enabled – from the construction of the tabernacle (Exodus 35:2-3) to the judging and defence of Israel (Judges 3:10). Acknowledging that these cannot be used as the basis for a pneumatological understanding of *all* work, because of their extraordinary nature, Volf nevertheless argues that, from the perspective of the new covenant, they point to the variety of tasks for which now '*all* God's people are gifted and called' (114). Implicit here, however, is the acknowledgement that, even under the new covenant, the gifting and enabling of the Spirit is restricted to God's people, even if now this includes all of them.

Volf's application of *charisms* to all human work stems from his underlying assumption that 'the Spirit of God is at work not only in the present anticipation of the new creation in the Christian community, but also in the world' (80). Yet, while the Spirit is present throughout creation, as the Spirit of life, as the Creator Spirit, he is present in the lives of believers in a unique way. To say anything less makes a nonsense of those New Testament passages which speak of the Holy Spirit as a 'gift' given to believers. Thus, while the Spirit of life may enable all human work and the Creator Spirit may give natural abilities to all, the *charisms* given to Christians must be qualitatively different from such natural abilities.

Acknowledging that skills are developed and acquired through work and personal development, Volf believes we can still see these in terms of *charisms* as long as *charisms* are not thought of as coming 'vertically from above'. 'Some capabilities,' he says, 'humans beings are born with, and many others they acquire' (130). Evidently, Volf sees these 'capabilities' as *charisms*. He cites Calvin, arguing from Exodus 31:2 that all human skills stem from the operation of the Spirit (see also Volf, 1991:144). Calvin, however, does not call such skills *charisms*. *Charisms* have a quality – whether they are 'extraordinary' or continuous with natural abilities – which sets them apart from human skills in general. They are, by definition, *given* for the building up of the church, and are given to those to whom the Spirit is especially given in redemption.

Following Volf, the Oxford Declaration on Christian Faith and Economics views work in the context of the giftings of the Spirit (see Volf, 1991:xi).

Nevertheless, in paragraph 15 the Declaration restricts the giftings of the Spirit to believers. '*For Christians*, work acquires a new dimension. God calls *all Christians* to employ through work the various gifts that God has given them. God calls people to enter the kingdom of God and to live a life in accordance with its demands. *When people respond to the call of God*, God enables them to bear the fruit of the Spirit and endows them individually with multiple gifts of the Spirit.' (Paragraph 15; emphasis added) At the same time, the Oxford Declaration says, 'Human beings are created by God as persons endowed with gifts, which God calls them to exercise freely ... God gives talents to individuals for the benefit of the whole community.' (Paragraphs 21 and 22) On the one hand, the Declaration restricts the giftings of the Spirit to those who have responded to the call to enter the kingdom. On the other hand, an ambiguity remains between giftings and natural talents.

In summary, Volf's theology of work depends upon seeing the natural abilities and skills of non-Christians as *charisms*, given by God to facilitate co-operation in the eschatological transformation. It is questionable, however, whether the New Testament understanding of spiritual gifts will allow this. Spiritual gifts are defined both in terms of their purpose and in terms of their source. Their purpose is to build up the church, a definition that does not allow the inclusion of all natural abilities, and one which excludes the abilities of non-Christians. And their source is the Holy Spirit. Arguably, all abilities and skills stem from the Creator Spirit. Nevertheless, spiritual gifts are clearly related in some way to the qualitatively different presence of the Spirit in Christians. One does not have to define in detail the nature of the relationship between natural abilities and spiritual gifts – and clearly there is often a continuity between the two – to affirm that spiritual gifts are qualitatively different. Whatever this difference is, its reason is clear: the unique presence of the Spirit in the lives of believers, mediating the presence of Christ and anticipating the eschatological future. Even where *charisms* are continuous with natural abilities, they take on a new quality born of the Spirit's empowering and sanctifying presence in the life of the believer. In other words, the uniquely Christian nature of *charisms* corresponds to the unique presence of the Spirit in the life of the Christian.

Volf's determination to include all human work in his eschatology of work endangers his determination to make his theology of work an eschatologically transforming theology. Volf asks himself whether work as 'co-operation with God in the eschatological transformation of the world' or 'work in the Spirit' are lofty words that mask an ideology of work, glorifying it at the expense of those who experience work as toil and exploitation? His answer is to affirm that not all work can be viewed as co-operation in eschatological transformation, but only that human activity which passes God's eschatological judgment will contribute to the new creation (1 Corinthians 3:12-15; Revelation 21:27; see also the Oxford Declaration on Christian Faith and Economics, paragraph 19). Because work is to be judged, argues Volf, relating human work to the new creation cannot function as an ideological glorification of work. While the co-operation with God in the eschatological transformation gives value and significance to human work, the judgment of work prevents its absolutisation.

This criterion in fact allows a positive appraisal of work as that which contributes to the future, even if it involves exploitation or drudgery now. He is realistic enough to acknowledge that much human work is done, not out of love, but out of self-interest. And so, Volf argues, that correspondence to the new creation is the criteria by which work is to be judged, not the attitude of love exhibited in the work. It is the effect of work, rather than its motive, which is key for Volf. Work done from envy does not lose its inherent value: 'the flames of "the absolutely searching and penetrating love of God" will envelop the evil worker while her work is purified and preserved' (121). Arguably, despite Volf's protestations, the transformation of the present is sacrificed to the transformation of the future. On the one hand, Volf wants to give value even to work which is experienced as toil – work has a significance beyond the self-fulfilment of the worker. On the other hand, he does not want to justify drudgery or exploitation as acceptable in the light of the future. He wants a mechanism that critiques such work, opening up the need for its transformation. Volf is left saying that 'those weighted down by the toil that accompanies most human work can rest assured that their sufferings "are not worth comparing with the glory" of God's new creation to which they are contributing (Romans 8:18)' – a comfort perhaps to those who will enjoy that glory, but sparse comfort for those who 'the flames of the absolutely searching and penetrating love of God will envelop' (121).

Briefly, if Volf's understanding of work is unsatisfactory, as we have been arguing, is there an alternative to charisms which takes on board the critique of callings which he advances? What is required is a perspective on work which ensures that all work – not just explicitly 'Christian' work – is valued in the economy of salvation and which, in addition, allows moral constraints to be placed upon work. Although this is not the place to develop in detail such an alternative, let me suggest that there is a simple rubric with which to view work, namely that all work should be viewed as service to others – as a dimension of love for one's neighbour. Unlike vocation, viewing work in terms of service survives mobility, since a change in employment means simply a change in the mode of one's service. Seeing work in terms of service to others also places moral constraints on work. Employment which does not serve the community can be judged from this perspective, and such an approach will insist that the social costs of production – the exploitation of workers or the environment – do not outweigh the service provided.

Conclusion

Volf self-consciously attempts to build on the theology of Moltmann. Taking Moltmann's theology of hope as his starting point, he attempts to develop a theology of work which is both transformational and eschatological. The attempt, however, is not entirely convincing. Volf's chosen route, making *charisma* the central motif for an understanding of work, breaks down when it comes to the work of non-Christians and work outside the ministry of the church. At the root of the problem is the difficulty in attributing eschatological participation to unbelievers who, unless one adopts the normally un-evangelical position of universalism, do not themselves participate in the eschatological new creation.

CHAPTER 9

The Future of the Present

Stephen Williams – The Limits of Hope

In Bauckham we have seen an evangelical who has interpreted and defended Moltmann; in Volf, an evangelical who has consciously sought to build upon his thought. We turn now to Stephen Williams, an evangelical who has been critical of Moltmann's use of eschatology. But Williams is significant, too, because he has also been critical of aspects of the use of eschatology in those evangelicals who have sought to re-emphasise social action. As we shall see, Williams entered the debates surrounding the Lausanne movement, questioning the value of the continuist position and entering into dialogue on the issue with Miroslav Volf. But his critique has been on broader fronts as well.

Williams neither denies the importance of social involvement, nor that hope has a proper effect upon Christian social activity. Rather, he distinguishes between the effect of the *fact* of the eschatological future and the effect of its *form* (1990i:26). The use of the word hope in the New Testament, he argues, is consistently unrelated to the products of social action (1986i:3). Williams asks what we mean when we speak of 'hope for humanity' or 'the redemption of all history'? Such language, or something like it, Williams detects in both Moltmann and in evangelical attempts to relate eschatology and mission. As such, his critique of both has a formal similarity. He recognises that in Moltmann such language belies an at least implicit universalism. 'By his general and perpetual conjunction of "universal salvation" with "all people" and in some apparently specific statements, Moltmann comes over as a dogmatic universalist in the sense of believing in the eventual salvation of all people' (1986ii:627; see also 1987:24-5). Such a statement is not true of evangelical contributors to the debate, and in some ways Williams' concern is to show the logic of their non-universalism in respect to social involvement. The evangelicals in Williams sights are those who attempt to make corporate or cosmic salvation a basis for social involvement. Indeed, he recognises that cosmic salvation, rather than individual eschatology, is the focus for Moltmann as well (1986ii:627).

His argument is that, whatever the truth of cosmic salvation, it cannot govern our attitude to the particulars we face day by day. If one is a non-universalist, one cannot speak of the certain hope of the New Testament in respect to every individual who may be the object of your social action. Even if one grants a universalist position with respect to people, cosmic salvation cannot govern all particulars. He suggests that the wider debate over universalism helps us focus the issues: 'According to non-universalists, eschatological totalities are not sum totalities: any talk of 'all humanity' is not talk of all humans where inclusion of salvation is under consideration. A grand totality, in such analysis, in not every particular.' (1989i:265; see also 1986i:3) Even universalists will not see in 'hope for history' a promise for all particulars. The picture of cosmic redemption in Romans 8 is not a promise of redemption for every tree and flower. 'In an important sense, then, "hope" does not govern our relationships to all particulars' (1989i:266). And as such, Williams sees a limit to hope as a basis for social responsibility.

Williams believes there has been a failure to distinguish between the promise and the temporally particular; between the certain, eschatological hope of biblical faith and uncertain, optimistic hope. Both Moltmann and some contributors to the evangelical debates have used eschatological categories to speak of hope within social movements, a hope that encourages their followers to act in expectation of historical change (1986i:3; 1989i:267; 1987:25-6). But, argues Williams, when used without a discrimination between biblical hope and the hope of social movements, '"hope" slithers around uncomfortably' (1989i:267). In other words, the expectation of historical change – which can be a powerful motive for action – is not the same as the eschatological hope of the New Testament. Even with the transforming presence and power of the kingdom in history, hope for imminent change within history remains at best a possibility. However valid and important such hope might be, it remains distinct from the certain hope of eschatological transformation created by the special divine revelation of promise. What is obscured by Moltmann's analysis 'is that some difference attaches to the passions kindled by promise and those kindled by possibility' (1989ii:7). Movements for social change do not all succeed, some meet with disappointment. But biblical hope 'does not disappoint us' (Romans 5:5; 1989ii:6).

Williams concern is, that, unless a distinction is made between hope for historical change and the certain hope of eschatological transformation, 'one may give false hope to the suffering' (1989ii:7). Movements for social change in history can suffer frustration, setbacks and ultimately failure. Without the necessary distinction outlined by Williams above, hope can collapse into despair. Attempts to employ hope to prevent the death of social activism in this way run the risk of killing hope – and with it social activism.

Williams goes further. In basing social involvement upon eschatology, Moltmann feels it important to speak of this-worldly hope. Hope for another world, argues Moltmann, does not foster action in this world, and such other-worldly hope too easily dissolves into escapism. And yet, Moltmann entertains the annihilation of the world in a nuclear catastrophe as a real possibility. This, suggest Williams, points to a very real contradiction in Moltmann. However concrete and non-ethereal the new creation may be, if this world has been annihilated, that new creation would be clearly be 'another world, genetically discontinuous with our world' (1986ii:628).

The Logic of Trinitarian Love

Instead of basing social action upon eschatology, Williams suggests we should recognise the limitation of hope in respect to social activity and restate the fundamental importance of love at the heart of missiology. We should 'distinguish between hope and love and think of Christian social action as directed by love rather that by hope' (1986i:3). 'Calculation and appraisal in terms of the eschaton may have its role in relation to social action, but it is totally unsafe to let it play its role until the principle of love for God and neighbour has taken proper root in the heart' (1989i:280). Love, argues Williams, should be primary as the basis of social concern because 'the scope of love is universal; the scope of hope is not' (1990i:25). We can thus speak of the limitation of hope. 'Love seems to govern the particular in a way different from that of hope' (1989i:267; see also 1986ii:630). Reflecting on the parable of the good Samaritan, Williams concludes, 'to be a neighbour or to love another is to meet the need of the needy according to the need when the needy is met' (1989i:269).

Furthermore, while God is not spoken of as being hope, he is spoken of as being love in the New Testament. Thus, an act of love is a 'participation in the divine *agapē*', and as such, 'love is a principle of conduct only because it is a principle of identity' (1989i:272; see also 1986i:3). Indeed, we can perhaps go further. Williams notes that at the end of the parable of the Good Samaritan, Jesus identifies the neighbour not, as we might expect, with the person in need, but with the active self. The implication of this, he believes, is that 'the self is not essentially an individual contingently related to the other, but essentially person-in-relationship'. By love, Williams does not mean a localised love for those with whom we have contact, but an all embracing love for neighbour, which aims, where necessary, at structural transformation (see 1986ii:630; 1989i:269-70; 1990ii), and a love for God which 'entails the holy yearning that all in his world should be as he wants it to be' (1990i:27).

Given that God is love, we can 'connect the fundamentally relational character of the self with the fundamentally relational character of deity who is love precisely in His inner-divine relationship, according to a trinitarian reading of the canon' (1989i:268-269). In other words, although 'love can be sustained, enriched and informed by hope' (1989i:275), it must be regarded as primary in social action as it reflects the love of God and, in its love for God, it is concerned for that which concerns God (1989i:278-80). In other words, the trinitarian identity of God is a more secure basis for social action than eschatology.

Williams concludes: 'Any reason for a substantial shift in perspective in the interests of mission must be very compelling ones indeed. Hope-based perspectives on mission constitute such a shift; whether anything like a compelling reason for this has been, or can be given, is a different matter.' (1986ii:630) This comment goes again to the core of our thesis, that hope is an ambiguous incentive for social involvement. Attempts to defend and develop Moltmann's theology of hope from an evangelical perspective are less than satisfactory. Although Williams is right to re-focus our attention upon love as the basis for social involvement, the task of rightly relating eschatology to mission, and to social concern in particular, still needs to be done. It is to evangelical attempts to do so that we now turn in the remainder of this chapter and the next. We will begin by examining the question of eschatological continuity, that is to say the nature and extent of continuity between pre- and post-eschaton existence, focusing upon the dialogue between two of the evangelicals we have already considered, namely, Volf and Williams.

Eschatological Continuity

In contrast to the individualism of much traditional popular evangelicalism with its central creed of a personal relationship with God, a common emphasis of the post-Lausanne discussions on social action is that salvation is corporate as well as individual. Texts such as Acts 3:19-21, Romans 8:19-22, Ephesians 1:9-10 and Colossians 1:19-20 are used to support the claim that salvation has this cosmic dimension; that the scope of Christ's redemptive work extends to the whole of creation. According to the *Grand Rapids Report*, 'salvation in the Bible is never a purely individualistic concept' (28). The Report looks at salvation under three headings 'new life ... new community ... new world' (28). The whole cosmos, both heaven and earth, are included in God's plan of salvation. 'We are looking forward not only to the redemption and resurrection of our bodies, but to the renovation of the entire created order, which will be liberated from decay, pain and death' (29).

While not a new theme to evangelical theology, it has been emphasised by those committed to social action because, it has been argued, a broader view of salvation should lead to a broader conception of mission. The Wheaton 1983 report describes the church as 'the community of the end time anticipating the End' (Par. 51). And René Padilla speaks of the church as 'the community of the kingdom ... through which, in anticipation of the end, the kingdom is concretely manifested in history' (1985ii:189). The church is the new humanity pointing towards the eschatological reconciliation of all things. It has the function, through its life and through its mission, of anticipating this cosmic eschatological salvation. At Lausanne, Padilla warned against conceiving salvation too much in other-worldly terms, as an escape by the soul from reality. Instead, prior to the eschaton, 'the new creation in Jesus Christ becomes history in terms of good works' (1975:130). In contrast to the 'eschatological paralysis' of other-worldliness, the gospel properly implies a commitment to our neighbour.

But it is not just the cosmic scope of salvation that has been emphasised. Arising from this has been an emphasis on the continuity between the present and the future. Continuity can be thought of at a moral level in the form of eschatological rewards. While the New Testament sees our eschatological fate as dependent upon our relationship to Christ, it also seems to indicate some sort of eschatological reward, although without being specific about the form these rewards might take. But, it is the issue of what we might call 'ontological continuity' around which debate has centred. Ontological continuity on an individual level (resurrection of the body) is universally affirmed among evangelicals. A number of those involved in the recent debates on social action, however, have sought to extend continuity to human activity and achievements. If salvation is cosmic in scope, they have argued, then work done in the world will be redeemed along with creation. And if there is continuity in this way, then our actions in the present have greater (that is eternal) significance.

> The new earth which is coming will not be an absolutely new creation, but a renewal of the present earth. That being the case, there will be continuity as well as discontinuity between our present culture and the culture, if so it will be called, of the world to come. (Hoekema, 1978:39)

> Because Christ has risen and brought in a new realm of love, deeds of love bear the marks of the new age and will find lasting fulfilment when that age is fully with us at the return of Christ ... Any deed in any sphere of life, be it social, political, economic, or religious, will remain if it is marked by the love of the new order. (Samuel and Sugden, 1985:145)

The argument for continuity is primarily exegetical, based on texts such as 1 Corinthians 3:10-15, Revelation 14:13, and 21:24,26. These say that a person's work may 'survive' the fire of judgment; that the deeds of those who die in the Lord 'will follow them'; that the kings of the earth 'will bring their splendour into [the new Jerusalem]' and that 'the glory and honour of the nations will be brought into it'. Hoekema concludes, 'It is clear from passages of this sort that what Christians do for the kingdom of God in this life is of significance also for the world to come' (1978:74).

In addition to the exegetical argument, there is an important theological argument. This is usually expressed by way of analogy to the resurrection of the body (see Beyerhaus, 1985:181; Hoekema, 1978:280; Goldsworthy, 1984:138; Samuel and Sugden, 1985:209; 1987:145), although, by implication, it derives from the resurrection of Christ himself. *The Grand Rapids Report* (which states the continuist position, while acknowledging that the consultation as a whole reached no agreement on the issue) says, 'the principle of continuity is evident in the resurrected body of Jesus' (41). The argument of the continuists is that the continuity of creation and human achievement can be seen as analogous to the continuity of individual, physical existence expressed as the resurrection of the body. Peter Beyerhaus, for example, says 'the new creation will be in an ontic continuation of identity with the present one; this is the significance of the message of the resurrection of the dead. Our personal resurrection is corresponded to by the promised liberation of everything created from the bondage of decay to the glorious liberation of the children of God.' (1985:181) Christian hope is not for release from physical existence, but the transformation of that existence into resurrected bodies and a new creation. If this involves continuity for the body, then why not also for the rest of creation? And why not for our stewardship of that creation? Our stewardship of creation in both its ecological and social dimensions, it is argued, finds its fulfilment in the eschatological new creation. What we do now in history finds significance in the new creation.

In the preface we noted how, at the Grand Rapids Consultation on the Relationship between Evangelism and Social Responsibility in 1982, Peter Kuzmic called for a dialogue between evangelical theology and Moltmann (1985:155). In that same essay, Kuzmic argues that in 'much of evangelical eschatology' – clearly too much in Kuzmic's view – there is an emphasis on a radical break between this present earth and the new creation. This 'total discontinuity' sees the earth as unredeemable and the new creation as 'a kind of *creatio ex nihilo*'. This, argues Kuzmic, represents 'a neglect or misunderstanding of the biblical doctrine of creation and the New Testament teaching on the present aspect of the kingdom of God' (151). While there is an emphasis upon discontinuity in the Bible, there is 'some continuity as well'. As such, 'we are to work for a better world already here and now, knowing that everything that is noble, beautiful, true and righteous in this world will somehow be preserved and perfected in the new world to come' (151). Kuzmic argues that eschatological continuity is one way of correcting the evangelical failure rightly to relate history and eschatology, which underlies the non-involvement in social issues (155). Instead, too often evangelicals 'de-eschatologize history or de-historize eschatology' (155). It is here that Kuzmic calls for his dialogue with Moltmann.

As we noted above, eschatological continuity is a key element in Volf's approach to work. In making it so, Volf, as we might expect, enters into the sort of dialogue with Moltmann suggested by Kuzmic. But in doing so, he highlights some of the problems involved in such a dialogue. The new creation is for Volf the criterion by which contemporary life should be judged, and the direction in which it should be pointed. He is careful to avoid the suggestion that the new creation will, in some way, develop from history: 'the radical newness of God's future creation frees us from having to press history into a utopian developmental scheme' (1991:84). Nevertheless, in making the new creation the criterion for judging history, Volf's stress is different from that of Moltmann. Moltmann stresses the entirely new of the future: the future is not *futurum*, that which develops from present trends, but *adventus*, that which comes towards us. Moltmann places the idea of the radical contradiction between present and future at the heart of his eschatological ethics. Indeed, Moltmann doubts the value of speaking of the kingdom of 'already' and 'not yet' because 'resignation knows that everything which "now already" exists will "no longer" exist tomorrow; for everything that comes into being passes away.' (*CoG*, 6) While Volf says that 'in the Christian community the new creation is presently being realised *only* in an anticipatory form' (1991:80, emphasis added), he has a much greater place for the idea of continuity between present and future. In Moltmann's thought continuity has an ambiguous place. Moltmann does talk of continuity, especially in his latter works. For example, he says in *The Coming of God*: 'In this Spirit, it is not just one part of life (whether it is be the soul or the ego) that is already immortal here and now; it is the whole of this mortal life, because that life is interpenetrated by eternal life, as by the spring that is its source.' (*CoG*, 71) Indeed, Moltmann suggests continuity will include 'the scars of mortality' (*CoG*, 84). And he speaks of resurrection as an opportunity to finish what was left unfinished in life. 'I shall again come back to my life, and in the light of God's grace and in the power of his mercy put right what has gone awry, finish what was begun, pick up what was neglected, forgive the trespasses, heal the hurts, and be permitted to gather up the moments of happiness and to transform mourning into joy' (*CoG*, 117) – a notion which sounds like a modified version of purgatory (*CoG*, 106)!

Nevertheless, it is by stressing contradiction, rather than continuity, that Moltmann is able to say that it is not the present which makes God questionable, but God who, through his word of promise, makes the present questionable. The contradiction between present and future, between present and promise, is the incentive for change felt by the believer. The problem with this, as we have already seen, is that any change is itself contradicted and relativized if the future is entirely new. For this reason Moltmann wants also to stress the this-worldly nature of Christian hope. And Bauckham, as we have previously noted, believes it is important for Moltmann to affirm continuity between this world and the new creation as a motive for action now (1987i:38; 1989:207). It seems difficult for Moltmann to do this given his emphasis on the future as entirely new. On the one hand, Moltmann makes the *futurum-adventus* distinction specifically to stress the discontinuity between the present and future, and so motivate change by relativising the present. On the other hand, he needs to maintain a measure of continuity to give that change significance. At best, one can say that this leads to a certain fluidity of expression. Volf recognises the implications of Moltmann's belief in a new creation *ex nihilo*. He says: 'Belief in the earthly locale of the kingdom suggests but does not necessitate continuity between the present and the future orders. One can have 'this-worldly' hope but expect that it will come about through the act of new creation *ex nihilo* rather than through the act of divine transformation of the present creation (so seemingly Moltmann in his *Theology of Hope*).' (1990i:29)

Volf's own understanding of continuity avoids the problems created by Moltmann's talk of the contradiction of history by the new creation. Volf's view of history is not wholly negative. The new creation will always relativize history (1990ii:16); so, for example, 'alienation from God will be overcome only in the new creation, all attempts to humanise work will be crowned with only partial success' (1991:163). Nevertheless, the 'normativeness of new creation enables us to evaluate (*and appreciate*) present achievements' (1991:84; emphasis added). As such, judging everything in the light of the new creation will not necessarily mean a wholly negative judgment on a given situation, even though it will always fall short of the new creation norm. At times we will discern progress; at other times deterioration. Volf speaks of 'a "kaleidoscope" theology of social life, according to which social arrangements shift in various ways under various influences (divine, human or demonic) without necessarily following an evolutionist or involutionist pattern' (1991:84). The affirmation of continuity between work in history and the new creation, argues Volf, means that eschatology gives significance to human work. Taking a lead from Moltmann (1991:98 fns. 31 and 32), Volf believes that human work should be viewed as co-operation with God in the transformation of creation, and not just its preservation (1991:89-102). More than once Volf cites Moltmann saying that human beings are 'co-workers in God's kingdom, which completes creation and renews heaven and earth' (1991:100 fn. 39 and 115 fn. 103). As Volf correctly observes (1991:xi), his influence is discernible in the Oxford Declaration on Christian Faith and Economics. The Declaration says: 'The deepest meaning of human work is that the almighty God established human work as a means to accomplish God's work in the world ... Human work has consequences that go beyond the preservation of creation to the anticipation of the eschatological transformation of the world.' (Paragraphs 17 and 18)

Yet, despite the regularity and confidence with which it has been expounded by evangelicals as they have re-emphasised social concern, the relating of eschatological continuity to social action has not been without its critics. The exegetical case is not as clear as its advocates often seem to assume. 1 Corinthians 3:10-15; Revelation 14:13; and Revelation 21:24,26 certainly seem to suggest a continuity of human achievement. In the case of the first two passages at least, however, this may well be in terms of converts resulting from proclamation. Furthermore, their very nature as eschatological statements raises hermeneutical questions. Without a more explicit hermeneutic of eschatological statements – something lacking in the evangelical discussions of continuity – the use for doctrinal or missiological purposes must be undertaken with caution.

Nevertheless, on balance, a *prima facie* reading of the biblical material seems to make some form of continuity for human achievements probable. Critics of the continuist position, however, have focused more upon the validity of eschatological continuity as an incentive for social involvement. It is the *fact* of eschatological continuity, but its *significance* that has been questioned. The fact that there is not a widespread unambiguous treatment of this issue and its implications in the New Testament would seem to suggest that such an incentive did not feature greatly in the missiology of the early church. Nevertheless, it has been assumed by those advocating a continuist position that this will provide an obvious incentive to mission in general and social involvement in particular.

> The affirmation of this neglected biblical teaching must then serve as an incentive to social involvement. (Kuzmic, 1985:152)

> This truth greatly increases the value and meaning of all that we do in harmony with our Creator; in that respect it enhances development also. (Sinclair, 1987:171)

> What all this means is that we must indeed be working for a better world now, that our efforts in this life toward bringing the kingdom of Christ to fuller manifestation are of eternal significance... our Christian life today, our struggles against sin – both individual and institutional – our mission work, our attempt to further a distinctively Christian culture, will have value not only for this world but even for the world to come. (Hoekema, 1978:39-40; see also p.287)

> Does it make any difference what we do before the end comes? It does, because the final kingdom will be the fulfilment of man's stewardship of this world. (Samuel and Sugden, 1985:208)

> In the light of the present and coming kingdom, Christians can invest their lives in the building of a historical order in the certainty that neither they nor their efforts are meaningless or lost. (Samuel and Sugden, 1987:146)

> Those who have the assurance of this continuity find in it a strong incentive to social and cultural involvement. (The Grand Rapids Report, 42)

These assumptions have been challenged by Stephen Williams. We have already seen how Williams is critical of the general attempt to relate eschatology to social involvement in Moltmann's thought and in the evangelical debates. He is similarly critical of attempts to focus this general emphasis in the assertion that eschatological continuity provides a powerful incentive for social involvement. Williams neither denies the importance of social involvement, nor that hope has a proper effect upon Christian social activity. Neither, indeed, does he necessarily challenge the validity of a continuist position. What he does question is the value of the continuist position as a motive in social action and, in particular, any insistence upon it as being necessary to a full-orbed understanding of social action. His argument has a number of strands.

First, Williams maintains that a continuist position adds little to the motive of love in Christian social ethics. This is the substance of an article entitled 'Hope, Love and Social Action' (1986i). Here he suggests that such a position 'may only reveal how impoverished our love is – a love whose energies are somewhat dissipated either by ignorance of or disbelief in "eternal consequences"' (3). Christian social action does not need these incentives to be effective in love. Thus, he suggests, 'what we hold on the continuity issue need not significantly affect our incentive for social change' (2). He asks what action, in practice, would be undertaken by a continuist that would not be undertaken by a discontinuist motivated by love? Or what qualitative difference would the action of a continuist have over against that of a discontinuist?

Second, Williams challenges the assumption that a discontinuist position is of necessity a pessimistic one in relation to this earth. The fact that you believe that this earth will be destroyed does not have to mean you hold little hope that there will be improvements in an imminent sense, especially if you believe the kingdom is present and active in history. 'One can be quite optimistic about what can be achieved in this world without insisting that it continues into the next' (1990i:26; see also 1989i:273-4).

Third, he also questions what meaning there is in speaking of human achievements being taken up into the new creation. What form will human achievements take in the new creation? How can we know whether a particular scientific or cultural achievement will merit inclusion and upon what criterion? 'At best the incentive seems to be that of a possibility, not that of a promise' (1990i:26). A labour sustained by possibility is not the same as a labour sustained by hope in the New Testament sense of the word hope. Williams acknowledges that we do not need to know *how* God will effect the transformation of continuous elements for them to operate as incentives. He adds, however, 'the deeper our agnosticism goes ... the more we should be inclined to ask whether we are on the right track as regards incentives for social responsibility' (1990i:26).

Williams' fourth argument relates to his general criticisms of hope as an incentive for social involvement. He argues that if one maintains a non-universalist position, as most evangelicals would, then the continuity incentive is seriously limited. There is, suggests Williams, 'an important distinction between hope and love ... The scope of love is universal; the scope of hope is not' (1990i:25).

Williams' first criticism, the suggestion that continuity as a motive for social action may reveal the impoverishment of our love, fails to recognise the importance that the concept of *reward* plays in the New Testament, not least in the teaching of Jesus. Now clearly, 'treasure in heaven' is not the same sort of incentive as a continuist incentive. It could be argued, however, that it is, if anything, less altruistic than a continuist position since its eternal significance lies in the effect upon the subject of the activity (personal reward), whereas with the continuist position the eternal significance lies in its effect upon the object of the activity. The New Testament unashamedly encourages us to look to the eternal consequences, in whatever form, of our acts of love.

Williams' second argument is clearly true. Social action does take place without the kind of incentive offered by the continuists. This, however, does not in itself invalidate the continuist position, even if it prevents it claiming too much.

More telling are the third and fourth strands of Williams' argument. The limitation of hope suggested by Williams, given a non-universalist position, does impinge upon the relevance of the continuist position. We might consider how an action to improve the social conditions of a particular individual, or community, can have eschatological significance, if that individual, or community, do not themselves enter the eschatological kingdom. It may well have significance for the agent of the action, in the sense which we have described as moral continuity (eternal reward). But it would seem that what we have called ontological continuity can only be posited if we resort to abstraction. The continuity of an action could only be realised apart from the concrete expression of that activity in history. Thus, while it could be said that we do not need to be specific about the form of continuity for it to motivate us, we must question the practical and concrete usefulness of the continuity argument for social action in the light of these ambiguities. Any continuity thus conceived looks more like the moral continuity of eschatological rewards than the ontological continuity proposed by the continuists.

This brings us to Williams' third argument, that continuists are forced to be so ambiguous in giving meaning to continuity that their claim to practical usefulness is undermined. This is perhaps his most substantial argument. Indeed, it is possible to take it further. We might ask, for example, whether the novels of Jane Austen will be available to be read in the new creation? Will works of art be on display? (see Mouw, 1983:19-20 for a suggestion along these lines). And if such cultural achievements are to be purged of any trace of human sin does this mean certain lines will be cut from a Shakespeare play or certain notes edited from a Beethoven symphony? And in the area of scientific achievement will we have light bulbs in the city where God himself is the light? It might be replied that such questions are simply frivolous: continuity will take place on a more abstract level. It is the spirit of cultural achievements, the love behind social activity, the commitment to the greater good and the advancement of human knowledge – purged of all impure motives – that will be continuous. Yet this appears to be more akin to moral continuity than to the ontological continuity that most continuists propose. Certainly it is no longer dependent on a renewed (as opposed to an *ex nihilo*) earth. Furthermore, we might ask how meaningful such talk is. It seems the more specific one tries to be in pinning down the nature of continuity the more abstract one is forced to be! And yet the more abstract one is, the less concrete becomes the motive for social or cultural action at a practical level.

A response to the criticisms of Williams has been made by Miroslav Volf in an article entitled 'On Loving with Hope: Eschatology and Social

Responsibility' (1990i; published together with Williams, 1990i). Volf believes that 'we must develop a Christian social ethic within the framework of the belief in eschatological continuity not because of practical (ethical) exigency but because of doctrinal constraints' (29). As such, Christian ethics cannot ignore, or choose to do without eschatology, for eschatology is at the core of the Christian faith.

Volf is no doubt right when he says that 'without theologically grounded belief in the intrinsic value and goodness of creation, positive cultural involvement hangs theologically in the air' (30). Again, arguably, he is right to assert that in the belief in the goodness of creation, the protological and eschatological perspectives are inseparably bound together (30). He is right to emphasise the centrality of a renewed earth in God's eschatological purposes. Nevertheless, it is less clear whether he can support a statement like:

> The expectation of the eschatological destruction of the world (and of everything human beings have created in it) is not consonant with belief in the value and goodness of creation: what God will annihilate must be either so bad that it is not possible to redeem it, or so insignificant that it is not worth being redeemed. It is hard to believe in the intrinsic value and goodness of something that God would completely annihilate. (30)

Attractive as this argument initially appears, it is, upon reflection, somewhat questionable. It leads Volf either towards universalism or towards a denial of the intrinsic value of a human individual. And, presumably, he has no wish to go in either direction. Questionable, too, is the concept of the freedom of God behind this statement: is God required to redeem that which is not too bad? Are human beings worth redeeming? – surely only from the perspective of grace. Arguably, God is not under any external compulsion to redeem anything because of any intrinsic value or worth it might have. It is surely better to see the eschatological perspective in terms of the reaffirmation and fulfilment of God's purposes in creation. The purposes of God are intrinsically good and God will fulfil these in the new creation. The very nature of God is such that what he elects to do (in, for example, creating the world), he accomplishes (in the new creation).

Yet arguably, God's purposes in creation involve humanity as stewards of that creation. Humanity has a central role in God's creational purposes. If the new creation is the fulfilment of those purposes, then it must also involve the fulfilment of humanity's participation, by the grace of God, in those purposes. This, however, raises an important point which is overlooked by Volf and others participating in the debate, namely, that *fulfilment is not the same as continuity*. Certainly it may well involve continuity, as those biblical texts which we have looked at seem to indicate. Nevertheless, as Williams is at pains to indicate, our knowledge of post-eschaton existence and the way in which God will transform reality into the new creation is so limited, that it is very difficult to give any substance to continuity as a motive for action. This highlights further weaknesses in Volf's defence of continuity.

In responding to Williams' question, When would belief in continuity make any real difference to a person's actions? Volf makes two points. First, Volf acknowledges, in what he calls 'a call to realism', that belief in continuity, and the call to love one's neighbour for that matter, do not necessarily feature highly in the motivation of most people. 'Hunger and pride are the main incentives for human work' (30). Instead, belief in continuity gives 'assurance and inspiration' (30). Yet he also wants to say that, belief in continuity not only inspires, but also directs our actions. While we cannot describe in detail *how* human actions may continue, we can ask *what kind* of actions will continue. Volf believes that 'love is the key for the anticipatory discernment of how our feeble works are related to the eschatological consummation of all things' (31). It is hard, however, to see how this can be reconciled with Volf's call to realism which leads him to say: 'human achievements do not lose their inherent value because they were done out of ethically impure motives' (30, fn. 7). If love is the criteria for eschatological continuity, then it would seem to exclude those acts done out of 'ethically impure motives'.

Volf's second response to the question of the practical use of belief in continuity is to say that 'such belief gives human beings important inspiration for cultural, social and ecological action, even when such action is not appreciated by one's neighbour' (30). People in such a position, Volf believes, can 'draw inspiration and strength from the belief that their noble efforts are not lost' (30). The problem with this is that when Volf describes how we might think of eschatological continuity, his three ways all involve a person making a *public* contribution to humanity now. First, he says we should think of 'the cumulative work of the whole human race', the human 'project' in which 'one generation stands on the shoulders of another, so that the accomplishments of each generation build upon those of the previous one' (31). Second, Volf argues that, while not every single human product will be integrated into the world to come (although it seems Volf continues to think that some will be), 'the worldly home of human beings', to which they contribute, will, as a whole, be integrated. Third, Volf argues that human activity contributes to the identity of human beings and, while that activity itself may not be continuous, the identity it creates is not lost on resurrected personality. These three ways may indeed help us to think of continuity correctly, yet it is hard to see what comfort these are to those whose work is unappreciated. How are succeeding generations to build upon work that is 'unappreciated' and 'lost'? What effect can unappreciated work have on human identity? Volf cannot have it both ways. Either continuity involves what he describes, and it gives little incentive to those whose work is unappreciated. Or continuity inspires those whose work is unappreciated, and it involves considerably more that Volf describes, or, one suspects, can reasonably defend.

As we have seen, at this point Volf parts company with Moltmann. Central to Moltmann's eschatological ethics is not continuity, but contradiction. The promise of the future places us in contradiction with the experience of the present, and so causes us to seek the change of that present. But, as Volf recognises, if the future is entirely new, any change is itself contradicted and relativised. Moltmann is left with rather ambiguous affirmations of the this-worldly nature of hope, which sit uneasily with the strong *futurum-adventus* distinction that he makes. Thus, although the causes differ, for both Moltmann and evangelical continuists the result is the same: motivation for cultural and social action, based on the form of the future, proves hard to express in any meaningful way. At best, we can say that in general terms continuity does take place. Any application of this, however, to specific activity is fraught with difficulties. The problem is, that despite the merits of the continuists position, what we know of the eschatological future is so limited that any argument based upon the form of the future is bound to flounder in ambiguity, and be difficult to articulate in a meaningful way.

In this chapter, we have indicated something of the dialogue that has taken place between evangelicals and Moltmann; and some of the problems that have emerged from that dialogue. At the same time, we have identified one dimension of evangelical attempts to relate eschatology to social action, namely that of eschatological continuity which we have called 'the future of the present'. In the next chapter we turn to the other side, considering 'the presence of the future'. What effect does the presence of the eschatological kingdom in history have upon the mission of the church?

CHAPTER 10

The Presence of the Future

In the previous chapter we focused on the issue of eschatological continuity, that is to say, 'the future of the present'. We turn now to 'the future in the present': the nature and implications of the presence of the kingdom of God in history prior to the parousia. We will first examine the way this question has arisen in the general evangelical debates over the theology of social involvement. This will set the scene for a discussion of the thought of three important evangelical contributors to the debate, namely Stephen Mott, Richard Mouw and Oliver O'Donovan.

The Centrality of the Kingdom

We have already noted how eschatology has been central to the post-Lausanne debates over the place of social concern in mission. The central feature of this eschatological orientation has been the kingdom of God. Traditionally, eschatological debates within evangelicalism have centred on the question of the millennium. It is striking, then, that as social action has been re-emphasised *the kingdom of God rather than the millennium has been the central eschatological motif.* Peter Kuzmic says, 'In evangelical eschatology, Jesus' teaching about the kingdom, which he enacted in his first coming, should certainly be more central than the millennial debates ... and the sensational preoccupation with the events surrounding his second coming' (1985:148). What Kuzmic believes *should* be the case, Kirk said in 1983 was the case: 'everywhere one turns in the church today the theme of the kingdom of God is being discussed' (1983:41).

A number of reasons can be given for this shift from the millennial to the kingdom as the key eschatological motif.

1. The interest among evangelicals in the kingdom of God reflects the debate within New Testament scholarship set in motion by the work of Johannes Weiss and Albert Schweitzer. Peter Kuzmic says, 'It is only more recently that, due to the importance of this concept in modern theological debates, some evangelicals are looking at the kingdom with greater seriousness.' (1985:148) The most important twentieth century evangelical contributor to this debate has been George Eldon Ladd. Ladd argued that the kingdom is the rule or reign of God over all of life. Furthermore, in contrast to the futurist orientation of

millennial debates, Ladd argued that the kingdom was both future *and* present. The kingdom has been inaugurated in Jesus, even if its consummation is still future. Ladd's book, *Jesus and the Kingdom* (later republished as *The Presence of the Future*, 1974) has been very influential. Both Vinay Samuel and Chris Sugden point to the crucial role it played in their thinking (Chester, 1993:38).

2. The kingdom has proved an attractive theme for evangelicals concerned to emphasise social action because it allows them to put an individual's relationship with God – the traditional focus of much evangelical soteriology – in a broader context, namely God's salvific rule over all of life. During the Lausanne Congress, a group of participants drew up 'a response to the Lausanne' which went further than the Covenant itself. This statement, entitled *Theology and Implications of Radical Discipleship*, defined the gospel as:

> God's Good News in Jesus Christ; it is Good News of the reign he proclaimed and embodies; of God's mission of love to restore the world to wholeness through the Cross of Christ and him alone; of his victory over the demonic powers of destruction and death; of his lordship over the entire universe; it is good news of a new creation, a new humanity, a new birth through him by his life-giving Spirit; of the gifts of the messianic reign contained in Jesus and mediated through him by the Spirit; of the charismatic community empowered to embody his reign of shalom here and now before the whole creation and make his Good News seen and known. It is Good News of liberation, of restoration, of wholeness, and of salvation that is personal, social, global and cosmic.

By defining the gospel in terms of the kingdom, or reign, of God, they made social change not only part of mission, but part of the gospel. It is this factor, above all others, which distinguishes the social thinking of the radical evangelicals from that of the evangelical social activists of the nineteenth century.

3. By setting social action in the eschatological context of the kingdom of God, evangelicals, particularly those from this radical wing, have been able to shape a view of social action which is oriented towards change. By placing the kingdom at the heart of social action, they find a rationale for radical social change in line with the radical nature of the kingdom and its future. This is in contrast to those evangelicals who root social involvement in the doctrine of creation, and who thus tend to be politically conservative, seeking to preserve the creation order. Tito Paredes says, 'No truly adequate theology of social change can be stated without the hope of the coming of the kingdom of God, in which social transformation will reach its perfect fulfilment' (1987:62).

4. Advocates of social action have argued that it is inhibited by an other-worldliness stemming from an overly-future eschatology. When the eschatological blessings are seen predominantly in future terms, it is alleged, mission is seen primarily in terms of preparing people, through conversion, for that future. Such an eschatology is portrayed as escapist, allowing Christians to sideline the radical demands of discipleship in the here and now. In contrast,

when the kingdom of God is seen as already present, albeit with its consummation still future, and as having implications for all of life, then social action is no longer seen as a diversion from the central task of mission.

Premillennialist eschatologies have particularly been singled out for criticism for too often creating a pessimistic attitude towards history and social change, and therefore social involvement. This accusation is all the more significant given the predominance of premillennialism in evangelical missiology, particularly in North America. The twentieth century has witnessed the growing predominance of North American evangelicalism in evangelical mission. At the time of the Edinburgh Conference in 1910, the USA and Canada already made up a third of the 21,000 Protestant missionaries world-wide. By 1925, half the world's 29,000 missionaries were North Americans (Noll, 1992:533). At the same time, North American missionary activity has itself shifted away from the mainline denominations to independent evangelical or fundamentalist missionary agencies. In 1953 half of North American missionaries were from churches affiliated to the National Council of Churches in the USA or the Canadian Council of Churches north of the border. By 1985 it was only ten per cent (Noll, 1992:533). Since these American independent agencies are more likely to be premillennialist in outlook or be sending premillennialist missionaries, the missionary expansion of the twentieth century has largely been marked by the spread of American versions of premillennialism and dispensationalism. This, it is argued, explains, at least in part, why evangelicalism in so many Third World countries suffers from the dichotomies and distortions of which Western evangelicalism has been accused by the advocates of social concern. These, they argue, lead to withdrawal from the world and to an escapist eschatology that awaits heaven while the world is going under (Kuzmic, 1985:147). As Third World evangelicalism has come of age, however, both in terms of the strength of the church and its influence upon missiology, the prevailing premillennialism has either been replaced, or at least challenged, by a focus upon the kingdom of God.

Both Peter Kuzmic and David Bosch have been highly critical of the essentially pessimistic attitude towards history of much – though not all – premillennialism. Speaking at the Consultation on the Relationship between Evangelism and Social Responsibility (Grand Rapids, 1982) – perhaps the key post-Lausanne conference on the question of the place of social action and eschatology in mission (see Chester 1993:121-124) – they both argued that such an outlook has been a major disincentive to social action. Social action is seen as able to achieve little when all hope of change on earth is relegated to the future millennial kingdom. Bosch argued that such an outlook had been a significant contributory factor to the abandonment of social action by evangelicals at the beginning of this century (Bosch, 1985:69-72; Kuzmic, 1985:137-147).

Nevertheless, the main debate has focused on the kingdom, without necessarily attempting to replace the millennial theme with the kingdom.

Advocates of evangelical social involvement have been slow to denounce premillennialism, perhaps because this would be counter-productive to their cause given the hold premillennialism has in many of part so the North American church and therefore also the evangelical missionary movement. The Grand Rapids report itself is cautious. It notes that the conference examined the question of 'whether there is any connection between our eschatological outlook and the attitude we adopt towards evangelism and social responsibility' (37). Although the report states that 'without doubt, our understanding of the millennium affects the way in which we view the world' (38), it fails to take this any further in the light of the deeply held and differing positions on the millennium at the conference. Furthermore, an emphasis upon the centrality of the kingdom, and upon its presence now, is by no means incompatible with premillennial beliefs. George Eldon Ladd, who more than anyone has influenced evangelical thinking on the kingdom of God, is a premillennialist. Although Ladd has argued hard for an inaugurated eschatology and for the reality of the presence of the kingdom now, he nevertheless believes that: 'The coming of God's Kingdom occurs in stages, not in a single event. First is a temporal kingdom of a thousand years when the resurrected saints reign with Christ. This is followed by what we may call the eternal Kingdom with its new heaven and new earth.' (1974ii:628)

These, then, are some of the reasons why the kingdom has dominated over the millennium in the eschatology of those evangelicals concerned to re-emphasise social involvement: it reflects wider theological debates; it sets social action in the broader context of God's purposes for the world; it orients social action towards radical change; and it provides an alternative to the other-worldly eschatologies of much evangelicalism, especially that of some premillennialists. Thus, while the kingdom has not necessarily been seen as an alternative to the millennial motif, it has replaced it as the central eschatological theme within these debates.

The Nature and the Extent of the Kingdom

The focus upon the kingdom of God raises the issue of 'the future in the present'. The nature and extent of the presence of the kingdom, prior to its consummation, has occupied a key place in evangelical debates. If, in Christ, the future kingdom has broken into history, what significance does this have for the life and mission of the church? If the kingdom is not only 'not yet' but also 'already', what form does it take in history? More specifically, if salvation has a corporate dimension, to what extent can this corporate dimension be experienced before the eschaton? Can we speak of the emergence of social justice and reconciliation as salvation? Two differing positions are discernible.

First, that there is corporate salvation now, but this is limited to the conscious confession of Christ. One of the leading advocates of this position is John Stott and, as he was the architect of the Lausanne Covenant and the Grand

Rapids Report, this view predominates in these documents. The Lausanne Covenant says that political liberation is not salvation (Section 5). The Grand Rapids Report speaks of salvation as 'new life ... new community ... new world' (28), but the new community is the church and the new world is spoken of only in future terms. Although the Report acknowledges that some found the use of salvation language appropriate for the emergence of justice and peace in the wider community, it continued, 'most of us, however, consider that is more prudent and biblical to reserve the vocabulary of salvation for the experience of reconciliation with God through Christ and its direct consequences' (29). John Stott himself insists that 'the kingdom of God in the New Testament is a fundamentally *christological* concept, and that as such it may be said to exist only where Jesus Christ is consciously acknowledged as Lord', although 'the righteous standards of the kingdom ... may to some extent spill over into the world as a result of Christian influence' (Sider and Stott, 1977:23).

This was also the position taken by Ronald Sider at the Grand Rapids consultation in 1982 (modifying his previous stance in Sider and Stott, 1977). In his paper, 'How Broad is Salvation in Scripture?' (1985; given jointly with James Parker), he says, 'If biblical usage is decisive, then we should use salvation language to refer only to what happens when persons confess Christ, experience the salvation he offers, and begin to live out the radical demands of his new kingdom' (105). Although he believes salvation is vertical and horizontal, personal and social, he believes it should nevertheless be restricted to the conscious confession of Christ. As such, 'salvation language should probably not be used to refer to the imperfect emergence of justice and peace in society at large before the return of Christ' (105). Similarly, while Sider refuses to be dogmatic, in the light of New Testament usage he concludes: 'It is important to note that *absolutely none* of the scores of New Testament texts on the kingdom of God speak of the presence of the kingdom apart from the conscious confession of Christ ... There seems no warrant in the New Testament for talking about the coming of the kingdom of God via societal change apart from confession of Christ.' (104)

A second, alternative position has however been taken, namely, that there is corporate salvation now and this is not limited to the conscious confession of Christ. The most prominent advocates of this position are Vinay Samuel and Chris Sugden. At Grand Rapids they argued that, because the church acknowledges the lordship of Christ, 'it experiences the salvation which the kingdom brings in a way that is different from the experience of the larger community'. Nevertheless, 'the kingdom activity in society beyond the church is not just its judgmental activity but also that which brings promise and grace' (1985:211). At the Consultation on the Theology of Development (1980) they similarly maintained that the kingdom is seen, not only in the church, 'but also in God's kingdom activity in the world beyond the church ... as the just relationships that belong to the kingdom are established in society' (1981:52). And at Wheaton 1983 they argued that 'one need not submit personally to the lordship of Christ to be able to experience [the kingdom's] grace and transformation in one's life' (1987:141). This is because: 'The kingdom, as it exists even now, is not an individual spiritual entity. It is corporate, and it permeates with its influence all historical life. There are many activities, structures, and movements in the world that already share in God's saving work by his grace.' (1987:141)

As an example, they point to the improved status of Indian women, which has happened through the work of the church in India, despite the women not having consciously confessed Christ. 'This transformation is still part of God's work of breaking down the dividing wall of hostility between separated groups, of creating in himself one new humanity in Christ in which there is neither male nor female' (1987:142). Although 'transformation is not salvation' in the sense of regeneration and justification, people who do not confess Christ can 'participate in the transformation that the kingdom brings' (1987:142). The term 'redemption' is appropriate for God's activity outside the church, when we see it not simply as the experience of regeneration, forgiveness and new life, but in wider terms as 'God's activity in fulfilling his intention for the world' (1987:153).

The example of the status of Indian women does not differ greatly from what John Stott calls the 'spill over' of kingdom values into society since it stems from the influence of those who confess Christ. The difference would appear to lie in the use of language. It is not clear whether Samuel and Sugden would be as happy to use salvation or kingdom language in cases where change does not involve the influence of Christians. This is not to say the differences are insignificant. Our choice of language can affect the value we give to things. The Grand Rapids Report reflects this semantic division when it says:

> Is it right to refer to the emergence of justice and peace in the wider community as 'salvation', and to attribute to the grace of Christ every beneficial social transformation? Some of us do not find salvation-language inappropriate for such situations, even when Christ is not acknowledged in them. Most of us, however, consider that it is more prudent and biblical to reserve the vocabulary of salvation for the experience of reconciliation with God through Christ and its direct consequences. (1982:29)

Bound up with the question of the extent of presence of the kingdom, is the question of the nature of God's activity outside the church. That God is active in the world is hardly an area of dispute. What has proved a point of contention, however, is the nature of that activity. Specifically, is this activity part of God's redemptive work in Christ or is it part of his activity as Creator and Judge? Is God at work outside the church on the basis of Christ's death and resurrection? Is God at work outside the church anticipating now, in the present, something of the future salvation?

At Lausanne John Stott argued that: '"Mission" does not cover everything

God does in the world. For God is the Creator and is constantly active in the world in providence and in common grace, quite apart from the purposes for which he sent his Son, his Spirit, his apostles, and his church into the world.' (1975i:68) Although the pursuit of socio-political justice is a legitimate aim of Christians, Stott argued at Lausanne that to call it salvation is to mix the roles of God as Creator and God as Redeemer; roles which the Scriptures keep distinct (1975i:74). The Lausanne Covenant itself places social concern very much in the context of God as Creator and Judge: 'We affirm that God is both the Creator and the Judge of all men. We therefore should share his concern for justice and reconciliation throughout human society, and for the liberation of men from every kind of oppression.' (Section 5) In a similar vein, Ronald Sider, while acknowledging that Jesus is Lord of all the world, asks: 'Is there not some necessary distinction between God's overall sovereign rule of history and the kingdom of God understood as the saving reality that broke into history so decisively in the person and work of Jesus Christ? God's creative and sustaining activity cannot simply be equated with his redemptive work.' (1985:104) *The Grand Rapids Report* concludes, given that Christ is the *de jure* King of the earth, but not yet its *de facto* King, 'we should reserve the expression "the kingdom of God" for the acknowledged rule of Christ, since this is the new thing he inaugurated at his coming, while referring to the more general 'sovereignty' of God over all things' (33).

In responding to the position of the Lausanne Covenant, Samuel and Sugden say, 'Our fundamental criticism of this "creation-based theology" is that it is divorced from redemption, from the eschatological recapitulation of all things in Christ which has been inaugurated with his coming' (1981:51). They believe it is weak for three reasons. First, it has no basis for entering the struggle between the weak and the strong in society. The First World approach to development, they argue, is to see it as a struggle to master natural resources in accordance with the creation mandate. In contrast, the Third World perspective sees history as a struggle between the strong and the weak in society. Second, it is liable to slip into a dualism between God's activity in the spiritual realm, which takes place upon the basis of the cross and resurrection, and God's activity in the physical realm, which takes place upon a different basis, that of his work of creation and providence. Third, the association of God's activity in the world with his work as Creator fails to provide 'the eschatological dimension' necessary to prevent us from seeking to preserve the created order while confining the role of redemption to a spiritual level.

Samuel and Sugden believe we can speak of God's activity in the world as salvific and based on Christ's work of redemption. Although the word 'world' is used in the New Testament to represent humanity in rebellion to God, it is also, they argue, used to refer to the arena of God's salvific activity. As such, we can speak of God having a redemptive and eschatological purpose for the world apart from the church. This work may not involve the use of God's people as his instrument, for God is not limited to the church in fulfilling his purposes. Thus, the work of Christ beyond the church is not inferior to the work of Christ in, and through, the church. Its basis is the same – the cross and resurrection – and so is its goal – 'the creation of a new humanity in Christ which openly acknowledges him as Lord' (1981:60). God's activity in the church and in the world is 'essentially the same work of lordship based on the death and resurrection of Christ moving both the world and the church to their consummation in the new earth' (1985:211).

Creation Ethics and Kingdom Ethics

Part of the significance of this discussion lies in the role it has played in an important current debate within evangelicalism. Two opposing positions have developed as evangelicals have re-emphasised social action. On the one hand, some have argued that our socio-ethical framework should be based upon creation and creational principles. Others, in contrast, have argued that the starting point for social ethics should be the kingdom of God. It has thus been characterised as a debate between 'creation ethics' and 'kingdom ethics'. (For a summary of both sides of the argument see Barclay and Sugden, 1990.)

Advocates of kingdom ethics start with the eschatological redemption of creation and, in the light of God's redemptive activity in the world, argue that our vision of the new creation should shape our attempts to transform society. The key question is, 'How can I take part in, express, and produce the quality of personal and corporate life that will be fulfilled in God's kingdom?' (Samuel and Sugden, 1987:146). Advocates of this approach point out that the kingdom of God was the focus for the ministry of Jesus. God's final purpose for creation is fulfilled in the kingdom, which has already invaded history through the life and ministry of Jesus. This focus on the kingdom, they claim, integrates the spiritual and material, the personal and social. And by placing the kingdom at the heart of social ethics, social ethics can be related to the gospel, to the announcement of the good news of the kingdom. Conversely, the proclamation of new life is related to the demonstration of that life in new relationships.

Advocates of the creation ethics approach believe the kingdom ethics approach cannot be reconciled with the Scriptures. In particular, as we have seen, they maintain the use of salvation and kingdom language for the activity of God outside the conscious confession of Christ is inappropriate in the light of the New Testament. Only believers can enter and share in the kingdom of God. Also, a kingdom ethics approach remains vague when applied to practical ethical issues – some following this approach, for example, can support armed rebellion, while others advocate pacifism. (In fact, the same accusation can be made against creation ethics; see Schluter and Clements, 1990:50-2.)

In contrast, then, those advocating creation ethics begin from the perspective of creation. Certain ethical principles can be derived from the order of created reality. These are ordained by God for the good of his creation. These creation ordinances are 'safeguarded' in the moral law and in particular in the

Decalogue. Oliver Barclay believes the advantage of such an approach to be threefold. First, creation provides an ethic for all – all people are part of creation; not all are part of the kingdom. Second, it can form the basis for practical policy. It is based on definite creational structures and enshrined in specific laws. Third, it can be commended to all. Creation ethics are not arbitrary for they have their basis in the order of created reality.

The Coming of the Kingdom

How are we to evaluate this debate (see also Chester, 2004, chapter 5)? That salvation is a corporate reality is not at issue. More complex is the question of whether the kingdom is present outside the confession of Christ. The language of the kingdom is used in the Gospels in more than one way. The kingdom can be seen as a sphere, or realm, of blessing created by the rule of God. The kingdom is spoken of as that which can be entered. The qualifications for entry, however, make it clear that entry is related to discipleship, to accepting the demands of the kingdom. In these senses, then, it is clearly inappropriate to speak of the kingdom outside the confession of Christ. Nevertheless, the most common sense in which the kingdom is used in the gospels is as the salvific rule of God, the rule of God which brings both blessings and demands. This sense of the kingdom, then, must be the focus for any discussion of whether the kingdom is present outside the confession of Christ.

When one asks, however, whether God rules outside the church, the question is cast in a different light. The Old Testament affirms that God is sovereign, not only in Israel, but over the whole world (see, for example, 1 Chronicles 16:31; 29:11-12; Psalm 9:7-8; 45:6; 47:7-9; 93:1-2; 103:19; 145:11-13; Isaiah 37:16). God rules and acts for good, both inside and outside the sphere of those who worship and serve him. Indeed, all good comes from him, and takes place within the context of his sovereignty.

The key question becomes, then, How did the kingdom come in the ministry of Jesus? How are we to account for the newness of the kingdom? If the Old Testament gives witness to the rule of God in history, then we can only make sense of the *coming* of the rule of God in Jesus, if that rule of God comes in *a new way*. If we say the kingdom has come in Christ, we must ask what is it that has come, and how does it contrast with the rule or sovereignty of God in the Old Testament? We must identify the new element in the rule of God which occurs with the coming of Christ. And having identified it, we can then ask if this new element is present outside the confession of Christ. It is our suggestion that this new element comprises two complementary components.

First, the kingdom has come because Christ has come. One might be tempted to say that the kingdom is present because the King is present. In fact, however, although he is clearly portrayed as King, particularly in the passion narratives, Christ's kingship is rarely directly related to the kingdom of God in the gospels. Nevertheless, it is evident from the Gospels that the kingdom is present in, and through, the person and ministry of Jesus. Jesus proclaims the presence of the kingdom, manifests its power in healings and exorcisms, and demonstrates its gratuitous nature in his relationships with sinners.

Second, the coming of the kingdom is the coming of the eschatological new age into history ahead of itself. The Jewish expectation of the coming of the kingdom was of the intervention of God in history establishing the new age of blessing. The secret of the kingdom is that this has happened in and through the ministry of Christ, even though it has not yet happened in its full and consummated sense. The eschatological age of salvation is already present in history.

In fact these two elements are intimately related for two reasons. First, Jesus is the Messiah. The messiahship of Jesus is something of a vexed question in New Testament scholarship. The extent to which the concept of an eschatological Messiah featured in Old Testament and Jewish thought is questioned. And, it raises the question of Jesus' own self-understanding. Clearly such questions are beyond the scope of this study. Nevertheless, we can say that, however widespread or otherwise it may have been, one feature of Jewish eschatological expectation was that a Messiah would come, a king in the line of David who would mediate the rule of God. Furthermore, the early church saw Jesus in these terms as is evidenced by the widespread use of the title 'Christ' or Messiah' for Jesus. The same is true for the christological title 'Son of Man', Jesus' preferred self-designation. Its meaning in contemporary Judaism is questioned, but if its background does lie in Daniel 7, as a number of the Gospels sayings suggest, then Jesus was clearly identified by the Gospel writers as the figure who receives authority from God and exercises dominion over the nations.

The second reason the coming of Jesus and the coming of the new age are related is that, after the resurrection and ascension of Jesus, his presence is mediated by the Holy Spirit. As such, the kingdom that was present in and through Christ is not now absent, but continues to be present as Christ's presence is mediated to his disciples by the Holy Spirit. Yet, it is at the same time clear, particularly from the writings of Paul, that it is the role of the Holy Spirit to mediate the firstfruits of the eschatological future life now in the life of the Christian and of the Christian community. This is why the gift of the Holy Spirit to all believers is a central feature of eschatological fulfilment (Joel 2:28-32 and Acts 2:1-21). In other words, these two aspects, the presence of Christ and the presence of the eschatological future rule of God, are both mediated by the Holy Spirit. They are different sides of the same reality. Furthermore, it is arguably the case that the kingdom was also present in the ministry of Jesus through the Holy Spirit (see Marshall, 1985:10). Jesus says, 'if I drive out demons by the Spirit of God, then the kingdom of God has come upon you' (Matthew 12:28).

We could well say, then, that what is new about the presence of the kingdom, certainly after Pentecost, is the Holy Spirit mediating the presence of

Christ and the eschatological life of the new age in the life of the Christian and of the Christian community. If we then return to our original question, Is the kingdom present outside the confession of Christ?, we can reformulate it in pneumatological terms, Is the Spirit at work outside the confession of Christ?

There is one sense, at least, in which the Spirit is at work outside the confession of Christ, for that very confession is the work of the Spirit. It is the Spirit who convicts 'the world of guilt in regard to sin and righteousness and judgment' (John 16:8). It is the Spirit who gives the new birth by which a person enters the kingdom of God (John 3:3-8) and which is itself a firstfruit of the redemption of creation (James 1:18). It is clear that God is at work through his Holy Spirit outside the confession of Christ in preparing people to accept the gospel and so experience the redemption that comes on the basis of Christ's work.

There is, however, no biblical material to support the contention that the Spirit mediates the eschatological new age outside the church. We may well want to say that the Creator Spirit is present in all human creativity, but this stems from creation rather than redemption. It is not an activity of the new age, *for it was true before the coming of the kingdom in Christ.* In fact, the New Testament evidence is that the work of the Spirit as mediator of the new age is a work specifically among believers and the Christian community. It is to believers that the Spirit is given as a seal and as a deposit of the life to come (2 Corinthians 1:21-22; Ephesians 1:13-14). Creation waits in frustration for its liberation and we, too, groan inwardly as we eagerly expect our redemption. The difference is that the Christian has already received the firstfruits of the Spirit (Romans 8:19-23). Thus, although they await their adoption as children of God, believers have already received the Spirit of sonship by which they cry '*Abba*, Father' (Romans 8:15-16).

The Rule of God in Creation and Redemption

Samuel and Sugden fear any distinction in the rule of God (as Creator and as Redeemer), yet the coming of the kingdom in Christ clearly requires some such distinction to be made. The coming of the kingdom in Christ must imply a new quality or type of rule. If not, then the coming of the kingdom is meaningless. This is why we speak of the kingdom as the *salvific* rule of God. This is not to say that God had not acted as Redeemer before. In such cases, however, God's acts of redemption were historically provisional and anticipatory. The generation that were liberated in the Exodus did not receive the rest of the promised land, but died in the wilderness because of their unbelief and disobedience. In contrast, the redemption of God effected in Christ is eschatologically certain – this is the meaning of Christian hope. And it is the fulfilment of Old Testament redemption.

There is, then, a necessary distinction between God's rule as Creator and Redeemer. While it is the same God who acts in both cases – God is one and wholly integrated in all his attributes and activities – nevertheless the activity of God does take different forms. The distinction between God's creative activity and his redemptive activity corresponds to the distinction maintained in the Reformed tradition between common grace and special grace. Indeed, whereas the distinction between God as Creator and God as Redeemer places the distinction within God, the distinction between common and special grace is helpful, for the grace of God is one, even if it operates in differing ways. The disadvantage of stating the distinction in this way is that special grace has traditionally been seen in largely individualistic terms.

To maintain this distinction between God's creative and redemptive activity does not require us, however, to go as far as John Stott when he says 'God is the Creator and is constantly active in the world in providence and in common grace, *quite apart* from the purposes for which he sent his Son, his Spirit, his apostles, and his church into the world.' (1986i:30; emphasis added) Instead we might say this: God is at work as Creator preserving creation *in order that* it might be redeemed through Christ in the new creation. God is at work as Judge in the world that people might take the opportunity to repent and know his grace. The Spirit is at work in people's lives bringing conviction that they might know the redemption of Christ. The key thing is that God works as Creator and Judge in order that he might work as Redeemer. His work as Creator *prepares* for his work as Redeemer. In respect to creation, he preserves and sustains it now in order that he might redeem it in the new creation. In respect to people, he works through his Spirit and as Judge that they might come to experience the redemption of Christ, and taste the justice and peace of the eschatological kingdom, as it is anticipated now, through the Holy Spirit, in the Christian community. God's activities as Creator are not 'quite apart' from his redemptive purposes; rather, they serve his redemptive purposes. Furthermore, because God's providential and redemptive activity are closely related, we must allow that in practice it will be all but impossible to indicate where God's creative activity becomes his redemptive activity. Any such judgments are, at best provisional, and at worst inappropriate.

It should be added that this argument is concerned with the *temporal* order of creation and redemption, and not the logical order of God's decrees. The argument stands, whether or not God had a purpose for creation apart from the fall (the supra-/infralapsarian controversy). In other words, we are not necessarily arguing that God creates in order to redeem, simply, that given the fall, he *sustains* his creation in order to redeem it.

Conclusion

This discussion highlights problems with both the kingdom ethics approach and creation ethics approach, outlined above. First, behind the thinking of those who advocate kingdom ethics there is a similarity to a wider trend in modern theology which is discernible in Moltmann, in Liberation Theology, and in much contemporary ecumenical thinking. This is the broadening of the concept of salvation away from simply the eternal fate of individuals, to encompass the transformation of communities, and indeed socio-political structures. As such, salvation is spoken of in terms of humanisation or socio-political liberation. Certainly this social aspect of salvation has been an important corrective of much previous individualism. As we have seen, the cosmic and corporate aspect of salvation are important features of biblical soteriology. Nevertheless, we have also argued that the language of the Bible restricts the present experience of salvation to those who confess Christ and to the community of faith. Evangelicals, by definition, feel themselves bound to the biblical witness in its entirety. Whatever the attractions of speaking of the kingdom of God and the salvific activity of God outside the community of faith, evangelicals, if they are to be true to their evangelicalism, need to measure the appropriateness of such language against the biblical witness. Our suggestion is that the use of salvation language for socio-political transformation is not warranted in the light of the Scriptures.

Again, criticisms developed in the previous chapter by Bauckham and Williams are pertinent here. Samuel and Sugden describe the transformation of the status of women in Indian society as 'part of God's work ... of creating in himself one new humanity in Christ' (1987:142). And René Padilla says 'the church anticipates the destiny of all humanity' (1985ii:196,199). This language echoes that of Moltmann, but in Moltmann it betrays his universalism. This universalism allows Moltmann to lessen the distinction between the church and the world, making the distinction temporal rather than eschatological. What the church experiences now is what humanity as a whole will experience at the eschaton, and as such, 'the church is not "the not-world"' (*CPS*, 84). For Moltmann the church exists, not for itself, but for the kingdom of God; and so he refuses to see the spread of the church as an end in itself (*CPS*, 11,69,84). Moltmann states explicitly that 'the economic, political and cultural liberations of men and women from exploitation, repression and alienation belong just as much to the work of redemption as the forgiveness of sins and hope for eternal life' (*SL*, 112). And likewise, Moltmann has no problem arguing that the Spirit is at work outside the church. The church, says Moltmann, 'has no monopoly in the operation of the Holy Spirit' (*SL*, 230).

> That makes Christianity alive to the operation of the Holy Spirit *extra muros ecclesiæ* – outside the church as well – and prepared to accept the life-furthering communities which people outside the church expect and experience ... There is certainly a line drawn between Christians and non-Christians through baptism and membership of the church, but as far as the natural and voluntary communities are concerned, there is in fact no inside and outside. There is only the complex web of life's relationship. (*SL*, 231)

This represents, however, an ecclesiology alien to evangelicalism. The evangelical tradition has always held that there is a fundamental distinction between the world, under the judgment of God, and the church. If they are to maintain these positions, as advocates of a kingdom ethics position would seem to want to do, then they need to be cautious in their use of such theological language. Certainly the church's experience of salvation anticipates the experience of creation as a whole (Romans 8:21, James 1:18). Yet the church is not the firstfruits of the new humanity, for it *is* the new humanity (Ephesians 2:15).

In the case of creation ethics, it is difficult to avoid the nagging doubt created by the absence of Christ and of the gospel in their ethical framework. Barclay can say, 'The truths of creation/providence provide a starting point for our thinking here, since God's purpose is to restore creation' (1990:18). It is clear, however, that the restoration of creation in Christ serves only to re-enforce the use of creation ethics. The coming of the kingdom, and the death and resurrection of Christ, do not substantially affect social ethics in a creation ethics approach. In contrast, Moltmann claims that if Jesus' proclamation had no socio-ethical content or claims, then he cannot be seen as God's Messiah fulfilling the Old Testament history of promise. In other words, to formulate ethics without reference to Christ calls into question his messiahship (see, for example, *WJC*, 116-119). Christ, as the supreme revelation of God and the fulfilment of God's word of promise, is the fundamental measure of all theology and ethics.

Neither a kingdom ethics, nor a creation ethics, approach is entirely satisfactory; and as such, more thought on this issue is required by those evangelicals engaged in the social ethics debate. An approach will have to be formulated which maintains a distinction between the activity of God as Creator and as Redeemer, and which also gives a central place to christology. Indeed, it is important to recognise that the kingdom and the new creation do not cancel the creation order, but rather fulfil God's purposes for it. Our socio-ethical framework need not be a choice between creation and kingdom, but rather can begin with creation restored, fulfilled and transformed in the kingdom of God. In other words, an ethical framework need not opt for one perspective only, but can be developed in the light of redemptive history as a whole, beginning with creation and ending with new creation.

In outlining the proposal of Stephen Mott, Richard Mouw and Oliver O'Donovan is the following chapter we will examine three differing evangelical attempts to develop just such an approach to social involvement. These attempts share a concern to develop an approach to social action on the basis of what Mouw calls 'the biblical drama' of creation, fall, redemption and consummation. The order in which they are examined is determined by, what in our view is, the progressively satisfactory nature of their proposals.

CHAPTER 11

Sin and Redemption: Stephen Charles Mott

Stephen Mott has been one of the more influential contributors to evangelical discussions on social ethics. Mott's essay on the use of the New Testament in social ethics (1984i/1984ii) played a key role in the development of a theological framework for the rediscovery of social involvement among evangelicals. Mott also shares with Moltmann and, as we shall see, Richard Mouw the influence of the sixties: he even quotes approvingly one of the great icons of the sixties, Che Guevara (1982:51). And like Volf, Mott was a contributor to the Oxford Conference on Christian Faith and Economics process, giving one of the main papers at the first Oxford conference in 1987 (see Mott, 1987; see also Mott, 1993i and Beisner, 1993, where Mott dialogues with Calvin Beisner on the Oxford Declaration's approach to justice). But Mott's main contribution to the on-going debates has been his book, *Biblical Ethics and Social Change* (1982) and it is upon this that our examination of Mott will focus, although reference will be made to his other works, especially his more recent book, *A Christian Perspective on Political Thought* (1993ii).

Biblical Ethics and Social Change is divided into two parts. The second looks at the different ways in which Christians may choose to involve themselves in social change. The first, which is more germane to our concerns, attempts to develop 'a biblical theology of social involvement' (ix).

The Social Reality of Sin

Mott begins by examining the social reality of sin. The New Testament term 'world' is one of the key ways in which the Bible describes evil. Although the term is used in different ways in the New Testament, its most striking use is of 'the twisted values which threaten genuine human life ... a system of values which are in opposition to God' (5-6). Not only does sin express itself at this social level, but Mott does not discount the effect of supernatural evil beings upon corporate life. His concern, however, is not to discuss whether angels and demons should be demythologised, but to come to terms with the social realities to which their biblical existence points. 'The biblical concepts of *cosmos* and the supernatural powers comprise an objective social reality which can function for good or for evil'. (10) The complexity of modern life means there are frequently problems for which there seem to be no solutions or for which attempts at solutions only create new problems. Mott cites Moltmann speaking of these phenomena as 'vicious circles' which is Moltmann's term for 'unjust systems' (see *SL*, 139). Mott speaks of 'hopeless economic, social and political pattern formations which drive life toward death' (13, citing Moltmann, *CG*, 293, 329).

Mott's point is not that we are without responsibility for social evil, but rather that we can only exercise responsibility through an awareness of the social reality of evil. Insensitivity to social evil often dulls our comprehension of our responsibility in regard to social sin. Mott cites familiar biblical texts (Isaiah 1:18 and Jeremiah 17:9) pointing out that, although often applied at the level of individual sinfulness, they come in the context of social sin and injustice. 'Social evil lies close to home. The powers which rule through the *cosmos* speak with a familiar voice.' (18) The reality of social evil does not take away our responsibility, rather it is only as we are aware of this reality that we can become genuinely responsible. Social involvement does not require Christians to weaken their piety, but rather to extend it into the social realm (see also Mouw, 1983:69-72). The drift of Mott's argument throughout the chapter is that if sin has social dimensions then our struggle against sin will include social involvement.

This emphasis upon the social dimensions of evil results in Mott taking a pragmatic approach to politics. He says, 'Power is denounced frequently in religious circles' (1993ii:13); but he has no sympathy for this. He appreciates that power can be used both for good and for evil and so, in *A Christian Perspective on Political Thought*, he distinguishes between what he calls 'defensive power' and 'exploitive power'. Defensive power is the power to carry out one's will in accordance with God's purposes; exploitive power is a selfish pervasion of this. Thus, if we are committed to social justice we must acknowledge the need for a third form of power, 'intervening power'. 'Intervening power restores defensive power by defeating exploitive power.' (1993ii:21) It is the failure to perceive the pervasiveness of exploitive power that leads some to advocate individualistic solutions or social non-involvement (1993ii:20).

This discussion of the social reality also sets the context for the coming of God's kingdom – which Mott consistently refers to as his 'Reign' – and its implications for Christian action. 'We serve a different order, the Reign of Christ, which he sets up in contrast to the prevailing way of life in the social order as supported by the fallen powers.' (1982:18) Christ has disarmed the powers (Colossians 2:15), but mutual hostility continues until their final subjugation at Christ's return. 'By faith we live in Christ's victory, yet we must continue to struggle.' (1982:18) The Reign of God, suggests Mott, should be seen as God's creative, intervening power (1993ii:21), although at the same time Mott suggests that God's intervening power is normally exerted through human beings fulfilling the mandate of creation (1993ii:22). Throughout Mott's work there is an implicit assumption that eschatology functions, not as an escapist force, but as a liberating force. Faced with an evil world order, we should not cocoon ourselves in hopes of the future, instead we are freed to serve and struggle by the presence and coming of a different order.

In *A Christian Perspective on Political Thought*, the tension between good and evil is particularly strong. Mott looks at power, human nature, intermediate social groups and government in turn. In each case, the focus is upon the tension between their goodness and their corruption. This is reflected in the chapter titles: 'The Goodness and Corruption of Power'; 'Doing Human Nature Justice'; 'Groups in Society: Danger and Deliverance'; and 'To Seek and to Distrust Government'. Significantly, in each case Mott draws political consequences from the corruption of each category rather than its essential goodness. Even Mott's treatment of love and justice is to some degree shaped by this tension. Although they are in continuity, 'the depth and pervasiveness of sin requires love to be expressed in justice (1993ii:93).

Eschatology and Human Action

Having begun with the extent of human sin, Mott turns to redemption, examining the relationship between God's grace and our action. Social action, he argues, is not a piety of works but starts with the cross. Social action builds upon God's grace (1982:22). God is the basis of Christian ethics, and the ground of his claim upon us is his grace in Christ. Having heard what God has done for us through his grace, we now hear his word of obligation. Not only are our social ethics based on grace, but they are also patterned on grace. They are to reflect the self-service and sacrifice of the cross, and God's unconditional love and acceptance of us. And it is through grace that we are empowered to serve God and others.

In some respects Mott's thought at this point mirrors that of Moltmann:

> The special grace of God in Christ's death and resurrection quickens our impatience with oppression and affliction. Because Christ was subjected to the depth of suffering and oppression in his death yet was raised victoriously, we can hope that the vicious circle of human suffering may be broken through by the sovereignty of God. Because in God's grace we 'have experienced healing in our life together, we cannot be content in the knowledge that there is brokenness and suffering in the world.' (30)

It is worthy of note, that this paragraph has a footnote reference to Moltmann, (*CG*, 317; and the citation is from Mouw, 1973:91). Like Moltmann, the believer is brought into contradiction with present reality – grace 'quickens our impatience', 'we cannot be content'. For Moltmann, however, the contradiction arises from the contrast between the present and the promise of the *future* while for Mott (and Mouw) it arises from the contrast between the brokenness of the world and our *present* experience of salvation – the 'healing in our life together' which we 'have experienced'. Yet, in common with Moltmann, there is a failure to reckon with the biblical themes of patience and endurance. Throughout the New Testament the promise (and present anticipation) of the future evokes patience and endurance. For Mott, as for Moltmann, it 'quickens our impatience'. Whatever the truth of this, it is clearly not the whole picture.

But perhaps more problematic is the statement that the resurrection of Christ gives 'hope that the vicious circle of human suffering may be broken'. Mott is more judicious that Moltmann. For Moltmann the resurrection is a wholly eschatological event without historical analogy, so that he can say that it is not susceptible to historical proof (or disproof), but only to eschatological proof. The problem is that it is then difficult to see what hope it brings to history. The resurrection may bring hope *for* history, for its ultimate transformation and consummation, but it is another matter to suggest that it brings hope *to* history, or *in* history, for transformation prior to the eschaton.

While citing Moltmann, Mott modifies his thought with the suggestion that 'the vicious circle of human suffering *may* be broken through the sovereignty of God' (emphasis added). If God can raise Christ in victory, the one who suffered and was oppressed, then he can do so for any who suffer or are oppressed. Yet experience suggests that, prior to the parousia, he does not always do so and so the best Mott can offer is that he may. Furthermore, when he does so it is, according to Mott, 'through his sovereignty'. It is difficult then to see what the resurrection adds to, say, the exodus from Egypt. If God can release a suffering and oppressed people through the exodus, then he can do so for any who suffer or are oppressed. The logic is the same.

Yet clearly the resurrection does add something. It brings the promise of eternal life and eschatological transformation. Mott offers an uncertain hope of historical change, while hope in the New Testament always speaks of the certain hope of eschatological redemption. If the eschatological kingdom of God has entered history through the resurrection of Christ, then we might be justified in suggesting that it can affect the behaviour of those who are part of that reign, and through them affect human history. But it is quite another thing to suggest that, in some general way, the resurrection brings hope for an end to (some) suffering and oppression in history. This is to confuse or merge proximate hope (optimism) and the certain eschatological hope for a new creation.

There is a similarity in structure between *Biblical Ethics and Social Change* and *A Christian Perspective on Political Thought*. And the chapter in the latter which corresponds to the chapter in *Biblical Ethics* on eschatology is entitled 'The Politics of Time'. The material on the Reign of God is very similar, but there is a much greater emphasis upon time and history – past, present and future. This emphasis is needed not only because different ideologies reflect different views of history, argues Mott, but more critically because Christ is at the centre of history. Understanding politics in the light of God's purposes in history counters those who would divorce salvation from responsible involvement (1993ii:97). Drawing heavily upon Reinhold Niebuhr (1964), Mott acknowledges that human beings cannot overcome the problems of history because of the limitations of human nature. We are finite and we have rejected trust in God. The result is that even as the kingdom of God grows in history, so there is a growth and intensification of evil. As such, 'regardless of their misuse, the concepts of the antichrist and the tribulation belong to a biblical perspective of history' (1993ii:99).

Given human rebellion and consequent evil, we are dependent on divine atonement. Through the incarnation of Christ, history has become the locus of salvation. Mott argues, for example, that it is significant that, in contrast to the Gospel of Thomas, the four canonical gospels are all narratives. The Gospel of Thomas consists of sayings without historical context, removing Jesus to a timeless, immaterial world. Mott concludes, 'The capacity of history to have meaning is reflected in all the events of salvation-history' (1993ii:101). The different events which lead to our final salvation 'weave into the fabric of history', even as they are transcended by the Reign of God. Salvation is not delivery from history, but involves it receiving its 'completeness' (1993ii:102). To see salvation as 'only the total, apocalyptic redemption of history' does not reflect the biblical heritage and forces politics to exist 'apart from grace' (1993ii:102).

Referring to Moltmann's *Theology of Hope*, Mott says that the promise 'draws the mind to the future in creative and obedient expectation' (1993ii:107). And again, like Moltmann, he argues that 'for much of its history the church has lost its powerful vision of the future'. He goes on to cite the famous passage from the prologue of *Theology of Hope* in which Moltmann argues that eschatology has all too frequently been seen as an appendix to dogmatics, rather than the medium of theological thought. Mott concludes: 'When the future Reign of God is taken seriously as a reality confronting the present, human energies are stimulated for efforts to bring about change in the certainty of the abiding meaning of such labour ... The Judæo-Christian idea of time encourages rational planning for the future. Since time is linear and contains purpose, preparation for the future is worthwhile.' (1993ii:107-8) Mott, however, does not correlate the idea of 'the future Reign' and 'rational planning'. The consequences of a linear view of time for rational planning are one thing, the consequences of the future Reign for such planning are another, and Mott does not spell these out. Mott himself acknowledges that 'optimism leads to shoddy planning' (1993ii:140). But how does hope for an ultimate future improve on optimism when it comes to planning for the imminent future? Mott does not say.

Furthermore, a 'certain future' might equally be taken to be a disincentive for present activity. If we are certain all will be well, why should we expend our energies in effecting historical change? Mott himself says that ' confidence about the future obfuscates the need for and possibilities of radical political change' (1993ii:141). He speaks here of the optimistic view of historical progress characteristic of liberalism. But why should Mott's confident hope for an ultimate future be any more conducive to radical change that the optimism of liberalism?

The Centrality of Love

If Christian ethics begins with God's grace, then its principle form, suggests Mott, is love. Christian ethics are grounded in love (1982:40). And love is social in dimension, for it is itself grounded in God's providential love for all. Love gives worth to every person. If God loves all people, all people have worth, even the weak and sinful for it was while we were weak and sinful that Christ died for us (Romans 5:6-10). It is not that God sees a worth in us that others have missed, but that through his love, he bestows worth on us. Although Mott speaks of the command to love being grounded in God's providential love to all, it is clear that the atonement features more strongly in his reasoning. He cites Paul Ramsey, 'call no man vile for whom Christ died' (1982:43).

If the command to love is to be grounded in the atonement, the question of its scope is raised. If, as Williams suggests, hope is limited as a social ethic because we cannot hope for the eschatological redemption of all, then surely, by the same token, an ethic based on the atonement will be limited by the scope of the atonement. If one holds to particular redemption, then will the scope of the command to love be limited to the elect? Mott argues not. Just as we can never know who the elect are and so we invite all to come to Christ, so likewise, not knowing the elect, we must love all *as if* they were those for whom Christ died – since they might be! Indeed, because the elect are chosen without regard for virtue, status and intellect, so we will love all without discrimination (1982:48).

If Mott claims that love is central to social ethics, what predominates in his thought is the theme of justice. Part Two of *Biblical Ethics and Social Change* is called 'Paths to Justice' with the implication that the pursuit of justice is the conclusion to the biblical theology of social involvement in Part One. And the theme of justice is of significance to our concerns since justice is, as we shall see, central to Mott's understanding of the implications of eschatology.

This emphasis on justice, however, does not represent an inconsistency with Mott's assertion that love is central, for he argues that justice and love are in continuity (1987:32; 1993ii:89-96). What love desires, justice demands. Just as love is the meaning of the law, so the justice expressed in the law gives content to love. 'An essential part of the Law, the meaning of which love discloses and the content of which is made complete in love, is justice' (1982:49). It is through justice that love can be expressed as a social ethic. 'Love creates images of itself potent for discerning social responsibility. Three elements in Christian love contained seeds of the recognition of human rights: equality, respect, and perception of common needs.' (1982:49)

The Partiality of Justice

Central to Mott's understanding of justice is its partiality (see Chapter 4: 'God's Justice and Ours', 1982:59-81; 1993i; 1993ii:74-88) and this has important consequences for his eschatology. Justice is not an impartial adjudication according to some abstract code or civic law, but a creative intervention on behalf of the needy. Justice 'requires taking the side of the poor against what has been advantageous to the rich' (1984i:23). This partiality of justice, Mott argues, is strongly expressed in the Mosaic law. Nevertheless, it is applicable to all ages, for it is rooted in the character of God who defends the fatherless and the widow, and whose righteousness is expressed in his salvific intervention on behalf of the poor and oppressed. Mott emphasises the partiality of justice because he sees poverty arising from social conflict, from the exercise of repressive power. His view of justice thus underlies his eschatology, for Mott sees the kingdom of God as an intervening power and as a kingdom of creative, partial justice.

This emphasis on the centrality of justice, and the partiality of that justice, has perhaps been Mott's key contribution to evangelical debates, albeit one which has not been without its critics. It featured prominently in his contribution to the first Oxford Conference on Christian Faith and Economics (1987). Indeed, those who responded to his paper feared an over-emphasis on this theme to the neglect of other themes, such as stewardship and wealth creation (see Wan, 1987 and Middelmann, 1987). The Oxford Declaration on Christian Faith and Economics (1990) says that 'biblical justice means impartially rendering to everyone their due in conformity with the standards of God's moral law' (Par. 38). At the same time, it says that Paul uses justice to describe 'God's creative and powerful redemptive love' (Par. 38) and that 'justice requires conditions such that each person is able to participate in society in a way compatible with human dignity. Absolute poverty ... denies people the basic economic resource for just participation in the community. Corrective action with, and on behalf of, the poor is a necessary act of justice' (Par. 40). The tension between the impartiality and partiality of justice, expressed in these statements, is resolved when the Declaration says: 'Justice requires special attention to the weak members of the community because of their greater vulnerability. In this sense justice is partial. Nevertheless, the civil arrangements in rendering justice are not to go beyond what is due to the poor or to the rich (Deuteronomy 1:17; Leviticus 19:15). In this sense justice is ultimately impartial.' (Par. 39)

After the second Oxford conference, Mott engaged in a dialogue with Calvin Beisner (see Mott, 1993i and Beisner, 1993). Beisner, a participant at the second Oxford Conference on Christian Faith and Economics, was critical of the Oxford Declaration. He accused it of expressing two mutually exclusive views of justice, namely, justice as impartial and justice as partial. The latter he vigorously refuted (see also Middelmann, 1987). In response, Mott mounts an equally vigorous defence of the view that biblical justice is partial.

Despite the focus on the biblical usage of the term 'justice', at the heart of their disagreements are differing perspectives on the root cause of poverty. So, while Beisner stresses the impartiality of biblical justice, he seems to have no problem with the notion that there is a sense in which justice is partial – that special attention be shown to the poor – in order for justice to be ultimately impartial. And, while Mott argues that it is impartial only by being partial, he states that the poor are not to receive more than their just claims. 'The bias toward the weak which is the most striking characteristic of biblical justice does not mean that God loves the poor more nor that they should receive more than their just claims. The poor are given priority only because their wretchedness requires greater attention if the equality called forth by the equal merit of all person in the community is to be achieved.' (1993i:24-5) Beisner criticises Mott's claim that justice requires the provision of basic needs to the poor. This, he claims, contradicts Paul's injunction that those who do not work should not eat (2 Thessalonians 3:10). He fears that such a claim means providing material and social goods regardless of desert (1993:16). But Mott side-steps this by asserting that 'those who can provide for their basic needs but chose not to are not needy' (1993i:26).

The real issue is that each has a different perspective on the cause of poverty. Beisner acknowledges that in the Bible justice comes to the aid of those who are poor because of oppression. But he sees poverty largely as arising from sloth, failure or misfortune. In such circumstances, charity grounded in grace is the appropriate response and this should not be confused with justice. Beisner fears seeing justice and love in continuity, since he thinks that this compromises the grace of the gospel.

Mott, as we have noted above, acknowledges that poverty can be caused by personal failure, but he sees it primarily in terms of social conflict. 'The image of society presumed in the Bible ... is of a society characterised by conflict between the mighty and the lowly ... The image of conflict in the Bible corresponds to its understanding of human nature. There sin is a deep principle which ... is reflected in the power of exploitation in social relations ... In the face of such social strife, justice requires an intervening power.' (1987:26-7) Or again: 'In the raging social struggles in which the poor are perennially victims of injustice and denied basic needs, God takes up the cause of the weak, and thus the followers of God do as well.' (1993i:25)

As we have noted already, Mott's emphasis on the social conflict and oppression which lie at the root of poverty, and, as a consequence, the partiality of biblical justice, are important for his eschatology. For when Mott draws out the implications of eschatology for social involvement, he emphasises the kingdom of God as a kingdom of justice.

The Radical Presence of the Reign of God

In order to capture the dynamic nature of the kingdom in New Testament, Mott consistently speaks of 'the Reign of God' rather than 'the kingdom of God' (1982:82-3). Throughout the Old Testament God was held to reign over the earth, but there arose a longing for that reign to be experienced in a fuller, more complete way. In Jesus that expectation is realised: the Reign is present (1982:83-8). Thus, while, as we shall see, Mott stresses that Jesus inherits the tradition of Old Testament teaching on social ethics, he also fulfils it.

As fulfilment Jesus' death and resurrection are the central acts of the coming of the Reign. The Reign breaks into the lives of those who share in the new life in Christ, and into the world as the Gospel of grace through faith which bursts national boundaries. As a guide to the tradition, Jesus confirms the demands for the ordering of life already given and expected. He radicalises them, and clarifies their true meaning ... for Jesus, these are not wisdom maxims or legal commentary for a static society. Jesus' counsels are nothing other than the principles of conduct of God's Reign emerging in concrete form. (1984i:24)

The presence of the Reign 'radicalises' God's demands. 'The demands of justice and peace have been heightened in urgency' (1987:33). 'The demand of God upon us is intensified by anticipation of the future' (1982:91). 'Present actions take on a new urgency in the light of the high demands of the new age' (1984ii:20). Why are the demands of God 'heightened' and 'intensified'? Why do they take on as 'new urgency'? There is something of rhetorical flourish in Mott, but the answer appears to be, although Mott does not use these terms, that every moment is now an eschatological moment. 'The presence of the Reign of God reveals the future as salvation and judgment, and the imminence of the future Reign reveals today as the day of decision and action.' (1982:88) 'The final fulfilment of human hopes [is] near, but instead of postponing concern for the present, those ideals and the accompanying judgment sharpen the demand on the present. The fruits of the Reign of God [are] expected now at the threshold of its arrival.' (1987:33) 'There is an eruption of the new into the present.' (1993ii:109)

Mott describes the church as the *avant-garde* of the future (1982:106, 129-30). 'The church is to be the community in which, through its behaviour and its mission, the Reign of God becomes visible, serving as precursor and *avant-garde* of the society that will be the fulfilment of all hope' (1982:106; Mott cites Padilla, 1985ii). 'It is the partial realisation of Christ's goal in history ...' (1982:130). Indeed, Mott states that the link between creation and redemption is the incarnation (1982:103), which he does little to develop except by saying that the church 'continues the incarnation' and so 'contributes to the cosmic task of reconciliation' (1982:103).

The ethics of Jesus are ethics of the Reign of God, not ethics of preparation or waiting (1982:89). And as we have seen, the coming of the Reign means Christians are now part of a new order, one that contrasts and conflicts with the present sinful order (1982:18). 'A new order is rivalling the old' (1984i:24). The coming of God's kingdom relativises the institutions of the present. Speaking of the corporate witness of the Christian community, Mott speaks of the 'withdrawal of support from practices contrary to the in-breaking of the reign' (1982:135) Indeed Mott, using language redolent of Moltmann, says: 'The expectation creates a tendency toward change. The fact that the hopes include relief for those suffering in their present economic and social conditions provides a massive critique of the present political realm. Present structures and institutional procedures should never be taken for granted.' (1987:31) The language evokes Moltmann's understanding of an objective, ontological tendency towards the future and a subjective experience in which believers are placed in contradiction to the present and oriented to the future. In Mott, however, it is probably best, despite his citing of Moltmann at this point, to think of this as 'an assumption of change'. A social ethic, in other words, which contains the perspective of the coming and future of the Reign of God will be one which is most naturally oriented towards change. The future of the Reign of God makes change desirable, its presence makes it possible. 'The Reign of God ... incorporates the imperative for social responsibility into God's goals for history' (1982:82).

The Realistic Practice of Justice

And yet, just as the Reign of God relativizes the present order and its institutions, so the application of the Reign of God and its ethics to that situation 'will be necessarily partial and realistically conceived' (1987:30; see also 1982:202-4; 1984ii:22-3 and 1987:33). Recognising this, our ethics will be realistic and practical. Reform may come 'through a cumulative series of partial steps' (1982:202). At the same time, 'we will not abandon the vision of the Reign of God, which still must guide us' (1987:30). 'The awareness that we cannot build a perfect society in history must not deflect us from the obligation to work for a better society' any more than our pursuit of personal righteousness is not deflected by our realisation that perfection is only attained with the return of Christ (1982:91). Given this tension, says Mott, 'we must be faithful to whatever possibility of implementation God opens to us in our historical moment' (1987:33). The purpose of God and our responsibility is, as it were, to 'narrow the gap' as opportunity allows (1982:90; see Williams' comments on this phrase, 1989i:263-4).

The centrality of justice in Mott's social thought spills over into his exposition of the implications of the eschatology. The Reign of God that has come in Christ is a reign of justice: 'justice is made part of the story of God's provision' (1982:82). The Old Testament focus on the partiality of justice finds fulfilment in the ministry of Jesus. 'Behind the New Testament lies an authoritative text which demonstrates deep concern for the social order, for justice, for the economic and social relationships of the powerful and the weak.

New Testament writers have interpreted new life in Christ in continuity with the Old Testament's social hopes and concerns.' (1984i:22) The writers of the New Testament interpreted their experiences in the light of the Old Testament 'including its message of justice' (1984i:22). Mott gives examples of the way in which the New Testament presupposes Old Testament teaching on justice and sees this as fulfilled in Christ and the coming of God's Reign (1982:93,97-100; 1984i:21-4; 1987:33). Thus, for example: 'Jesus is linked to the Old Testament social tradition in which the leaders of Israel are called to account for their violation of God's covenant through acts of injustice ... Groups in the Old Testament who are recipients of justice, such as the sick, the poor, and the widow ... frequently appear in the Gospels ... To identify such classes of victims presupposes some perception of the social organism which exploits or excludes them.' (1984i:22) As a consequence, 'the Reign of God ... makes the injustices and exploitations inherited from the past outdated as remnants of a past which is already being destroyed' (1993ii:109). Or again: 'The Reign of God breaking into history brings a demand for justice that must affect the political outlook of those who seek this Reign' (1982:100).

The Extent of the Kingdom in the Present

If the coming of the Reign of God means the coming of a reign of justice, does this mean that the coming of justice, when this is seen in society, is a sign of the coming of that Reign? The statement cited above suggests that key to the relationship between the Reign of God and the emergence of justice in society are the 'demands' of those 'who seek this Reign'. Other statements by Mott, however, appear to go further. 'The political task receives a new dynamic with the Reign of God breaking into history. The new social order that God is creating intermingles with and acts upon and against the old order, which it will some day replace.' (1982:194) Is this an assertion that the eschatological Reign of God exists outside of the church? Again, it could be read as implying that the Reign of God 'intermingles' with the old order through the work and witness of those who acknowledge that Reign. It could, but it is not the most obvious reading. The same is true of the following: 'This triumph of God is actual in history to the extent that the destructive demonic forces are broken. If we limit the presence of the Reign to action within the church, we neglect this work of God upon the forces which govern social history. Historical struggles are not irrelevant to the coming of God's full Reign.' (1982:96) Although Mott again employs something of a rhetorical flourish, it would seem that he is referring to what others might label the providence of God in history. This raises the question of the newness of God's Reign. How is the 'work of God upon the forces which govern social history' new or different from his actions, say, in the exodus? And, if social advance is to be understood as the Reign of God, how are we to understand its contingency?

It is perhaps significant that, when Mott begins to amplify the relevancy of 'historical struggles' to the fullness of God's Reign, he speaks of 'the small victories *in which we share*' (1982:96, emphasis added). While the kingdom of God may not be restricted to action 'within' the church in a narrow ecclesiastical sense, it is an open question whether we should see it in more than action in and through the church. The 'spill-over' effect of the kingdom, of which the Grand Rapids Report speaks, may not be action 'within' the church but it nevertheless remains action 'through' the church, through those who acknowledge the king. In *A Christian Perspective on Political Thought* Mott is more explicit: 'Even historical change outside of the church and *outside of the church's influence* upon its culture relates to the presence of the kingdom. The scope of God's kingdom work is not confined to the church.' (1993ii:111; emphasis added)

Mott recognises the problems involved in identifying such kingdom activity. Nevertheless, he argues that God's redemptive work and secular history should not be viewed in a dualistic way as two separate histories. Neither, he argues, should they be seen as one, for the unity of history will only be established with the final reconciliation at the end of history. In the meantime 'glimpses of that unity appear' (1993ii:111). 'The Reign is in creation itself in the measure that the creation follows the sovereign's orders, even in subconscious conformity' (1993ii:111). As such, 'where this conformity reflects an advance in justice, it participates from afar in the Reign of Christ' (1993ii:111). Mott, following Tillich, speaks of 'hidden forms of grace in secular life'.

Again, we might ask how we should distinguish the conformity of creation to the sovereign's orders from God's general providence? Or how we might distinguish the hidden forms of grace from God's providence and common grace? The point is not that God is not at work outside of the church – he has been since the first day of creation. The point is that in Christ the kingdom of God has come in a *new* way; the future has entered history. Mott, in his assertion that the kingdom is present outside the church, cannot account for this newness. He himself says, 'within the church Satan has been defeated in a decisive way not found beyond it ... the church provides *unique* visibility for God's Reign. (1993ii:111; emphasis added).

The Absence of a Doctrine of Creation

The emphasis in Mott on the social conflict and oppression which lie at the root of poverty is significant for it implies that poverty is not addressed simply by more effective stewardship or a more creative use of resources. This link between poverty and powerlessness is an important one, as are the conclusions Mott draws from it. But absent in Mott is a corresponding ethic of stewardship, of responsible work or wealth creation. In contrast, for example, are the 'Agra Affirmations on Christian Faith, Market Economics and the Poor' – one outcome of the third Oxford Conference on Christian Faith and Economics. Of the 31 theological affirmations made in that statement, twelve come under the title 'God, the creator and owner of all, entrusts his creation to human beings' (1995:5).

This omission in Mott is symptomatic of the somewhat ambiguous treatment that the theme of creation receives in Mott's thought. That creation has social implications Mott does not deny, but it does not figure prominently. Mott, for example, as we have noted, roots human dignity in the atoning love of God. Only secondarily, and in passing, does he mention, the creation of people in the image of God (though see also 1993ii:27). More significantly, his 'theology of social involvement' follows what Mouw calls 'the biblical drama' – sin, redemption and eschatology – but includes no chapter on creation. This is true in other essays by Mott (see, for example, 'The Contribution of the Bible to Economic Thought' (1987) where there is a focus upon the Mosaic law and upon Jesus, but not upon creation).

One symptom of this ambiguity is Mott's assertion that 'to the old order there *must* be enmity' (1982:18, my emphasis). What is meant by the 'old order'? Mott acknowledges that, although affected by sin, the social order and social institutions are not intrinsically evil, as Paul makes clear in Romans 13 (1982:15). Yet if the institutions are created good, can our relationship to them be simply one of enmity? Mott clearly means the old order as it stands in opposition to God, 'the social order as supported by the fallen powers'. But without a more thorough discussion of creation we are offered no basis upon which to distinguish this from the created order to which we are to submit. Are political and social institutions to be written off entirely as a result of the fall? Mott's own discussion of creative reform through politics suggests otherwise (1982:192-208).

Discussing the possibility of 'strategic non-co-operation' (1982:142-166), Mott acknowledges that there is, within the Scriptures, a tension between the injunctions to submit to those in authority and those which call for non-conformity to this age. 'The command to submit reflects God's intention that the basic structures of society be instruments of good for his creation. The command to non-conformity is a recognition of the organisation of social life in opposition to God.' (1982:142) Having begun his discussion with the social reality of sin, however, it is 'the social life in opposition to God' that predominates over the 'instruments of good'.

In this respect Mott's approach contrasts with that of Mouw, whose thought his own closely resembles in many other ways. As we shall see, unlike Mott, Mouw begins his discussion of politics and the biblical drama with creation, and he works hard to establish that social and political institutions were created inherently good. He is no less realistic than Mott about the social impact of sin and the reality of social evil, but at the same time clearly maintains the normativeness of the creation order.

Creation and Sin

Part of the problem for Mott may lie in his dependence upon Tillich, and thus a tendency to conflate creation and fall, a feature we have seen in Moltmann's theology. Mott acknowledges at the beginning of *A Christian Perspective on Political Thought* (1993ii:) that he has drawn heavily upon the work of the Christian realists, including Paul Tillich. And Tillich's influence is discernible in Mott's exposition of power. But Tillich's understanding of Being and Non-being is also clear in Mott's understanding of human freedom and finitude (see 1993ii:29). 'Because of our finiteness and freedom, we are insecure. We are insecure because of our finiteness lest we come to meaninglessness ...We are also insecure because of freedom. We are anxious lest we be not what we ought to be.' (1993ii:30) At times, Mott sees our finitude as an expression of our limited power and knowledge. But at other times, echoing Tillich, he sees it as the threat of non-being, of death. The result is a merging of creation and fall. 'Eden shows that the source of evil lies in the very factors that makes us human/creatures, our freedom and our finiteness ... In our freedom ... we failed ... Dignity and risk are correlates ... Freedom means possibility, which is identical to temptation. Eden also shows the relationship between the source of evil and consciousness of our finiteness. In the garden we were tempted to overcome the confines assigned to us.' (1993ii:29)

Mott draws back from a total conflation. 'The dilemma of history goes much deeper,' he says, 'than our created limitations'. The root problem is 'our attempts to throw off those limitations placed upon us by our Creator'. (1993ii:98) Yet, even here, Mott argues that 'finite freedom creates the opportunity for sin' (1993ii:98). In one sense, Mott is content to say that finite freedom allows the possibility of sin: 'In the face of such insecurity one can either trust God ... or one can continue in anxiety ... The resource to trusting in God, however, may be rejected. It follows that unbelief, the rejection of God, not anxiety, is the root of sin.' (1993ii:30) And yet at times he goes further, 'Sin arises in the very conditions of our being a creature ... Sin appears in our very essence' (1993ii:29). And so 'God vicariously suffered and died for human iniquity' because 'no human power could provide a solution for the condition of finiteness and freedom that is at the basis of historical existence' (1995:99). What created the need for divine atonement? Human sin and rebellion? Or are we to see a more fundamental and underlying problem, namely 'the condition of finiteness and freedom'? Mott seems to suggest the latter. It is an ambiguity that reflects the ambiguous place that creation has in Mott's thought.

Although the theme of creation is not allowed to stand on its own, it does feature in Mott's discussion of eschatology. The Reign of God initiates 'a renewal of the situation at the creation' (1984ii:22; see also 1987:25). 'The coming of this new rule of God is that salvation in which God's creation is renewed in such a way that creation and redemption become merged'

(1984i:23). Or again: 'Creation and salvation do not exist as distinct spheres of divine action ... Divine actions are interrelated and God's purpose in history has a unity (1982:101-2). Yet what Mott is saying is simply that the eschatological future is not a second work of God replacing the original creation, but the fulfilment of God's purposes in creation.

In his essay, 'The Use of the New Testament' (1984ii), Mott takes up Ernst Troeltsch's distinction between absolute and relative natural law. 'Natural law,' says Mott, 'reflects the conviction that moral obligation should correspond to the nature of the world as God created and maintained it' (22) – although, as we have suggested, this 'moral obligation' does not feature significantly in Mott's own thought. He continues by arguing that absolute natural law reflects creation as God intended it to be, while relative natural law takes into account the effects of the fall. There is a sense in which this distinction can guide Christian action in a pluralistic society. Nevertheless, Mott in effect uses the distinction to show that the in-breaking of the kingdom re-relativises, that is to say, re-enforces the relativization of, relative natural law.

> By drawing normatively upon the original state, Jesus shows that these ideal standards continue to govern human relationships beyond the fall. God's Reign breaking into history is restoring lost creation ... We may say that in New Testament ethics concrete commands ... correspond to the concessions of relative natural law and have value in the situations for which they are intended. They are, however, in tension with the demands of creation reiterated in the new order. Thus the absolute natural law remains available in its critical function. (1984ii:22)

The tendency in Mott's thought, although he does not state it in these terms, is to suggest that, with the coming of sin into the world, the creation ethic is no longer normative, or at least no longer practicable. It becomes normative again, however, with the in-breaking of God's kingdom when the restoration of creation begins.

In his later work, *A Christian Perspective on Political Thought*, Mott is harder on relative natural law, regarding it as an acceptance of the fall, used by the comfortable, to justify the necessities of a fallen world like inequitable property distribution and war (94). The result is that the guiding principle of Christian social involvement becomes the maintenance of the present order. Social change is seen either as impossible or likely to lead to further anarchy and sinfulness. Attempts at change are therefore confined to individuals. Mott comments, 'This attitude makes more sense for individuals who are already materially and socially comfortable in life' (94; see also 116-8,130).

With Mott, as with Moltmann (and Volf), it is axiomatic that theology should be employed to effect social change. Like Moltmann, Mott is sensitive to the Marxist accusation that theology, and in particular eschatology, functions as a disincentive to social change, as opiate for the people. He believes that Western forms of Christianity – both liberal and evangelical – must be 'reformed' if they are to provide a spiritual base for social change because they 'have been permeated with the individualism of the conquering middle class' (149). For Mott, the future of the Reign of God legitimises change, while the reality of social evil makes change necessary, and the presence of the Reign of God makes change possible. That first statement, however, that the Reign of God legitimises social change, remains problematic. The linkage remains ambiguous. As with Moltmann, there is the suspicion that Mott expects too much from eschatology because he sees too little in creation.

CHAPTER 12

The Biblical Drama: Richard Mouw

One of the more prominent evangelical thinkers on social involvement from the Reformed tradition has been Richard Mouw. In particular, Mouw's book *Politics and the Biblical Drama* has had a widespread influence upon the debates that have shaped the recommitment to social involvement by evangelicals. But Mouw has not simply contributed to the debate from outside as it were. He himself was a participant at the Chicago Workshop in 1973. The conferences described at the beginning of chapter seven as the major contributors to, and indicators of, the shift in evangelical thinking towards social concern represent only international gatherings. Around the world, national and regional conferences have had an equally important impact within their localities. The Chicago Workshop was perhaps the most significant of these for the United States, bringing together the younger generation, shaped by the radical movements of the sixties, with more mainstream evangelical figures. Mouw has also continued to feed into evangelical debates through regular contributions to *Christianity Today*.

Mouw addresses himself to the same social and cultural context addressed by Moltmann's *Theology of Hope*. *Politics and the Biblical Drama* was written in 1976 when, says Mouw, 'Western culture [was] experiencing a mood of political and institutional disillusionment'; a mood which expressed itself in 'challenges to traditional modes of human interaction' (16). Family, classroom and church had all been questioned. In the preface to his earlier book, *Political Evangelism* (1973), Mouw describes the commitment of large numbers of young people in the 'sixties to non-violent witness for the cause of justice and peace – a commitment that was often costly. It was a commitment borne of the hope that 'we shall overcome someday'. Writing in 1973, however, Mouw describes how many have lost that conviction and have become cynical and embittered. He comments: 'A hope based on mere conviction or feeling cannot long be sustained. The Christian's social-political hope goes deeper than this. The Christian's belief that "we shall overcome" is firmly rooted in his experience of the objective person and work of Jesus Christ.' (92-93) Indeed, Mouw describes how his concern to develop a political theology arose from his own personal struggles with the issues of his generation. His conservative evangelical background, he claims, did not equip him with the concerns over social injustice, racism and militarism that characterised his time as a graduate student in secular universities. Out of this experience, rose a commitment to political involvement, but to a 'political involvement firmly grounded in submission to the Word of God in obedience to the Lord of the church' (1973:7).

As the title suggests, in *Political Evangelism* Mouw was determined to see personal evangelism and political engagement as part of 'the *unity* of the mission of the church in the world' (8). By speaking of 'political evangelism', Mouw sought not only to correct those who either disparage political activity in favour of evangelism or so narrow the scope of evangelism as to marginalize it, but also to correct those who accept both, but in a way that makes political involvement less central to the Christian calling.

Mouw's response is to go back to the biblical drama, to answer questions about the ground and nature of social relationships and political patterns in the light of the biblical drama's central acts: creation, fall, redemption and consummation.

Creation

When Mouw examines creation, he begins with the image of God. Conceding that the significance of this has created a complex and indecisive debate, Mouw nevertheless believes there is still much to be learnt from such attempts. He believes that it is clear that 'sociality and dominion play a central role in God's creative will for human beings' (1976:28). As such, he concludes that 'human beings were created for positive social co-operation with each other, to perform certain tasks with respect to the rest of creation, in obedience to the will of the Creator' (1976:28). In other words, being made in the image of God implies not just sociality, but sociality in certain ways, namely, co-operation in the task of dominion over creation in obedience to the Creator.

Mouw asks the question, Was there a political order prior to the fall? (1976:32-36). He rejects the argument that politics is about coercion, and that, since there was no coercion prior to the fall, there was no political order, no master-servant or ruler-subject relationships. Mouw argues that there are master-servant relationships in the redeemed community and in the consummated kingdom. There was clearly no civil government in Eden with a population of just two, but this does not mean that there was no provision for civil government. Mouw speculates what might have happened without sin and with a growing population (1976:36; see also 1973:45-47). Why should there not emerge an intermediary level – a hierarchy – between God and individuals in the political sphere?

Mouw's concern is to show that politics is rooted in creation. The speculation is clearly just that, speculation. It could as easily be speculated that the family would have remained the sole social structure. Indeed, Mouw's speculation has more to do with the consummated order than the opening chapters of Genesis. 'How it will be' reveals – at least to some extent – 'how it would have been without sin.' (1976:33) Mouw's argument that social structures would have developed if there had been no fall cannot be proved. He himself provides elsewhere the basis for an alternative reading when he describes how God takes historical development into account in his eschatological purposes. If God can take Israel's rebellious request for a human king and make that kingship a feature of the messianic promises, then God could take all political institutions and make them part of the eschatological kingdom. Mouw's argument, however, is not dependent on what may or may not have happened apart from the fall. It is sufficient for him to show that there is a viable alternative to the suggestion that the political order is the product of the fall: the result of, or a counter-measure to, the intrusion of sin into human affairs. The central feature of Mouw's argument is not what might or might not have happened without the fall, but rather that political structures are not necessarily the tainted product of human sinfulness.

It is important for Mouw to affirm the pre-fall nature of political institutions, particularly when he comments on the Anabaptist-Reformed dialogue on politics (1976:97-116). If all political structures are products of the fall, if they are all manipulative and oppressive to some degree, then, as John Howard Yoder argues, Christian are bound to resist their power, albeit in Yoder's case, by revolutionary subordination (1972). If, however, political structures were part of God's original intention in creation, it seems legitimate to call them to function in accordance with that intention, albeit recognising the provisionality of human politics prior to the parousia (1976:105). In response to those who argue that it is illegitimate to attempt an imposition of theocratic ideals in a non-theocratic context, Mouw points to the prophets Amos and Jeremiah who, in addressing the nations surrounding Israel, were calling upon those non-theocratic nations to acknowledges at least some theocratic principles.

The Fall

If political structures are not the product of the fall, Mouw is under no illusions that the fall has a profound effect on the political order. The Serpent portrays God as a deceiving despot: an accusation which, if true, would legitimise human rebellion. But, not only does the biblical account of creation and fall paint a very different picture of God, the story of redemption challenges this false notion of the lordship of God.

> The story of the reclamation of fallen humanity directly confronts the revisionist doctrine of God [put forward by the Serpent] that precipitated the fall into sin. Over and over, human beings must hear the refrain, "You have misunderstood; that is not what it means to be a 'lord'". Finally God himself must become a member of sinful humanity, so that human beings can once again cry out in surprised joy: "At last! flesh of my flesh and bone of my bone!" "The Word became flesh and dwelt among us, full of grace and truth" (John 1:14). The lie of

the Tempter is decisively exposed when the incarnate Son says, "Look! This is what it means to be a 'lord'": and "he emptied himself, taking the form of a servant ... and become obedient unto death, even death on a cross" (Philippians 2:7-8). (1976:41)

Not only has humanity accepted the lie of the Serpent, but it has additionally sought to conform to this false model of lordship. 'Having revised their concept of "lordship" from the idea of a loving creator to that of a selfish despot, Adam and Eve aspired to this latter kind of lordship' (1976:41). The result is a concern for 'control' and 'management' in which politics and technology become ends in themselves, or law becomes more important than relationships (1976:46-48). This institutional oppression can take many forms, from clumsy bureaucracy to institutions created to satisfy the selfish desires of a powerful few (1976:50).

Mouw, however, insists that the fact that oppression can take corporate or institutionalised forms does not mean to say that institutional machinery, or decision-making procedures, are bad *per se*. We are not compelled to 'maximise spontaneity'. As he concluded from his discussion of creation, some form of standardised decision-making procedure might be appropriate in a sinless state of affairs (1976:51).

There is a link between these corporate expressions of sin and personal forms of oppression. 'Corporate injustice and the neurotic patterns that characterise collective interaction are results of the institutionalisation of this personal rebellion.' (1976:49) Nevertheless, 'these institutionalisations of the personal sinful project can come to have a life of their own'. As such, argues Mouw, simply 'changing hearts' is not sufficient to change society as many conservative evangelicals argue. 'If the manipulative patterns which are built into the very structures of social relationships are not changed, all of the effects of sin have not been challenged.' (1976:47-8) Indeed, Christianity itself can express what Mouw calls 'neurotic patterns', the most common example being legalism in which law takes the place of the relationship between the Creator and his human creatures.

Redemption

Mouw, then, outlines the effect of the fall upon human society and politics. But sin is not the last word: God has graciously acted to reclaim what was lost. 'Just as God's initial address to humanity was *as a plurality* to a plurality, so the work of redemption is one whereby the Triune God creates a new *people* ... The new community of the "people of God" constitutes the reinstatement of the social bond broken and distorted by human rebellion.' (1976:53) And so Mouw moves from the fall to redemption, and specifically to the church. His chapter on redemption is entitled 'Redeemed Society: The Church's Life and Mission'. The church, argues Mouw, occupies a central place in the revelation of God's social and political purposes for humanity, not simply because it is itself a social structure, but because it is to be a model for civil political structures *and* an agent for change. Parallels between ecclesiological and political structures are not coincidental. The church 'is intended by its very existence to be a model, even a revelation, of God's will for corporate life' (1976:56). This present calling to be a model of, and agent for, change is set in the context of its past and future relations. The church is a token of the past because in its midst God is renewing the creative purpose which was marred by sin. At the same time, the church is the sign, the firstfruits, of the kingdom which is to come (1976:56).

In *Political Evangelism*, Mouw says Christ's 'redemptive and reconciling activities do reach, of course, beyond the bounds of the church' (1973:107). Yet, says Mouw, we see this only 'in some mysterious way, incomprehensible to us' (1973:108). In fact, what Mouw has in view is 'his creating and sustaining power'. 'As we look and reflect on the apparent chaos and fragmentation of the world around us, it is not easy to see his power at work ... It is so much a mystery that to confess that he is working in and through these events would be to mouth empty platitudes were it not often so desperately important that we believe in *his creating and sustaining power.*' (1973:107-8; emphasis added) Indeed, when Mouw goes on to ask where Christ is among 'the hatred and sirens and bombs and angry cries', his answer is: 'Look at the church, it is there that we can experience the *hope* of glory' (1973:108).

> God in Jesus Christ is working out his purposes in the world. It is not obvious that he is doing so. But he is. And he has not left us without a witness, without a sign, of the glory that will some day be revealed in and through all that he has done. For the work he is carrying on secretly and mysteriously throughout the created order, even in this present time, is of a piece with the work he is doing openly in the body, the church. (1973:109)

On the one hand, Mouw confines the anticipation of the hope of glory to the church. And he restricts salvation to the confines of the church. 'It is no mere arbitrary stipulation on God's part that "outside the church there is no salvation." God calls us to the community in which he is restoring the fellowship for which man was created.' (1973:109) And political hope is focused in Christ, the shepherd-ruler. As such, 'for Christians the anticipation of the new political order must take shape in obedience to the rule of Jesus Christ' (1983:37).

On the other hand, however, Mouw says that Christ's activities inside and outside the church are 'of a piece'. The difference is simply that one is open, the other secret and mysterious. Does this mean that, just as the church anticipates the kingdom of glory, so the world also anticipates the kingdom of glory? Mouw says that Christ's 'redemptive and reconciling activities do reach, of course, beyond the bounds of the church.' And he speaks of 'the complexities of a world that is ... in the process of being rescued by God's redeeming work' (1973:35). What this activity might look like he does not say. Indeed, it is so mysterious and incomprehensible as to be impossible to discern. He speaks of the hatred and the bombs, but offers no analysis of whether Christ's redemptive activity might lie behind the emergence of reconciliation or peace in wider society.

In 1976 in *Politics and the Biblical Drama*, Mouw again argues that the kingdom exists outside the church, but his view appears to have changed, although the parameters of his discussion are different. He says that 'the institutional church is one among many manifestations of the kingdom of God' (1976:64). The key word here is 'institutional'. In *Politics and the Biblical Drama*, what Mouw means by arguing that the kingdom exists outside the church is that the kingdom exists outside the *institutional* church. What he has in mind are bodies such as Christian colleges, the Christian family, businessmen's groups and so on.' When thinking of church in contrast to kingdom, we do well to consider the church as denoting all past, present, and future manifestations of the *institutional* church, with the kingdom comprised of all else that falls under the rule of Christ, but also *including* the institutional church.' (1976:64)

Although Mouw gives a high priority to the institutional church, he sees the church itself as broader than simply its institutional form. In fact, Mouw himself acknowledges that 'the distinction between church and kingdom, as thus explained, is exactly similar to our distinction between the narrow and broad senses of church' (1976:64). Kingdom in this sense appears to be equivalent to the invisible church on earth. Thus, although Mouw can speak of the kingdom existing outside of the church, he nevertheless maintains that the kingdom exists 'under the rule of Christ'. In so doing, he captures the intuitive hesitation that many have with equating the kingdom with the church, for the immediate perception of the church is the church in its institutional forms. And, unlike Mouw, many do not hold these in high regard.

Mouw's emphasis upon the presence of the kingdom outside the institutional church, but within the rule of Christ in the form of what we might call mediatory groups (Christian professional fellowships and recreational groups) has important practical consequences. Mouw believes they provide a vehicle for authentic Christian involvement in, and reflection upon, business, politics, sport and so on. Too often, believes Mouw, when it comes to corporate witness, Christians polarise between official ecclesiastical statements and personal witness. Such groups allow – or should allow – for proper Christian reflection on their respective spheres and co-operative action (1976:66).

In *Political Evangelism* Mouw argues that the redemptive work of Christ 'must be directed to all dimensions of human life' (1973:14). All Christians, and particularly those involved in political processes, must concern themselves with political structures and policies in the name of Christ. This is because (i) sin is not limited to our 'private' lives; (ii) social problems cannot be solved by simply changing individual lives without regard to social structures; (iii) the message of the church to individuals cannot ignore the social context they inhabit; (iv) evangelism must be concerned with the whole person; and (v) there is a reality – a moral or political 'climate' – which cannot be explained simply in terms of the sum of the activities of individuals (1973:14-19,49; see also 1983:61-5).

Turning to the mission of the church itself, Mouw draws a parallel between the dimensions of mission and the three marks of the church. Just as the church is a listening community – marked by the preaching of the word – so it is a proclaiming community. Just as it is served by Christ through the sacraments, so it is to serve the world. And just as it is a disciplined community, so it is to discipline the world, calling it to follow the way of God. These three dimensions correspond, argues Mouw, to the biblical 'offices' of prophet, priest and king. Mouw recognises that some churches emphasise personal evangelism, others incarnational themes and Christian presence, and others the importance of influencing legislation. Mouw, however, argues that 'each of these emphases is in fact an important aspect of the church's mission in the world ... they complement each other' (1976:68). The result is that the mission of the church 'is a very complex one' (1976:81).

The tension Christians face in the political realm between biblical ideals and the reality of what is politically achievable in a plural society, the tension between faithfulness and compromise, arises, Mouw argues, from the eschatological tension between 'the "no longer" of the rule of Satan and the "not yet" of the fulness of the kingdom' (1973:98). 'There are times when flexibility will require that the Christian must work for gradual change, labouring patiently within the system. There are other times when faithfulness to the demands of the gospel will require protest, judgment, and a refusal to walk the way of expediency. To decide what is required in a given situation will often be difficult.' (1973:100) Mouw's point is that these tensions cannot be resolved prior to the consummation of the kingdom. 'There is no simple formula for deciding' (1973:100). We must learn to live with the tensions.

Consummation

Having surveyed the shape of the political and social conclusions that Mouw draws from the first three stages in the biblical drama, we turn to the area of most concern to us, namely the consummation of the biblical drama. We have already seen that, for Mouw, the eschaton impacts the first three stages. The consummation reveals that political structures are implied by the creation of humanity in the image of God, and not simply the result of the fall. Eschatology is not wholly concerned with the future consummation for the kingdom is already present. This has political implications, for this reality is not confined to the institutional church, but is present among mediatory groups – mediating that is between the church and the world. Such mediatory groups should play a key role in the corporate witness of the Christian in the social, business and political spheres. The tensions in the political task of the church reflect the tension between the presence and coming of the kingdom. Though not going as far as Moltmann in saying that 'Christianity is eschatology', Mouw does regard eschatology as having 'an integral relationship to the rest of theology'. Eschatology, says Mouw, 'deals with the creation *restored*, sin as *eliminated*, and redemption as *completed*' (1976:117).

Mouw claims, in the preface to *Political Evangelism*, that 'the political attitudes of evangelical Christianity have been based on an inadequate theology in the areas of ecclesiology and eschatology' (1973:8). Indeed, there is an eschatological dimension to Mouw's critique of evangelical ecclesiology. Mouw enters his discussion of ecclesiology and eschatology by examining the reasons given by Christians for not getting involved in politics. Two are relevant to our discussion of eschatology and social involvement. First, some will say, 'The redemption of the world does not hang on politics'. Mouw's immediate response is to agree, but to add that neither does it hang on preaching – even though preaching is key – but rather upon the sovereignty of God. He also adds that 'under the guise of awaiting the transformation of all things they have enthusiastically supported the status quo' (1973:33) More importantly, Mouw asks, If redemption does not hang on politics, how *are* God's redemptive purposes brought to fruition? The answer, he suggests, is that 'God has chosen to call apart a people as the instrument for revealing his kingdom' (1973:24). Notice that, first, God has chosen a *people*: our communal witness to Christ's work is the means God uses (ecclesiology). And second, this witness directs people to the *kingdom* of God, both present and coming (eschatology). The use of a political term, the kingdom, 'indicates that the total transformation of all things which God intends for his creation includes a transformation of the political realm as well as other realms' (1973:24). As such, the coming of Christ is not only a threat to individual sinners, but to the political status quo. 'The early disciples of the risen Lord were persecuted because they gave him a title – 'Lord' – that earthly politicians coveted.' (1973:25) Mouw emphasises that the redemptive work of Christ includes a political redemption. And as such, the testimony of the church must be that 'the new life is also a new *political* life' (1973:25).

Evangelism, according to Mouw, should not be equated simply with the verbal articulation of the gospel message. Even on an individual level it can involve asking questions, demonstrating love and so on. This paves the way for Mouw's definition of evangelism. 'Evangelism is concerned to show forth the full glories of the kingdom of God among men, with an eye to the day when the kingdom will reign over the entire earth.' (1973:76) In other words, Mouw defines evangelism in terms of eschatology, both realised and future.

A second 'misconception' that undermines Christian political involvement, addressed by Mouw, arises from premillennialism – a strongly eschatological system, but one which is commonly also strongly a-political. 'Clearly amillennialism and postmillennialism provide a basis for Christian political activity,' says Mouw (1973:28). With amillennialism, the kingdom that is coming with the return of Christ has already come, and its presence and power can be seen now, albeit in fragmentary ways. With postmillennialism, there is an expectation that the church's influence will increasingly pervade the earth prior to Christ's return. Thus, in both cases, there is the expectation that Christian political activity can bear fruit to the glory of God prior to the return of Christ. This Mouw assumes.

With premillennialism, however, there is often 'a belief that very little progress can be made in this area short of the return of Christ' (1973:28). So, for example, no attempt is made to protest against military exploits because there is little hope for peace until the Prince of peace returns. Mouw attempts neither to settle the millennial debate, nor to argue whether a pessimistic view of political change is inherent, or necessary, to premillennial beliefs. Instead, he argues, that since we can never be certain that we live immediately prior to the return of Christ, we can never be certain to what extent society is immune to change. More importantly, the fact that little or no change is conceivable does not release us from the divine mandate, nor our calling to be faithful to the heavenly vision, a vision in which Christ's atoning work redeems all areas of life.

In *Politics and the Biblical Drama* Mouw goes further, challenging one particular stream of premillennialism, namely dispensationalism. He argues that this particular brand of premillennialism is in fact far from a-political. Dispensationalists believe that the biblical drama is political, but that God's political purposes are tied to the nation of Israel. In practice, Mouw points out, this means that 'few Christians have so detailed a "Christian foreign policy" as do dispensationalists' (1976:119). This 'foreign policy' often implies that Christians should not criticise the policy of the current Israeli government – an attitude which, Mouw points out, is in stark contrast with that of the Old Testament prophets!

Having approached the subject from the perspective of common arguments against involvement in politics, Mouw looks more directly at ecclesiology and eschatology – the two central themes of Mouw's corrective of evangelical theology.

Mouw asks, What is the primary purpose for which God has gathered people in the church? On the one hand, some (Mouw cites Lewis Sperry Chafer) have argued that it is simply for fellowship; that service belongs to individual Christians and that therefore the church *qua* church has no task, and therefore also no political task. In response, Mouw argues that the establishment of a community is indeed central to the biblical drama, but it is a community whose *corporate* life is to reveal God to the world, to be a light to nations. The people of God, under both the old and new covenants, are to be 'a *model* of collective obedience to the will of God ... a paradigmatic community, whose life together demonstrates the triumphs of God's grace in human communal existence'

(1973:40-1).

In complete contrast, others have argued that the church has no purpose apart from mission. They equate the church with the mission of the church, speaking of 'the church as mission'. Mouw cites the Dutch theologian J.C. Hoekendijk:

> The church exists only *in actu*, in the execution of the apostolate, i.e. in the proclamation of the gospel of the kingdom to the world ... In no way can *mission* be viewed as *one* among other tasks to which the church is called. A church that knows that she is a function of the apostolate and that her very ground of existence lies in the proclamation of the kingdom to the world, does not engage in missions, but she herself becomes mission, she becomes the living outreach of God to the world. That is why a church without mission is an absurdity. As soon as the church fails to become mission in the totality of her being, she thereby proves that she has been denaturalised into a temple or into some sort of association for the cultivation of one's personal religious life. (1964:43-44; cited by Mouw, 1973:39)

The Dutch apostolate theology of J.C. Hoekendijk and A.A. van Ruler were a significant influence on the development of Moltmann's thought. Richard Bauckham comments, 'From this school of Reformed theology, Moltmann learned to think of the church as constituted by its mission to the world in the service of the coming universal kingdom of God' (1987i:5). As we have noted, Moltmann sees the church as a provisional reality which will one day be superseded by the kingdom. Because Moltmann makes the distinction between the church and world a provisional one, the church becomes the mission of the church. The church exists in mission and the purpose of this mission is the fostering of every anticipation of the kingdom – whether inside the church or not. As such, the aim of mission 'is not to spread the church but to spread the kingdom' (*CPS*, 11).

Mouw finds problems with this view of the church, describing it as 'an inadequate understanding of the church' (1973:39). The church is more than activity, it is a community; albeit one that has the activity of mission at the heart of its life. In practice this means that Mouw wants to stress 'the importance of the church's building up its own community as a necessary preparation for its larger witness (1973:47). In essence Mouw's response to both views is the same: he emphasises that the church is the focus for God's purposes. This is true now, in history, *pace* Lewis Sperry Chafer. But it is true eschatologically. Once universal salvation is anticipated, traditional ecclesiology breaks down. Once condemnation is removed from the eschatological day of judgment, the church can no longer be understood as a community of people called out from the world. Its experience of salvation is simply the experience of hopefulness, initiation into the knowledge that everything will be all right for everybody at the end of the day. And so, a new meaning must be sought for the church. It becomes activity. It is no longer a community, the fellowship of the redeemed. Instead it is motion towards the future. For all that he stresses the mission of the church, Mouw's soteriology prevents him identifying ecclesiology and missiology in the way that Moltmann does.

In *Politics and the Biblical Drama*, Mouw takes issue not only with the eschatology of dispensationalism, but also, on the other extreme, with that of 'a certain strain of contemporary "radical Christianity"'. Mouw particularly highlights the thinking of William Stringfellow who identifies the United States with the Babylon described in Revelation 18. American life, argues Stringfellow, is completely given over to the way of death. Within this Babylon, there are manifestations of the holy Jerusalem among radical and confessional movements (though rarely in the institutional church). Mouw, however, believes that Stringfellow's ideological commitments mean that he fails to see the positive tendencies in American life. According to Stringfellow, the picture of Babylon is one which describes a political and cultural condition to which all nations tend, a condition especially true of contemporary America. Mouw, however, with his commitment to both pre-fall political structures, and the redemption of those structures, cannot take such a negative view of the state. There may well be Babylonian elements within contemporary America, but there is not the rigid connection between Babylon and America assumed by Stringfellow. Stringfellow's position leaves him with no hope for America. Mouw believes the Babylonian elements will be destroyed, but that in the process the political structures of America, in common with other political structures, will be redeemed.

The redemption or transformation of political structures is an important theme for Mouw. In his 1983 book, *When the Kings Come Marching In*, he focuses on what he calls 'the transformation of culture emphasis in Isaiah 60' (1983:vii). Isaiah 60, says Mouw, should shape our view of heaven. We too easily confuse, suggests Mouw, the interim state of a soulless body with the final goal of the biblical drama in which the city is central. There is discontinuity, but 'the Holy City is not *wholly* discontinuous with present conditions'. There are 'some patterns of continuity' (1983:6).

As we have seen, the continuity between pre- and post-eschaton existence has been an important issue among evangelicals. Mouw takes a continuist position, rooting it in the creation mandate to fill the earth. This makes Mouw's approach to the continuist issue distinct in an important way. Mouw looks for continuity, not just in the good that humans undertake in history, but in every aspect of human activity. Not only will continuity involve that which we recognise now as good, but also military technology, idolatrous art and so on. Swords will become ploughshares. 'The fruits of history – even sinful history – will be gathered into the City, and made into fitting vessels for service' (1983:20). In the end time God will purge his creation of all rebellion and idolatry. The wicked will be condemned, but 'God will not destroy the things which they have put to their own rebellious uses'. Instead the new Jerusalem will be adorned with 'the glory and honour of the nations' (Revelation 21:26; 1983:16). And so, for example, when Isaiah 60 speaks of trade, even though it will be transformed, it will nevertheless be trade. In the judgment of God it is not trading ships *per se* which are judged, but their rebellious and idolatrous functions. The prophet is optimistic about the future of culture, but not in such a way as would encourage his hearers to embrace pagan culture. Does this mean every trading ship will be in heaven? Does the picture in Isaiah 11 of reconciliation between animals mean everyone's pet dog will be in heaven? Anticipating such questions, Mouw argues that Isaiah's interest is not personal but cosmic: he is interested in the future of 'corporate structures' and 'cultural patterns' (1983:9).

Mouw roots his commitment to a continuist position in the creation mandate to fill the earth. Why is God interested in gathering the glory of the nations into the new Jerusalem? Because, as the Psalmist says, 'The earth is the Lord's and the fulness thereof'. The 'filling' of the earth, which is the outworking of the command in Genesis 1:28 that humanity fill the earth, belongs to God. This, argues Mouw, is more than just a command to have children ('be fruitful') but to bring order to the garden, to be creative as a reflection of the Creator, to take what God has made and 'add' to it (see 1983:16). But humanity rebelled against God, and as a result human cultural formation has developed in faithless and distorted ways. Even so God has not abandoned his creation, and through his Son redeems the entire cosmos from the effects of sin. The 'filling' of creation which rightfully belongs to him will be reclaimed, purged and restored (see 1983:17).

When Revelation speaks of the kings of the earth coming into the city, we need not see this as only believing monarchs, nor as a hint at universal salvation, argues Mouw. Rather, they are representative of the political structures and cultural development. They represent these structures in their acknowledgement of Christ and his lordship, and in their cultural richness and diversity – the 'filling' – which God is redeeming as part of the new creation (see 1976:132-3 and 1983:24-26,31-32). Again, Mouw's approach is rooted in the biblical drama; the four stages of creation, fall, redemption and consummation. 'God intended from the beginning that human beings would 'fill the earth' with the processes, patterns and products of cultural formation. And this intention has in no way been cancelled by human sin. God will redeem and transform that which is presently perverted and distorted by human disobedience to his will.' (1983:xvi)

In this way, God will 'take into account the facts of sinful human development' (1983:17). 'The Holy City is the Garden-plus-the-"filling"' (1983:17). 'In an important sense, then, the "world", the *cosmos*, which Jesus came to save was bigger that the world which he originally created.' (1983:66) Thus, for example, in asking for a king, the people of Israel reject the kingship of God. Nevertheless, the failure of Israel's kings leads not simply to the promise of a return to pre-Saul divine rule, but the promise of divine rule through a king-greater-than-David (1983:29-30). In a similar way, argues Mouw, the judgment of Babel has led to the richness of linguistic and cultural diversity which will be reflected in the new Jerusalem (1983:48). Indeed, Mouw argues that creation provides an inadequate basis for opposition to racial discrimination: we need to point to the reconciling work of the cross and John's vision of people from every tribe, people and language joining together to worship the Lamb (1983:50-2).

The commitment of God to the redemption of the cultural 'filling' of creation means, argues Mouw, that God takes historical development seriously in his plans for the new creation. 'When the end-time comes there will be an acknowledgement that the historical process has occurred, with all this means in terms of cultural and institutional life ... historically-developed institutions will be "received" into the kingdom of God' (1976:136). Or again: 'God will gather in the ships of Tarshish ... because he takes history seriously' (1983:18). Indeed, not only is the City the Garden-plus-the-'filling', but at the heart of that City is not simply the second person of the Trinity, but the Lamb, what Mouw calls 'the Logos-plus-the-Cross' (1983:61).

Mouw is not unaware of the difficulties of a continuist position. What this continuity will look like, he concedes, 'remains mysterious' (1983:20). What will be the character of the event, or process, described as the 'healing of the nations'? Mouw acknowledges that 'any answer to this question must be speculative' (1976:137). He speaks of the reference in Revelation 21 to the kings of the earth as 'an allusion' and 'a puzzling one' at that (1976:130). Nevertheless, he argues that just as swords become ploughshares so 'Marxist posters will become aesthetic objects which will enhance the beauty of the City. Perhaps missiles will become play areas for children' (1983:19-20). The pattern is the same as that for personal destiny: just as we will experience continuity of identity even as our bodies are transformed, so likewise will the 'filling' of history.

Indeed, not only is Mouw aware of the difficulties of a continuist position, he also acknowledges that, strictly speaking, it cannot be proven. Speaking of his contention that human activity will be transformed and incorporated into the new creation, Mouw concedes, 'I do not think that I will be able to "prove" this contention in any strict sense' (1983:xvi). He acknowledges that someone might easily say of his key texts (Isaiah 60, Revelation 21) that they should not be submitted to such detailed examination, but should instead be understood 'typologically' or as 'doxological hyperbole' (1983:xvi). Mouw claims only that his reading of the texts is plausible and a reading which 'illuminates many other elements of the biblical story' (1983:xvi).

What impact should this eschatological vision have upon Christian mission? What are the implications for discipleship? The critics of Christian hope are right, acknowledges Mouw, in suggesting that belief in the afterlife has often functioned to reinforce the status quo. Mouw argues, however, that this is not, as the Marxists would suggest, its real function. There is no getting round the 'pie in the sky' element in Christian eschatology, but this is not to be an excuse for inaction, but a comfort in failure.

In his end time predictions, Isaiah describes concrete historic realities. According to Mouw, Isaiah 60 is predictive, but it is prediction addressed to the particular hopes and fears of Isaiah's context.

> When Christian people have experienced political oppression, they have often longed for a day of political vindication. They have viewed God as a righteous judge who will someday set the political record straight. On the other hand, those Christian who have been relatively satisfied with the political status quo have tended to think of the afterlife in rather a-political terms. Isaiah is on the side of the politicisers of the afterlife. (1983:23-4; see also 30-31)

The predictive elements of biblical prophecy do not arise from a passive attitude to the present. The vision that the prophets have of the future is shaped by their bitter experience of the present. The image and types with which they describe the future are those drawn from their contrast to the present. Future prophecy cannot, therefore, be separated from historical involvement.

> Is it difficult to find justice? Well, someday justice will rush in like a mighty river ... The prophet is not someone who curtains himself off from the world in order to gaze into a crystal ball; he is someone whose hopes are forged out of the intense agonies of historical involvement – and who is thereby made capable of discerning the shape, often in terms of images and types, of the fulfilment which the Lord of history will bring to pass. (1976:122-3)

Biblical prophecy, then, does not arise from historical passivity. And nor does it lead to passivity. The announcement of the future, both of blessing and judgment, has as its aim repentance. When the future is made known, it is in order that there might be change in history.

Mouw concludes *When the Kings Come Marching In* with a reflection on Hebrews 13:14 and John Bunyan's *Pilgrims Progress*. Bunyan's vision of the Celestial City, and the pilgrimage towards it, has proved an inspiration to generations of Christians. Mouw acknowledges that Bunyan's portrayal of the Christian life is very individualistic. Although Bunyan's vision is not wrong, it is, argues Mouw, incomplete. 'When the Christian life is viewed as a-lonely-journey-through-a-hostile-world, it is difficult to find a context for thinking about economic injustice or racial discrimination.' (1983:70) Nevertheless, Mouw argues that we should not ditch Bunyan for two reasons. First, the pietistic perspective, despite its defects, is an important one. Second, many of the alternatives prove inadequate because they fail to ground the vision of the Christian life, as Bunyan does, in the individual's experience of God's preserving mercies. Bunyan begins in the right place, in a piety expressed as a commitment to holiness, to obedience to God's word, to following Jesus. The question is, What does the word of God say? What does following Jesus involve? What are the political consequences of such commitment? In other words, Mouw wants to harness this piety, a piety already shaped by the vision of the Celestial city, and shape it by the vision of the City in its political dimensions so that it expresses the full range of what it means to be a Christian disciple.

What, then, does 'seeking the city' involve? Turning to Hebrews 13:14, Mouw suggests that it means sharing the rejection of Jesus (verse 13). And it means 'doing good', particularly identification with the poor ('to share with others' in verse 16). It is no coincidence, argues Mouw, that Isaiah's vision of the new Jerusalem is preceded by, and followed by, chapters whose focus is upon the problems of economic and social injustice (Isaiah 58-59, 61). Mouw outlines activities which are proper to this 'seeking' the City: calling human institutions to obedience to the Creator, proposing programmes of racial justice, working to bring healing and obedience within the Christian community, and so on. The Bible links the vision of the future with practical commands to help and identify with the poor. In this way, 'we can experience something of the light of God's glory – a light which will someday shine eternally in the Holy City' (1983:75-76).

Although Mouw has identified himself as one who believes that Christ will transform culture, he ends by qualifying this. We should expect this transformation and we should not wait for it passively. Nevertheless, Mouw continues, 'while the Bible does teach – or so I believe – that Christ will transform culture in the end time, there is no clear biblical command to Christians to "transform culture" in any general way' (1983:76). In other words, Mouw refuses to place the responsibility for the transformation of culture upon Christians, even in part. We share in the mission of God through our responsibility to evangelise, but Mouw hesitates to make a similar statement about the transformation of culture. Whatever our theoretical formulations regarding 'Christ and culture', we cannot avoid the clear mandate of the Scriptures. We must actively seek the City by suffering abuse outside the camp (1983:76). At times Mouw holds out the prospect that what we do now will be related to the eschatological transformation of all things. 'Our present efforts as citizens of Zion will culminate in the final victory of the Lamb whose light will fill the City.' (1983:77). At other times he is more cautious: 'God will allow our present activities to count as preparatory signs of his coming kingdom.' (1976:139)

How, then, might a 'transformationalist' approach make a difference in practice from one which holds that the present order will be destroyed, and the new creation will be entirely new? The answer, suggests Mouw, is 'on the level of attitude and mood'. Participation is 'not a mere "holding" action but a legitimate means of *preparation* for life in the kingdom' (1976:138). Or again: 'If, in a fundamental and profound sense, God has not given up on human culture, then neither must we' (1983:21). 'Because we look for a city which is yet to come, we will not be able to place our ultimate trust in the systems of the present age. But because the tree may sprout leaves for the healing of the kinds of nations of which we are presently citizens, we cannot completely dissociate ourselves from that which God has promised to heal.' (1976:137) 'The tensions and ambiguities involved in the perspective we have been developing ... reflect similar ones in God's own attitude toward the present condition of his creation' (1976:138). God is going to both redeem and judge the present order. Our attitude, says Mouw, must 'be neither more optimistic than God's nor less optimistic.' (1976:138)

With Mouw we have a much more workable use of eschatology in social concern because of its integration into the biblical drama as a whole. His discussion of the continuist position is stronger than that proposed by others evangelicals because of its link to creation (a link others avoid for fear of reinforcing the status quo). The new creation is the consummation of the 'filling' ordained at creation. In other words, eschatology cannot be applied to social and cultural involvement in isolation from the biblical drama as a whole. Mouw acknowledges that the difference eschatology makes is one of 'attitude and mood' (1976:138). This is important but it falls short of a programme for social concern. Eschatology does affect attitude and mood, but it is the attitude and mood of a prior commitment to social concern. When social concern is established on other grounds, eschatology heightens and sustains such activity. But when social action has not been established in people's minds, eschatology can serve to bolster escapist quietism.

CHAPTER 13

Creation and Resurrection: Oliver O'Donovan

Resurrection and Moral Order (1986i) by Oliver O'Donovan, Regius Professor
of Moral and Pastoral Theology at Oxford University and one of Britain's
leading evangelical theologians, has already been hailed as a classic. Although
not strictly about mission, *Resurrection and Moral Order* is about ethics and
thus, given the renewed commitment by evangelicals to social involvement as a
function of mission, has made an important contribution to evangelical
thinking. Indeed, O'Donovan argues that the essential character of Christian
ethics is love, and this, he goes on to argue, is an outward-looking, missionary
love (242).

A Gospel Ethic

More significantly, *Resurrection and Moral Order* is an attempt to develop an
ethical framework based on the gospel. Hence the subtitle, 'An outline for
evangelical ethics' (although O'Donovan seems happy to let this stand also as a
reference to the evangelical stream of the contemporary church of which he is
part). The alternative is ethics without the gospel, which is no longer
missiological, nor, O'Donovan argues, truly Christian. 'The foundations of
Christian ethics must be evangelical foundations; or, to put it more simply,
Christian ethics must arise from the gospel of Jesus Christ. Otherwise it could
not be *Christian* ethics.' (11) This is how the main text of *Resurrection and
Moral Order* opens, and it forms the starting point for his whole argument.
Such an approach ties ethics in to the central events of redemptive history; of
the 'biblical drama'. O'Donovan continues: 'A belief in Christian ethics is a
belief that certain ethical and moral judgments belong to the gospel itself; a
belief, in other words, that the church can be committed to ethics without
moderating the tone of its voice as a bearer of glad tidings.' (12) Christian
morality is not an attempt to walk a middle way between law and license – that
is, to oscillate between two sub-Christian forms of life. Christianity takes a
different path altogether: 'the path of integrally evangelical ethics which
rejoices the heart and gives light to the eyes because it springs from God's gift
to humanity in Jesus Christ.' (12)

Resurrection and the Moral Order of Creation

More specifically, for to suggest that ethics springs from God's gift to humanity
is too imprecise, O'Donovan argues that 'Christian ethics depends upon the
resurrection of Jesus Christ from the dead' (13). He acknowledges that in New
Testament moral teaching appeal is made to all aspects of Christ's life, but
argues that it is necessary 'to uncover the hidden relation of things that gives
the appeal force' (13). 'We are driven to concentrate on the resurrection as our
starting-point because it tells of God's vindication of his creation, and so our
created life' (13). The resurrection reverses Adam's decision to die: his choice
of sin and therefore death. But it also affirms God's decision to give Adam life.
'It is God's final and decisive word on the life of his creature, Adam.' (13)
Apart from the resurrection, it might have been possible that the creature's
decision to uncreate itself, and the rest of creation, meant that God's work of
creation was flawed beyond hope. But, since God has raised Jesus, who as the
last Adam shared our createdness, from the dead, then we should not think in
terms of a gnostic hope of redemption *from* creation, but, instead, of the
redemption *of* creation. 'The deviance of [Adam's] will, its fateful leaning
towards death, has not been allowed to uncreate what God created.' (14) The
moral order is no longer a threat, the criterion of judgment, but becomes for us
a blessing. 'Jesus' moral authority is evangelical in the fullest sense, since the
moral order which he proclaims is the kingdom of God, the theme of his
message of salvation. It is a moral order in which the arbitrariness of sinful
man's relation to God's purposes has been overcome and done away with.'
(155)

In their proclamation of the resurrection of Christ, the apostles proclaimed
the resurrection of humanity. If that were all, it would be a gospel of sorts, but a
purely gnostic and world-denying one, far removed from the reality of the
apostolic message. But in proclaiming the resurrection of humanity, the
apostles also proclaimed the renewal of creation (31). We might ask of
O'Donovan, What does the resurrection add to the created order? Does a reaffirmation amount to very much? One could write a book re-affirming the
created order – what would be qualitatively different about God doing so in the
resurrection? The answer is that, without the resurrection, it appears to be
genuinely open to question whether one should base moral obligations on an
order so marred by human sin. Whatever it might have been, the created order
could now be viewed as redundant, as we wait for redemption *from* it. But, if
resurrection means the renewal of the created order, then clearly it has a future,
and therefore a continuing moral validity.

O'Donovan does not, he says, want to isolate the resurrection from the other
saving of events proclaimed in the gospel. The cross pronounces God's 'No' to
life in the flesh, just as the resurrection pronounces his 'Yes' to life in the
Spirit. And the ascension makes explicit the transformation of human life,
revealing in the gospel a world-transcending aspect. Yet, if these dimensions

are not to collapse into gnostic other-worldliness, they need to be interpreted from the perspective of the resurrection as the affirmation of the created order.

> These aspects, of abnegation and transcendence in personal ethics, of criticism and revolution in social ethics, are prevented from becoming negative and destructive by the fact that they are interpreted from the centre, the confirmation of the world-order which God has made. Man's life on earth is important to God; he has given it its order; it matters that it should confirm to the order he has given it. (14-5)

The resurrection points forward to the end of history, when the particular fate of the Resurrected one is universalized in the general resurrection of the dead. 'The sign that God has stood by his created order implies that this order, with humanity in its proper place within it, is to be totally restored at the last.' (15) But eschatology does not deny, or replace, the created order. O'Donovan draws attention to the writer to the Hebrews' eschatological reading of Psalm 8 (Hebrews 2:5-9), a Psalm which outlines humanity's ordering within creation (38). The writer does not deny, or replace, the understanding of creation in Psalm 8, argues O'Donovan. 'Rather, he sees in Christ, and in the order of the world to come, the vindication and perfect manifestation of the created order which was always there but never fully expressed.' (53) In other words, the eschatological order is not an innovative order, but one which fully vindicates and fulfils the original order; a realisation which could not be achieved in the fallen state of humanity and the universe. The very term 'redemption' presupposes a created order which is recovered or restored (see also 1979:29). This contrasts with Moltmann's thought. Moltmann, with his conflation of creation and fall, emphasises the innovative nature of the new creation, rather than its restored character. As Brian Walsh points out, the prefix 're-' (*re*demption, *re*storation, *re*newal, *re*covery etc.) figures little in Moltmann's soteriology (Walsh, 1987:61).

O'Donovan's emphasis on the restoration, rather than denial or replacement of the creation order, underlies his comments on Helmut Thielicke's important work *Theological Ethics*. Thielicke sets out, like O'Donovan, to frame an evangelical ethical foundation which is shaped by Christian proclamation. This ethical foundation is based on three aspects. First, the eschatological mystery, that is, the tension between time and eternity, between this age and the age to come. Second, the christological mystery, that is, the tension between the deity and humanity of Christ. And third, the sacramental mystery, that is, the tension between the sign and the thing signified. O'Donovan expresses his appreciation for Thielicke's enterprise, and particularly his commitment to ground ethics in theology. He remains uneasy, however, about the repeated emphasis on 'unresolved tension'. This applies to the first aspect, the eschatological, but applies less comfortably to the christological and sacramental. O'Donovan doubts, for example, whether it is appropriate to speak of the incarnation as a 'tension' between the divine and human natures of Christ. This, he argues, betrays the fact that for Thielicke the eschatological motif is the dominant one. O'Donovan argues that there are problems with this. It could be constructive, where it is a recognition of the co-existence of the new age and the old. He suspects, however, that in Thielicke the tension is so strong that 'the new age loses its comprehensibility, and hence its worldliness and becomes merely a transcendent mystery, alien and critical' (145) – a criticism redolent of those levelled against Moltmann, particularly against his early emphases. The result is that when Thielicke discusses Jesus' ethical teaching in the Sermon on the Mount, he reformulates Luther's doctrine of two kingdoms in eschatological terms, describing the Sermon on the Mount as 'the law of the coming age', the purpose of which is to 'unsettle' us and highlight the fallenness of this age. While this gives the Sermon an 'existential immediacy', O'Donovan feels that 'in the end we have only the uncomfortable sense that the Sermon on the Mount is, after all, not relevant to our lives in the world except in so far as it reminds us of their provisionality' (145). The result is that Thielicke's evangelical ethics sound 'troublingly like a gospel of deliverance *from* the world rather than *of* it' (145). While the new age remains in Thielicke's thinking, it assumes no form in this age except the 'formless form of protest'. We are left 'to be guided by emergency orders' (145). Thus, Thielicke gives the Mosaic Law a continuing significance for Christians instead of seeing Christians now being under the fulfilment of that Law in Christ. The result is that we are left living under an authority other than Christ's. O'Donovan suspects that at the heart of the problem is a weakness in the understanding of the incarnation. A question is placed over whether the divine really assumed human form. 'We may focus the question like this: Did the Sermon on the Mount, with its "extraplanetary" demand, actually take on form in the human life of Jesus of Nazareth?' (146) If so, then we should see this not simply as transcendent protest, but as a pattern for Christian life in the world.

While it is central to his argument that the whole of creation, and not just humanity, is restored, O'Donovan believes 'we cannot speculate what "redemption" will imply for the non-human creation' (55). 'We must not allow the idea to float free in independence of "the revealing of the sons of God"' (55). Thus, O'Donovan sees the restoration of creation in the context of the restoration of humanity. What is recovered is not just humanity, but 'humanity in his context of the ruler of the ordered creation that God made' (54-5).

O'Donovan does not see redemption as a mere restoration. Redemption does more than take us back to the Garden of Eden. 'It leads us on to that further destiny to which, even in the Garden of Eden, we were already directed.' (55) 'Man is summoned to a destiny that is not given immediately in his creation ... "to reign eternally with Christ in heaven"' (56; citing Athanasius). The givenness of creation included its own goal and purposes. Thus: 'the eschatological transformation of the world is neither the mere repetition of the created world nor its negation. It is its fulfilment, its *telos* or end.' (55) The

Gospels speak of Christ's resurrection as both his restoration from the dead and his glorification at God's right hand. In the same way, the resurrection vindicates the created order in a double sense, by restoring it and by transforming it.

By the renewal of creation, O'Donovan means not merely the raw material of which the world was made, but the order and coherence in which it was composed. 'It is not created energy as such that is vindicated in the resurrection of Christ, but the order in which created energy was disposed by the hand of the Creator' (31). O'Donovan identifies two directions in this ordering: (i) teleological order, ordering-to, in which one thing serves another, it is its end; and (ii) generic order, ordering-alongside, in which one thing is like another to varying degrees.

O'Donovan anticipates the objection that generic morality is irreconcilable with a belief that morality is the demand of God's will, which must be free and unbound. A generic morality ties God's will down to an eternal and necessary structure over which he has no more power to command. The details of O'Donovan's response need not concern us since they do not relate to our theme of eschatology and mission (38-45). In responding, however, O'Donovan acknowledges, and indeed argues, that 'it is not acceptable to think of God as being under a necessity to create the world as it is, not ever a necessity arising from within his own being' (39). While 'we may perhaps dare to speak, by way of analogy and hesitantly' of divine love having to express itself in creation, we cannot go further and speak of God having to create this world. To do so is to make creation no longer a 'creation', but an 'emanation', 'a reflection of the inner law of God's being'. This, suggests O'Donovan, is the first step towards pantheism. Although O'Donovan does not mention him by name, the parallel with the criticisms advanced against Moltmann and his Hegelianism is striking. As we have seen, Moltmann's theology does tend towards making the world necessary to the self-becoming of God and thus, if not towards pantheism, then explicitly towards panentheism.

Starker still is the contrast between O'Donovan's commitment to moral obligations based on the creation order and Moltmann's rejection of creation ordinances. O'Donovan, however, in part meets Moltmann's objections by centring his ethics not upon creation *per se*, but creation affirmed in the resurrection of Jesus Christ. The important point, however, is that Moltmann merges creation and fall. Sin enters the world because of the threat of the *nihil* present in creation. Sin follows death. If the created order leads to sin, it can hardly stand as a basis for moral concepts. In contrast, for O'Donovan, creation and fall remain two distinct events in the biblical drama. Sin has marred the created order, requiring restoration of that order in Christ. And sin has obscured our perception of that order, requiring revelation of that order in Christ. But the created order continues to place moral obligations upon us. O'Donovan, who confesses a 'personal predilection' for Augustine (18), would no doubt concur with him when he says, in contrast to Moltmann, 'it is by sin that we die, and not by death that we sin'.

Beyond Creation Ethics and Kingdom Ethics

His emphasis upon the resurrection as the affirmation of the created order means that O'Donovan makes a decisive contribution to the creation ethics and kingdom ethics debate. As we have seen, the debate over the extent of the kingdom prior to the parousia has had important implications for evangelical missiology. Some have argued that the kingdom is present outside the conscious confession of Christ and that it should therefore be central to our approach to mission in its social dimensions. Others have argued that the kingdom is not present outside the conscious confession of Christ prior to the parousia and that therefore, instead of the kingdom, the doctrine of creation should shape our approach to social issues.

O'Donovan rejects the very framework of the debate as a false polarisation. For in the resurrection of Christ, creation and the kingdom are linked in affirmation and fulfilment (see also O'Donovan, 1979:30-1). 'This way of posing the alternatives is not acceptable, for the very act of God which ushers in his kingdom is the resurrection of Christ from the dead, the reaffirmation of creation' (1986i:15). A kingdom ethics which is set up in opposition to creation ethics cannot be based on the kingdom as understood in the New Testament where the kingdom fulfils creation. O'Donovan sees in such an approach a false dualism in which the progress, or completion, of history in the kingdom of God is not the fulfilment of creation but a denial of its beginnings. But a creation ethics set up in opposition could not be evangelical ethics, since it would exclude the good news that God has acted to bring what he has made to fulfilment.

> In the resurrection of Christ, creation is restored and the kingdom of God dawns. Ethics which starts from this point may sometimes emphasise the newness, sometimes the primitiveness of the order that is there affirmed. But it will not be tempted to overthrow or deny either in the name of the other. (15; see also 1979:31 for an example of how this might work)

> Christian ethics looks backwards and forwards, to the origin and to the end of the created order. It respects the natural structures of life in the world, while looking forward to their transformation. (58)

O'Donovan cites 1 Peter. Peter characterises the Christian life as a life of hope, but at the same time calls for submission 'for the Lord's sake' to every institution of human life, especially those of government, work and marriage. There is no conflict here, suggests O'Donovan, because 'a hope which envisages the transformation of existing natural structures cannot consistently attack or repudiate those structures' (58). At the same time, the 'conservatism' of 1 Peter is not without critical distance, for there is an awareness of the need for redemption. In other words, the transformation of created structures means one cannot condemn them, since they will be transformed rather than being replaced. But neither can you regard them uncritically, since they will be transformed rather than being left unchanged.

When we sketched the contours of the creation ethics and kingdom ethics debate, we noted that advocates of creation argue that one of the strengths of the creation ethics position is that it can be offered as an ethic for all people rather than simply for those who participate in the kingdom of God. In a similar way, O'Donovan argues that since it is creation that is reaffirmed by the resurrection, Christian ethics are not simply opted into by those who so choose, but are relevant for all. In other words, his emphasis upon the gospel as the starting point of Christian ethics does not make them ethics for Christians only. He avoids the choice between an ethic which includes the gospel but excludes non-believers, and a general ethic which includes all people but excludes the gospel.

Moral Order and Voluntarism

O'Donovan outlines his view of ethics in contrast not only to the creation ethics and kingdom ethics debate, but also in opposition to both 'voluntarism' and 'historicism'. Voluntarism sees morality as a creation of man's will by which he imposes order on his life, both individually and socially. The result is that moral disagreements can at best reveal differing commitments, incapable of ultimate resolution (see 16-7;35-7; see also 1979:22-25). This voluntarism has its Christian versions. 'In this modern "faith-ethic", Christian moral obligation becomes a function of the believer's decision, something that he has opted into.' (16) It is relevant only to a closed circle. The unbeliever cannot even be expected to respect prohibitions against adultery or murder since, lacking the faith-commitment of believers. he has no reason to respect his neighbour's marriage or life. This, argues O'Donovan, is evidently mistaken, if only because so many unbelievers do respect the marriages and lives of their neighbours, and so many non-Christian cultures require them to do so. But the real problem is 'a failure to reckon with creation' (16). Even though humanity has rejected the divinely-given order of creation, it nevertheless stands over against us and makes its claims upon us. The very fact that we experience creation as broken points to the fact that it is a broken order rather than unordered chaos (88). The key point is that 'Christian ethics has an objective reference', since it is concerned with the givenness of the created order (17). 'The summons to live in [the divinely-given creation order] is addressed to all humanity, because the good news that we *may* live in it is addressed to all humanity.' (17) Ethics therefore is, as was argued in the classical ethics of Plato, Aristotle and the Stoics, closely related to metaphysics. The way the universe *is* determines how we *ought* to live in it. 'Christian moral thought must respond to objective reality – the reality, that is, of a world-order restored in Christ, the reality which the gospel declares.' (101) So, for example, in O'Donovan's book on just war, he states: 'God's peace is the original ontological truth of creation. We must deny the sceptical proposition that competition and what metaphysicians call "difference" are the fundamental realities of the universe, a proposition which the creation, preservation and redemption of the world make impossible to entertain' (2003:3). How O'Donovan's develops his approach to just war need not concern us. The point is that in developing it he is concerned with 'the original ontological truth of creation', with 'the fundamental realities of the universe'. Notice, too, how appeal is made to different stages in the biblical drama.

Moral Order and Historicism

Historicism, in contrast to voluntarism, rejects the notion that morality is to be based upon generic orderings independent of time-place particularity. Instead, it argues that morality must respond, not to uniform structures that stand apart from history, but to the free agency of God in history. O'Donovan does not want to deny the free will of God in history, nor that history is meaningful as the stage for salvation-history. Instead, he argues that 'for history to be meaningful history, and for God's freedom to be gracious freedom, there must also be order which is not subject to historical change' (45). If there is no order independent of history then history becomes 'uninterpretable movement, the denial of what has been in favour of what is to be' (45). The very fact that time is understandable as 'history' indicates an unchanging, given moral order.

Since historicism denies a transhistorical natural ordering, it defines teleology in historical terms rather than generic terms (58-67). The concept of an 'end' is essentially a concept of development in time. The natural order is but a moment in the historical process. Its value is not inherent, but lies in it being raw material for transformation. Again, O'Donovan argues that history can have no meaning if all is history. In contrast, O'Donovan argues that creation is complete, in other words, the creation order is a given which forms the basis of historical existence. 'The world is established, it shall never be moved.' (Psalm 96:10) The traditional distinction between 'creation' and 'providence' is designed to safeguard this very fact. There is a distinction between the givenness of the creation order and historical contingency. God's work of providence and redemption continues, but, as the Sabbath should remind us, God's work of creation is complete. He is not continuously creating. The eschatological does not call into question this completion, as the writer to the Hebrews realized. Instead we are called to *enter* the Sabbath rest of God (Hebrews 4:3-11). 'Historical fulfilment means our entry into a completeness which is already in the universe.' (62)

In contrast, Moltmann argues that evolutionary theories compel the church to 'take up once again the neglected doctrine of the *creatio continua*' (*GC*,

207). For Moltmann, continuous creation presents no problem, because he sees creation from the beginning as 'an open system'; although he does emphasise the need to distinguish between creation-in-the-beginning and continuous creation, the former being without preconditions. Moltmann believes the notion of creation created, then preserved, and then restored, is inadequate from the perspectives of both evolution and eschatology. God is doing a new thing in preparation for the consummation. Moltmann also lays great emphasis on the Sabbath as the climax of creation (*GC*, 276-96), but not to emphasise the completeness of creation, but rather that its climax is other than in humanity. The teleology of creation is other than humanity, an assertion important for Moltmann's 'ecological doctrine of creation'.

O'Donovan's critique of historicism continues with him arguing that, if natural teleology is historical, then it follows that the end of things can be known in history, and that therefore we can discern the direction of history. With such a scheme the inscrutability of God's ways is lost. And lost, too, is Christian proclamation of 'the mystery hidden from ages in God' (Ephesians 3:9). But, argues O'Donovan, the fulfilment of history is not generated from within the latencies and possibilities of history, but from outside. God's grace is not just his activity in history, but his activity in history from outside of history. 'God is not merely responding to necessities intrinsic to [the world], but is doing something new.' (64) This is why the Christian view of history is eschatological, rather than simply teleological. 'The destined end is not immanently present in the beginning or in the course of movement through time, but is a "higher grace" which, though it comes from the same God as the first and makes a true whole with the first as its fulfilment, nevertheless has its own integrity and distinctness as an act of divine freedom.' (64-5) If the destiny of the world is immanently present within it, then we cannot speak of its fulfilment through 'Christ alone'. Historical events are destined for fulfilment in the kingdom of God, not because of an intrinsic tendency within them, but through the redeeming work of Christ. 'Our complaint against historicism is that it has made every act of providence by definition an act of salvation.' (66)

At this point O'Donovan turns to Moltmann – his only explicit interaction with Moltmann in *Resurrection and Moral Order*. He begins by commending the distinction made by Moltmann in *Hope and Planning* (1971) between the promise and providence of God. For example, 'The promise of God is not based on the providence of God, but rather the providence of God serves the fulfilment of the promise of God'. When the promise disintegrates into general providence it 'becomes merely the expression, the revelation, of the divine planning-mentality for history' (1971:184; cited O'Donovan, 66). O'Donovan goes on, however, 'I must admit that I am simply puzzled to know how a thinker who can make this point with such sharpness can then go on to maintain, in the same essay: "Both hope and planning have their foundation in suffering and in dissatisfaction with the present" (p. 178), and even, "Hope invokes itself in an evolutionary contradiction to present reality" (p. 194).'

(1971:184; cited O'Donovan, 66) O'Donovan cannot understand how hope, based on the resurrection of Christ, can be founded on dissatisfaction. For Moltmann, however, this dissatisfaction is created by the promise implicit in the resurrection of Christ. Hope would not be hope if its object were not something different to the present. O'Donovan, in contrast, believes 'our dissatisfaction with the present is overwhelmed by the glorious vindication of creation which God has effected in Christ' (1971:184; cited O'Donovan, 66). O'Donovan, however, does highlights key ambiguities in Moltmann's thought. The failure to make clear the ontological status of his language, means that in his early thought one is never entirely sure whether Moltmann's eschatological rhetoric is much more than a radical and revolutionary historicism, albeit a christologically focused one. His attempts to clarify this are not helped by the way his trinitarian history of God looks like Hegelian process, in which the future is not determined from outside of history, but is inherent within history; albeit a history within God. Hope reaches towards the impossible, but, says Moltmann, this is in fact 'the not yet possible'. This, suggests O'Donovan, means that in Moltmann revolutionary transformation still belongs immanently in history, even if only the far-sighted take it into account. Hope is then differentiated from planning only by degree.

The consequences of historicism for morality, O'Donovan believes, are far reaching (63,67-75). Classic Christian morality is based on a universal order of meaning and value, given in creation and fulfilled in the kingdom of God. Historicism denies the existence of such an order, seeing it as an historical phenomenon. Sin is no longer defined in relation to the good natural order, but as historical imperfection, from which we are to advance. Instead of the threefold pattern of good creation, an evil fall and an end of history, in which evil is negated and the created good transcended, we have a dualist opposition between a historical 'from' and 'towards'. The goal of history is that man become aware of himself as an historical being and take control of the processes of history. The result is that historicism is 'systematically interventionist' (69; see also 1979:29). Again, this is a problem we have identified in Moltmann. With creation merging with fall in Moltmann, the threefold pattern of classical Christian moral thought becomes the dualist opposition of 'from' and 'towards'. Moltmann's rejection of creation ordinances makes the present inevitably suspect. Moltmann cannot accept a moral authority within the given, objective moral order, an identification central to O'Donovan. Since the present is contradicted by the promise, the resulting ethics are inevitably ethics of change – and preferably radical change since the future is radically new.

O'Donovan also criticises historicism for its social thought which, he claims, lacks a strong eschatology. Classic Western theology and political thought has started with the assertion that the kingdoms of this world are not the kingdom of our God and of his Christ. In other words, there is opposition between the City of God and the earthly city. This opposition has prevented theocratic or totalitarian concepts of government. All earthly government is relativised by the City of God. Only the government of God can reconcile the world. This does not mean the secular state can be independent of God. Instead, because it does not have to reconcile all things, it can get on with its task of bearing witness to the justice of God. Nor does it mean an individual can cultivate a private piety while avoiding the claims of society. Instead, he can contribute to society that knowledge of good which he learns from the heavenly kingdom. O'Donovan acknowledges that it is paradoxical that he should accuse historicism of lacking a strong eschatology, for historicism claims to re-establish the importance of the kingdom in political thought. In fact, claims O'Donovan, 'its use of eschatological categories is characteristically to *legitimise* the immanent tendencies of history rather than to *criticise* them' (73). With no locus of value outside history, the kingdom must receive its definition from the processes of history.

Knowing the Created Order

O'Donovan's concern in the case of both voluntarism and historicism is the same: to defend the objective reality and givenness of the created order, which he argues is the basis of moral concepts (see 1979:23). The objective reality of the God-given created order is, however, only one side of Christian moral concepts. Humanity's fallenness points not only to his rejection of that order, 'but also to an inescapable confusion in his perceptions of it' (1986i:19). A simple call to 'life in accord with nature' requires epistemological qualification. Empirically, those non-Christian cultures in which, as O'Donovan has already noted, we see respect for features of the created order, also display a neglect of other features of that order. 'We must reckon upon the opacity and obscurity of that order to the human mind which has rejected knowledge of its Creator.' (1986i:19; see also 81-2) What is 'natural' is not self-evident to us. Nevertheless, despite the epistemological problems facing a natural ethic, we should not conclude that it lacks an *ontological* basis (see also 1979:26-7). There is an objective ground to which moral life can respond.

The epistemological problems are not insurmountable. Knowledge of the created order is possible through Christ. We know that the natural order has claims upon us because of God's revelation in the resurrection of Christ. We can only distinguish between nature and convention, between natural ethics and primitive superstition, through Christ. The certainty we can have about the created order depends upon God's self-disclosure of himself and his works. Through revelation, and only through revelation, we can overcome the epistemological barriers to an ethic that conforms to nature. 'True knowledge of the moral order is knowledge "in Christ"' (85). Moral knowledge is also 'co-ordinated' with obedience. 'There can be no true knowledge of that order without loving acceptance of it and conformity to it, for it is known by participation and not by transcendence' (87). Moral discernment therefore 'must begin with the initial conversion of the mind in repentance and... be constantly renewed in repentance as well.' (93)

Even 'natural knowledge' with which, O'Donovan acknowledges, all people are endowed, is only truly apprehended in Christ. Hence O'Donovan avoids the term 'Natural Law', because it does not differentiate between universality of being and universality of knowledge (85). An unbeliever can grasp aspects of the moral order – the structure of the family, for example. Nevertheless, such knowledge is incomplete unless the created order is grasped as a whole, including in its relation to the Creator. We are not forced to choose between an ethic which is grounded in creation, but only dimly perceived through natural knowledge, and a revealed ethic that lacks ontological grounding (and is therefore implicitly voluntarist). In fact, these two false polarisations live together when it is argued that the church should pursue one morality in the public arena (based on natural knowledge) and another internally (based on revelation).

Moral Conflict

In the world the true and the false are in conflict. The true participation of humanity in creation, as represented by Jesus, ends with his death, as the corrupted order defends itself against correction. The meaning of the cross *in itself* – a meaning presupposed by the further meanings which the resurrection brings to light – is that obedient participation cannot freely continue in the world, but must conflict with disobedience, and so be driven out. Even when Jesus is vindicated, this penultimate word is not forgotten, his resurrection body bears the nail marks. All who would follow him must take up their cross. 'The path to full participation lies through being excluded.' (95) The result is that others, or our own fallen humanity, do not allow us to participate fully in the created order without some degree of compromise. To compromise in this way, however, argues O'Donovan, is to fail to imitate Christ. '[Christ's followers] are called to accept exclusion from the created good as a necessary price of a true and unqualified witness to it.' (96) Though not developed by O'Donovan, this statement has interesting implications for debates about appropriate lifestyles. The created order might in itself validate a lifestyle enriched by a beautiful home, good food, travel and so on. But witness to the created order in a fallen and hostile world might require that we sacrifice some of these blessings. (Although disallowing compromise in this primary sense, O'Donovan outlines two features of moral deliberation where 'compromise' in a secondary sense may apply. The first is in the application of moral criteria to specific situations, where those situations involve features which are 'deplorable and which impose unwelcome constraints upon our actions' [96], forcing us to 'compromise' between the ideal and the actual. The second is in 'the definition of norms for the conduct of public life' [97].)

Eschatology and Moral Order

We are beginning to see how O'Donovan's approach to making moral judgments is shaped by redemptive history. Starting with the gospel, we see in the resurrection an affirmation of the created order. The objective reality of this order is the basis for moral decision. The fall, however, makes us wary of our perception of that order, pointing us to the need for revelation. But the evangelical character of morality is not complete, argues O'Donovan, until we add another word, namely that of eschatology. 'From the resurrection we look not only back to the created order which is vindicated, but forwards to our eschatological participation in that order.' (22) Indeed, O'Donovan adds that, were we to follow Paul, this word would have been placed first. And in reality, as we have seen, the restoration and vindication of the created order in the resurrection of Christ underlies O'Donovan's entire argument so that eschatology is constantly to the fore.

For O'Donovan eschatology is closely related to pneumatology since 'of that final enjoyment we have a present anticipation through the Pentecostal gift of the Holy Spirit' (22). The resurrection not only reaffirms and restores the created order, it also makes possible 'life in the Spirit'. The result in *Resurrection and Moral Order* is a discussion of the Spirit and Christian freedom (22-27). For without the anticipatory presence of the Holy Spirit, the resurrection remains two steps removed from a moral ethic: first, because it is a promise of an, as yet, unrealised world-redemption; and second, because it points to a 'world-order' and 'humanity' which are too easily viewed in a non-moral way, as objective realities distant or detached from 'me'. Instead. 'the Pentecostal gift means that the renewal of the universe touches me at the point where I am a moral agent.' (23; see also 101) This subjective aspect has two complementary features: 'First, that the Spirit makes the reality of redemption, distant from us in time, both *present* and *authoritative*; secondly, that he evokes our *free* response to this reality as moral agents.' (102). Thus, through the Holy Spirit, there is a movement from the objective to the subjective mode, in which the awaited world-redemption is already present in anticipatory form. In this way 'the Spirit brings God's act in Christ into critical opposition to the falsely structured reality in which we live.' (104) Through the Spirit our world is judged even as it is also being recreated.

Love as the Ethic of the Restored Created Order

According to O'Donovan, 'the Spirit forms and brings to expression the appropriate pattern of free response to objective reality' (25). And this 'appropriate pattern' is *love*. 'Love is the overall shape of Christian ethics, the form of human participation in created order.' (25) This love which is enabled by the Spirit is the same love of Christ who in his creative freedom did not overthrow the created order, but redeemed it, rescuing it from the emptiness to which it had been subjected. This love defines the task of ethics: '[Love] is itself ordered and shaped in accordance with the order that it discovers in its object, and this ordering of love it is the task of substantive Christian ethics to trace.' (25-6) Or again: 'love is the principle which confers unifying order both upon the moral field and upon the character of the moral subject.' (226) Participation in the divine love is the goal of humanity and creation, and Christian love in the present is oriented to that end. The focus upon love is along the lines suggested by Williams, as we noted above. Both O'Donovan and Williams place love, rather than hope, at the centre of social ethics. But it is not love divorced from hope. Love, says O'Donovan, is 'the appropriate response' to the vindication and restoration of the creation order which finds its fulfilment in the new creation.

Before we return to O'Donovan's exposition of love in an eschatological context, we need to examine another dimension of the freedom given by the Spirit. According to O'Donovan, 'human freedom consists not only in the power to act alone, but in the power to act together, as a co-operating fellowship' (163). According to O'Donovan, the church is humanity acting. It does not merely speak God's word. It also hears God's word, enters his kingdom by faith and begins to be conformed to its life. 'It is humanity, and not an angel.' (164) O'Donovan rejects what he calls 'angel-ecclesiology'. If the church's role is simply to witness to the kingdom, then when that kingdom has come, its role will be over. If its task is simply to speak God's word of redemption, then when redemption is complete, that task will be done. But the church not only announces the coming of God's kingdom, it is the kingdom already taking shape. It not only points to the eschatological redemption of humanity, it is the new humanity. This is the 'ultimate significance of the community in God's redeeming purposes' (164). And this is a significance which, as we have seen, is lost in Moltmann's theology. In Moltmann, the church is not the 'not-world'; rather it is the avant-garde of the future of all humanity. The distinction between church and world is temporal (indeed temporary), rather than eschatological. O'Donovan maintains this distinction without lapsing into the self-serving view of mission which Moltmann fears.

> The new reality confirms, clarifies and vindicates the reality which was always there, presupposed even in its denial by sin, the reality of human brotherhood. Far from denying universal love of man for man, the love of the believer for Christ and for his fellow-believer is the form in which it is restored and re-enters the world. For the church anticipates restored humanity, and all humanity lies implicitly in the church. To love the church, therefore, is to venture out beyond its present borders, to claim those who lie outside them for their place in the City of God. (242)

In other words, the eschatological nature of this love means it is not the closed love of an exclusive community, but a *missionary love*.

Love is hopeful in the sense that it carries with it 'a sensed incompleteness' and depends upon the anticipated future to make it intelligible. In the language of the Gospels, love has a 'reward'. If love is a participation in the restored creation and in the divine life, we might ask what higher good could constitute our reward? O'Donovan answers, 'only a good that is essentially one with this good, a renewal and perfection of this good which we now have.' (248-9) In other words, citing Augustine, 'he himself is our reward'. We do not experience a private redemption apart from the public redemption of the cosmos. And in the present, even though the life of love is not intrinsically a burden, it does involve us in burdens, for it is life in conformity to the cross. The pattern of labour and reward corresponds to that of cross and resurrection.

Hope and Faith

While hope starts with the incomplete and imperfect present, and looks in expectation to its completing and perfecting in the future; faith moves in the opposite direction, starting with the final judgment's affirmation of the created order, and turns to the present with that affirmation as a given. Faith moves to the present, rather than from it, giving practical substance to what is hoped for. Faith 'corrects' hope's perception of the present, as incomplete and imperfect, by regarding it in the light of the affirmation of its future completeness and perfection (253). 'Justification' binds ethics and eschatology together. 'To conceive God's final judgment of grace upon man's life as the hope of *righteousness* is to insist that any rightness which may belong to human act or character derives from this final judgment.' (253) In other words, to use language not used by O'Donovan, justification precedes sanctification in Christian experience, even though justification is eschatological and sanctification is historical. Our sanctification, O'Donovan argues, depends not simply on the change wrought in conversion, nor simply in the on-going operation of divine grace, but in that last and decisive word which is the object of faith. And this is the word already spoken in the resurrection of Jesus (Romans 4:25). It is not that a person does what they can to earn God's verdict of 'Yes'. Rather, a person is only able to please God because God will most definitely say 'Yes'. Indeed, O'Donovan argues that 'the improper divorce of sanctification from justification bequeathed Protestant churches their characteristic tension between a gospel with no concern for life in the world, and a concern for life in the world which has lost touch with the gospel' (254).

Moltmann also gives the final judgment a christological focus, but, while remaining non-committal, concludes that the 'Yes' in Christ suggests that the final judgment may not involve condemnation. In contrast, O'Donovan continues to assert that with the 'Yes' of the final judgment is also a 'No'. While God says 'Yes' to humanity in Christ, he has also said 'No' to all refusal of Christ. This 'No' does not qualify the 'Yes', making it ambiguous or incomplete. 'In rejecting all that rejects him, God has rejected nothing of humanity and nothing of the created universe, but only that which denies and detracts from them.' (256) God is not dependent upon his creatures and they have no claim over him – 'not even the claim that if he will not capitulate to it on its own terms, something will be lacking from his restored creation' (256).

Conclusion

In a paper delivered at the National Evangelical Conference on Social Ethics in 1978, a gathering of over 100 British evangelicals, under the chairmanship of John Stott, and described as 'the first national evangelical venture into the field of social ethics to be held in Britain' (see Chester, 1993:93,180-1), O'Donovan said: 'There are, of course, notoriously, two ways of living in expectation. We can believe in the value of intermediate transformation, "preparing the way for the Lord", and so commit ourselves to a life of activity; or we can feel that the ultimate transformation renders all penultimate change irrelevant, and so resign ourselves to a life of hopeful suffering. (1979:26) O'Donovan comments that, although they appear opposed, they have one important thing in common, namely, a negative view of the *status quo*. Neither, he claims, sees in the present a natural order to which we can respond in love and obedience. The purpose of the world is imposed upon it, either by our activity or by God's intervention.

The comment is revealing in more ways than one. It confirms our central thesis, namely that eschatology offers an ambiguous motive for social transformation. The future confirms the commitment to social change for some, while relegating the need for such change for others. It can lead equally – and Christian history confirms the point – to 'a life of activity' and to 'a life of hopeful suffering'. Our study has shown that those arguing that eschatology leads *of necessity* to the former have failed to prove their point adequately. This is not meant to suggest that eschatology should lead to resignation but that eschatology is ambiguous as a motive for social involvement – although nor should it be assumed in the light of the New Testament emphasis on patience and endurance that 'a life of hopeful suffering' is always inappropriate.

O'Donovan's comment also point to the fact that he himself essentially has a positive view of the present, or at least a positive view of the possibilities open in the present. It is overstating it to say that O'Donovan offers a creation-redemption-consummation pattern (compared, for example with the tendency in Mott towards a sin-redemption-consummation pattern). The fall has epistemological implications: the creation order is no longer clearly perceived by humanity. But even when O'Donovan's warnings about confusing epistemology and ontology are taken into account (1979:26-7,32-3), the ontological implications of the fall are less clearly spelt out. O'Donovan points out that to speak of the disorder in the world presupposes an original order. The point is well taken, and O'Donovan's central thesis – the vindication of that creation order in the resurrection – is a crucial corrective to kingdom ethics. Nevertheless, that original order is now *dis*ordered. Its restoration is assured as a result of the resurrection, but is not yet fully accomplished. Sin is still a very present reality – there is, as O'Donovan acknowledges, 'disruption within nature' (1979:26).

Related to this is the criticism made against O'Donovan that his moral foundations neglect the cross (Williams, 1988:89-90). O'Donovan says that the meaning of the cross is that discipleship involves confrontation and exclusion, but he does so in the context of the conflict between the true and the false – epistemological categories. There exists in the New Testament a pattern of cross-resurrection in which, while the resurrection promises a glorious future, the cross is the mark of both Christian discipleship in the present (it is the supreme expression of love) and the continuing presence of sin (it is the supreme expression of evil). It is this eschatology of the cross which we will explore in our concluding chapter.

PART THREE

An Eschatology of the Cross

CHAPTER 14

United with the Crucified and Risen Christ

We have seen progressively more satisfactory attempts, in Mott, Mouw and O'Donovan respectively, to relate eschatology and transformational mission. In the process, however, eschatology has increasingly become an integral part of an overall picture rather than the central theme. There is a shift away from an eschatological approach to mission towards an approach shaped by the 'biblical drama', by redemptive history as a whole. Just as eschatology cannot be excluded from missiology, so eschatology alone cannot shape mission or social ethics. By itself it is highly ambiguous.

Much of the discussion of eschatology in relation to mission is shaped by a fear of it acting as a disincentive to social involvement. There has been a high degree of sensitivity, both in Moltmann and among evangelicals, to the Marxist critique of Christian hope as opium for the people. The attempt has been made, therefore, to shape eschatology so that it functions as a basis for social involvement, rather than leading to other-worldly escapism. Our study has shown, however, that such attempts, while having much to commend them, are not entirely successful. Eschatology, in and of itself, remains ambiguous in its relationship to social involvement. Ultimately even Moltmann himself acknowledges this in *The Coming of God*: 'Every hope is equivocal. It can fill the present with new power, but it can also draw power away from the present. It can lead to resistance – and also to spiritual escape.' (*CoG*, 153) A certain hope of future transformation appears to act as an incentive to change in history for some, while for others it acts as a disincentive. Criticisms can be made of both extremes of such a polarisation. It is hard to avoid the suspicion, however, that one's presuppositions about social transformation count more than one's eschatology.

Moltmann starts by adopting Marx's assertion that philosophy must serve the case of transformation. For Moltmann this becomes the assertion that theology – and therefore eschatology, since eschatology is the medium of Christian theology – must serve social transformation. The point is that the commitment to social transformation is presupposed and therefore prior to the discussion of eschatology. The same, one suspects, is true of those evangelicals who have sought to reaffirm social involvement. In attempting this reaffirmation, they are aware of the world-denying eschatology of many of those who deny the importance of social involvement. It has been important, therefore, for them to develop an alternative eschatological approach. Again, the commitment to social change is prior to the discussion of eschatology. Moltmann believes, 'The *pro-missio* of the universal future *leads of necessity* to the universal *missio* of the church to all nations' (*TH*, 225, emphasis added). But Moltmann is not concerned to provide an eschatological basis for transformation, but rather to show how eschatology might affect a prior commitment to transformation. That is to say, his commitment to transformation is not based upon his reflection upon eschatology, but is axiomatic to his thought. As such, for Moltmann, the question is not whether eschatology leads to change, but how eschatology can be used in the service of change. Chapman believes that Moltmann provides 'less an "ethic", in the sense of selecting among competing moral options, and more an "ethos", in the sense of a theological preparation of attitudes prior to choosing' (1983:458). For Moltmann Christian hope can never be 'the opium of the people'; instead it is 'the power and ferment of emancipation here and now' (1969:79). His fear of a quietistic and escapist hope leads him to neglect the New Testament association of hope with patience, endurance and long-suffering. Yet this need not be a quietistic long-suffering; it can also be the endurance and long-suffering of love which patiently labours even in the face of disappointment.

Writing in 1976, Walter Capps asks 'What ever happened to hope?' He describes how the widespread interest in hope vanished between the 'sixties and the 'seventies (Capps, 1976). Hope appeared to evaporate in the face of historical disappointment (see *CG*, 2; 1980:13-4). A generation later, Moltmann contributed to a seminar looking at hope and postmodernism entitled 'the future of hope' (Volf and Katerberg, 2004). He looks at the way biblical and extra-biblical apocalyptic visions were secularised in the Enlightenment. But postmodernity now views the Enlightenment project with suspicion because of its role in Third world poverty, environmental destruction, two world wars and the various holocausts of the twentieth century. Modernity's vision of human progress now lacks credibility. As a result, acknowledges Moltmann, postmodernism is sceptical about visions for the future and of eschatology in all its variations (2004ii). Can we talk about the failure of hope? Does hope have a future? Was the *Theology of Hope* simply an expression of its time? Could it be that Moltmann's failure to make hope practical and, in particular, to distinguish between and relate immanent and ultimate hopes, that led to the failure of the theology of hope to transcend its cultural context.

In this respect it is interesting that in a lecture given in 1974, entitled 'The Crucified God and the Apathetic Man' (see 1975:69-84), Moltmann does not counter disillusionment and apathy with a renewed enthusiasm for hope. Indeed, rather than contrasting apathy with hope, he contrasts it with *pathos*. Rather than turning to the resurrection, he turns to the passion of Christ and of God. It is not man as a being of hope, but *homo sympathetica* who is now to the fore. The same shift is evident in *The Crucified God*, even though this must be seen in continuity with *Theology of Hope* (see also the comments of Dumas,

1978:97). Could it be that love, and in particular participation in the passion of God, rather than hope, is the underlying motive for mission? The centrality of hope is not repudiated, but is it really hope 'in the service of love' (1969:121)?

Our criticisms are not meant to suggest that eschatology has no place in social ethics or missiology; nor that the attempts by Moltmann and evangelicals to relate eschatology and missiology have been wholly in vain. Despite our criticism, it is our conviction that eschatology is an important feature of transformational missiology. Nevertheless, eschatology can also function as a disincentive to social change, if social change has not been established on other grounds. In others words, as a motive for mission, and social transformation in particular, hope is ambiguous. Given that such a motive can be is established on other grounds, hope can have an important and creative role to play. In particular, hope has the potential to sustain the long-suffering, endurance of love.

John Calvin: Love Sustained by Hope

We turn now to the thought of John Calvin in order to demonstrate an alternative way in which eschatology can be related to mission, including social involvement. Our concern is not to provide a definitive exposition of Calvin or contribute to the understanding of his thought, but rather make some concluding remarks on our theme by reference to primary sources of Calvin's thought and the biblical text. We will propose what we believe to be a missing dimension in the debates outlined above. We will attempt to show how an emphasis upon future blessing need not function as 'opium for the people', but can, if such action is established on other grounds, reinforce one's commitment to social involvement. Contrary to the thrust of the arguments examined previously, we want to assert that a form of other-worldliness – not in the sense of belief in a wholly new, ethereal future, but in the sense of patient hope for a radically new future beyond history – can actually promote this-worldly activity. We will examine Calvin's understanding of the role of eschatology in the life of the believer, in particular the union of the believer in the death and resurrection of Christ. We will then extend and apply this to the Christian life in a broader context, that is to say, to the life of the Christian in the world and the mission of the church.

Calvin is an appropriate point of departure for such an endeavour. Moltmann cites Calvin in the 'meditation on hope' which functions as an introduction to *Theology of Hope,* and indeed to Moltmann's eschatological theology as a whole (15-36). Moltmann elicits Calvin's support at the starting point of his theological programme. Indeed, it may be that Moltmann's *meditation on hope* is intended as a parallel to Calvin's *meditatio vitae futuræ* – meditation on the future life (see especially *Institutes,* 3.9). Nor is this the only significant parallel, intended or otherwise, for Karl Barth, in what proved to be the programmatic work for his early theology – his commentary on Romans

(1933:19-20) – quotes from the very same passage in Calvin's writings (Calvin's comments on Hebrews 11:1). The passage which Moltmann cites (*TH*, 18-19) is as follows:

> Eternal life is promised to us, but it is promised to the dead; we are told of the resurrection of the blessed, but meantime we are involved in corruption; we are declared to be just, and sin dwells within us; we hear that we are blessed, but meantime we are overwhelmed by untold miseries; we are promised an abundance of all good things, but we are often hungry and thirsty; God proclaims that he will come to us immediately, but seems to be deaf to our cries. What would happen to us if we did not rely on hope, and if our minds did not emerge above the world out of the midst of darkness through the shining Word of God and by his Spirit? (*Comm. on Hebrews 11:1*)

'Calvin', says Moltmann, 'perceived very plainly the discrepancy involved in the resurrection hope.' (18) 'Present and future, experience and hope, stand in contradiction to each other in Christian eschatology, with the result that man is not brought into harmony and agreement with the given situation, but is drawn into conflict between hope and experience.' (18) To a certain extent this is true of Calvin. The Christian, as he or she aspires heavenwards, is in conflict with this world. There is a discrepancy in resurrection hope between present and future.

Yet Moltmann's fundamental contradiction between present and future is for Calvin only an apparent contradiction. While there might appear to be a contradiction between hope and experience, with the eye of faith we perceive that, through our union with Christ, we already share the glory of the future. Commenting on faith as the demonstration of things unseen, Calvin says, 'these two things *apparently contradict* each other, but yet they *agree perfectly* when we are concerned with faith,' (*Comm. on Hebrews 11:1*; emphasis added) Moltmann's real contradiction leaves him, as we have seen, without adequate mediating categories between the present and future. For Calvin, however, the present and future are linked by our union with Christ. Through his resurrection and ascension, Christ now enjoys the glory of heaven, and we, through our union with him, share this by faith. Our resurrection life is now hidden under our present experience of the cross. This means that, whereas in *Theology of Hope* the accent is on faith and hope expressing themselves in an agitation for change, for Calvin they are frequently linked with *patience*. 'Patience necessarily follows hope. If it is burdensome to lack the good which one desires, we must faint from despair, unless we sustain and comfort ourselves by patience. Hope, therefore, always brings patience with it ... Hope is sustained only by patience. The salvation of believers, therefore, is fulfilled only by patience.' (*Comm. on Romans 8:25*; see also, for example, *Comm. on 1 Thessalonians 1:3*)

Faith, for Calvin, is trusting in God's mercy and believing his promises which means that it is always related to hope and always gives rise to hope

(*Inst.*, 3.2.7; see also 3.2.41-42). At the same time, hope sustains faith. Faith trusts in what it does not see, what is hidden, and so is sustained by hope's expectation of the manifestation of Christ and the fulfilment of God's promises. 'Hope strengthens faith ... refreshes faith ... sustains faith ... invigorates faith again and again with perseverance.' (*Inst.* 3.2.42; see also *Comm. on 1 Corinthians 13:13*) Faith, then, for Calvin, is eschatologically determined for it looks to Christ who is our hope and resurrection. 'Our faith can only stand if it looks to the coming of Christ ... this, I say, is the only way to sustain our faith, so that we may patiently wait for the promised life.' (*Comm. on 1 John 3:2*; see also, for example, *Comm. on Ephesians 2:6*) Citing Calvin again – faith 'hastens beyond this world' – Moltmann comments, Calvin 'did not mean by this that Christian faith flees the world, but he did mean that it strains after the future' (*TH*, 19). This understanding, while arguable (there are those who believe that Calvin had a world-denying ethic), seems conditioned by Moltmann's fear that any other-worldly eschatology will be detrimental to participation in the world now. This fear makes Moltmann's use of Calvin highly selective, for Calvin also speaks of a 'contempt for the present life' (*Inst.* 3.9.1,3).

Yet, for Calvin, eschatology did not lead in practice to the quietism which many seem to fear will be the correlate of an emphasis on patience (see Holwerda, 1984:312). For Calvin the patience of hope is always connected with the work of faith and labour of love (1 Thessalonians 1:3). What sort of faith arises from hope? 'It is an earnest faith, full of power, so that it shirks no task when our neighbours are in need of help.' (*Comm. on 1 Thessalonians 1:3*) It is clear that for Calvin it is not those whose affections are rooted in this earth who exercise love for others to the full. Rather, it is those who, through their union with Christ in his death, deny themselves and mortify the flesh; and who, through their union with Christ in his resurrection, have set their hearts on things above so that they are liberated from the pursuit of their own interests and can truly persevere in love and seek the heavenly life now. T.F. Torrance says, in contrast 'to the deep element of quietism in Luther's whole position ... Calvin's eschatology was activist, stressing the mighty acts of God in Christ and *therefore* the work of the church in obedience and joy, in thankful assurance of victory waiting for the final act of redemption.' (1954:91)

We are 'to wait quietly and in haste', enduring but not being slothful. Confident in a better life ahead, the believer is able to remain steadfast in good works: 'the resurrection hope has the effect of making us not grow tired of doing good' (*Comm. on 1 Corinthians 15:58*; see also *Comm. on 2 Peter 3:12*). The important point is that, whereas for Moltmann a very real contradiction exists between present and future, for Calvin that contradiction is only apparent. The future glory of the resurrection life is present now in a hidden way. The Christian life, then, is the outworking of that hidden reality in lives lived under the cross. The kingdom is already hidden in the life of the Body and the lives of its members. The renewal of all things and the restoration of universal order has begun in the believer's experience and in the unity of the church. Holwerda says that in Calvin: 'The history of salvation which becomes visible in the church contains within it the meaning of the history of the world. And the renewal manifesting itself in the body of Christ is the renewal that embraces the whole of creation.' (1984:337)

The purpose of our examination of Calvin is to show how Calvin's understanding of the believer's union with Christ in his death and resurrection provides an important perspective on the question of eschatology and mission today. As such, we will first examine in more detail the role of eschatology in the life of the believer in Calvin's thought. Second, we will seek to extend the thought of Calvin and apply his understanding of eschatology in the Christian life to the mission of the church and the life of the believer in the world.

Union with Christ

The union of the believer with Christ, so important to Calvin's understanding of justification, is also at the heart of his understanding of the Christian life. Calvin speaks of the 'double grace' of union with Christ, namely justification and regeneration (*Inst.*, 3.11.1). Through regeneration we are being restored to the true humanity, the true image of God and the true natural order seen in Christ. This means that eschatology is central to Calvin's understanding of the Christian life, and that his eschatology is thoroughly christocentric, since all stems from the believer's union with Christ in his death and resurrection. At the same time Calvin speaks of the Holy Spirit as 'the root and seed of heavenly life in us' (*Inst.* 3.1.2) because it is through the Spirit that we are united to Christ. Union with Christ is appropriated by the believer through faith and faith is the principal work of the Holy Spirit; the Spirit is the source of faith. As a result the Holy Spirit is the surety and beginning of the life of the future in our experience now. The whole discussion of the effect of our union with Christ upon the Christian life, remembering that the *Institutes* follow the pattern of the Apostles' Creed, comes under the article of the Spirit.

The pattern for the Christian life is determined by our union with Christ in his death and resurrection so that there exists in the believer's life a pattern of suffering followed by glory (see, for example, *Inst.*, 3.8.1; *Comm. on Romans 6:5 and 7; on Romans 8:30; on Philippians 3:10; on 1 Peter 1:11; on 1 Peter 4:12*). Just as we now share in Christ's sufferings, so we will share in his glory when this revealed (see *Comm. on Philippians 3:10*; see also *Comm. on Romans 8:29*; *Comm. on 2 Timothy 2:11*; *Comm. on Hebrews 2:10*). Not that suffering is a precondition or the means of salvation – Christ's death is uniquely salvific. Rather our suffering is 'a manifest token or proof ... an extraordinary consolation ... evidence of our salvation' (*Comm. on Philippians 1:28*). This is not naturally perceptible, but when by faith we perceive our union with Christ, all evidence of participation with Christ in his suffering and death becomes evidence that we will also participate with him in his glory and life.

Following the same pattern, repentance, according to Calvin, consists of two parts: *mortification* and *vivification* (*Inst.*, 3.3.5; see also 3.3.8). Mortification is that self-denial and patient cross-bearing which arise from our participation with Christ in his death. Vivification, on the other hand, is the desire and power to live a holy life which arise from our rebirth, from our participation with Christ in his resurrection. Through partaking in Christ's death the old self is crucified; through partaking in his resurrection we are raised to newness of life (*Inst.*, 2.16.13; 3.3.9).

Although Calvin focuses on the individual, our union with Christ is not the union of individuals with Christ, but our union together as the body of Christ. Indeed, Calvin frequently speaks of the union or conformity between the Head and the members of the Body (see *Comm. on John 15:10; on Colossians 1:24; on Hebrews 2:10*). And he speaks, too, of the renewal of the earth and the restoration to order of all things (see, for example, *Comm. on John 13:31; on Romans 8:19-22; on Hebrews 7:17*) which is already a reality in the Body of Christ (see *Comm. on Ephesians 1:10*).

Union with Christ in His Death

Although not all believers will die as martyrs for Christ's sake, all have been saved through Christ that we might be conformed to his image, express his pattern, and follow his example (see, for example, *Inst.*, 3.6.3, *Comm. on Matthew 20:23; on John 15:10; on Romans 8:29*). There is to be a 'conformity' (*Comm. on John 15:10; on Hebrews2:10*) or 'analogy' (*Comm. on 2 Corinthians 6:2*) or 'correspondence' (*Comm. on Colossians 1:24*) between the Head and the members of the Body. Calvin recognises that this will not involve an imitation of every aspect of Christ's activity. We do not follow, for example, that which stems from his divinity. Instead, it is Christ's self-denial and cross-bearing which lie at the heart of the *imitatio Christi*. Yet this conformity to Christ is not just a case of following his example, rather it is that which arises from our union with him in his death and resurrection. 'Our ingrafting signifies not only our conformity to the example of Christ, but also the secret union by which we grow together with him, in such a way that he revives us by his Spirit, and transfers his power to us.' (*Comm. on Romans 6:5*; see also *Comm. on Romans 6:4; on 1 Peter 4:1*) As we shall endeavour to show, this understanding of conformity to Christ in his death can shape our approach to socio-political involvement.

The pattern of dying with Christ has two aspects – an inward process and an outward process. Calvin speaks of a twofold mortification (*Comm. on Colossians 3:5*), a twofold likeness to the death of Christ (*Comm. on 1 Peter 4:1*), and even of two distinct communions in the death of Christ (*Comm. on Romans 6:7; Comm. on Philippians 3:10*). We are conformed to Christ through our external circumstances, in particular through afflictions and sufferings, and through an inward process of mortifying self-will and the desires of the corrupt nature within us (see, for example, *Comm. on Colossians 3:5; on 1 Peter 4:1*). In the *Institutes* he deals with the Christian life as participation in the death of Christ under these two headings: *The Denial of Ourselves* (3.7) and *Bearing the Cross* (3.8).

1. The Denial of Ourselves

Since the fall, the natural tendency of a person is to desire that which is sinful and contrary to God's will (see, for example, *Inst.*, 2.1.8-9) and to place one's affection firmly on this earth. As such, argues Calvin, in order to live to God we must deny ourselves (see *Comm. on Galatians 5:17*). Indeed, Calvin goes so far as to speak of a self-loathing. This self-loathing stands in contrast to the self-love engendered by our sinful nature. As such, the anger and hatred which we naturally direct towards God and towards others should be directed instead towards ourselves (*Comm. on Ephesians 4:26*). Calvin also speaks of 'this earthly prison of the body' (*Inst.*, 3.6.5; 3.9.4) and 'the prison house of the flesh' (*Inst.*, 3.25.1). This, however, is not a Platonic deprecation of the body (*pace* McNeill, *Institutes*, 3.7.5, fn. 9). Rather it is evident from the context that Calvin has in mind the body of death (Romans 7:24) or the body of sin (Romans 6:6) of which Paul speaks. Calvin longs for the day when we will be released from the sinful desires of the flesh and when our bodies will be resurrected gloriously new.

2. Bearing the Cross

The ordinary sufferings of life can, according to Calvin, be used, under the hand of God, for the furtherance of our sanctification. In particular, they help us to turn from the things of this earth and fix our attentions on the life to come. Nevertheless, when he speaks of cross-bearing Calvin primarily thinks of that suffering and affliction which derives from our being united with Christ: the hostility of the world which we endure for the sake of righteousness. It is only in this sense that we can truly be said to participate in the death of Christ (see *Comm. on 2 Corinthians 1:5*). If we are united with Christ, then we must expect to share in something of the sufferings which he endured patiently for our sakes (*Comm. on Isaiah 53:7; on 1 Peter 2:23*). Although this is seen primarily in the cross, Calvin believes that Christ's 'whole life was nothing but a sort of perpetual cross' (*Inst.*, 3.8.1).

The important thing is that such suffering is a very real participation in the death of Christ (see, for example, *Comm. on Matthew 10:38; on 2 Corinthians 1:5; on Philippians 3:10*). This fact – that our afflictions are a real participation in the death of Christ – is 'a great consolation' for us as we suffer (*Comm. on Philippians 3:10*), not least because if we share in his death, we will also, by God's grace, share in his life and glory (see, for example, *Comm. on 2*

Corinthians 1:5; on Philippians 3:10). Through our afflictions 'our fellowship with Christ is confirmed' (*Inst.*, 3.8.1). Suffering, then, in causing us to look beyond this world and in causing us to rely all the more on the promises of God, strengthens us in our hope (*Inst.*, 3.8.3). And conversely, as we meditate on the life to come, so we are enabled to bear the cross now in hope.

Union with Christ in His Resurrection

Through our union with Christ we participate not only in his death, but also in the life and glory of the resurrection. Christ's resurrection is a pledge of our resurrection for Christ has not risen for himself, but for us (see, for example, *Comm. on 1 Corinthians 15:22; on 2 Timothy 2:8; on Hebrews 7:25*). Likewise, because of our unity with Christ in faith, we share in his ascension into heavenly glory. 'Christ did not ascend to heaven privately for himself, to dwell there alone, but rather that it might be the common inheritance of all the godly, and that in this way the Head might be united to the members.' (*Comm. on John 14:2*) What has been begun in the Head must be completed in all the members.

But there is, for Calvin, a very real sense in which we participate even now in the resurrection, and indeed in Christ's ascension to glory. Although we do not yet live in heaven as Christ does, yet 'he makes the new life, which we live on earth after our regeneration, match his life in heaven' (*Comm. on Romans 6:10*). While the fulness of the kingdom of God will be the renewal of the whole world, the kingdom is already present in 'the inward and spiritual renewing of the soul' and the quickening of God's 'elect to heavenly newness' (*Comm. on Romans 6:10*). Christ 'now reigns when he regenerates his people into the heavenly life, and fashions them anew to the image of God.' (*Comm. on Luke 19:12*) In other words, while the consummation of the kingdom is future, it has already begun in the lives of God's people. Through the work of Christ 'the whole world was renewed and all things restored to order' (*Comm. on John 13:31*; see also, for example, *Comm. on Ephesians 1:10; on Heb 7:17*) and this is present in the life of his Body and the lives of its members. Thus, although we have not yet been raised with Christ as we will be when he comes, yet even now we already have 'the firstfruits in Christ' (*Comm. on 1 Corinthians 15:23*; see also *Comm. on John 7:38; on 1 Timothy 4:8*).

Hidden Life

Nevertheless, despite our present experience of the resurrection, we never outgrow the cross, and indeed it is the experience of the cross which predominates in our present life. 'The resurrection of Christ does lead us away from the cross.' (*Comm. on Galatians 6:14*) Although the inward aspect of our union with Christ is being renewed by the Spirit, outwardly it does not manifest itself. Or rather, outwardly it manifests itself in the suffering of the cross, rather than the glory of the resurrection. As such, the idea of 'hiddenness' is very important in Calvin's thought. Our new life in Christ, our participation with him in glory, is a present reality, but it is a hidden reality. 'Our life is now hidden in Christ, and will remain hidden, as if it were buried, until Christ shall appear from heaven.' (*Comm. on 1 Peter 1:7*; see also *Inst.*, 2.9.3; *Comm. on Hebrews 11:1*) Only by faith do we understand that we share in Christ's ascended glory, for this 'is not yet seen with eyes'. 'Our salvation is still hidden in hope, yet in Christ we possess blessed immortality and glory.' (*Comm. on Ephesians 2:6*) Christ alone 'is the mirror in which we can contemplate that which the weakness of the cross obscures in us.' (*Comm. on Ephesians 1:20*)

Is salvation future or present? On the one hand, Christ has been raised from the dead and has ascended into glory and we are united with him through faith. On the other hand, the cross is the essential mark of Christian experience here on earth. The answer, then, that Calvin would give is that salvation is present but hidden; that it is future but possessed now in Christ by faith. It is possessed now by Christ, and by us through our union with Christ by faith (see *Comm. on Ephesians 2:6*). This means that the Christian life is lived in the tension between the commencement and completion of our salvation and of the reign of Christ. It means, too, that we have no reason for complaint if our present life is one of affliction, for our resurrection life is a hidden life (see *Comm. on Colossians 3:3*). Finally, if the kingdom of God and our resurrection life are now hidden, the *parousia* of Christ will, in contrast, involve the revelation of his glory and power over all things and the manifestation of our life (see, for example, *Inst.*, 2.16.17; *Comm. on Luke 19:12*).

Meditation on the Future Life

The meditation on the future (or heavenly) life, *meditatio vitae futuræ*, is a central aspect of godly living, according to Calvin (see *Comm. on Acts 20:21*). Since Calvin is reluctant to speculate on the nature of our future life (see, for example, *Inst.*, 3.25.8,10-11; *Comm. on Romans 8:21; on 2 Peter 2:10*), this meditation is more on the *fact* of our future life, than on its *form*. It is the recollection of our status as pilgrims in this world. 'Although believers are now pilgrims on earth, yet by their confidence they surmount the heavens, so that they cherish their future inheritance in their bosoms with tranquillity.' (*Comm. on Romans 5:2*) It is the remembrance that we are aliens and strangers on earth (Hebrews 11:13, 1 Peter 1:1, 2:11), those who are looking for a better country (Hebrews 11:16). 'Christ bids the disciples be ready and equipped for the road, that they may travel with speed through the earth and not look for any fixed and quiet resting-place anywhere but in heaven ... God does not grant the title of sons except to those who admit they are strangers on the earth: they must not only always be ready for pilgrimage, but actually keep moving in the way to eternal life.' (*Comm. on Matthew 24:43*; see also *Comm. on 1 Corinthians 15:58; on 2 Corinthians 5:1*).

The meditation on the future life is closely linked with the ascension of Christ. Since Christ has ascended into heavenly glory and we are, by faith, united with him, so we must aspire towards, and fix our eyes upon, that heavenly glory. Since he has ascended 'we must ascend unless we want to be separated from him' (*Comm. on John 20:18*). And how do we ascend to heaven? By meditation on the heavenly life, the focus of which is the ascended Christ. As such, the meditation of the future life is an extension of our union with Christ in his resurrection (see *Comm. on Colossians 3:1*). Commenting on Philippians 3:20, Calvin exhorts his readers to 'life up your hearts, that they may be with the Lord!' (*Comm. on Philippians 3:20*). He goes on to say, 'there is no part of us that ought not to aspire after heaven with wholehearted desire' (*Comm. on Philippians 3:21*; see also *Comm. on Matthew 6:21*). For Calvin the Lord's Supper is the central means of confirming and strengthening our communion or fellowship with Christ in his death and resurrection. As such, he added to the Eucharist liturgy, at the point of communication, these words: 'Let us raise our hearts and minds on high where Jesus Christ is in the glory of his Father, and from whence we look for him at our redemption' (Jasper and Cuming, 1975:142).

The negative counterpart of the meditation on the future life is contempt for this earth. If self-loathing is a feature of self-denial (the inward aspect of conformity to Christ in his death), then a contempt for this earth is a feature of cross-bearing (the outward aspect of conformity to Christ in his death). 'Whatever kind of tribulation presses upon us, we must ever look to this end: to accustom ourselves to contempt for the present life and to be aroused thereby to mediate upon the future life.' (*Inst.*, 3.9.1) Contempt for earth is in effect a precondition for true meditation on the future life: 'the mind is never seriously aroused to desire and ponder the life to come unless it be previously imbued with contempt for the present life' (*Inst.*, 3.9.1; see also *Comm. on Luke 24:31*). It is to this end that God permits his children to suffer affliction, that is that they might not set their hearts on things below but on things above (see *Comm. on Matthew 27:27; on 2 Corinthians 4:16*). Indeed Calvin suggests that there is a sense in which we long for death (*Inst.*, 3.9.4).

It is for this reason that Calvin has been accused of holding a world-denying ethic in which the world and the present are swallowed up in eschatology (see Quistorp, 1955:52). Calvin himself, however, is careful not to encourage a hatred of the present life – that would be ingratitude to God the Creator (*Inst.*, 3.9.3). This means that Calvin can say we must have contempt for this earth, while also arguing that it is made by God not just for our necessities, but in order to give us pleasure and enjoyment (*Inst.*, 3.10.2). In fact, Calvin devotes a whole chapter of the *Institutes* (3.10, the chapter immediately following *Meditation on the Future Life*) to a discussion of how we should rightly enjoy the present life without being ensnared by it. Indeed, far from denying this world, only those who truly aspire to heaven live in this world as they should, for 'believers ought to lead a heavenly life in this world' (*Comm. on*

Philippians 3:20). Torrance, commenting on Calvin's *contemptus præsentis vitæ,* says that this attitude to this world 'does not in any sense mean a depreciation of our earthly life – how could it, for it is God's *kindness,* his *good creation,* even though it is marred by our sin? – but such handling of our present life that its future renewal or restoration is already made to govern the present.' (1956:141) Holwerda, too, defends Calvin from the accusation that he is world-denying: 'Calvin's so-called unworldliness is in actuality a seeking for renewal and life in Christ who is now in heaven. Meditation on the future life is not a rejection of this created world in favour of another heavenly world unrelated to this one, but it is always a seeking of Christ in whom the renovation of this world has occurred.' (Holwerda, 1984:326-7) It is only as we taste of the future life prepared for us in Christ that we truly learn to appreciate this earthly life as a gift of God's mercy. And, conversely, present blessings whet our hope and desire for heavenly blessings *(Inst.,* 3.9.3). 'In short, it is not in itself wrong to love this life, provided we only journey in it as foreigners, always intent on our bourne. For the true way to love life is when we remain in it as long as God pleases and are prepared to change our home as soon as he tells us – or, to put it in a word, when we, so to say, carry it in our hands and offer it to God as a sacrifice.' *(Comm. on John 12:25)*

Our exposition of Calvin's understanding of the believer's union with Christ in his death and resurrection is an attempt to lay some foundations. In the final chapter we will extend and apply Calvin's understanding of the role eschatology plays in the Christian life to the Christian life in a broader context; that is to say, to the life of the Christian in the world and the mission of the church.

CHAPTER 15

An Eschatology of the Cross

The Way of the Cross

When Calvin works out the implications of our participation in the death of Christ for the Christian life, he confines himself largely to self-denial, mortification and cross-bearing. As we have seen, the first two concern what Calvin calls the inward process of conformity to the cross of Christ, the latter to the outward process. Where we wish to extend Calvin's thought is in respect to this latter aspect, our outward participation in the death of Christ, what Michael J. Gorman has called 'cruciformity' (2001). For Calvin this consists primarily in the suffering and persecution we endure as Christians, and it largely serves the process of inward mortification and self-denial. While we would not dispute either of these truths, we wish to add, firstly, our participation with Christ in his death consists not just simply in cross-bearing (*tolerantia crucis*), but more broadly in following the way of the cross (the *via crucis*). As such, secondly, the cross is at the heart of Christian discipleship and the Christian's relationship with the world. That our participation with Christ in his death affects our relationship to the world is certainly not disputed by Calvin. Self-denial, although primarily a denial of self in relation to God, also, for Calvin, involves a denial of self in relation to one's neighbour; and, as such, is necessary for true love for others (*Inst.*, 3.7.4-6). Nevertheless, the fact remains that in Calvin the *tolerantia crucis* predominates over the *via crucis*.

The aim of mission given in what is commonly called the Great Commission is to 'go and make disciples' (Matthew 28:19) and to be a disciple is to follow Jesus. It involves imitating Jesus (1 Thessalonians 1:6), being 'christlike'. Indeed, to the Romans Paul says, 'clothe yourselves with the Lord Jesus Christ' (Romans 13:14). Yet clearly we are not to imitate Jesus in every respect. On one hand, he was an unmarried Jewish male and an itinerant preacher in first century rural Palestine. On the other hand, he was the Son of God, who accomplished the salvation of the world. Both in the specifics of his human vocation, and in his divine nature and salvific role, we clearly cannot follow him. Rather we follow the example of his sacrificial love, submission and service which characterised his entire ministry, but is seen supremely in the cross. The essential mark of Christian discipleship is the cross of Jesus Christ.

Thus when Paul says we are to be imitators of God, he spells this out by saying that we are to 'live a life of love, just as Christ loved us and gave himself up for us as a fragrant offering and sacrifice to God' (Ephesians 5:1 2). Christ's love for us, in his sacrificial giving of himself, is our model as we seek to live 'a life of love'.

Perhaps Jesus' most programmatic statement on discipleship is Mark 8:34 (= Matthew 16:24 = Luke 9:23), where Jesus says, 'If anyone would come after me, he must deny himself and take up his cross and follow me'. In each gospel this saying follows the prediction of the sufferings of the Son of Man, and as such, this saying links discipleship – taking up one's cross – with the cross of Christ. Those that would follow him must deny themselves just as he did and take up their cross (see also Matthew 10:38 = Luke 14:27). Only those who lose their lives will gain them (see also Matthew 10:39 and John 12:24-26). Only those who are not ashamed of the Son of Man – a Son of Man who suffers and is killed – will be those of whom the Son of Man is not ashamed. Ernest Best shows that 'cross-bearing' could not have been a literal part of discipleship (i.e. martyrdom by crucifixion) for all those who would follow Jesus, although it does have that potential (Best, 1981:38-39). Indeed, Luke's account adds the word 'daily', implying a metaphorical understanding. The important point is that cross-bearing, although 'a precise point in the life of Jesus ... is symbolic of all his loving activity' (Best, 1981:39).

The broader context of this saying in Mark's gospel is a section built around the journey to Jerusalem (8:27-10:45) which Anderson entitles: 'The will of God for Jesus and his disciples: the way of suffering' (1976:205). There may indeed be a parallel between the way to Jerusalem (the way *to* the cross) and the way of discipleship (the way *of* the cross). The important thing to note is that Mark has built this section on discipleship around three predictions by Jesus of his sufferings and death (8:31; 9:31; 10:33-34). Thus, for example, when James and John ask Jesus for positions of honour in his glory, Jesus responds by emphasising the necessity of suffering. And when the other ten become indignant, Jesus teaches them that leadership in the kingdom community is not to follow the pattern of the Gentiles, who lord it over those under them. Instead, it is to be based on the pattern of Jesus himself: 'the Son of Man did not come to be served, but to serve, and to give his life as a ransom for many' (Mark 10:45; Mark 10:41-45 = Matthew 20:24-28 = Luke 22:24-27; see also Mark 9:33-37 = Matthew 18:1-5 = Luke 9:46-48; Matthew 23:11-12). Whoever would be great in the community of Christ must be a servant, and whoever would be first must be the slave of all (Mark 10:44). The pattern is the life of service of the Son of Man, seen supremely in his self-giving on the cross as a ransom for many.

The cross, then, is at the heart, not only of our redemption, but also of our ethics, of our life in the world. Nor is it just in the Gospels that the cross is presented as the standard and pattern for Christian behaviour. Paul speaks of Christians sharing in Christ's sufferings (see, for example, Romans 8:17).

Certainly this involves the possibility of persecution (see, for example, Acts 14:22; 1 Thessalonians 3:2-4). But the way of the cross is more than simply accepting and facing persecution. It forms the heart of much of Paul's teaching on the Christian life. In urging the Corinthian Christians to give generously, Paul points to the cross (2 Corinthians 8:9). The attitude of those in the church of Rome towards those among them who are weak is to be governed by Christ's example (Romans 14:15; 15:1-7; see also 1 Corinthians 10:31-11:1). In Ephesians 5 husbands are told to love their wives as Christ loved the church and gave himself up for her (Ephesians 5:25). Whether the subject is giving, relationships within the church or marriage, the cross forms the basis of Paul's teaching.

Certainly Paul saw his own ministry as a participation in the sufferings of Christ. He speaks of wanting to know 'the fellowship of sharing in [Christ's] sufferings, becoming like him in his death' (Philippians 3:10). He labours to the extent that he is 'being poured out like a drink offering' (Philippians 2:17). The sufferings of Christ 'flow over into our lives' (2 Corinthians 1:5); sufferings shared by the Corinthians (2 Corinthians 1:6-7) and Philippians (Philippians 1:29-30). In his love for the Thessalonians, he shared with them not only the gospel, but his life as well (1 Thessalonians 2:7-8). Paul always accommodates himself to those he is seeking to win for Christ (1 Corinthians 9:19-23; Acts 16:3). Although such cross-centred living often involved persecution and imprisonment for Paul, it is clear that it was more than this: it was also the sacrificial giving of himself in the service of others. And it is this which is at the heart of Paul's view of his own ministry and mission. 'We always carry around in our body the death of Jesus, so that the life of Jesus may also be revealed in our body. For we who are alive are always being given over to death for Jesus' sake, so that his life may be revealed in our mortal body. So then, death is at work in us, but life is at work in you.' (2 Corinthians 4:10-12; see also 1 Corinthians 2:1-2; 15:31; 2 Corinthians 1:6; 1 Thessalonians 1:5)

Twice in 2 Corinthians, Paul, in defending his ministry, feels the need to accredit that ministry. The striking thing is that he does this not by listing his successes, but with a litany of his sufferings and difficulties (2 Corinthians 6:3-10; 11:21-12:10). In contrast to the 'super-apostles' with their emphasis on power and eloquence, for Paul the mark of genuine Christian discipleship and ministry is the way of the cross, of suffering and the giving of one's life in the service of others and of Christ. And likewise, the Christian community is made up, not of those who are wise, powerful and noble, but those who accept the foolishness, weakness and shame of the cross (1 Corinthians 1:18-31). Richard Bauckham comments: 'Paul's theological breakthrough in 2 Corinthians was to understand this weakness of the bearer of the gospel in relation to the content of the gospel. If God's definitive salvific act occurred through the weakness of the crucified Jesus, then it should be no surprise that the saving gospel of the crucified Jesus should reach the Gentiles through the weakness of his apostle.' (1982:5)

The pattern is similar in Peter's first epistle. 1 Peter 2:13-3:12 takes the form of a series of applications centred around 2:21-25 which speak of our calling to follow the example of Christ. The particular emphasis of these verses is on submission, even when we suffer for doing good, just as Christ submitted to his sufferings, even though he suffered, not for his own sins, but for ours. The suffering and submission modelled on the cross that Peter has in mind is much greater than just persecution, although it includes persecution.

In the Johannine corpus the emphasis is slightly different. Discipleship is primarily seen in terms of love expressed through obedience to the commands of the Father and the Son. It is based upon the law of love (John 13:34; 15:12; 1 John 4:21; 2 John 5). This love is to be modelled upon the love of God and of Jesus (John 13:14,34; 1 John 2:6; 3:16; 4:11,16). Yet significantly for John, love is defined in terms of the cross: 'This is how we know what love is: Jesus Christ laid down his life for us. And we ought to lay down our lives for our brothers.' (1 John 3:16; see also John 15:13 and 1 John 4:9-11). Jesus shows his love for the disciples in washing their feet, the activity of the meanest of servants (John 13:1-11). It is clear that the cross overshadows this event: the love shown here is the love which will be revealed supremely in the cross. Sitting down, Jesus tells the disciples that in spurning the privileges of his position as Teacher and Lord and humbling himself to wash their feet, he has set them an example that they should follow (John 13:12-15). Furthermore, the foot-washing sets the context for the giving of the new commandment: 'Love one another. As I have loved you, so you must love one another' (John 13:34).

So then, the way of the cross, the *via crucis*, and especially the love demonstrated in the cross, is the essential mark of Christian discipleship under the lordship of Christ. This can certainly involve persecution, but its characteristics are broader in scope. It is characterised by humility, submission, service and suffering. It is to deny oneself and to live for others, both in the church and in the world. If this appears to be a return to pietism with its emphasis on being like Jesus, we are not troubled, for, like Mouw, we believe the basic instinct of pietism to be a good one. Our desire is to see that instinct extended into the social realm in recognition of Christ's lordship over all of life. Citing John Bunyan's *The Pilgrim's Progress*, Mouw comments:

> These are powerful expressions of a Christian piety whose implications are, in the best sense of the word, 'radical'. In constructing a proper foundation for 'Christian social action' or 'political witness' or 'cultural involvement', we would be hard-pressed to find a better place to begin. Pious Christians are not to be faulted for insisting on the need for 'a practical subjection to the power of the Word', or for desiring to follow the footprints of Jesus. Rather, they must be challenged – and we along with them – to reflect carefully on the implications of these sentiments. (1983:73)

Towards a Political Theology of the Cross

The frequent failure of pietism to extend the example of Christ and the pattern of the cross into the social realm finds a suggestive parallel in Moltmann's assertion that Martin Luther failed to formulate his *theologia crucis* as social criticism. 'In political terms, its limit lay in the fact that while as a reformer Luther formulated the *theologia crucis* in theoretical and practical terms against the medieval institutional church, he did not formulate it as social criticism against feudal society in the Peasant Wars of 1524 and 1525.' (*CG*, 72; see also 1984i:104; *ET*, 23-24) Certainly the Lutheran two kingdoms model is not well thought of by those seeking a high level of political and social involvement by the church. This is because of its radical separation of the spheres of the church and world which was developed as a reaction to the all-embracing authority of the Medieval church. There are those today who, as an alternative to the separation of church and world, and in contrast to the Medieval church which sought to make the world part of the church, seek to make the church part of the world. Moltmann, for example, as we have noted previously, argues that the church 'is not "the not-world"' (*CPS*, 83). Instead of the world being subsumed under the church, the church is subsumed under the world. It is simply the beginning of the liberation of all men and women.

To those who believe the church represents the new humanity in contrast to a world under the judgment of God, such a theology is unacceptable. But what is the alternative? How are we to work out Calvin's principle of the lordship of Christ over all of life, while maintaining the autonomy of the world, or at least without seeking a return to a situation in which the church dictates to the world? How can the church be involved in politics without recreating Christendom?

Let us return to the *via crucis*. As we have shown, Christian discipleship is to follow the way of the cross. As such, Christian involvement in the world is not to be at the level of power, but at the level of weakness (see Bonhoeffer, 1971:359-62). That is to say, the church *qua* church does not seek power or influence in a secular sense (2 Corinthians 10:4), although individual Christians may seek political office. It does not seek power over the world, instead it seeks opportunities to serve the world. As it follows the *via crucis*, the church participates 'in the powerlessness of God in the world' (Bonhoeffer, 1971:362). It stands with the weak and the powerless. It speaks out on behalf of those whose voice is not heard. It seeks justice for the poor. It lives by the first beatitude: Blessed are the poor, and the poor in spirit, for theirs is the kingdom of God.

This is in keeping with Romans 13 and 1 Peter 2. The church does not seek to usurp the God-given authority of the state; it does not challenge the state for power. But this does not mean it never challenges the state to exercise its God-given authority in a godly way, nor that it never questions the rule of the state as it declares a different set of values – the values of the kingdom – through its words and deeds among the poor, and as it models those values in its community life. The subversive nature of its message is inevitable, since it proclaims to those in power the values of weakness and foolishness; and it sings of a time when the proud will be scattered, rulers deposed, the humble raised, the hungry filled and the rich sent away empty (Luke 1:51-53). As it gives witness to the good news of the kingdom in this way, it may well be that it is persecuted. The church enters the political realm not to seek power, not to make itself powerful or secure, but to be weak and vulnerable in love, and to be in solidarity with those who are weak and powerless. The power of the kingdom is seen under the sign of the cross. And in this way the church exercises the power and lordship of God *tectum sub cruce et sub contrario*, dwelling in suffering and what is contrary (see Chester, 2004, 149-165; Smith, 2003i and Hall, 1995).

Towards an Eschatology of the Cross

To suggest that the essential mark of Christian discipleship is the cross of Jesus Christ is to suggest, by implication, that the essential mark of Christian discipleship in the present is *not* power and glory. It is to suggest that resurrection power and glory belong to the future. The way of the cross must be seen in eschatological perspective. While the Christian life is lived in the power of the resurrection, resurrection glory remains a hidden reality until the apocalypse – the 'revelation'. Those who commit themselves to the *via crucis* are sustained by the hope of glory. If the *via crucis* is not to be abandoned because of disillusionment, or in favour of present self-interest, then it must be accompanied by an *eschatologia crucis*. With the way of the cross there must be an eschatology of the cross.

So far we have been speaking of suffering as that which is voluntarily accepted by disciples as they deny themselves and take up their crosses daily. Suffering, however, is clearly not always of this nature. It is not always, or even commonly, voluntarily accepted, nor meritorious. More usually, it is inflicted upon the sufferer against his or her will. In this sense suffering is always to be worked against. Yet the basic assertion holds true: present reality bears the mark of the cross. This is so because the cross is at one and the same time both the fullest expression of love and the fullest expression of evil. The cross is more than an example for us to follow. It represents the judgement of God upon sin. On the cross, Christ was made sin for us, and, as such, he encompassed the full effects of sin, including its punishment, in his own body, so that through his resurrection he might redeem the world. Yet this redemption remains essentially future, and, as such, the world continues to suffer under the power and effects of sin; in others words, it exists under the cross. Just as the world experiences godforsakenness, so Christ cried from the cross, 'My God, my God why have you forsaken me'. This is no coincidence. Christ experiences the full power and effects of sin, of godforsakenness, in order to redeem the world.

In his ministry, Jesus proclaimed that the kingdom of God had come. Its power was already at work transforming lives, bringing peace and healing to people. Likewise, through the cross and resurrection we are already reconciled both with God and with one another in the Body of Christ. The kingdom, as it were, takes shape ahead of itself in the life of the Christian community. Moreover, the power of the resurrection in the lives of this community and their experience of love spills over into society. Nevertheless, the redemption of creation, effected through the work of Christ, is ultimately future. Thus, in Romans 8 Paul says, 'the creation waits in eager expectation for the sons of God to be revealed ... the creation *will be* liberated from its bondage to decay and brought into the glorious freedom of the children of God' (Romans 8:19-21; see also Acts 3:21). As such, although the kingdom of God can be, and is, anticipated now, its full peace, righteousness and joy remain a future reality. The kingdom is neither spiritual nor heavenly (as opposed to earthly), rather it is hidden. The manifestation of its glory is future. Calvin says, the kingdom 'has not been made clearly manifest; rather it lies in the shadow of the cross and is violently opposed by [Christ's] enemies.' (*Comm. on 2 Timothy 4:1*)

Thus, if we are not to succumb to what we might call a *eschatologia gloriæ*, we must acknowledge that the kingdom of God in the world will always bear the mark of the cross. Luther distinguished between a *theologia gloriæ*, a theology of glory, which seeks the revelation of God in the power and glory of his actions, and a *theologia crucis*, a theology of the cross, which sees the ultimate revelation of God in the cross, seeing there by faith, power in weakness, victory in failure and glory in shame. Likewise, we must distinguish between an *eschatologia gloriæ*, which seeks the glory and victory of the resurrection, without accepting the reality of the cross in the present, and an *eschatologia crucis*, which looks forward to glory and victory, while seeing them as present now, in a hidden form, as shame and weakness. The redemption of the world as a whole is a future reality, and as such, no part of the political spectrum can realistically offer utopia prior to the *parousia*. According to Calvin, the fault of the disciples was to hold what we have called an *eschatologia gloriæ*. That is to say, their fault was 'to confuse the completeness of Christ's kingdom with its beginning, and to wish to acquire on earth what should be sought in heaven' (*Comm. on Matthew 24:3*). Calvin comments, 'It is enough that the faithful receive a taste of these good things now, that they may cherish the hope of their full enjoyment in the future' (*Comm. on Matthew 24:4*).

The cross judges any claim to the establishment of that which will rightly happen only after the eschaton. If the present can not escape the shadow of the cross, then it can also not experience the fulness of the resurrection. Thus, while it is wrong to suppose we can know nothing of the resurrection now, we must hold to an *eschatologia crucis*. This will function as an eschatological proviso, guarding against fulfilment eschatologies (what we might call 'overly-realized eschatologies'). And it will protect us also from de-historized, or spiritualised, eschatologies of an eternal present, which lay claim to the experience of the resurrection at the expense of, or by by-passing, the redemption of the earth from the experience of the cross (what we might call 'eschatologies of escape'). Thus it is that Calvin speaks of hope not only sustaining faith, but also restraining it (*Inst.*, 3.2.42). In other words, the very fact that we hope means we have not yet received our full redemption (Romans 8:24-25) and, as such, hope guards faith against falling into an *eschatologia gloriæ*. Faith must be accompanied by patience.

Suffering Followed by Glory

We have already seen how, for Calvin, our union with Christ in his death and resurrection means that, although we experience the resurrection in some measure already, there exists in the believer's experience the pattern of suffering followed by glory. This is so because the experience of the resurrection is, for the believer as for the cosmos, essentially future (the difference is that the believer has already received a foretaste of the resurrection). This pattern of suffering followed by glory can be expressed as the way of the cross followed by the glory of the resurrection. This means, too, that the pattern of Christian experience conforms to the pattern of Christ's own experience.

Jesus' response to the request of James and John for position of authority clearly indicates that he saw suffering as a necessary prelude to glory (Mark 10:35-40 = Matthew 20:20-23). Peter exhorts his readers to 'rejoice that you participate in the sufferings of Christ, so that you may be overjoyed when his glory is revealed' (1 Peter 4:13). This pattern of suffering followed by glory runs throughout 1 Peter (see 1 Peter 1:6-7; 1:11; 4:13; 5:1; 5:2-4; 5:6 and 5:10). One dimension of it is that of submission followed by vindication. Christ submitted to his unjust sufferings, trusting himself to God (2:23), and as a result was vindicated by God (3:17-22). Likewise, Christians are to entrust themselves to God, confident in future glory (4:12-19).

We find this suffering-glory pattern in Paul too. In Romans 8 he says, '... we share in [Christ's] sufferings in order that we may also share in his glory. I consider that our present sufferings are not worth comparing with the glory that will be revealed in us.' (Romans 8:17-18) The pattern of suffering followed by glory is a pattern the Christian shares with Christ. And, furthermore, it is a necessary pattern. We share in the sufferings of Christ *in order that* we might share in his glory. It is because of this suffering-glory pattern that Paul can argue that suffering leads ultimately to hope (Romans 5:3-4). In the light of such hope, Paul can say that 'just as the sufferings of Christ flow over into our lives, so also through Christ our comfort overflows' (2 Corinthians 1:5,7). Richard Bauckham comments: 'Paul's experience might often seem outwardly unremarkable. But because he sees the death and resurrection of Jesus as the key to his life, as to everything else, he can find there a pattern which makes

Christian sense of his experience. The shape which everyone needs to give to his experience on order to understand it Paul found in the cross and resurrection of Jesus ... All the ups and downs of his ministry were for Paul experiences *of God*, events in which he experienced an identification with Jesus in his dying and rising.' (1982:5)

It is because the way of the cross is a prelude to the glory of the resurrection that we can speak of an *eschatologia crucis* in the experience of believers. 'The resurrection does not lead us away from the cross.' (Calvin, *Comm. on Galatians 6:14*) Our redemption remains hidden until the *parousia*, the day of 'revelation'. Although adopted by God, justified, forgiven, and renewed by the Holy Spirit, Christians do not yet *appear* any more blessed than others, except to the extent that their hidden hope expresses itself in joy and confidence in God. Indeed, Christians more often appear worse off, whether because of the *tolerantia crucis* or as a result of the self-denial and the sacrificial love of the *via crucis*. This is what it means to experience the resurrection under the sign of the cross. Our participation in the resurrection and life of Christ, and our inward vivification by the Spirit, are not outwardly discernible; or rather they manifest themselves outwardly in our experience of the cross, whether the *tolerantia crucis* or the *via crucis*. As such, our salvation, our participation in the resurrection, is currently a hidden reality. This is what the Reformers meant when they spoke of the kingdom as *tectum sub cruce et sub contrario*, dwelling in suffering and what is contrary. The transforming power and rule of God are present now in a hidden way in the lives of believers and of the Christian community, and are manifest as the Christian community experiences the cross through the *tolerantia crucis* and *via crucis*.

Power to Be Weak

Yet the pattern of suffering followed by glory is not the full picture. The believer and the Christian community do experience the resurrection now in a real sense. It is the ministry of the Holy Spirit which completes the picture. In his sermon on the day of Pentecost Peter identifies the coming of the Spirit as a fulfilment of Joel's prophecy concerning the last days. The giving of the Spirit is an eschatological reality. Through the Spirit the expectation of the last days is fulfilled, even prior to the eschaton. Eternal life, the life of the future age, is present now through the mediation of the Spirit (John 6:63; 7:38-39). 'It is the gift of the Spirit which pre-eminently distinguishes the new dispensation from the old ... It is the Spirit who mediates divine life to men ... The Spirit was a gift of the new age.' (Barrett, 1955:148,271-2; see also Ladd, 1974ii:257-9,288-9) Paul describes the Spirit as a deposit, guaranteeing what is to come (2 Corinthians 1:22; 5:5; Ephesians. 1:13-14), and as the seal of our redemption (Ephesians. 1:13; 4:30; and possibly 2 Corinthians 1:22). Our redemption, says Paul, is future, but in the present we are given the Holy Spirit as a deposit and guarantee. The Spirit guarantees the promises of God (2 Corinthians 1:20-22).

Again, in Romans 8:23 Paul says we have the firstfruits of the Spirit. The harvest, so to speak, of salvation, effected by the resurrection, is given in part to us now by the Holy Spirit. Our redemption is clearly seen by Paul here as being future (Romans 8:24-25), but in the present we have the firstfruits of the Spirit. That is to say, we have a first instalment, a foretaste, of the life of the future kingdom. Thus, for example, in Romans 8:23 Paul can say that we wait for our adoption as sons, while in 8:14-17 Paul can say we are God's children and already cry '*Abba*, Father' because we have received the Spirit of adoption (see also Galatians 4:6).

The role of the Holy Spirit, then, in the life of the believer and in the life of the Christian community is to mediate the life of the future and the power of the resurrection. The Christian life is not a life of victory and power, but nor is it simply a life of weakness. It is a life of *power in weakness*, a life lived in conscious dependence upon the power of God mediated by the Holy Spirit. James Dunn writes: 'As for Jesus so for Paul, the Spirit is the power of the new age already broken into the old, not so as to bring the old to an end or render it wholly ineffective, but so as to enable the believer to live in and through the old age in the power and in the light of the new.' (J.D.G. Dunn, ' *pneuma*', *NIDNTT*, 3:701)

Through the Holy Spirit we experience the power of the resurrection in order to follow the way of the cross. It is, as it were, power to be weak – not weakness in the sense of allowing sin once more to rule over us, but weakness as it is used by Paul when he says that he glories in his weakness (2 Corinthians 12:9-10; 13:9); that is to say, weakness as human frailty which becomes an opportunity for God to work in us (see, for example, 2 Corinthians 4:7; 12:7-10) and weakness as a characteristic of the way of the cross.

In Philippians 3:10-11 Paul expresses his desire to know the power of the resurrection now as he follows the way of the cross and so to attain to the future experience of resurrection: 'I want to know Christ and the power of his resurrection and the fellowship of sharing in his sufferings, becoming like him in his death, and so, somehow, to attain to the resurrection of the dead.' In 2 Corinthians 13 Paul reminds his readers that Christ 'was crucified in weakness, yet lives by God's power' (13:4). 'Likewise', he continues, 'we are weak in him, yet by God's power we will live with him to serve you.' (13:4) Resurrection power is given, not that we might be served, but that we might serve. Likewise, we receive resurrection life not that we might live to ourselves, but that we might live for Christ (2 Corinthians 5:15). We receive freedom not that we might 'indulge the sinful nature', but that we might 'serve one another in love' (Galatians 5:13). In Colossians 1:11 Paul discloses that his prayer for his readers is that they might have power so that they might 'have great endurance and patience'. And in 2 Timothy 1:8 Timothy is invited to suffer for the gospel 'by the power of God'. To love, to serve, to endure, to suffer: this is not the language of triumphalism, nor of victory, but it is the language of resurrection power.

It is in this way that we steer between defeatism and hopelessness on the one hand, and triumphalism on the other. Triumphalism is, in reality, overly-realised eschatology, an eschatology of glory. It suggests we can experience now, in the present or in the imminent future, that which truly belongs to the eschaton. It trumpets 'victorious Christian living' in which stress is placed upon Christian victory and joy at the expense of a stress upon the needs of the world and the on-going power of sin in the world. An eschatology of the cross is a constant reminder that discipleship, prior to the *parousia*, is always to follow the way of the cross and patiently to bear that cross, albeit in hope and in the present power of the resurrection mediated by the Spirit.

Yet the alternative to triumphalism is not hopelessness and inactivity. By the Holy Spirit, the power of the resurrection is at work in our lives and in the life of the Christian community. The eschatological kingdom has already entered history in the person and ministry of Christ, a ministry conducted in the power of the Spirit. Now his presence is mediated by the Holy Spirit. As such, the Spirit mediates the life of the future kingdom now in the life of the Christian community. The Christian lives in the power of the future, mediated by the Holy Spirit, and in that power seeks to serve the needs of the world. Eschatology need not be the opiate of the people.

But we must never separate the power of the resurrection from the way of the cross. The Christian's attitude to the world is not one of victory, but one of service and sacrificial love. The essential mark of Christian mission in the world is the cross (see Smith, 2003ii:114-129; Gorman, 2001; and Hall, 2003); that is to say, it is a mission which takes place in the power of the Spirit, but which is characterised by service, love and submission and conducted with gentleness and respect. As such, it will not be characterised by 'aggressive evangelism', nor power politics. In this mission, hope does not fill us with optimistic dreams, but rather sustains us. It fosters endurance, enabling us to be long-suffering in the reality of life in a world marred by sin.

For all that we have learnt from the proposals of Moltmann and evangelicals, their desire to use hope as an incentive to social change has tended to create a missing element in their approaches, namely that of patience, of the long-suffering of love in a world awaiting its full redemption. We need not be afraid of an 'other-worldly' eschatology, if that eschatology sustains discipleship shaped by the cross. Nor should we be afraid of declaring to the poor and oppressed the coming of a kingdom of justice and plenty. If this is 'pie in the sky' then so be it – we must not minimise the extent to which the 'pie' is good news. It is worse to offer people hope for the imminent future which cannot be sustained in the reality of a world marred by sin (see Williams 1989ii:5-10). The sacrificial love modelled for us in the cross is enough to prevent this making us complacent about the plight of the poor now in history.

Conclusion

Mission would not be possible without the transforming power and presence of God's kingdom. It derives its mandate from the authority over all the earth given to the risen Christ. Discipleship must hold in tension the presence of God's kingdom, which makes discipleship possible, and the future glory of that kingdom upon which we fix our hope. The former makes some change in history *possible*. The latter is the good news that glorious change in the future is *certain*. Asked, in an interview, to comment on his contention that Christians are optimists, but not utopians, John Stott replied that we are not utopians because 'we cannot build the kingdom of God on earth. We are waiting for the new heaven and the new earth, which will be the home of righteousness and peace' (1995:23). He continued: 'But meanwhile I am an optimist, because I do not think pessimism and faith are easy bedfellows. I believe that God is at work in the world, I believe that the gospel is the power of God unto salvation to every believer, and I believe that the church can be salt and light in the community.' (23)

One might question whether 'optimism' is the best term to use of as a correlate of faith, but Stott's statement is suggestive. Eschatology has to do with both the future of God's kingdom and with its presence. While hope is the characteristic Christian response to the future dimension, it is faith which is the characteristic response to the present dimension. According to Paul, the object of hope is, by definition, that which 'we do not yet have' (Romans 8:24-25). When we speak of the relationship between eschatology and mission, we must speak of the presence of the kingdom, but the correlate of this is not hope, but faith – a knowledge of, and confidence in, a hidden reality. This is a helpful distinction, for underlying the misgivings raised throughout this thesis is the danger that arises when the ultimate hope of a new creation is confused, or deliberately used interchangeably, with proximate hopes. To suggest, for example, that eschatology can energise movements for social change with hopeful expectation represents just such a confusion. It cannot be sustained in the light of the biblical evidence. The eschatological future hope is certain and arises from the promise of God. It does not disappoint us (Romans 5:5). Historical hopes are susceptible to disappointment and arise at best from faith in the presence of God's kingdom, and at worst from unfounded optimism.

It may be important to say that faith in the power of God and the presence of his kingdom should lead to an expectation which motivates us to action – although such an expectation will be qualified by a recognition of the sovereignty of God and the continuing presence of sin. But to say this is not new. It was, after all, William Carey's contention that we should 'expect great things from God and attempt great things for God'. But to relate such proximate expectations with the certain eschatological hope of the New Testament creates confusion and the danger of disappointment, as well as leading to a neglect of the themes of patience and endurance, which are vital if missionary activity, prompted by faith and love, is to be sustained.

In this concluding chapter, we have sought to outline a way of relating eschatology and mission which is distinct from those advanced by Moltmann and in the recent evangelical social debates. The aim has not been to provide a definitive alternative. Instead we have sought to demonstrate that an eschatology that gives due weight to future blessings and, though the word is not a helpful one, the 'other-worldly' dimensions of eschatology, need not serve as a disincentive to social involvement. Indeed, such as eschatology can sustain us as we follow the way of the cross. Thus we have sought to include the New Testament correlates of hope, namely patience and endurance. Moltmann himself, when speaking of the mystics, says: 'It is not out of a gnostic contempt for the world that the mystics face human beings with the alternative: God and the world; it is in the interests of undivided love.' (*SL*, 206) Or again: 'True life means here *love* and there *glory* ... Only the love which passionately affirms life understands the relevance of this hope, because it is through that that this love is liberated from the fear of death and the fear of losing its own self. The resurrection hope makes people ready to live their lives in love wholly, and to say a full and entire Yes to a life that leads to death.' (*CoG*, 66) We might equally say that it is not out of a contempt for present activity that the New Testament emphasises the future dimensions of hope; but in the interests of undivided love, of patient and enduring service.

Eschatology is an ambiguous basis for social involvement. For some it appears to act as an incentive towards anticipatory or preparatory change; for others it appears to act as a disincentive. Ultimately, whether hope functions as an incentive or disincentive has less to do with how much relative stress is given to the present or future dimensions of eschatology, or how their relationship is conceived, than it has to do with prior commitments.

'We always thank God for all of you, mentioning you in our prayers. We continually remember before our God and Father your work produced by faith, your labour prompted by love, and your endurance inspired by hope in our Lord Jesus Christ.' (1 Thessalonians 1:3) When Paul tells the Thessalonians that he continually remembers before God their work and labour, this work and labour are not inspired by hope, but produced by faith and prompted by love. Faith and love are the basis for good works, for social involvement. But this does not mean hope is relegated. Writing to the Colossians, the Apostle speaks of 'the faith and love that spring from the hope that is stored up for you in heaven' (Colossians 1:5). And in 1 Thessalonians, he thanks God for the *endurance* of the Thessalonians which is inspired by hope in Christ. That which is produced by faith and prompted by love, is sustained by hope. 'You turned to the God from idols to serve the living and true God, and wait for his Son from heaven, whom he raised from the dead – Jesus, who rescues us from the coming wrath.' (1 Thessalonians 1:9-10)

Bibliography

Agra Affirmations
1995   'Agra Affirmations on Christian Faith, Market Economics and the Poor', a
        report from the Third Oxford Conference on Christian Faith and Economics,
        Transformation, Vol. 12, No. 3, pp. 5-7

Alves, Rubem A.
1969   *A Theology of Human Hope* (New York: Corpus)

Anderson, G.H. and Stransky, T.F. (eds.)
1976   *Mission Trends: Third World Theologies* (New York/Grand Rapids:
        Paulist/Eerdmans)

Anderson, Hugh
1976   *The Gospel of Mark*, New Century Bible Commentary (London: Marshall,
        Morgan and Scott)

Attfield, D.G.
1977   'Can God be Crucified? A Discussion of J Moltmann', *Scottish Journal of
        Theology*, Vol. 30, pp. 47-57

Baker, David W. (ed.)
2001   *Looking into the Future: Evangelical Studies in Eschatology* (Grand Rapids:
        Baker)

Barclay, Oliver
1970   *Whose World?*, published under the pseudonym A N Triton (Leicester: IVP)
1990   'The Theology of Social Ethics: A Survey of Current Positions', *Evangelical
        Quarterly*, Vol. 62, No. 1, pp. 63-86

Barclay, Oliver and Sugden, Chris
1990   'Biblical Social Ethics in a Mixed Society', *Evangelical Quarterly*, Vol. 62,
        No. 1, pp. 5-18

Barrett, C.K.
1955   *The Gospel according to St John* (London: SPCK)
1985   *Church, Ministry, and Sacraments in the New Testament* (Exeter: Paternoster)

Barth, Karl
1933   *The Epistle to the Romans* (Oxford: OUP)

Barth, Markus
1974   *Ephesians, A New Translation with Introduction and Commentary*, Vol. 1
          Ephesians 1-3, Anchor Bible (New York: Doubleday)

Bartholomew, Craig, Jonathan Chaplin, Robert Song and Al Walters (eds.)
2002   *A Royal Priesthood? A Dialogue with Oliver O'Donovan* (Carlisle/Grand
          Rapids: Paternoster/Zondervan)

Bauckham, Richard
1977   'Moltmann's Eschatology of the Cross', *Scottish Journal of Theology*, Vol.
          30, pp. 301-311
1978   'The Rise of Apocalyptic', *Themelios*, Vol. 3, No. 2, pp. 10-23
1980   'Jürgen Moltmann', *One God in Trinity*, ed. P. Toon and J.D. Spiceland
          (London: Bagster), pp. 111-132
1982   'Weakness – Paul's and Ours', *Themelios*, Vol. 7, No. 3, pp. 4-6
1983   *Jude, 2 Peter*, Word Biblical Commentary (Waco, Texas: Word)
1984   '"Only a suffering God Can Help": Divine Passibility in Modern Theology',
          Themelios, Vol. 9, No. 3, pp. 6-12
1986   'Bibliography: Jürgen Moltmann', *Modern Churchman*, Vol. 28, pp. 55-60
1987i   *Moltmann: Messianic Theology in the Making* (Basingstoke: Marshall,
          Morgan and Scott)
1987ii   'Theodicy from Ivan Karamazov to Moltmann', *Modern Theology*, Vol. 4, No.
          1, pp. 83-97
1988   'Moltmann, Jürgen', *New Dictionary of Theology*, eds. Sinclair B. Ferguson
          and David F. Wright (Leicester: IVP), pp. 439-40
1989i   'Moltmann's *Theology of Hope* Revisited', *Scottish Journal of Theology*, Vol.
          42, pp. 199-214
1989ii   'Jürgen Moltmann', *The Modern Theologians: An Introduction to Christian
          Theology in the Twentieth Century*, Volume 1, ed. David F. Ford (Oxford:
          Basil Blackwell), pp. 293-310
1990   'In Defence of *The Crucified God*', *The Power and Weakness of God*, ed.
          Nigel Cameron (Edinburgh: Rutherford House), pp. 93-118
1991   'Moltmann's Messianic Christology', a review article of *The Way of Jesus
          Christ* (J Moltmann), *Scottish Journal of Theology*, Vol. 44, pp. 519-531
1993i   *The Theology of the Book of Revelation* (Cambridge: CUP)
1993ii   *The Climax of Prophecy: Studies in the Book of Revelation* (Edinburgh: T. &
          T. Clark)
1995   *The Theology of Jürgen Moltmann* (Edinburgh: T. & T. Clark)
1997   'Must Christian Eschatology be Millenarian? A Response to Jürgen
          Moltmann' in K.E. Brower and M.W. Elliot (eds.), *'The Reader Must
          Understand': Eschatology in the Bible and Theology* (Leicester, Apollos), pp.
          263-278; also published as 'The Millennium' in Richard Bauckham (ed.), *God
          Will Be All in All: The Eschatology of Jürgen Moltmann* (Edinburgh: T. & T.
          Clark, 1999), pp. 123-148
1998   *God Crucified: Monotheism and Christology in the New Testament* (Carlisle:
          Paternoster)
1999   (ed.), *God Will Be All in All: The Eschatology of Jürgen Moltmann*
          (Edinburgh: T. & T. Clark)

Bauckham, Richard and Trevor Hart
1999   *Hope Against Hope: Christian Eschatology in Contemporary Context* (London: DLT)

Beasley-Murray, George R.
1986   *Jesus and the Kingdom of God* (Grand Rapids/Exeter: Eerdmans/Paternoster)
1987   *John*, Word Biblical Commentary (Texas: Word Books)

Bebbington, D.W.
1989   *Evangelicalism in Modern Britain* (London: Unwin Hyman)

Bediako, Kwame
1989   'World Evangelisation, Institutional Evangelicalism and the Future of the Christian World Mission', *Proclaiming Christ in Christ's Way*, ed. Vinay Samuel and Albrecht Hauser (Oxford: Regnum), pp. 52-68

Beisner, Calvin
1993   'Justice and Poverty: Two Views Contrasted', *Transformation*, Vol. 10, No. 1, pp. 16-22

Bentley, J.
1976   'The Christian Significance of Atheist Ernst Bloch', *Expository Times*, Vol. 88, pp. 51-54

Berkhof, Hendrikus.
1966   *Christ the Meaning of History* (London: SCM)

Berkouwer, G.C.
1977   *A Half Century of Theology* (Grand Rapids: Eerdmans, 1974, ET 1977)

Best, Ernest
1981   *Following Jesus: Discipleship in the Gospel of Mark, Journal for the Study of the New Testament*, Supplement Series No. 4 (Sheffield: JSOT Press)
1986   *Disciples and Discipleship: Studies in the Gospel according to Mark* (Edinburgh: T. & T. Clark)

Beyerhaus, Peter
1985   'A Biblical Encounter with Some Contemporary Philosophical and Theological Systems', *In Word and Deed*, ed. Bruce Nicholls (Exeter: Paternoster), pp. 165-188

Bloch, Ernst
1986   *The Principle of Hope* (Oxford: Blackwell)

Blocher, Henri
1984   *In the Beginning* (Leicester: IVP, 1979, ET 1984)
1985   'Christian Thought and the Problem of Evil, Part 2', *Churchman*, Vol. 99, pp. 101-130

1990   'Divine Immutability', *The Power and Weakness of God*, ed. Nigel Cameron (Edinburgh: Rutherford House), pp. 1-22

Bonhoeffer, Dietrich
1964   *Ethics*, ed. E. Bethge (London: Fontana, 1949, ET 1955, 1964)
1971   *Letters and Papers from Prison*, ed. E Bethge (London: SCM, 1951, ET 1953, 1971)

Boff, Leonardo and Boff, Clodovis
1984   *Salvation and Liberation* (New York: Orbis, 1979, ET 1984)

Bonino, José Miguez
1975   *Revolutionary Theology Comes of Age* (London: SPCK)

Bosch, David
1980   *Witness to the World: The Christian Mission in Theological Perspective* (London: Marshall, Morgan and Scott)
1985   'In Search of a New Evangelical Understanding', *In Word and Deed*, ed. Bruce Nicholls (Exeter: Paternoster), pp. 63-83
1987   'Towards Evangelism in Context', *The Church in Response to Human Need*, eds. Vinay Samuel and Chris Sugden (Oxford: Regnum), pp. 180-192

Braaten, C.E.
1976   'A Trinitarian Theology of the Cross', *Journal of Religion*, Vol. 56, pp. 113-121

Bragg, Wayne
1987   'From Development to Transformation', *The Church in Response to Human Need*, eds. Vinay Samuel and Chris Sugden (Oxford: Regnum), pp. 20-51

Branson, Mark Lau and Padilla, C. René (eds.)
1986   *Conflict and Context* (Grand Rapids: Eerdmans)

Brown, David.
1985   *The Divine Trinity* (London: Duckworth)

Brown, Raymond
1966,1971 *The Gospel according to John*, Anchor Bible, Vol. 29, *I-XII*, 1966, Vol. 29A, *XIII-XXI*, 1971 (New York: Doubleday)

Brower, K.E. and M.W. Elliot (eds.)
1997   *'The Reader Must Understand': Eschatology in the Bible and Theology* (Leicester, Apollos)

Bruce, F.F.
1961   *The Epistle to the Ephesians* (London: Pickering & Inglis)

Brunner, Emil
1949   *The Christian Doctrine of God: Dogmatics Vol. 1* (London: Lutterworth)

Caird, G.B.
1980   *The Language and Imagery of the Bible* (London: Duckworth)

Calvin, John
Inst.   *The Institutes of Christian Religion*, 2.Vol's (The Library of Christian
          Classics, Vols. XX and XXI), trans. F.L. Battles, ed. J.T. McNeill
          (Philadelphia/London: Westminster Press/SCM, 1961)
Comm.   *Calvin's Commentaries, The New Testament*, 12 Vols., ed. D.W. and T.F.
          Torrance (Edinburgh: St Andrew's Press, 1959-1966, 1972)
Letters *Letters of John Calvin*, selected from the Bonnet edition of Calvin's letters
          (Edinburgh: Banner of Truth, 1980)

Cameron, Nigel M. de S. (ed.)
1989   *Issues in Faith and History*, Scottish Bulletin of Evangelical Theology –
          Special Study 3 (Edinburgh: Rutherford House)
1990   *The Power and Weakness of God*, Scottish Bulletin of Evangelical Theology –
          Special Study 4 (Edinburgh: Rutherford House)

Capps, Walter H.
1972   *Time Invades the Cathedral: Tensions in the School of Hope*, foreword by
          Jürgen Moltmann (Philadelphia: Fortress Press)
1976   *Hope Against Hope: Moltmann to Merton in One Theological Decade*
          (Philadelphia: Fortress Press)

Chan, Simon
1985   'Second Thoughts on Contextualisation', *Evangelical Review of Theology*,
          Vol. 7, No. 1, pp. 50-54

Chapman, G. Clarke
1974   'Moltmann's Vision of Man', *Anglican Theological Review*, Vol. 56, pp. 310-
          330
1979   'Black Theology and Theology of Hope: What have they to say to each
          other?', G S Wilmore and J H Cone (eds.), *Black Theology: A Documentary
          History, 1966-1979* (Maryknoll, New York: Orbis), pp. 193-219. First
          published in *Union Seminary Quarterly Review*, 29 (1974), pp. 107-129
1983   'Hope and the ethics of formation: Moltmann as an interpreter of Bonhoeffer',
          Studies in Religion/ Science Religieuses, Vol. 12, pp. 449-460

Chester, Tim
1993   *Awakening to a World of Need: The Recovery of Evangelical Social Concern*
          (Leicester: IVP)
2001   'Christ's Little Flock: Towards an Ecclesiology of the Cross,' *Evangel* 19:1,
          pp. 13-21

2002i   'Church Planting: a Theological Perspective,' *Multiplying Churches:*
          Reaching Today's Communities through Church Planting, ed. Stephen
          Timmis (Fearn, Ross-shire: Christian Focus), pp. 23-46
2002ii   editor, *Justice, Mercy and Humility: Integral Mission and the Poor* (Carlisle:
          Paternoster)
2003   'What Makes Christian Development Christian?' *Evangel* 21:1, supplement,
          pp. i-ix
2004   *Good News to the Poor* (Leicester: IVP)
2005   *Delighting in the Trinity* (Oxford: Monarch)

The Chicago Declaration
1974   *International Review of Mission*, Vol. 63, No. 250, pp. 274-275; also
          published in C René Padilla and Chris Sugden (eds.), *Texts on Evangelical*
          Social Ethics (Nottingham: Grove Booklets, 1985)

Cho, J. Chongnahm
1985   'The Mission of the Church: Theology and Practice', *In Word and Deed*, ed.
          Bruce Nicholls (Exeter: Paternoster), pp. 215-238

'Concerned Evangelicals'
1987   'Evangelical Witness in South Africa', *Transformation*, Vol. 4, No. 1, pp. 17-
          30

Cohn, Norman
1970   *The Pursuit of the Millennium* (London: Paladin, first published 1957)

Cook, David
1990   'Weak Church, Weak God', *The Power and Weakness of God*, ed. Nigel
          Cameron (Edinburgh: Rutherford House), pp. 69-92

Cook, William
1985   'Reflections on Wheaton '83', *Evangelical Review of Theology*, Vol. 9, No. 1,
          pp. 27-31

Cope, Christopher
1990   'The Relationship between Evangelism and Social Responsibility in
          Evangelical Thought from the Wheaton Conference of 1966 to the Wheaton
          Conference of 1983', MPhil Thesis, University of Manchester

Costas, Orlando
1974   *The Church and Its Mission: A Shattering Critique from the Third World*
          (Wheaton: Tyndale) 1982 *Christ Outside the Gate* (Maryknoll, New York:
          Orbis)
1983   'Proclaiming Christ in the Two Thirds World', *Sharing Jesus in the Two*
          Thirds World, ed. Samuel Vinay and Chris Sugden (Bangalore: PIM), pp. 1-15

Cotterell, Peter and Turner, Max
1989   *Linguistics and Biblical Interpretation* (London: SPCK)

Cousins, Ewert H. (ed.)
1973   *Hope and the Future of Man*, the papers of the Conference on Hope and the Future of Man, New York, October 1971 (London: Teilhard Centre for the Future of Man)

Cox, Harvey
1968   'Ernst Bloch and "The Pull of the Future"', *New Theology No. 5*, eds. M.E. Marty and D.G. Peerman (New York: Macmillan), pp. 191 203; first published as a forward to Ernst Bloch, *Man on his Own: Essays in the Philosophy of Religion* (New York: Herder & Herder)
1970   'The Problem of Continuity', *The Future of Hope*, ed. F Herzog, (New York: Herder and Herder), pp. 72-80

Cranfield, C.E.B.
1977   *The Gospel according to St Mark*, Cambridge Greek Testament Commentary (Cambridge: CUP)

Crowe, Philip
1967   *Keele '67: The National Evangelical Anglican Congress* (London: Falcon)

Cullmann, Oscar
1962   *Christ and Time* (London: SCM, 1946, ET 1951, Rev Ed 1962)
1963   *The Christology of the New Testament* (London: SCM, 1957, ET 1963)

Cupitt, Don
1980   Review of *The Future of Creation* (J Moltmann), *Theology*, Vol. 83, pp. 215-216

Dawsey, James M.
1990   'The Biblical Authority of the Poor', *Expository Times*, Vol. 101, pp. 295-298

Dayton, Edward R.
1987   'Social Transformation: The Mission of God', *The Church in Response to Human Need*, eds. Vinay Samuel and Chris Sugden (Oxford: Regnum), pp. 52-61

Dillistone, F.W.
1974   'The Theology of Jürgen Moltmann', *Modern Churchman*, Vol. 18, pp. 145-150

Douglas, J.D. (ed.)
1975   *Let the Earth Hear His Voice*, the papers of Lausanne 1974 (Minneapolis: World Wide Publications)

1990   *Proclaim Christ Until He Comes: Calling the Whole Church to Take the Whole Gospel to the Whole World*, the papers of the International Congress of World Evangelism, 1989 (Lausanne II) (Minneapolis: Worldwide Publications)

Dumas, André
1978   *Political Theology and the Life of the Church* (London: SCM)

Dunn, James D.G.
1978   *Jesus and the Spirit* (London: SCM)

Ebeling, Gerhard.
1970   *Luther* (London: Collins, 1964, ET 1970)

Eckardt, Burnell J.
1985   'Luther and Moltmann: The Theology of the Cross', *Concordia Theological Quarterly*, Vol. 49, No. 1, pp. 19-28

Eckhardt, A.R.
1976   'Jürgen Moltmann, the Jewish People, and the Holocaust', *Journal of the American Academy of Religion*, Vol. 44, pp. 675 691

Edwards, Jonathan
1774   *A History of the Work of Redemption* (Edinburgh: Banner of Truth, 2003)

Ellison, H.L.
1953   *The Centrality of the Messianic Idea for the Old Testament*, The Tyndale Old Testament Lecture for 1953 (Leicester: RTSF Monograph)

Erskine, Noel
1979   'Christian Hope and the Black Experience', *Hope for the Church: Moltmann in Dialogue with Practical Theology*, Jürgen Moltmann with M Douglas Meeks, Rodney J Hunter, James W Fowler, Noel L Erskine, ed. Theodore Runyon (Nashville: Abingdon), pp. 112-127

Escobar, Samuel
1972   'The Social Responsibility of the Church', *Is Revolution Change?*, ed. Brian Griffiths (Leicester: IVP), pp. 84-111
1975   'Evangelism and Man's Search for Freedom, Justice and Fulfilment', *Let the Earth Hear His Voice*, ed. J D Douglas (Minneapolis: World Wide Publications), pp. 303-326; also published in *Mission Trends: Third World Theologies*, eds. G.H. Anderson and T.F. Stransky (New York/Grand Rapids: Paulist/Eerdmans, 1976, pp. 104-110

Fiorenza, F.P.
1968   'Dialectical Theology and Hope', *Heythrop Journal*, Vol. 9, pp. 143-163, 384-399; Vol. 10, pp. 26-42

France, R.T.
1986   'Liberation in the New Testament', *Evangelical Quarterly*, Vol. 58, pp. 3-23
1990   *Divine Government: God's Kingship in the Gospel of Mark* (London: SPCK)

Gilkey, Langdon
1970   'The Universal and Immediate Presence of God', *The Future of Hope*, ed. F. Herzog (New York: Herder and Herder), pp81-109
1976   *Reaping the Whirlwind: A Christian Interpretation of History* (New York: Seabury)

Gill, Athol
1976   'Christian Social Responsibility', *The New Face of Evangelicals*, ed. C. René Padilla (London: Hodder & Stoughton)

Gladwin, John
1977   'Politics, Providence and the Kingdom', *Churchman*, Vol. 91, pp. 47-57

Gollwitzer, Helmut
1974   'Liberation in History', *Interpretation*, Vol. 28, pp. 404-421

Gorman, Michael, J.
2001   *Cruciformity: Paul's Narrative Spirituality of the Cross* (Grand Rapids: Eerdmans)
2004   *Apostle of the Crucified Lord: A Theological Introduction to Paul and His Letters* (Grand Rapids: Eerdmans)

Gorringe, Timothy
1999   'Eschatology and Political Radicalism: The Example of Karl Barth and Jürgen Moltmann' in Richard Bauckham (ed.), *God Will Be All in All: The Eschatology of Jürgen Moltmann* (Edinburgh: T. & T. Clark, 1999), pp. 87-114

The Grand Rapids Report
1982   *Evangelism and Social Responsibility*, the conference report of the Consultation on the Relationship between Evangelical and Social Responsibility, Grand Rapids 1982 (Exeter: Paternoster)

Guelich, Robert A.
1989   *Mark 1-8:26*, Word Biblical Commentary (Texas, Word Books)

Gustafson, James
1974   *Theology and Christian Ethics* (Philadelphia: Pilgrim Press)

Gutierrez, Gustavo
1974   *A Theology of Liberation* (London: SCM, 1971, ET 1974)

Hall, Douglas John
1995   *The End of Christendom and the Future of Christianity* (Harrisburg, Pennsylvania: Trinity)
2003   *The Cross in Our Context: Jesus and the Suffering World* (Minneapolis: Fortress)

Harvey, Van A.
1970   'Secularism, Responsible Belief, and the "Theology of Hope"', *The Future of Hope*, ed. F Herzog (New York: Herder and Herder), pp. 126-153

Hathaway, Brian
1990   'The Kingdom Manifesto', *Transformation*, Vol. 7, No. 3, pp. 6-11

Helm, Paul
1990   'The Impossibility of Divine Passibility', *The Power and Weakness of God*, ed. Nigel Cameron (Edinburgh, Rutherford House), pp. 119-140

Hengel, Martin
1971   *Was Jesus a Revolutionist?* (Philadelphia, Fortress Press)
1975   *Victory over Violence* (London: SPCK)

Henry, Carl F.H. and Mooneyham, Stanley (eds.)
1967   *One Race, One Gospel, One Task*, 2 Vol. s, The official reference volumes of Berlin 1966 (Minneapolis: World Wide Publications)

Henry, Carl
1981   'American Evangelicals in a Turning Time', in *Theologians in Transition*, ed. J.M. Wall (New York: Crossroad), pp. 41-49

Herzog, Frederick (ed.)
1970   *The Future of Hope: Theology as Eschatology*, the papers of the Duke Consultation on 'The Task of Theology Today', 4th-6th April, 1968 (New York: Herder and Herder)

Hick, John
1976   *Death and Eternal Life* (London: Collins)

Hill, William J.
1982   *The Three-Personed God: The Trinity as a Mystery of Salvation* (Washington, DC: Catholic University Press of America)

Hodgson, P.C.
1971   *Jesus – Word and Presence: An Essay in Christology* (Philadelphia: Fortress Press)

Hoekema, A.A.
1978   *The Bible and the Future* (Exeter: Paternoster)

Hoekendijk, J.C.
1964   *The Church Inside Out* (Philadelphia: Westminster)

Hoekstra, Harvey T.
1979   *Evangelism in Eclipse* (Exeter: Paternoster)

Holwerda, David E.
1984   'Eschatology and History: A Look at Calvin's Eschatological Vision', in *Readings in Calvin's Theology*, ed. Donald K. McKim (Grand Rapids: Baker), pp. 311-342

Howard-Brook, Wes and Anthony Gwyther
2002   *Unveiling Empire: Reading Revelation Then and Now* (Maryknoll, NY.: Orbis)

Hudson, Wayne
1982   *The Marxist Philosophy of Ernst Bloch* (London: Macmillan)

Hunsinger, George
1973   'The Crucified God and the Political Theology of Violence', *Heythrop Journal*, Vol. 14, pp. 266-279, 379-395

Irish, J.A.
1975-76 'Moltmann's Theology of Contradiction', *Theology Today*, Vol. 32, pp. 21-31

Jantzen, G.M.
1982   'Christian Hope and Jesus' Despair', *King's Theological Review*, Vol. 5, pp. 1-7

Jasper, David
1987   'The Limits of Formalism and the Theology of Hope: Ricoeur, Moltmann and Dostoyevsky', *Journal of Literature and Theology*, Vol. 1, No. 1, pp. 1-10

Jasper, R.C.D. and Cuming G.J.
1975   *Prayers of the Eucharist: Early and Reformed* (London: Collins)

Jayasooria, Denison
1990   'Spirit and Kingdom: History and Study Process', *Transformation*, Vol. 7, No. 3, p.5

Johnston, Arthur P.
1978   *The Battle for World Evangelism* (Wheaton: Tyndale)
1985   'The Kingdom in Relation to the Church and the World', *In Word and Deed*, ed. Bruce Nicholls (Exeter: Paternoster), pp. 109-134
Kerstiens, Ferdinand
1970   'The Theology of Hope in Germany Today', *Concilium*, 9/6, pp. 101-111

Kettler, Christian D.
1991   *The Vicarious Humanity of Christ and the Reality of Salvation* (Lanham, New York/ London: University Press of America)

Kirk, Andrew
1980   *Theology Encounters Revolution* (Leicester: IVP)
1983   *A New World Coming* (Basingstoke: Marshalls)

Kuzmic, Peter
1985   'History and Eschatology: Evangelical Views', *In Word and Deed*, ed. Bruce Nicholls (Exeter: Paternoster), pp. 135-164

Kyle, Richard
1998   *Awaiting the Millennium: A History of End-Time Thinking* (Leicester: IVP)

Ladd, George Eldon
1974i   *The Presence of the Future* (London: SPCK)
1974ii   *A Theology of the New Testament* (Guildford, Lutterworth)

Lane, William L.
1974   *The Gospel of Mark*, The New International Commentary on the New Testament (Grand Rapids: Eerdmans)

The Lausanne Covenant
1975   The statement of Lausanne 1974, published with the conference documents in *Let the Earth Hear His Voice*, ed. J D Douglas (Minneapolis: World Wide Publications); also published in Sugden, 1981:176-184

Lausanne II: Report of the Social Concern Track
1990   'Social Concern and Evangelisation at Lausanne II', *Transformation*, Vol. 7, No. 3, p.2

Lincoln, Andrew
1981   *Paradise Now and Not Yet* (Cambridge: CUP)
1990   *Ephesians*, Word Biblical Commentary (Dallas, Texas: Word Publ.)

Lohse, Bernhard
1986   *Martin Luther* (Edinburgh: T. & T. Clark, 1980, ET 1986)

Luther, Martin
Luther's Works, American Edition, ed. Jaroslav Pelikan, Hilton C. Oswald and Helmut T. Lehmann (Vols. 1-30, St Louis: Concordia, 1955-; Vols. 31-55, Philadelphia: Fortress, 1957-)

McAfee Brown, Robert
1988   *Spirituality and Liberation* (London: Spire)

McGrath, Alister E.
1985   *Luther's Theology of the Cross* (Oxford: Blackwell)
1986   *The Making of Modern German Christology: From the Enlightenment to Pannenberg* (Oxford: Blackwell)
1990   *A Life of John Calvin: A Study in the Shaping of Western Culture*, Oxford: Blackwell)

McIntyre, John
1988   Review of *God in Creation*, *Scottish Journal of Theology*, Vol. 41, pp. 268-273

Mackey, J.P.
1983   *The Christian Experience of God as Trinity* (London: SCM)

Macquarrie, John
1970   'Eschatology and Time', *The Future of Hope*, ed. F Herzog (New York: Herder and Herder), pp. 110-125
1978   *Christian Hope* (London/ Oxford, Mowbrays)
1980   'Today's Word for Today: I. Jürgen Moltmann', *Expository Times*, Vol. 92, pp. 4-7
1990   *Jesus Christ in Modern Thought* (London: SCM)

Marshall, I. Howard
1977   'Slippery Words I: Eschatology', *Expository Times*, Vol. 89, No. 9, pp. 264-269
1985   'The Hope of the New Age: the Kingdom of God in the New Testament', *Themelios*, Vol. 11, No. 1, pp. 5-15

Martin, Ralph
1972   *Mark: Evangelist and Theologian* (Exeter: Paternoster)

Meeks, M. Douglas
1974   *Origins of the Theology of Hope* (Philadelphia: Fortress Press)
1981   'Trinitarian Theology: A Review Article', *Theology Today*, Vol. 38, pp. 472-477

Middelmann, Udo
1987   'The Contribution of the Bible to Economic Thought: A Response to Stephen Mott', *Transformation*, Vol. 4, Nos. 3 and 4, pp. 36-40

Migliore, Daniel L.
1979   'The Trinity and Human Liberty', *Theology Today*, Vol. 36, pp. 488-497

Milbank, John
1986   'The Second Difference: For a Trinitarianism without Reserve', *Modern Theology*, Vol. 2, No. 3, pp. 213-234

Moltmann, Jürgen
Major works
TH   *Theology of Hope: On the Ground and the Implication of a Christian*
         Eschatology (London: SCM, 1965, ET 1967)
CG   *The Crucified God: The Cross of Christ as the Foundation and Criticism of*
         Christian Theology (London: SCM, 1973, ET 1974)
CPS   *The Church in the Power of the Spirit: A Contribution to Messianic*
         Ecclesiology (London: SCM, 1975, ET 1977)
TKG   *The Trinity and the Kingdom of God: The Doctrine of God* (London: SCM,
         1980, ET 1981)
GC   *God in Creation: An Ecological Doctrine of Creation*, The Gifford Lectures
         1984-1985 (London: SCM, 1985, ET 1985)
WJC   *The Way of Jesus Christ: Christology in Messianic Dimensions* (London:
         SCM, 1989, ET 1990)
SL   *The Spirit of Life: A Universal Affirmation* (London: SCM, 1991, ET 1992)
CoG   *The Coming of God: Christian Eschatology* (London: SCM, 1995, ET 1996)
ET   *Experiences in Theology: Ways and Forms of Christian Theology*
         (Minneapolis, MN.: Fortress Press, 2000, ET 2000)
Other works
Articles reprinted in volumes of collected essays are generally not listed separately. For
a fuller bibliography of Moltmann's works see James L. Wakefield, *Jürgen Moltmann:*
A Research Bibliography (Lanham, MD.: Scarecrow Press, 2002).
1969   *Religion, Revolution and the Future* (New York: Charles Scribner's Sons)
1970i   'Theology as Eschatology', *The Future of Hope: Theology as Eschatology*, ed.
         F. Herzog (New York: Herder and Herder), pp. 1-50
1970ii 'Towards the Next Step on the Dialogue', *The Future of Hope: Theology as*
         Eschatology, ed. F. Herzog (New York: Herder and Herder), pp. 154-164
1970iii 'Introduction', *Man on his Own*, Ernst Bloch (New York: Herder and Herder),
         pp. 19-29
1971   *Hope and Planning* (London: SCM)
1972   'The 'Crucified God': A Trinitarian Theology of the Cross', *Interpretation*,
         Vol. 26, pp. 278-299
1972   'The 'Crucified God': God and the Trinity Today', *Concilium*, Vol. 8, No. 6,
         pp. 26-37.
1973i   *Theology and Joy* (London: SCM)
1973ii 'Hope and the Biomedical Future of Man', *Hope and the Future of Man*, ed.
         Ewert H. Cousins (London: Teilhard Centre for the Future of Man), 89-105
1973   'Response to the Opening Presentations', *Hope and the Future of Man*, ed.
         Ewert H. Cousins (London: Teilhard Centre for the Future of Man), pp. 55-59
1974i   *Man: Christian Anthropology in the Conflicts of the Present* (London: SPCK)
1974ii 'The Cross and Civil Religion', *Religion and Political Society*, Jürgen
         Moltmann, H.W. Richardson, Johannes-Baptist Metz, W. Oelmüller, M.D.
         Bryant (New York: Harper and Row) pp. 9-47
1974   'The Liberating Feast', *Concilium*, 2/10 = *Politics and Liturgy*, ed. H. Schmidt
         and D. Power (London: Concilium), pp. 74-84
1975   *The Experiment Hope* (London: SCM)

1977   'God's Kingdom as the Meaning of Life and of the World', *Concilium*, Vol.
         117 = *Why did God make me?*, ed. H. Küng and J. Moltmann (New York:
         Seabury Press, 1978), pp. 97-103
1978i   'The Confession of Jesus Christ': A Biblical Theological Consideration',
         Concilium, Vol. 118 = *An Ecumenical Confession of Faith?*, ed. H. Küng and
         J. Moltmann (New York: Seabury Press, 1979), pp. 13-19
1978ii   *The Open Church: Invitation to Messianic Lifestyle* (London: SCM)
1979i   *The Future of Creation* (London: SCM)
1979ii   'The Diaconal Church in the Context of the Kingdom of God', *Hope for the
         Church: Moltmann in Dialogue with Practical Theology*, Jürgen Moltmann
         with M. Douglas Meeks, Rodney J. Hunter, James W. Fowler, Noel L.
         Erskine, ed. Theodore Runyon (Nashville: Abingdon), pp. 21-36
1979iii 'The Life Signs of the Spirit in the Fellowship Community of Christ', *Hope
         for the Church: Moltmann in Dialogue with Practical Theology*, Jürgen
         Moltmann with M. Douglas Meeks, Rodney J. Hunter, James W. Fowler, Noel
         L. Erskine, ed. Theodore Runyon (Nashville: Abingdon), pp. 37-56
1979iv   'Response', *Hope for the Church: Moltmann in Dialogue with Practical
         Theology*, Jürgen Moltmann with M. Douglas Meeks, Rodney J. Hunter,
         James W. Fowler, Noel L. Erskine, ed. Theodore Runyon (Nashville:
         Abingdon), pp. 128-136
1979v   'Theology as Mystical Experience', *Scottish Journal of Theology*, Vol. 32, pp.
         501-520
1980   *Experiences of God* (London: SCM)
1981i   'The Motherly Father: Is Trinitarian Patripassianism Replacing Theological
         Patriarchalism?', *Concilium*, 143 = *God as Father?*, ed. Edward Schillebeeckx
         and Johannes Baptist Metz (Edinburgh: T. & T. Clark), pp. 51-56
1981ii   *Jewish Monotheism and Christian Trinitarian Doctrine*, a dialogue by Pinchas
         Lapide and Jürgen Moltmann (Philadelphia: Fortress Press)
1981   'The Challenge of Religion in the '80's', in *Theologians in Transition*, ed.
         J.M. Wall (New York: Crossroad), pp. 107-112
1983i   *The Power of the Powerless* (London: SCM)
1983ii   'Hope', *A New Dictionary of Christian Theology*, ed. Alan Richardson and
         John Bowden (London: SCM), pp. 270-272
1983   'Cross, Theology of the', *A New Dictionary of Christian Theology*, ed. Alan
         Richardson and John Bowden (London: SCM), pp. 135-137
1983   'Perseverance', *A New Dictionary of Christian Theology*, ed. Alan Richardson
         and John Bowden (London: SCM), pp. 441-442
1983   'Theodicy', *A New Dictionary of Christian Theology*, ed. Alan Richardson and
         John Bowden (London: SCM), pp. 564-566
1983   'Commentary on "To Bear Arms"', *Human Rights: A Dialogue between the
         First and Third Worlds*, eds. R.A. Evans and A.F. Evans (Maryknoll, New
         York: Orbis/ Guildford: Lutterworth Press), pp. 48-52
1983   'Editorial: Can there be an Ecumenical Mariology?', *Concilium*, Vol. 168 =
         Mary in the Churches, ed. H. Küng and J. Moltmann (Edinburgh: T. & T.
         Clark), pp. xii-xv
1984i   *On Human Dignity* (London: SCM)
1984ii   *Humanity in God*, Elisabeth Moltmann-Wendel and Jürgen Moltmann
         (London: SCM)

1984   'Theology in Germany Today', in *Observations on 'The Spiritual Situation of the Age'; Contemporary German Perspectives*, ed. J. Habermas (Cambridge, Mass./London: MIT Press), pp. 181-205

1984   'Teresa of Avila and Martin Luther: The turn to the mysticism of the cross', *Studies in Religion*, Vol. 13, pp. 265-278

1984   'The Fellowship of the Holy Spirit – Trinitarian Pneumatology', *Scottish Journal of Theology*, Vol. 37, pp. 287-300

1985   'The Expectation of His Coming', *Theology*, Vol. 88, pp. 425-428

1985   'The Inviting Unity of the Triune God', *Concilium*, Vol. 177 = *Monotheism*, ed. C. Geffré and J.-P. Jossua (Edinburgh: T. & T. Clark), pp. 50-58

1988i   'The Possible Nuclear Catastrophe and Where is God?', *Scottish Journal of Religious Studies*, Vol. 9, pp. 71-83

1988   *Theology Today* (London: SCM)

1988   'The Ecological Crisis: Peace with Nature', *Scottish Journal of Religious Studies*, Vol. 9, pp. 5-18

1989   *Creating a Just Future* (London: SCM)

1991   *History and the Triune God* (London: SCM)

1994   *Jesus Christ for Today's World* (London: SCM)

1995   with Johann-Baptist Metz, *Faith and the Future – Essays on Theology, Solidarity and Modernity* (Maryknoll, NY: Orbis)

1997   *The Source of Life: Holy Spirit and the Theology of Life* (London: SCM)

1998   'Political Theology and Theology of Liberation' in Joerg Rieger (ed.) *Liberating the Future: God, Mammon and Theology* (Minneapolis: Fortress Press), pp. 60-80

1999i   various essays in Richard Bauckham (ed.), *God Will Be All in All: The Eschatology of Jürgen Moltmann* (Edinburgh: T. & T. Clark, 1999)

1999ii   *God for a Secular Society: The Public Relevance of Theology* (Minneapolis: Fortress Press)

2003   *Science and Wisdom* (London: SCM)

2004i   *In The End – The Beginning : The Life of Hope* (Minneapolis: Fortress Press)

2004ii   'Progress and Abyss: Remembrances of the Future of the Modern World' in Miroslav Volf and William Katerburg (eds.), *The Future of Hope: Christian Tradition Amid Modernity and Postmodernity* (Grand Rapids: Eerdmans), pp. 3-26

Mondin, B.
1972   'Theology of Hope and the Christian Message', *Biblical Theology Bulletin*, Vol. 2, pp. 43-63

Morse, Christopher
1979   *The Logic of Promise in Moltmann's Theology* (Philadelphia: Fortress Press)

Mott, Stephen Charles
1982   *Biblical Ethics and Social Change* (New York/Oxford: OUP)

1984i   'The Use of the Bible in Social Ethics II: The Use of the New Testament – Part 1', *Transformation*, Vol. 1, No. 2, pp. 21-26

1984ii   'The Use of the Bible in Social Ethics II: The Use of the New Testament – Part 2', *Transformation*, Vol. 1, No. 3, pp. 19-25

1984i and 1984ii: later reprinted as *Jesus and Social Ethics*, Grove Booklets on Ethics No. 55 (Bramcote, Notts.: Grove Books, 1984)
1987   'The Contribution of the Bible to Economic Thought', *Transformation*, Vol. 4, Nos. 3 and 4, pp. 25-33
1993i   'The Partiality of Biblical Justice', *Transformation*, Vol. 10, No. 1, pp. 23-29
1993ii *A Christian Perspective on Political Thought* (New York/Oxford: OUP)

Mouw, Richard
1973   *Political Evangelism* (Grand Rapids: Eerdmans)
1976   *Politics and the Biblical Drama* (Grand Rapids: Baker)
1983   *When the Kings Come Marching In: Israel and the New Jerusalem* (Grand Rapids: Eerdmans)

Muller, R.A.
1981   'Christ in the Eschaton: Calvin and Moltmann on the Duration of the *Munus Regium*', *Harvard Theological Review*, Vol. 74, pp. 31 59

Müller-Fahrenholz, Geiko
2000   *The Kingdom and the Power: The Theology of Jürgen Moltmann* (London: SCM)

Murray, Iain
1971   *The Puritan Hope* (Edinburgh: Banner of Truth)

Neill, Stephen
1980   'Religion and Culture – An Historical Perspective', *Down to Earth*, ed. John Stott and Robert Coote (London: Hodder & Stoughton), pp. 1 13

Neuhaus, Richard John
1990   'Democracy – A Christian Imperative', Transformation, Vol. 7, No. 4, pp. 1-4,18-19

Nicholls, Bruce
1980   'A Personal Response to the Consultation on the Theology of Development', *Evangelical Review of Theology*, Vol. 4, No. 2, pp. 270-273
1985   (ed.), *In Word and Deed*, the conference papers of *The Consultation on the Relationship between Evangelism and Social Responsibility*, Grand Rapids 1982 (Exeter: Paternoster)

NIDNTT
        The New International Dictionary of New Testament Theology, ed. Colin Brown (Exeter: Paternoster, 1971, English Edition 1976, 1986)

Niebuhr, Reinhold
1964   *The Nature and Destiny of Man: A Christian Interpretation*, Vol. 2 (New York: Scribner's)

Noll, Mark A.
1992   *A History of Christianity in the United States and Canada* (Grand Rapids/London: Eerdmans/SPCK)

O'Brien, Peter T.
1982   'Principalities and Powers and their Relationship to Structures', *Evangelical Review of Theology*, Vol. 6, No. 1, pp. 50-61

O'Collins, G.
1968   'The Principle and Theology of Hope', *Scottish Journal of Theology*, Vol. 21, pp. 129-144

O'Donovan, Oliver
1979   'The Natural Ethic', *Essays in Evangelical Social Ethics*, ed. David F Wright (Exeter: Paternoster), pp. 19-38
1986i   *Resurrection and Moral Order: An Outline for Evangelical Ethics* (Leicester: IVP)
1986ii 'The Political Thought of the Book of Revelation', *Tyndale Bulletin*, Vol. 37, pp. 61-94
1996   *The Desire of the Nations: Rediscovering the Roots of Political Theology* (Cambridge, CUP)
2002   *Common Objects of Love: Moral Reflections and the Shaping of Community* (Grand Rapids: Eerdmans)
2003   *The Just War Revisited* (Cambridge: CUP)

O'Donovan, Oliver and Joan Lockwood O'Donovan
2003   *Bonds of Imperfection: Christian Politics, Past and Present* (Grand Rapids: Eerdmans)

O'Donnell, J.J.
1982   'The Doctrine of the Trinity in Recent German Theology', *Heythrop Journal*, Vol. 23, pp. 153-167
1983   *Trinity and Temporality: The Christian Doctrine of God in the Light of Process Theology and the Theology of Hope* (Oxford: OUP)

Olson, R.
1983   'Trinity and Eschatology: The Historical Being of God in Jürgen Moltmann and Wolfhart Pannenberg', *Scottish Journal of Theology*, Vol. 36, pp. 213-227

Oxford Declaration
1990   'The Oxford Declaration on Christian Faith and Economics', the report of the Third Second Oxford Conference on Christian Faith and Economics (1990), *Transformation*, Vol. 7, No. 2, pp. 1-9

Padilla, C. René
1975   'Evangelism and the World', *Let the Earth Hear His Voice*, ed. J.D. Douglas (Minneapolis: World Wide Publications), pp. 116 146; also published in *Mission Between the Times*, René Padilla (Grand Rapids: Eerdmans, 1985), pp. 1-44
1976   (ed.), *The New Face of Evangelicals: An International Symposium on the Lausanne Covenant* (London: Hodder & Stoughton)
1980   'Hermeneutics and Culture – A Theological Perspective', *Down to Earth*, ed. John Stott and Robert Coote (London: Hodder & Stoughton), pp. 63-78
1985i   'How Evangelicals Endorsed Social Responsibility 1966-1983', *Transformation*, Vol. 2, No. 3, pp. 28-32; also published by Grove Booklets (Nottingham)
1985ii *Mission Between the Times* (Grand Rapids: Eerdmans)
1989   'The Politics of the Kingdom of God and the Political Mission of the Church', *Proclaiming Christ in Christ's Way*, ed. Vinay Samuel and Albrecht Hauser (Oxford: Regnum), pp. 180-198

Padilla, C. René and Sugden, Chris (eds.)
1985   *Texts on Evangelical Social Ethics, 1974-1983* (Nottingham: Grove Booklets)

Page, Ruth
1984   Review of *The Trinity and the Kingdom of God* (J Moltmann), *Scottish Journal of Theology*, Vol. 37, pp. 97-98

Pannenberg, W.
1984 *Christian Spirituality and Sacramental Community* (London: Darton, Longman and Todd)

Pawlikowski, J.
1984   'The Holocaust and Contemporary Christology', *Concilium*, No. 175; also printed in *The Holocaust as Interruption*, ed. E S Fiorenza and D Tracy (Edinburgh: T. & T. Clark), pp43-49

Pannell, William
1989   'Is Dr King on Board?', *Proclaiming Christ in Christ's Way*, ed. Vinay Samuel and Albrecht Hauser (Oxford: Regnum), pp. 199-207

Paredes, Tito
1987   'Culture and Social Change', *The Church in Response to Human Need*, eds. Vinay Samuel and Chris Sugden (Oxford: Regnum), pp. 62-84

Perriman, Andrew
1991   'The Pattern of Christ's Sufferings: Colossians 1:24 and Philippians: 3:10-11', *Tyndale Bulletin*, Vol. 42, No. 1, pp. 62-79

Piper, J.
1979   'Hope as the Motivation of Love in 1 Peter, 1 Peter 3:9-12', *New Testament Studies*, Vol. 26, pp. 212-231

Preston, R.H.
1975   'Reflections on Theologies of Social Change' *Theology and Change: Essays in Memory of Alan Richardson*, ed. R H Preston (London: SCM), pp. 143-166

Quistorp, Heinrich
1955   *Calvin's Doctrine of the Last Things* (London: Lutterworth Press)

Richardson, Alan
1973   *The Political Christ* (London: SCM)

Ricoeur, P.
1981   'Freedom in the Light of Hope', *Essays on Biblical Interpretation*, ed. L.S. Mudge (London: SPCK), pp. 155-182

Rieger, Joerg (ed.)
1998   *Liberating the Future: God, Mammon and Theology* (Minneapolis, MN: Fortress Press)

Ringgren, Helmet
1956   *The Messiah in the Old Testament*, Studies in Biblical Theology, No. 18 (London: SCM)

Robinson, John A.T.
1957   *Jesus and His Coming* (London: SCM)

Runia, Klaas
1984   *The Present-Day Christological Debate* (Leicester: IVP)

Runyon, Theodore (ed.)
1979   *Hope for the Church: Moltmann in Dialogue with Practical Theology*, Jürgen Moltmann with M. Douglas Meeks, Rodney J. Hunter, James W. Fowler, Noel L. Erskine, ed. Theodore Runyon, the papers of the 43rd Ministers' Week, 1978, 'A Theology of Hope and Parish Practice', Emory University's Candler School of Theology (Nashville: Abingdon)

Samuel, Vinay and Hauser, Albrecht (eds.)
1989   *Proclaiming Christ in Christ's Way: Studies in Integral Evangelism*, the papers of the Stuttgart Consultation on Evangelism, 1987; presented as a *Festschrift* for Walter Arnold (Oxford: Regnum)

Samuel, Vinay and Sugden, Chris
1981   'Toward a Theology of Social Change', *Evangelicals and Development*, ed. Ronald Sider (Exeter: Paternoster), pp. 45-68
1983   (eds.), *Evangelism and the Poor* (Oxford: Regnum) 1983 (eds.), *Sharing Jesus in the Two Thirds World* (Bangalore: PIM)
1985   'Evangelism and Social Responsibility – A Biblical Study on Priorities', *In Word and Deed*, ed. Bruce Nicholls (Exeter: Paternoster), pp. 189-214

1987   (eds.), *The Church in Response to Human Need*, the Conference report and papers of *The Consultation on the Church in Response to Human Need*, Wheaton 1983 (Oxford: Regnum)
1987   'God's Intention for the World', *The Church in Response to Human Need*, eds., Vinay Samuel and Chris Sugden (Oxford: Regnum), pp. 128-160

Schluter, Michael and Clements, Roy
1990   'Jubilee Institutional Norms: A Middle Way between Creation Ethics and Kingdom Ethics as the Basis for Christian Political Action', *Evangelical Quarterly*, Vol. 62, No. 1, pp. 37-62

Schnackenberg, Rudolf
1965   *God's Rule and Kingdom* (New York/London: Herder and Herder/Burns and Oates, ET 2nd ed.)

Schuurman, Douglas J.
1987   'Creation, Eschaton, and Ethics: An Analysis of Theology and Ethics in Jürgen Moltmann', *Calvin Theological Journal*, Vol. 22, pp. 42-67
1991   *Creation, Eschaton, and Ethics: The Ethical Significance of the Creation-Eschaton Relation in the Thought of Emil Brunner and Jürgen Moltmann*, American University Studies, Series VII, Theology and Religion, Vol. 86 (New York: Peter Lang)

Schweitzer, Albert
1945   *The Quest for the Historical Jesus* (London: A. & C. Black, 1906, ET 1910, 1945)

Sider, Ronald
1977   *Rich Christians in an Age of Hunger* (London: Hodder & Stoughton); also published as a synopsis published in *Evangelical Review Theology*, Vol. 4, No. 1 (1980), pp. 70-83
1980   *Christ and Violence* (Tring: Lion)
1981   (ed.), *Evangelicals and Development*, the papers of The Consultation on the Theology of Development, Hoddesdon 1980 (Exeter: Paternoster)
1982   (ed.), *Lifestyle in the Eighties*, the papers of The Consultation on Simple Lifestyle, Hoddesdon 1980 (Exeter: Paternoster)
1985   with James Parker, 'How Broad is Salvation in Scripture?', *In Word and Deed*, ed. Bruce Nicholls (Exeter: Paternoster), pp. 85-108
1993   *Evangelism and Social Action* (London: Hodder & Stoughton)

Sider, Ronald and Stott, John
1977   *Evangelism, Salvation and Social Justice* (Nottingham: Grove Books) Sider's contribution first published in *International Review of Mission* (1975), Vol. 64, No. 255, pp. 251-267; also published in *Evangelical Review of Theology*, Vol. 2, No. 1 (April 1978), pp. 70-88

Sider, Ronald *et al*
1985   'Editorial: Christian Faith and Politics', *Transformation*, Vol. 2, No. 3

Sinclair, Maurice
1987   'Development and Eschatology', *The Church in Response to Human Need*,
        eds. Vinay Samuel and Chris Sugden (Oxford: Regnum), pp. 161-174

Smalley, Stephen
1978   *John: Evangelist and Interpreter* (Exeter: Paternoster)

Smith, David W.
2003i   *Mission After Christendom* (London: DLT)
2003ii *Against the Stream: Christianity and Mission in an Age of Globalization*
        (Leicester: IVP)

Smith, Stephen
1984   'Hope, Theology of', *Evangelical Dictionary of Theology*, ed. Walter Elwell
        (Basingstoke: Marshall Pickering), pp. 532-4

Steuernagel, Valdir R.
1988   'The Theology of Mission in its Relation to Social Responsibility within the
        Lausanne Movement', DTh thesis, Lutheran School of Theology, Chicago,
        Illinois
1990   'Social Concern and Evangelisation', *Transformation*, Vol. 7, No. 1, pp. 12-16

Stringfellow, William
2004   *An Ethic for Christians and Other Aliens in a Strange Land* (Eugene, OR.:
        Wipf & Stock, first published 1973)

Stott, John R.W.
1975i   'The Biblical Basis of Evangelism', *Let the Earth Hear His Voice*, ed. J.D.
        Douglas (Minneapolis: World Wide Publications), pp. 65-78
1975ii *Explaining the Lausanne Covenant* (Lausanne Occasional Papers) 1979
        God's New Society: The Message of Ephesians (Leicester: IVP)
1984i   *Issues Facing Christians Today* (Basingstoke: Marshall, Morgan and Scott)
1984ii 'Seeking Theological Agreement', *Transformation*, Vol. 1, No. 1, pp. 21-22
1986i   *Christian Mission in the Modern World* (Eastbourne: Kingsway, 1975, 1986)
1986ii *The Cross of Christ* (Leicester, IVP)
1989   'A Note about the Stuttgart Statement on Evangelism', *Sharing Christ in
        Christ's Way*, ed. Vinay Samuel and Albrecht Hauser (Oxford: Regnum), pp.
        208-211
1995   'Life in the Spirit of Truth: Interview with Roy McCloughry', *Third Way*, Vol.
        18, No. 8, pp. 14-23

Stott, John R.W. and Coote, Robert (eds.)
1980   *Down to Earth: Studies in Christianity and Culture*, the papers of Willowbank
        '78 (London: Hodder & Stoughton)

Sturm, Douglas
1982   'Praxis and Promise: On the Ethics of Political Theology', *Ethics*, Vol. 92, No.
        4, pp. 733-750

Sugden, Chris
1981   *Radical Discipleship* (Basingstoke: Marshall, Morgan and Scott)
1989   'Evangelicals and Wholistic Evangelism', *Proclaiming Christ in Christ's Way*, ed. Vinay Samuel and Albrecht Hauser (Oxford: Regnum), pp. 29-51. A shorter version of this article is published in *Transformation* (1989), Vol. 7, No. 1, pp. 9-12 under the title 'Theological Developments since Lausanne I'

Thompson, W.D.J. Cargill
1966   'Martin Luther and the "Two Kingdoms"', *Political Ideas*, ed. David Thomson (Harmondsworth: Penguin)

Tomlin, Graham
1999   *The Power of the Cross: Theology and the Death of Christ in Paul, Luther and Pascal* (Carlisle: Paternoster)

Torrance, T.F.
1956   *Kingdom and Church* (Edinburgh: Oliver and Boyd)

Transformation – The Church in Response to Human Need
1984   The statement of Wheaton '83, published in *Transformation*, Vol. 1, No. 1, pp. 23-28; also, published under the same title, Grove Booklets on Ethics, No. 62 (Bramcote, Nottingham, 1986); and with the conference papers in *The Church in Response to Human Need*, ed. Vinay Samuel and Christ Sugden (Oxford: Regnum, 1987), pp. 254-65

Travis, Stephen
1980   *Christian Hope and the Future of Man* (Leicester: IVP)

Volf, Miroslav
1983   'Doing and Interpreting: an Examination of the Relationship between Theory and Practice in Latin American Liberation Theology', *Themelios*, Vol. 8, No. 3, pp. 11-19
1989   'Church, State and Society: Reflections on the Life of the Church in Contemporary Yugoslavia', *Transformation*, Vol. 6, No. 1, pp. 24-32
1990i   'On Loving with Hope: Eschatology and Social Responsibility', *Transformation*, Vol. 7, No. 3, pp. 28-31
1990ii 'Democracy and the Crisis of the Socialist Project: Towards a Post-Revolutionary Theology of Liberation', *Transformation*, Vol. 7, No. 4, pp. 11-16
1991   *Work in the Spirit: Toward a Theology of Work* (New York: OUP)
1996   *Exclusion and Embrace: A Theological Exploration of Identity, Otherness and Reconciliation* (Nashville: Abingdon)
1998   *After Our Likeness: The Church as the Image of the Trinity* (Grand Rapids: Eerdmans, 1998)
1999   'After Moltmann: Reflections on the Future of Eschatology' in Richard Bauckham (ed.), *God Will Be All in All: The Eschatology of Jürgen Moltmann* (Edinburgh: T. & T. Clark, 1999), pp. 87-114

2002   'Community Formation as an Image of the Triune God' in Richard N.
          Longenecker (ed.), Community Formation in the Early Church and in the
          Church Today (Peabody: Hendrickson)

Volf, Miroslav and William Katerburg (eds.)
2004   The Future of Hope: Christian Tradition Amid Modernity and Postmodernity
          (Grand Rapids: Eerdmans)

Von Rad, Gerhard
1975   Old Testament Theology, 2 Vols. (London: SCM, 1957, ET 1962, Rev Ed
          1975)

Wallace, Ronald S.
1959   Calvin's Doctrine of the Christian Life (Edinburgh/London: Oliver and Boyd)

Wallis, Jim
1983   The New Radical (Tring: Lion)

Walsh, Brian J.
1987   'Theology of Hope and the Doctrine of Creation: An Appraisal of Jürgen
          Moltmann', Evangelical Quarterly, Vol. 59, pp. 53-76

Wan, Milton W.Y.
1987   'The Contribution of the Bible to Economic Thought: A Response to Stephen
          Mott', Transformation, Vol. 4, Nos. 3 and 4, pp. 34-5

Weber, Eugen
1999   Apocalypses: Prophecies, Cults and Millennial Beliefs Through the Ages
          (London: Hutchinson)

Webster, J.B.
1985   'Jürgen Moltmann: Trinity and Suffering', Evangel, Vol. 3, No. 2, pp. 4-6

Wells, Paul
1990   'God and Change: Moltmann in the Light of the Reformed Tradition', The
          Power and Weakness of God, ed. Nigel Cameron (Edinburgh, Rutherford
          House), pp. 53-68

Wendel, Francois
1963   Calvin: The Origins and Development of his Religious Thought (London:
          Collins)

Wenham, David
1980   'The Christian Life: A Life in Tension? – A Consideration of the Nature of
          Christian Experience in Paul', Pauline Studies, Festschrift for F.F. Bruce, eds.
          D.A. Hagner and M.J. Harris (Exeter: Paternoster), pp. 80-94

Williams, Stephen
1986i   'Hope, Love and Social Action', *Evangel*, Vol. 4, No. 3, pp. 2-4
1986ii   'Reformed Perspective on Mission and Hope', *Reformed World*, Vol. 39, No. 4, pp. 625-31
1987   *Jürgen Moltmann: A Critical Introduction* (Leicester: RTSF Monograph)
1988   'Outline for ethics: a response to Oliver O'Donovan', *Themelios*, Vol. 13, pp. 86-91
1989i   'The Limits of Hope and the Logic of Love: On the Basis of Christian Social Responsibility', *Tyndale Bulletin*, Vol. 40, No. 2, pp. 261-281
1989ii   'On Giving Hope in a Suffering World: Response to Moltmann', *Issues in Faith and History*, ed. Nigel Cameron (Edinburgh: Rutherford House), pp. 3-19
1990i   'The Partition of Love and Hope: Eschatology and Social Responsibility', *Transformation*, Vol. 7, No. 3, pp. 24-27
1990ii   'Structural Change', *Third Way*, Vol. 13, No. 5, pp. 8-9
1995   'The Pilgrim People of God: some General Observations', *Irish Biblical Studies*, Vol. 17, pp. 129-137
1997i   'Thirty Years of Hope: A Generation of Writing on Eschatology' in K.E. Brower and M.W. Elliot (eds.), *'The Reader Must Understand': Eschatology in the Bible and Theology* (Leicester, Apollos), pp. 263-278
1997ii   'Evangelicals and Eschatology: A Contentious Case,' *Interpreting the Bible: Historical and Theological Studies*, ed. A. N. S. Lane (Apollos), pp. 291-308.

Wolterstorff, Nicholas
2004   'Seeking Justice in Hope' in Miroslav Volf and William Katerburg (eds.), *The Future of Hope: Christian Tradition Amid Modernity and Postmodernity* (Grand Rapids: Eerdmans), pp. 77-100

World Council of Churches
1973   *Meeting in Bangkok, International Review of Mission*, Vol. 62, No. 246; includes *The Bangkok Report*
1974   *Evangelism 1974: A Symposium, International Review of Mission*, Vol. 63, No. 249
1980   *Melbourne Conference Notes, International Review Mission*, Vol. 69, No. 275
1980   *Melbourne Reports and Notes, International Review of Mission*, Vol. 69, Nos. 276 & 277
1980   *Your Kingdom Come*, the papers of Melbourne '80 (Geneva: WCC)

Woodhouse, John
1988   'Evangelism and Social Responsibility', *Christians in Society: Explorations 3*, B.G. Webb (ed.) (Homebush West, NSW, Australia: Lancer Books/Moore Theological College), pp. 3-26

Yoder, John Howard
1972   *The Politics of Jesus* (Grand Rapids: Eerdmans)

Young, N.
1976   Creator, Creation and Faith (London: Collins)

Index

Capps, Walter, 200
Carey, William, 222
Cassidy, Michael, 94
Chapman, G. Clarke, 85, 88, 90,
    200
charisms, 106, 110-117
Chicago, 163
Christendom, 59, 63, 73, 215
Chronicles, 1&2, 141
church, the, 3-5, 8-10, 13, 17, 19,
    21-23, 25, 33, 40-42, 44, 47, 49,
    51-52, 54, 59-60, 62, 68, 75-80,
    82-85, 89, 93, 95, 101-103, 105,
    109, 111-115, 117, 122, 127,
    132-133, 135-139, 141-146,
    151, 155, 157-158, 163-164,
    166-173, 179, 186, 190, 192,
    200-201, 203-204, 210, 213-
    215, 222
church leadership, 25
Colossians, 17, 30, 122, 148, 205,
    208-209, 220, 223
coming, 5, 10-12, 15, 24, 29, 35,
    40, 43, 53-54, 60, 62, 73, 76, 81-
    82, 85, 88-90, 94, 96, 102-103,
    106-107, 114, 123, 127, 133-
    134, 136-137, 139, 141-143,
    146, 148, 155, 157, 160-161,
    170-172, 174, 177, 182, 192,
    203, 219, 221, 223
communion, 79, 209
community, 16-17, 34-35, 37-39,
    41, 45, 66, 75, 77-79, 84, 89,
    108, 113-116, 122, 125, 129,
    134, 137-138, 142-145, 153-
    156, 164, 166-167, 169, 171-
    172, 177, 192, 212-213, 216-
    217, 219, 220-222
conformity, 5, 14, 30, 81, 153,
    158-159, 189, 193, 205, 209,
    211
consciousness, 8, 52, 160
Constantine, 59, 84
Consultation on the Relationship

between Evangelism and Social
    Responsibility 1982, the, 94-95,
    105, 124, 135, 137
consumerism, 28
consummation, 10, 12, 107, 131,
    134-136, 140, 146, 150, 164,
    169, 174, 178, 187, 194, 207
continuity, 13-14, 19, 30, 42, 81,
    85-87, 96, 105, 108, 115, 119,
    122-133, 149, 152, 154, 157,
    173-175, 178, 200
contradiction, 9, 14, 24, 53-54, 56,
    73, 80-81, 83, 85-88, 90, 99,
    121, 125-126, 132, 149, 156,
    187, 202-203
conversion, 14, 103
Corinthians, 1 & 2, 11, 14, 30, 109,
    111, 112, 113, 115, 123, 126,
    143, 203, 205, 206, 207, 208,
    209, 213, 215, 218, 219, 220
cosmos, the, 6, 9, 14, 30, 75, 122,
    147-148, 174, 193, 218
Cox, Harvey, 28
creation, 8-10, 13, 15-18, 34-37,
    44-47, 49, 53, 55-56, 58, 61, 63,
    67-68, 69, 70, 75, 79, 85-88, 96,
    101, 103, 106-110, 113-116,
    121-128, 130, 134, 138-141,
    143, 144, 146, 148, 153, 155,
    158-162, 164-166, 169-170,
    173-175, 177-190, 192-194,
    204, 209-210, 217
Croatia, 105
cross, the, 3-4, 8-11, 13-14, 16-17,
    22-23, 25-26, 29-31, 33-37, 41-
    49, 54-56, 62-63, 65-69, 71-75,
    77-78, 80-84, 86, 98-103, 134,
    139-140, 149, 166, 175, 180,
    190, 193, 195, 197, 199-200,
    202, 203, 205-209, 211-221, 223
cruciformity, 62-63, 211
culture, 5, 14, 31, 41, 54, 59, 85,
    94, 113, 123, 127-132, 145, 158,
    163, 173-175, 177-178, 200, 214

Paternoster Biblical Monographs
(All titles uniform with this volume)
Dates in bold are of projected publication

Joseph Abraham
Eve: Accused or Acquitted?
A Reconsideration of Feminist Readings of the Creation Narrative Texts in Genesis 1–3
Two contrary views dominate contemporary feminist biblical scholarship. One finds in the Bible an unequivocal equality between the sexes from the very creation of humanity, whilst the other sees the biblical text as irredeemably patriarchal and androcentric. Dr Abraham enters into dialogue with both camps as well as introducing his own method of approach. An invaluable tool for any one who is interested in this contemporary debate.
2002 / 0-85364-971-5 / xxiv + 272pp

Octavian D. Baban
Mimesis and Luke's on the Road Encounters in Luke-Acts
Luke's Theology of the Way and its Literary Representation
The book argues on theological and literary (mimetic) grounds that Luke's on-the-road encounters, especially those belonging to the post-Easter period, are part of his complex theology of the Way. Jesus' teaching and that of the apostles is presented by Luke as a challenging answer to the Hellenistic reader's thirst for adventure, good literature, and existential paradigms.
2005 */ 1-84227-253-5 / approx. 374pp*

Paul Barker
The Triumph of Grace in Deuteronomy
This book is a textual and theological analysis of the interaction between the sin and faithlessness of Israel and the grace of Yahweh in response, looking especially at Deuteronomy chapters 1–3, 8–10 and 29–30. The author argues that the grace of Yahweh is determinative for the ongoing relationship between Yahweh and Israel and that Deuteronomy anticipates and fully expects Israel to be faithless.
2004 / 1-84227-226-8 / xxii + 270pp

Jonathan F. Bayes
The Weakness of the Law
God's Law and the Christian in New Testament Perspective
A study of the four New Testament books which refer to the law as weak (Acts, Romans, Galatians, Hebrews) leads to a defence of the third use in the Reformed debate about the law in the life of the believer.
2000 / 0-85364-957-X / xii + 244pp

Mark Bonnington
The Antioch Episode of Galatians 2:11-14 in Historical and Cultural Context
The Galatians 2 'incident' in Antioch over table-fellowship suggests significant disagreement between the leading apostles. This book analyses the background to the disagreement by locating the incident within the dynamics of social interaction between Jews and Gentiles. It proposes a new way of understanding the relationship between the individuals and issues involved.

2005 / 1-84227-050-8 / approx. 350pp

David Bostock
A Portrayal of Trust
The Theme of Faith in the Hezekiah Narratives
This study provides detailed and sensitive readings of the Hezekiah narratives (2 Kings 18–20 and Isaiah 36–39) from a theological perspective. It concentrates on the theme of faith, using narrative criticism as its methodology. Attention is paid especially to setting, plot, point of view and characterization within the narratives. A largely positive portrayal of Hezekiah emerges that underlines the importance and relevance of scripture.

2005 / 1-84227-314-0 / approx. 300pp

Mark Bredin
Jesus, Revolutionary of Peace
A Non-violent Christology in the Book of Revelation
This book aims to demonstrate that the figure of Jesus in the Book of Revelation can best be understood as an active non-violent revolutionary.

2003 / 1-84227-153-9 / xviii + 262pp

Robinson Butarbutar
Paul and Conflict Resolution
An Exegetical Study of Paul's Apostolic Paradigm in 1 Corinthians 9
The author sees the apostolic paradigm in 1 Corinthians 9 as part of Paul's unified arguments in 1 Corinthians 8–10 in which he seeks to mediate in the dispute over the issue of food offered to idols. The book also sees its relevance for dispute-resolution today, taking the conflict within the author's church as an example.

2006 / 1-84227-315-9 / approx. 280pp

Daniel J-S Chae
Paul as Apostle to the Gentiles
*His Apostolic Self-awareness and its Influence on the Soteriological Argument
in Romans*
Opposing 'the post-Holocaust interpretation of Romans', Daniel Chae competently demonstrates that Paul argues for the equality of Jew and Gentile in Romans. Chae's fresh exegetical interpretation is academically outstanding and spiritually encouraging.
1997 / 0-85364-829-8 / xiv + 378pp

Luke L. Cheung
The Genre, Composition and Hermeneutics of the Epistle of James
The present work examines the employment of the wisdom genre with a certain compositional structure and the interpretation of the law through the Jesus tradition of the double love command by the author of the Epistle of James to serve his purpose in promoting perfection and warning against doubleness among the eschatologically renewed people of God in the Diaspora.
2003 / 1-84227-062-1 / xvi + 372pp

Youngmo Cho
Spirit and Kingdom in the Writings of Luke and Paul
The relationship between Spirit and Kingdom is a relatively unexplored area in Lukan and Pauline studies. This book offers a fresh perspective of two biblical writers on the subject. It explores the difference between Luke's and Paul's understanding of the Spirit by examining the specific question of the relationship of the concept of the Spirit to the concept of the Kingdom of God in each writer.
2005 / 1-84227-316-7 / approx. 270pp

Andrew C. Clark
Parallel Lives
The Relation of Paul to the Apostles in the Lucan Perspective
This study of the Peter-Paul parallels in Acts argues that their purpose was to emphasize the themes of continuity in salvation history and the unity of the Jewish and Gentile missions. New light is shed on Luke's literary techniques, partly through a comparison with Plutarch.
2001 / 1-84227-035-4 / xviii + 386pp

Andrew D. Clarke
Secular and Christian Leadership in Corinth
A Socio-Historical and Exegetical Study of 1 Corinthians 1–6
This volume is an investigation into the leadership structures and dynamics of first-century Roman Corinth. These are compared with the practice of leadership in the Corinthian Christian community which are reflected in 1 Corinthians 1–6, and contrasted with Paul's own principles of Christian leadership.
2005 / 1-84227-229-2 / 200pp

Stephen Finamore
God, Order and Chaos
René Girard and the Apocalypse
Readers are often disturbed by the images of destruction in the book of Revelation and unsure why they are unleashed after the exaltation of Jesus. This book examines past approaches to these texts and uses René Girard's theories to revive some old ideas and propose some new ones.
2005 / 1-84227-197-0 / approx. 344pp

David G. Firth
Surrendering Retribution in the Psalms
Responses to Violence in the Individual Complaints
In *Surrendering Retribution in the Psalms,* David Firth examines the ways in which the book of Psalms inculcates a model response to violence through the repetition of standard patterns of prayer. Rather than seeking justification for retributive violence, Psalms encourages not only a surrender of the right of retribution to Yahweh, but also sets limits on the retribution that can be sought in imprecations. Arising initially from the author's experience in South Africa, the possibilities of this model to a particular context of violence is then briefly explored.
2005 / 1-84227-337-X / xviii + 154pp

Scott J. Hafemann
Suffering and Ministry in the Spirit
Paul's Defence of His Ministry in II Corinthians 2:14–3:3
Shedding new light on the way Paul defended his apostleship, the author offers a careful, detailed study of 2 Corinthians 2:14–3:3 linked with other key passages throughout 1 and 2 Corinthians. Demonstrating the unity and coherence of Paul's argument in this passage, the author shows that Paul's suffering served as the vehicle for revealing God's power and glory through the Spirit.
2000 / 0-85364-967-7 / xiv + 262pp

Scott J. Hafemann
Paul, Moses and the History of Israel
The Letter/Spirit Contrast and the Argument from Scripture in 2 Corinthians 3
An exegetical study of the call of Moses, the second giving of the Law (Exodus 32–34), the new covenant, and the prophetic understanding of the history of Israel in 2 Corinthians 3. Hafemann's work demonstrates Paul's contextual use of the Old Testament and the essential unity between the Law and the Gospel within the context of the distinctive ministries of Moses and Paul.
2005 / 1-84227-317-5 / xii + 498pp

Douglas S. McComiskey
Lukan Theology in the Light of the Gospel's Literary Structure
Luke's Gospel was purposefully written with theology embedded in its patterned literary structure. A critical analysis of this cyclical structure provides new windows into Luke's interpretation of the individual pericopes comprising the Gospel and illuminates several of his theological interests.
2004 / 1-84227-148-2 / xviii + 388pp

Stephen Motyer
Your Father the Devil?
A New Approach to John and 'The Jews'
Who are 'the Jews' in John's Gospel? Defending John against the charge of antisemitism, Motyer argues that, far from demonising the Jews, the Gospel seeks to present Jesus as 'Good News for Jews' in a late first century setting.
1997 / 0-85364-832-8 / xiv + 260pp

Esther Ng
Reconstructing Christian Origins?
The Feminist Theology of Elizabeth Schüssler Fiorenza: An Evaluation
In a detailed evaluation, the author challenges Elizabeth Schüssler Fiorenza's reconstruction of early Christian origins and her underlying presuppositions. The author also presents her own views on women's roles both then and now.
2002 / 1-84227-055-9 / xxiv + 468pp

Robin Parry
Old Testament Story and Christian Ethics
The Rape of Dinah as a Case Study
What is the role of story in ethics and, more particularly, what is the role of Old Testament story in Christian ethics? This book, drawing on the work of contemporary philosophers, argues that narrative is crucial in the ethical shaping of people and, drawing on the work of contemporary Old Testament scholars, that story plays a key role in Old Testament ethics. Parry then argues that when situated in canonical context Old Testament stories can be reappropriated by Christian readers in their own ethical formation. The shocking story of the rape of Dinah and the massacre of the Shechemites provides a fascinating case study for exploring the parameters within which Christian ethical appropriations of Old Testament stories can live.
2004 / 1-84227-210-1 / xx + 350pp

Ian Paul
Power to See the World Anew
The Value of Paul Ricoeur's Hermeneutic of Metaphor in Interpreting the Symbolism of Revelation 12 and 13
This book is a study of the hermeneutics of metaphor of Paul Ricoeur, one of the most important writers on hermeneutics and metaphor of the last century. It sets out the key points of his theory, important criticisms of his work, and how his approach, modified in the light of these criticisms, offers a methodological framework for reading apocalyptic texts.
2006 / 1-84227-056-7 / approx. 350pp

Robert L. Plummer
Paul's Understanding of the Church's Mission
Did the Apostle Paul Expect the Early Christian Communities to Evangelize?
This book engages in a careful study of Paul's letters to determine if the apostle expected the communities to which he wrote to engage in missionary activity. It helpfully summarizes the discussion on this debated issue, judiciously handling contested texts, and provides a way forward in addressing this critical question. While admitting that Paul rarely explicitly commands the communities he founded to evangelize, Plummer amasses significant incidental data to provide a convincing case that Paul did indeed expect his churches to engage in mission activity. Throughout the study, Plummer progressively builds a theological basis for the church's mission that is both distinctively Pauline and compelling.
2006 / 1-84227-333-7 / approx. 324pp

David Powys
'Hell': A Hard Look at a Hard Question
The Fate of the Unrighteous in New Testament Thought
This comprehensive treatment seeks to unlock the original meaning of terms and phrases long thought to support the traditional doctrine of hell. It concludes that there is an alternative—one which is more biblical, and which can positively revive the rationale for Christian mission.
1997 / 0-85364-831-X / xxii + 478pp

Sorin Sabou
Between Horror and Hope
Paul's Metaphorical Language of Death in Romans 6.1-11
This book argues that Paul's metaphorical language of death in Romans 6.1-11 conveys two aspects: horror and hope. The 'horror' aspect is conveyed by the 'crucifixion' language, and the 'hope' aspect by 'burial' language. The life of the Christian believer is understood, as relationship with sin is concerned ('death to sin'), between these two realities: horror and hope.
2005 / 1-84227-322-1 / approx. 224pp

Rosalind Selby
The Comical Doctrine
The Epistemology of New Testament Hermeneutics
This book argues that the gospel breaks through postmodernity's critique of truth and the referential possibilities of textuality with its gift of grace. With a rigorous, philosophical challenge to modernist and postmodernist assumptions, Selby offers an alternative epistemology to all who would still read with faith *and* with academic credibility.
2005 / 1-84227-212-8 / approx. 350pp

Kiwoong Son
Zion Symbolism in Hebrews
Hebrews 12.18-24 as a Hermeneutical Key to the Epistle
This book challenges the general tendency of understanding the Epistle to the Hebrews against a Hellenistic background and suggests that the Epistle should be understood in the light of the Jewish apocalyptic tradition. The author especially argues for the importance of the theological symbolism of Sinai and Zion (Heb. 12:18-24) as it provides the Epistle's theological background as well as the rhetorical basis of the superiority motif of Jesus throughout the Epistle.
2005 / 1-84227-368-X / approx. 280pp

Kevin Walton
Thou Traveller Unknown
The Presence and Absence of God in the Jacob Narrative
The author offers a fresh reading of the story of Jacob in the book of Genesis through the paradox of divine presence and absence. The work also seeks to make a contribution to Pentateuchal studies by bringing together a close reading of the final text with historical critical insights, doing justice to the text's historical depth, final form and canonical status.
2003 / 1-84227-059-1 / xvi + 238pp

George M. Wieland
The Significance of Salvation
A Study of Salvation Language in the Pastoral Epistles
The language and ideas of salvation pervade the three Pastoral Epistles. This study offers a close examination of their soteriological statements. In all three letters the idea of salvation is found to play a vital paraenetic role, but each also exhibits distinctive soteriological emphases. The results challenge common assumptions about the Pastoral Epistles as a corpus.
2005 / 1-84227-257-8 / approx. 324pp

Alistair Wilson
When Will These Things Happen?
A Study of Jesus as Judge in Matthew 21–25
This study seeks to allow Matthew's carefully constructed presentation of Jesus to be given full weight in the modern evaluation of Jesus' eschatology. Careful analysis of the text of Matthew 21–25 reveals Jesus to be standing firmly in the Jewish prophetic and wisdom traditions as he proclaims and enacts imminent judgement on the Jewish authorities then boldly claims the central role in the final and universal judgement.
2004 / 1-84227-146-6 / xxii + 272pp

Lindsay Wilson
Joseph Wise and Otherwise
The Intersection of Covenant and Wisdom in Genesis 37–50
This book offers a careful literary reading of Genesis 37–50 that argues that the Joseph story contains both strong covenant themes and many wisdom-like elements. The connections between the two helps to explore how covenant and wisdom might intersect in an integrated biblical theology.
2004 / 1-84227-140-7 / xvi + 340pp

Stephen I. Wright
The Voice of Jesus
Studies in the Interpretation of Six Gospel Parables
This literary study considers how the 'voice' of Jesus has been heard in different
periods of parable interpretation, and how the categories of figure and trope may
help us towards a sensitive reading of the parables today.
2000 / 0-85364-975-8 / xiv + 280pp

Paternoster:
thinking faith

Paternoster
9 Holdom Avenue,
Bletchley,
Milton Keynes MK1 1QR,
United Kingdom
Web: www.authenticmedia.co.uk/paternoster

Paternoster Theological Monographs
(All titles uniform with this volume)
Dates in bold are of projected publication

Emil Bartos
Deification in Eastern Orthodox Theology
An Evaluation and Critique of the Theology of Dumitru Staniloae
Bartos studies a fundamental yet neglected aspect of Orthodox theology: deification. By examining the doctrines of anthropology, christology, soteriology and ecclesiology as they relate to deification, he provides an important contribution to contemporary dialogue between Eastern and Western theologians.
1999 / 0-85364-956-1 / xii + 370pp

Graham Buxton
The Trinity, Creation and Pastoral Ministry
Imaging the Perichoretic God
In this book the author proposes a three-way conversation between theology, science and pastoral ministry. His approach draws on a Trinitarian understanding of God as a relational being of love, whose life 'spills over' into all created reality, human and non-human. By locating human meaning and purpose within God's 'creation-community' this book offers the possibility of a transforming engagement between those in pastoral ministry and the scientific community.
2005 */ 1-84227-369-8 / approx. 380 pp*

Iain D. Campbell
Fixing the Indemnity
The Life and Work of George Adam Smith
When Old Testament scholar George Adam Smith (1856–1942) delivered the Lyman Beecher lectures at Yale University in 1899, he confidently declared that 'modern criticism has won its war against traditional theories. It only remains to fix the amount of the indemnity.' In this biography, Iain D. Campbell assesses Smith's critical approach to the Old Testament and evaluates its consequences, showing that Smith's life and work still raises questions about the relationship between biblical scholarship and evangelical faith.
2004 / 1-84227-228-4 / xx + 256pp

Tim Chester
Mission and the Coming of God
Eschatology, the Trinity and Mission in the Theology of Jürgen Moltmann
This book explores the theology and missiology of the influential contemporary theologian, Jürgen Moltmann. It highlights the important contribution Moltmann has made while offering a critique of his thought from an evangelical perspective. In so doing, it touches on pertinent issues for evangelical missiology. The conclusion takes Calvin as a starting point, proposing 'an eschatology of the cross' which offers a critique of the over-realised eschatologies in liberation theology and certain forms of evangelicalism.
2006 / 1-84227-320-5 / approx. 224pp

Sylvia Wilkey Collinson
Making Disciples
The Significance of Jesus' Educational Strategy for Today's Church
This study examines the biblical practice of discipling, formulates a definition, and makes comparisons with modern models of education. A recommendation is made for greater attention to its practice today.
2004 / 1-84227-116-4 / xiv + 278pp

Darrell Cosden
A Theology of Work
Work and the New Creation
Through dialogue with Moltmann, Pope John Paul II and others, this book develops a genitive 'theology of work', presenting a theological definition of work and a model for a theological ethics of work that shows work's nature, value and meaning now and eschatologically. Work is shown to be a transformative activity consisting of three dynamically inter-related dimensions: the instrumental, relational and ontological.
2005 / 1-84227-332-9 / xvi + 208pp

Stephen M. Dunning
The Crisis and the Quest
A Kierkegaardian Reading of Charles Williams
Employing Kierkegaardian categories and analysis, this study investigates both the central crisis in Charles Williams's authorship between hermetism and Christianity (Kierkegaard's Religions A and B), and the quest to resolve this crisis, a quest that ultimately presses the bounds of orthodoxy.
2000 / 0-85364-985-5 / xxiv + 254pp

Keith Ferdinando
The Triumph of Christ in African Perspective
A Study of Demonology and Redemption in the African Context
The book explores the implications of the gospel for traditional African fears of occult aggression. It analyses such traditional approaches to suffering and biblical responses to fears of demonic evil, concluding with an evaluation of African beliefs from the perspective of the gospel.
1999 / 0-85364-830-1 / xviii + 450pp

Andrew Goddard
Living the Word, Resisting the World
The Life and Thought of Jacques Ellul
This work offers a definitive study of both the life and thought of the French Reformed thinker Jacques Ellul (1912-1994). It will prove an indispensable resource for those interested in this influential theologian and sociologist and for Christian ethics and political thought generally.
2002 / 1-84227-053-2 / xxiv + 378pp

David Hilborn
The Words of our Lips
Language-Use in Free Church Worship
Studies of liturgical language have tended to focus on the written canons of Roman Catholic and Anglican communities. By contrast, David Hilborn analyses the more extemporary approach of English Nonconformity. Drawing on recent developments in linguistic pragmatics, he explores similarities and differences between 'fixed' and 'free' worship, and argues for the interdependence of each.
2006 / 0-85364-977-4 / approx. 350pp

Roger Hitching
The Church and Deaf People
A Study of Identity, Communication and Relationships with Special Reference to the Ecclesiology of Jürgen Moltmann
In *The Church and Deaf People* Roger Hitching sensitively examines the history and present experience of deaf people and finds similarities between aspects of sign language and Moltmann's theological method that 'open up' new ways of understanding theological concepts.
2003 / 1-84227-222-5 / xxii + 236pp

John G. Kelly
One God, One People
*The Differentiated Unity of the People of God in the Theology of
Jürgen Moltmann*
The author expounds and critiques Moltmann's doctrine of God and highlights
the systematic connections between it and Moltmann's influential discussion of
Israel. He then proposes a fresh approach to Jewish–Christian relations building
on Moltmann's work using insights from Habermas and Rawls.
2005 / 0-85346-969-3 / approx. 350pp

Mark F.W. Lovatt
Confronting the Will-to-Power
A Reconsideration of the Theology of Reinhold Niebuhr
Confronting the Will-to-Power is an analysis of the theology of Reinhold
Niebuhr, arguing that his work is an attempt to identify, and provide a practical
theological answer to, the existence and nature of human evil.
2001 / 1-84227-054-0 / xviii + 216pp

Neil B. MacDonald
Karl Barth and the Strange New World within the Bible
Barth, Wittgenstein, and the Metadilemmas of the Enlightenment
Barth's discovery of the strange new world within the Bible is examined in the
context of Kant, Hume, Overbeck, and, most importantly, Wittgenstein.
MacDonald covers some fundamental issues in theology today: epistemology,
the final form of the text and biblical truth-claims.
2000 / 0-85364-970-7 / xxvi + 374pp

Keith A. Mascord
Alvin Plantinga and Christian Apologetics
This book draws together the contributions of the philosopher Alvin Plantinga to
the major contemporary challenges to Christian belief, highlighting in particular
his ground-breaking work in epistemology and the problem of evil. Plantinga's
theory that both theistic and Christian belief is warrantedly basic is explored and
critiqued, and an assessment offered as to the significance of his work for
apologetic theory and practice.
2005 / 1-84227-256-X / approx. 304pp

Gillian McCulloch
The Deconstruction of Dualism in Theology
With Reference to Ecofeminist Theology and New Age Spirituality
This book challenges eco-theological anti-dualism in Christian theology, arguing that dualism has a twofold function in Christian religious discourse. Firstly, it enables us to express the discontinuities and divisions that are part of the process of reality. Secondly, dualistic language allows us to express the mysteries of divine transcendence/immanence and the survival of the soul without collapsing into monism and materialism, both of which are problematic for Christian epistemology.
2002 / 1-84227-044-3 / xii + 282pp

Leslie McCurdy
Attributes and Atonement
The Holy Love of God in the Theology of P.T. Forsyth
Attributes and Atonement is an intriguing full-length study of P.T. Forsyth's doctrine of the cross as it relates particularly to God's holy love. It includes an unparalleled bibliography of both primary and secondary material relating to Forsyth.
1999 / 0-85364-833-6 / xiv + 328pp

Nozomu Miyahira
Towards a Theology of the Concord of God
A Japanese Perspective on the Trinity
This book introduces a new Japanese theology and a unique Trinitarian formula based on the Japanese intellectual climate: three betweennesses and one concord. It also presents a new interpretation of the Trinity, a co-subordinationism, which is in line with orthodox Trinitarianism; each single per-son of the Trinity is eternally and equally subordinate (or serviceable) to the other persons, so that they retain the mutual dynamic equality.
2000 / 0-85364-863-8 / xiv + 256pp

Eddy José Muskus
The Origins and Early Development of Liberation Theology in Latin America
With Particular Reference to Gustavo Gutiérrez
This work challenges the fundamental premise of Liberation Theology, 'opting for the poor', and its claim that Christ is found in them. It also argues that Liberation Theology emerged as a direct result of the failure of the Roman Catholic Church in Latin America.
2002 / 0-85364-974-X / xiv + 296pp

Jim Purves
The Triune God and the Charismatic Movement
A Critical Appraisal from a Scottish Perspective
All emotion and no theology? Or a fundamental challenge to reappraise and realign our trinitarian theology in the light of Christian experience? This study of charismatic renewal as it found expression within Scotland at the end of the twentieth century evaluates the use of Patristic, Reformed and contemporary models of the Trinity in explaining the workings of the Holy Spirit.

2004 / 1-84227-321-3 / xxiv + 246pp

Anna Robbins
Methods in the Madness
Diversity in Twentieth-Century Christian Social Ethics
The author compares the ethical methods of Walter Rauschenbusch, Reinhold Niebuhr and others. She argues that unless Christians are clear about the ways that theology and philosophy are expressed practically they may lose the ability to discuss social ethics across contexts, let alone reach effective agreements.

2004 / 1-84227-211-X / xx + 294pp

Ed Rybarczyk
Beyond Salvation
Eastern Orthodoxy and Classical Pentecostalism on Becoming Like Christ
At first glance eastern Orthodoxy and classical Pentecostalism seem quite distinct. This ground-breaking study shows they share much in common, especially as it concerns the experiential elements of following Christ. Both traditions assert that authentic Christianity transcends the wooden categories of modernism.

2004 / 1-84227-144-X / xii + 356pp

Signe Sandsmark
Is World View Neutral Education Possible and Desirable?
A Christian Response to Liberal Arguments
(Published jointly with The Stapleford Centre)
This book discusses reasons for belief in world view neutrality, and argues that 'neutral' education will have a hidden, but strong world view influence. It discusses the place for Christian education in the common school.

2000 / 0-85364-973-1 / xiv + 182pp

Hazel Sherman
Reading Zechariah
The Allegorical Tradition of Biblical Interpretation through the Commentary of
Didymus the Blind and Theodore of Mopsuestia
A close reading of the commentary on Zechariah by Didymus the Blind
alongside that of Theodore of Mopsuestia suggests that popular categorising of
Antiochene and Alexandrian biblical exegesis as 'historical' or 'allegorical' is
inadequate and misleading.
2005 / 1-84227-213-6 / approx. 280pp

Andrew Sloane
On Being a Christian in the Academy
Nicholas Wolterstorff and the Practice of Christian Scholarship
An exposition and critical appraisal of Nicholas Wolterstorff's epistemology in
the light of the philosophy of science, and an application of his thought to the
practice of Christian scholarship.
2003 / 1-84227-058-3 / xvi + 274pp

Damon W.K. So
Jesus' Revelation of His Father
A Narrative-Conceptual Study of the Trinity with Special Reference to
Karl Barth
This book explores the trinitarian dynamics in the context of Jesus' revelation of
his Father in his earthly ministry with references to key passages in Matthew's
Gospel. It develops from the exegeses of these passages a non-linear concept of
revelation which links Jesus' communion with his Father to his revelatory words
and actions through a nuanced understanding of the Holy Spirit, with references
to K. Barth, G.W.H. Lampe, J.D.G. Dunn and E. Irving.
2005 / 1-84227-323-X / approx. 380pp

Daniel Strange
The Possibility of Salvation Among the Unevangelised
An Analysis of Inclusivism in Recent Evangelical Theology
For evangelical theologians the 'fate of the unevangelised' impinges upon
fundamental tenets of evangelical identity. The position known as 'inclusivism',
defined by the belief that the unevangelised can be ontologically saved by Christ
whilst being epistemologically unaware of him, has been defended most
vigorously by the Canadian evangelical Clark H. Pinnock. Through a detailed
analysis and critique of Pinnock's work, this book examines a cluster of issues
surrounding the unevangelised and its implications for christology, soteriology
and the doctrine of revelation.
2002 / 1-84227-047-8 / xviii + 362pp

Scott Swain
God According to the Gospel
Biblical Narrative and the Identity of God in the Theology of Robert W. Jenson
Robert W. Jenson is one of the leading voices in contemporary Trinitarian theology. His boldest contribution in this area concerns his use of biblical narrative both to ground and explicate the Christian doctrine of God. *God According to the Gospel* critically examines Jenson's proposal and suggests an alternative way of reading the biblical portrayal of the triune God.
2006 / 1-84227-258-6 / approx. 180pp

Justyn Terry
The Justifying Judgement of God
A Reassessment of the Place of Judgement in the Saving Work of Christ
The argument of this book is that judgement, understood as the whole process of bringing justice, is the primary metaphor of atonement, with others, such as victory, redemption and sacrifice, subordinate to it. Judgement also provides the proper context for understanding penal substitution and the call to repentance, baptism, eucharist and holiness.
2005 / 1-84227-370-1 / approx. 274 pp

Graham Tomlin
The Power of the Cross
Theology and the Death of Christ in Paul, Luther and Pascal
This book explores the theology of the cross in St Paul, Luther and Pascal. It offers new perspectives on the theology of each, and some implications for the nature of power, apologetics, theology and church life in a postmodern context.
1999 / 0-85364-984-7 / xiv + 344pp

Adonis Vidu
Postliberal Theological Method
A Critical Study
The postliberal theology of Hans Frei, George Lindbeck, Ronald Thiemann, John Milbank and others is one of the more influential contemporary options. This book focuses on several aspects pertaining to its theological method, specifically its understanding of background, hermeneutics, epistemic justification, ontology, the nature of doctrine and, finally, Christological method.
2005 / 1-84227-395-7 / approx. 324pp

Graham J. Watts
Revelation and the Spirit
*A Comparative Study of the Relationship between the Doctrine of Revelation
and Pneumatology in the Theology of Eberhard Jüngel and of
Wolfhart Pannenberg*
The relationship between revelation and pneumatology is relatively unexplored.
This approach offers a fresh angle on two important twentieth century
theologians and raises pneumatological questions which are theologically crucial
and relevant to mission in a postmodern culture.
2005 / 1-84227-104-0 / xxii + 232pp

Nigel G. Wright
Disavowing Constantine
*Mission, Church and the Social Order in the Theologies of John Howard Yoder
and Jürgen Moltmann*
This book is a timely restatement of a radical theology of church and state in the
Anabaptist and Baptist tradition. Dr Wright constructs his argument in dialogue
and debate with Yoder and Moltmann, major contributors to a free church
perspective.
2000 / 0-85364-978-2 / xvi + 252pp

Paternoster
9 Holdom Avenue,
Bletchley,
Milton Keynes MK1 1QR,
United Kingdom
Web: www.authenticmedia.co.uk/paternoster